Working Capital Management

Working Capital Management

JOHN J. HAMPTON

College of Insurance

CECILIA L. WAGNER

Seton Hall University

WILEY

JOHN WILEY & SONS

New York · Chichester · Brisbane · Toronto · Singapore

Hampton, John J.
Working Capital Management

Hampton, John J. and Cecilia L. Wagner
p. 544

ISBN: 0-471-60260-4

Printed in the United States of America

The management of current assets and liabilities has long been a relatively underdeveloped area of finance. For many years, few researchers examined short–term assets and liabilities or developed theories with respect to their fundamental nature. Many professors did not recognize that there are substantive areas and complex issues that need to be understood and explained.

During recent years, we have seen changes in this situation. Cash management has become a critical area where innovation can make a crucial difference in the success of a company. Decisions to extend credit to consumers and businesses can bankrupt a company if done improperly. An adequate level of short–term assets is essential if management is to be free to focus on the firm's primary products or services. The sources of short–term borrowing can provide flexibility to the firm but must be analyzed in terms of costs and restrictions. All of these areas, along with others, have grown in importance in the management of modern firms.

Working Capital Management addresses the full range of managing cash, credit, receivables, inventory, and short–term sources of funds. The following features should be noted:

1. **Mixture of Theory and Practice.** This book is built on a conceptual base of the financial literature. It contains the current theoretical contributions throughout. It also reflects actual practices of cash managers, credit analysts, treasurers, and bankers, as it blends a real world approach with the theoretical foundation.

2. **Realistic Cases.** The theory and techniques are brought together in cases at the end of most chapters. The reader has the opportunity to apply the ideas in the chapter to solve the problems posed in each case.

3. **Spreadsheet Formats.** Much of the analysis in working–capital areas requires the movement from specific detail to final outcomes. The electronic spreadsheet is a particularly suitable tool for processing data and converting it to useful information. The electronic spreadsheet is fully integrated into all areas of the book.

4. **Decision Making Orientation.** The chapters lead the reader to understanding the need to make decisions in the varying areas of working–capital. How much cash is needed? Where can the firm raise

the money and how much will it cost? Does the firm have an adequate level of current assets compared to its current liabilities? This book does not simply discuss working–capital issues; it encourages an analysis of individual situations and the determination of correct solutions to problems.

Many people have contributed to the development of this book. In 1979 it began as a cash management workbook. It was joined by a credit management workbook in 1981. These two documents were used in seminars throughout the nation and comments were received from instructors and practicing managers. In 1983, the two workbooks were sufficiently developed so they could be used in courses on working capital. The authors wish to express their appreciation to the professors, students, and readers who provided constructive criticisms and suggestions for improvement.

Working capital management is a challenging and exciting area of finance. Increasingly, professors and practicioners are recognizing the need to study this area and share ideas and experiences. This book is designed to assist in that process and facilitate an introduction to a once overlooked area of financial management.

John J. Hampton
New York City, New York

Cecilia L. Wagner
South Orange, New Jersey

About the Authors

John J. Hampton is Provost and Professor of Finance, at the College of Insurance in New York City. He is the author of six books and several journal articles. He has consulted widely with corporations and banks in the areas of cash management and credit administration. He holds a doctorate in business from the George Washington University.

Cecilia L. Wagner is Assistant Professor of Finance at Seton Hall University in New Jersey. She is the author of several journal articles. She has conducted seminars on the management of records and using computers to solve cash and credit problems. She holds a doctorate in international business from the University of International Business and Economics in Beijing.

Contents

I   FRAMEWORK   **1**

1   Working Capital Policies   **3**

Nature of Working Capital   4
Working Capital Strategies   9

II   THE BANKING SYSTEM   **23**

2   Understanding the Flow of Money   **25**

Money and the Money Supply   25
Features of U.S. Commercial Banking   31
Measures of U.S. Money Supply   35
Money Creation   38
Seton National State Bank Case   45

3   Managing Disbursements and Collections   **51**

Cash Management System   51
Managing Collections   55
Managing Disbursements   64
Cash Management Problems   66
Chicago National Bank   70
Olean National Corporation   75

**4   Commercial Bank Packages
    for Cash Management**   **79**

Citicash Manager Package   80
PNB Compulink Package   88
Phoenix-Hecht Services   100

III   CASH MANAGEMENT   **105**

5   Cash Forecasting   **107**

Traditional Forecasting Techniques   107
Increasing the Accuracy of Forecast   119

ix

Tonnervae, Inc. Case		**133**
Morgan Computer Corporation Case		**136**

6 Cash Forecasting: Advanced Techniques   **141**

Simulation Models	**141**
Determining the Optimal Cash Balance	**149**
Saltlake Resources Incorporated Case	**157**
Union Packaging and Products Case	**159**

7 Investing Excess Cash: **163**
A Risk Return Framework

Expected Return	**163**
Calculating Return with an Electronic Spreadsheet	**166**
Risk and Return	**170**
Measuring Risk	**174**
Foreign Investments	**182**
A Portfolio Approach	**185**
Northern Cliffs Manufacturing Case	**192**

8 International Cash Management   **195**

Foreign Exchange Market	**195**
Premiums and Discounts in Forward market	**198**
Arbitrage in Foreign Exchange Markets	**205**
Why Do Arbitrage Profits Occur?	**205**
Hedging Foreign Currency Transactions	**206**
Guidelines on When to Hedge	**215**
Hedging with Organized Exchanges	**215**
Foreign Exchange Restrictions	**220**
Taurus Asian Products Case	**222**
Fielding Offshore Funds Case	**224**

IV ANALYZING WORKING CAPITAL   **227**

9 Cash Flow Analysis   **229**

Financial Statements	**229**
Balance Sheet	**230**
Income Statement	**237**
Flow of Funds Statement	**242**
Elliot Company Case	**252**

10 Working Capital Adequacy   **259**

Nature of Financial Analysis   **259**
Working Capital Ratios   **263**
A Spreadsheet Model of Working Capital Adequacy   **269**
Wallace Products Case   **277**
Lopez and Lopez Inc. Case   **279**

11 Economics of Short Term Financing   **283**

Short Term Financing   **283**
Economics of Short Term Loans   **290**
Effective Cost of Working Capital   **296**
Harper Company Case   **302**

12 Sources of Near Term Financing   **305**

Miscellaneous Short Term Credit   **305**
Receivable Financing   **309**
Madison Manufacturing Case   **317**

V   CREDIT AND COLLECTIONS   **321**

13 Analyzing Credit Capacity of Customers   **323**

Elements of Credit Capacity   **323**
Liquidity Indicators   **327**
Profitability Indicators   **331**
Capital Indicators   **338**
Pizza King Inc. Case   **343**

14 Developing Credit Policies   **359**

Receivable Policies   **359**
Cost-Volume-Profit Approach to Credit   **365**
Establishing Credit limits   **373**
Harding Supply Company Case   **381**
U.S.A. Distributors Company Case   **385**

15 Collection Policies and Government Regulations   **389**

Truth in Lending   **389**
Fair Credit Billing Act   **396**
Equal Credit Opportunity   **398**
Fair Debt Collection Practices   **407**
Western Finance Company Case   **414**

VI CONSUMER AND BUSINESS LENDING   **417**

16 Consumer Loans   **419**

Overview   **419**
Credit Capacity of Borrowers   **424**
City Central State Bank Case   **427**

17 Small Business Loans   **439**

Overview   **439**
The Credit Decision   **441**
North Jersey Carpet Company Case   **447**

18 Credit Scoring Systems   **457**

Overview   **457**
Benefits and Weaknesses   **459**
Lyle Electronics Company Case   **462**

VII INVENTORY   **471**

19 Inventory Management   **473**

Nature of Inventories   **473**
Inventory Management   **479**
Total System   **486**
Draper Corporation Case   **488**

20 Inventory Planning   **491**

The Production Side   **491**
The Marketing Side   **493**
The Inventory Data Base   **498**
Inventory Reports   **501**
Robin Sporting Goods Case   **508**
Mini Vehicles Case   **512**

VIII APPENDIX A   **517**

Index   **523**

I.

Framework

Working Capital Policies

The connotation of energy in the term *working capital* is indeed accurate. It refers to the resources of the firm that are used to conduct operations— to do the day-to-day "work" that makes the business successful. Without cash, bills cannot be paid. Without receivables, the firm cannot allow timing differences between delivering goods or services and collecting the money to pay for them. Without inventories, the firm cannot engage in production, nor can it stock goods to provide immediate deliveries. As a result of the critical nature of current assets, the management of working capital is one of the most important areas in determining whether a firm will be successful.

The effective management of working capital requires both medium-term planning and immediate reactions to changes in forecasts and conditions. At the same time, the area of working-capital management has historically represented a relatively small portion of finance. Traditionally, finance textbooks reflected the scholarly literature, with a major emphasis on investment policy, sources of financing, and portfolio theory. The concepts and practices from these areas were assumed to apply to the tasks of managing cash, receivables, and inventory. In textbooks the chapters on managing current assets are still noticeably lighter in content than those on other topics.

The light coverage of working-capital management was more acceptable in the 1950s than it is today. The difference has come about because the level of complexity in business has increased. Cash was once kept in the bank, with few opportunities to manage it aggressively. Today, cash moves around the world chasing overnight interest, as the treasurer seeks new investments that offer liquidity and profitability. Receivables were once the byproduct of standardized terms of trade, with limited possibilities to make them more liquid. Inventories were viewed as a component of operations and were largely left in the hands of the plant manager. Thanks to the Japanese and the high cost of idle assets, totally new systems for inventory management have been developed that significantly increase efficiency and profits.

In this book, we will address working capital management in a comprehensive fashion, with some limitations. These include

1. **Emphasis on Cash and Receivables.** The term *working capital* has three major categories of assets— cash, receivables, and inventories. In this book greater weight is given to the first two. Inventory management

3

has become a fully developed area of professional study. Mathematical techniques are highly developed and can provide the basis for extensive study. Here inventories are treated as a component of working capital, but mathematical techniques are not covered in great detail.

2. **Emphasis on Practical Techniques.** Conceptually, current assets play the same role as any other resources of the firm. Hence, the theory of managing working capital is essentially identical to the concepts for managing the firm. In this book, we will not repeat the theoretical framework. Instead, the focus will be on practical approaches to managing working capital so as to maximize the net present value of the firm.

NATURE OF WORKING CAPITAL

In order to manage working capital, we must understand the nature of current assets. Of particular importance are concepts dealing with the need for current assets and their relationships to other areas of the firm. In this section, we will examine the nature of working capital from different viewpoints.

Current Assets and Current Liabilities

The term *working capital* refers to the current assets of the firm— those items that can be converted into cash within the next year. **Net working capital** is defined as the difference between current assets and current liabilities. Both liquid assets and liabilities are important in working-capital management. Liquidity may be viewed as the near-cash resources (current assets) available to pay near term bills (current liabilities). Thus, all current accounts should be covered in the study of working capital.

Figure 1-1. Current Assets and Liabilities, Nonfinancial Corporations (1985).

	Billions of Dollars	Percent
Cash and Government Securities	190	0.11
Notes and Receivables	636	0.37
Inventories	664	0.39
Other Current Assets	215	0.13
TOTAL CURRENT ASSETS	1,705	1.00
Notes and Accounts Payable	626	0.54
Other Current Liabilities	538	0.46
TOTAL CURRENT LIABILITIES	1,164	1.00
NET WORKING CAPITAL	540	
Ratio of Current Assets to Current Liabilities		1.46

Source: Federal Reserve Bulletin, March 1986.

The relationship of current accounts can be seen in the data presented in Figure 1-1. Nonfinancial corporations in the United States hold $1.7 trillion in current assets. Their current liabilities exceed $1.1 trillion. It is clear that working capital is an important component of a corporation's financial resources. Inventories and receivables are the two most important components of current assets, each making up between 35 and 40 percent of the total. Cash is less significant at approximately 10 percent of current assets. These relationships have been fairly consistent in recent years.

Most firms hold more current assets than liabilities. The ratio in Figure 1-1 shows $1.46 of assets for each $1 of liabilities. This produces a total net working capital of $540 billion. The actual relationship of assets to debts varies considerably by industry. Service firms will not have large inventories, and financial corporations might have larger cash positions. Still, we generally expect a firm to have more current assets than liabilities.

Circulating Working Capital

The term **circulating assets** refers to the fact that the value represented by working capital circulates among the firm's current assets. This is shown in Figure 1-2. In a simple sense, cash is used to purchase inventories that are sold on credit and become receivables that are collected in the form of cash.

The figure also shows the circulation where current liabilities are used to provide financing for a portion of current assets. The example is for a manufacturing firm, in which payables finance labor and raw materials and cash and accrued expenses finance overhead. At the end of the manufacturing process, finished goods are held and then sold on credit. Receivables are collected and become cash.

The circulating nature of current assets is a key concept in working-capital management. Some current assets are more liquid than others; that is, they will be converted into cash sooner. Cash is the most liquid, since no conversion is needed. Receivables are next, since they only have to be collected to become cash. Inventories are the least liquid, with finished goods being more liquid than raw materials.

Permanent and Variable Working Capital

A firm's working capital may be viewed as having two components.

1. **Permanent Working Capital.** This category represents cash, receivables, and inventories required on a continuing basis over the entire year. It may be viewed as the minimum current assets needed to carry on operations at any time.

2. **Variable Working Capital.** This category reflects additional current assets needed at peak periods during the operating year. Additional inventory may be needed to support higher sales during the selling season. Receivables must increase once the goods have been sold. Extra cash may be needed to pay for increased supplies and labor activity preceding the period of high activity.

Figure 1-2. Circulating Nature of Current Assets.

Assets Only

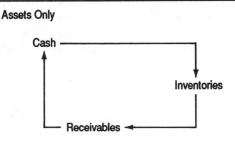

Assets and Liabilities, Manufacturing Example

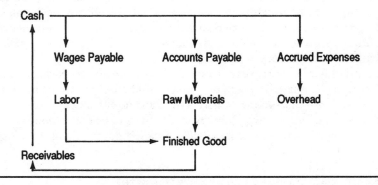

Figure 1-3 graphically displays permanent and variable working capital for a firm during a two-year period. In this example, the firm is growing, so its permanent working-capital level has risen from the first year to the second. It appears that April represents a cyclical low for this firm. Its permanent working capital in year one appears to be $1 million, rising to $1.2 million in the second year. The needs above the $1 and $1.2 million levels represent variable working capital.

Figure 1-3. Permanent and Variable Working Capital.

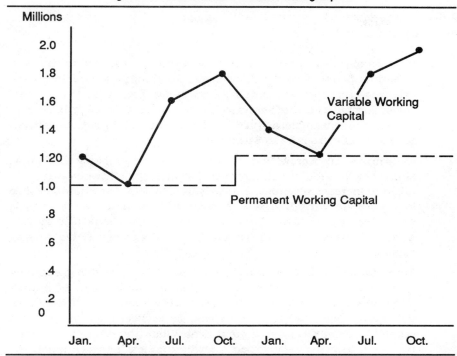

Figure 1-4. Sources of Changes in Working-Capital Needs.

Source of Change	Working Capital Affected	Reason
Sales Volume	Permanent	Different levels of cash, receivables, and inventory are needed at new sales level.
Seasonal or Cyclical Factors	Variable	Receivables and inventory must be available on temporary basis.
Technological Developments	Permanent	Level of inventory must support the new production capability.
Philosophy of the Firm	Both	Some policies tie up working capital; others free it.

Needs for Working Capital

A firm's requirements for working capital are largely determined by 4 factors, as shown in Figure 1-4. These are

1. **Volume of Sales.** A firm finances cash, receivables, and inventory in order to support efforts to achieve sales. Over long periods of time, most firms maintain current assets in a fairly steady proportion to its annual sales. Normally, current assets will be held in a ratio of 20 to 40 percent of sales. As an example, a firm with $10 million in sales will hold current assets ranging from $2 to $4 million.

   As a firm's sales grow, the current assets will probably also grow. Management should certainly plan for such growth when steps are taken to increase revenues. Similarly, an efficient firm should be able to reduce its current assets if sales decline. If the sales drop is permanent, the permanent level of working capital should also decline. At peak seasons, we would also expect a reduction of variable working capital.

2. **Seasonal or Cyclical Factors.** Most businesses experience seasonal fluctuations in the demand for their products or services. Such variations in sales will affect the level of variable working capital. Similarly, the overall economy tends to experience cyclical fluctuations, with economic activity varying a great deal. When the economy enters a recession, most firms can expect a decline in sales. In this situation, the need for permanent working capital will be lessened. A boom period in the economy will have the opposite effect. Once the cycle is completed, the firm might expect permanent working capital to change once again.

3. **Technological Developments.** Changes in technology, particularly with respect to the production process, can have sharp impacts on the need for working capital. If the firm automates an assembly line so that it processes raw materials at a faster rate than previously, the permanent need for inventory will be changed. If the high-speed assembly line requires more raw materials for efficient runs, permanent inventory will increase. If the new line uses less expensive materials or processes them quickly so that large finished goods inventories are not needed, permanent inventory will be reduced.

4. **Philosophy of the Firm.** The firm's policies will affect the levels of permanent and variable working capital. If the firm has a philosophy of aggressive collections, its receivables will be lower than those for a similar firm that is lax on collections. A cautious firm may maintain larger cash levels than a firm that is willing to operate with less liquidity. In both of these examples, the permanent and variable needs for working capital will be affected.

Levels of Working Capital

Once the needs for working capital are noted, more specific factors will determine the actual levels of cash, receivables, and inventories that are maintained. Some of these operational factors are

1. **Size of the Company.** Large firms have markedly different working capital needs than small firms. This is true for a number of reasons. Large firms can take advantage of a wider range of resources when they run low on cash or are unable to collect receivables. Smaller firms, on the other hand, are more affected by the failures of a few customers to pay their bills. As a general statement, larger firms with many sources of funds may need less working capital as compared to total assets or sales.

2. **Activities of the Firm.** The nature of the business affects the level of working capital. A firm that provides services will not have a need for inventories. A firm that sells for cash will not maintain receivables.

3. **Availability of Credit.** The global economy provides many possible sources of credit, with different maturities, repayment requirements, and even currencies available. If a firm can borrow locally to finance shortfalls, it will need less cash on hand. If the operating unit cannot depend on borrowing on short notice at reasonable rates, the parent may be forced to maintain larger liquid balances of cash equivalents.

4. **Attitude Toward Profits.** Most funds involve a cost to the firm. Thus, a relatively large amount of current assets tends to reduce the overall profit. Some firms are willing to accept greater liquidity risks in order to achieve higher profits. Other firms are not highly focused on maximizing profits and do not manage liquid assets aggressively. These behaviors affect the level of working capital.

5. **Attitude Toward Risk.** The reverse side of the attitude toward profits involves risk. The greater the level of working capital, the lower the risk. Cash provides safety for paying bills. Inventories provide less risk of running out of goods to sell. Firms that are averse to risk may maintain more current assets than firms willing to accept higher levels of risk.

WORKING-CAPITAL STRATEGIES

The management of working capital should be coordinated with the overall objectives of the firm. Cash, receivables, and inventory as well as the financing mix for these current assets must be part of the total approach to earning adequate long-term profits and managing financial resources. In this section, we will identify some of the conceptual strategies that can be used in managing current assets and liabilities.

Risk Return Tradeoff

The goal of working-capital management is to support the long-term operational and financial goals of the business. In effect, this involves recognizing the relationship between risk and return. Three elements must be included in analyzing the tradeoff between risk and return when managing working capital.

1. **Insolvency.** This condition occurs when a firm can no longer pay its bills and must default on obligations and possibly declare bankruptcy. A firm without adequate levels of working capital may have to face this risk.

2. **Profitability of Assets.** Different levels of current assets will have varied effects on profits. A high level of inventory will require high carrying costs. At the same time, the firm will have a wide range of goods to sell and may be able to generate higher sales and profits. Each decision on the level of cash, receivables, and inventory should consider the effects of different levels.

3. **Cost of Financing.** When interest rates are high, it costs more to carry inventory than when rates are low. Large cash balances may not earn the return that is possible if the cash is converted into operating assets. The cost of debt and the opportunity costs of alternative investments are items to consider when evaluating working-capital levels.

Figure 1-5 shows liquidity risk with high and low levels of current assets. If cash, receivables, and inventories are maintained at low levels, the risks of insolvency or failing to support operations to make profits are high. As working capital rises, the liquidity risk declines.

Figure 1-6 shows the effect on profits with high and low levels of working capital. At low levels, operations are not supported properly, so profits are low. At some optimum, return to the firm will peak. Above this point, the firm will have idle or sluggish current assets, involving unnecessary financing costs. Thus, profits will decline.

Figure 1-5. Risk and the Level of Working Capital.

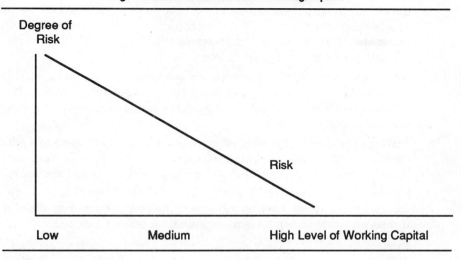

Figure 1-6. Return and the Level of Working Capital

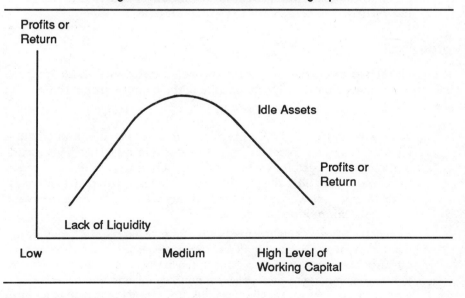

Left Side Risks

The risk-return tradeoff required for effective working-capital management can be further delineated by examining the balance sheet. The risks related to current assets are called **left side risks,** because assets are placed on the left-hand side of the balance sheet. These risks are

1. **Inadequate Cash.** The firm must pay its routine and ordinary bills, have cash for emergencies, and also have cash to take advantage of special large discounts or other opportunities. If cash levels are not adequate, the firm faces danger of default or an inability to take advantage of profitable opportunities.

2. **Inadequate Credit.** Most products are sold on credit; that is, purchasers have 10 to 60 days to pay for them. Such credit results in the creation of receivables. If the firm lacks the funds to allow such credit, sales will be hurt.

3. **Inadequate Inventory.** Raw materials should be purchased in sufficient quantity to allow efficient production runs. Finished goods should be available to fill orders. Without the appropriate level of inventory, costs may be unnecessarily high and sales may suffer.

4. **Excessive Current Assets.** All assets involve a financing cost. If unneeded working capital is maintained, profits are reduced.

5. **Frozen Assets.** Worldwide firms maintain levels of current assets in different countries and reflect them in a variety of currencies. It is not uncommon for foreign nations to forbid the repatriation of funds to a parent company in another country. The danger of cash that cannot be used where it is needed is a current asset risk.

Right Side Risks

The risks related to current liabilities are called **right side risks**, because liabilities are placed on the right-hand side of the balance sheet. These risks are

1. **Excessive Payables.** When the firm purchases inventory on credit, a payable is created. Because some firms are relatively lax when extending credit, it is possible for a firm to order more inventory than is needed in the near term. Still, the payable must be eliminated in 10 to 60 days. With idle, excessive inventory, the firm may not have the cash to pay the bills. This can produce a default.

2. **Excessive Short-Term Borrowing.** To finance assets, the firm may tap a number of short-term lenders. It may even secure permission in advance to borrow at a future time. If too many such arrangements are made, the firm may use short-term sources for borrowed funds when long-term sources would offer less risk. Too many loans with near-term maturities can be a serious exposure.

3. **Excessive Long-Term Debt.** During most economic periods, the cost of money borrowed for the long-term is higher than money borrowed for the short term. If the firm does not take advantage of lower cost payables

and other current liabilities, its profits will decrease This is the reverse side of the coin. Excessive short-term borrowing involves liquidity risks; excessive long-term borrowing may involve profitability risks.

4. **Excessive Equity.** This situation is similar to that associated with long-term debt. If the firm is not taking advantage of lower cost current liabilities, it fails to use leverage. This reduces risk but hurts profits.

5. **Foreign Exchange Fluctuations.** For foreign subsidiaries, most firms borrow the local currency in local capital markets. They also make credit purchases and create payables in local currencies. In some cases, the value of the currency may rise compared to the dollar or other currency of the parent company. If the goods are sold in another country for dollars or a different currency, the liabilities may become quite costly. This is an exposure for multinational firms.

Strategies to Reduce Risk

Part of the excitement of working-capital management is devising and implementing strategies to reduce risk. Generally, the firm employs a variety of approaches. Some of the major strategies are

1. **Minimize Current Liabilities.** This straightforward approach reduces the exposure from near-term obligations. If the firm does not incur large payables and it avoids short-term borrowing, it faces minimal risk from defaulting on these obligations. This strategy requires the firm to make use of long-term sources of funds, debt and equity, to finance the bulk of its working capital.

2. **Minimize Financing Costs.** This strategy takes maximum advantage of payables and low-cost, short-term, debt to finance working capital. Firms following this approach are willing to accept higher levels of risk of default than firms that finance current assets with long-term sources of funds.

3. **Maximize Total Value of Firm.** This strategy ties working-capital management into the total financial strategy of the firm. In the financial literature, the generally accepted goal of management is to maximize the net present value of the total firm. This is achieved by maximizing the long-term earnings prospects while incurring an acceptable level of risk. In this framework, the firm would be careful to ensure adequate liquidity while allowing for some risks because the firm restricts the level of current assets and employs short-term financing where economical.

Policies for Financing Working Capital

Within the framework of the above strategies, the firm must develop policies for financing its current assets. The common approaches employ a combination of short- and long-term sources. When inventory is purchased on credit terms, accounts payable become the source of financing. Similarly, funds to finance cash or receivables can be arranged by issuing a 10-year bond.

Matching an item of working capital to a specific source of funds must be done in a policy framework. It does not make sense, for example, to say that a long-term bank loan provides the money to finance any single asset. A dollar is a dollar and all money goes into a pool of funds that finance all assets. From this pool, the firm draws money to finance its resources, whether current or fixed assets. As a policy statement, however, we can match categories of financing with categories of assets to ensure rational overall financing for working capital.

Figure 1-7. Three Sets of Guidelines for Sources of Funds to Finance Working Capital.

Permanent and Variable Working Capital

Item	Source
Variable Working Capital	S-T
1/3 Permanent Working Capital	S-T
2/3 Permanent Working Capital	L-T
Fixed Assets	L-T

Major Current Asset Accounts

Item	Source
Cash and Receivables	S-T
Inventories	L-T
Fixed Assets	L-T

Total Current Assets

Item	Source
1/2 Current Assets	S-T
1/2 Current Assets	L-T
Fixed Assets	L-T

In a balance sheet framework, firms can identify guidelines for financing working capital. These guidelines will provide the policy to be followed by the treasurer. The three possible guidelines shown in Figure 1-7 are mutually exclusive. Thus, a firm can follow one norm but not all three. The rationales for each set of guidelines are

1. **Permanent and Variable Current Assets.** This approach recognizes the seasonal nature of working capital. Variable working capital is financed from short-term sources that can be reduced to zero when the funds are not needed. Permanent working-capital needs are met by a combination of short- and long-term sources of funds. In the figure, it is assumed that one-third of variable working capital would be financed with short-term funds. The balance would be financed with long-term debt and equity.

2. **Major Current Asset Accounts.** This approach distinguishes between the different current assets. Cash and receivables are the most liquid assets and are or will be available soon to pay bills. A firm may match these against current liabilities, which also have near-term maturities. Inventories, on the other hand, are less liquid and are converted to cash over a longer time period. These assets and other less liquid assets can be financed from long-term sources.

3. **Total Current Assets.** This guideline does not distinguish among current asset accounts but recognizes the difference between current and fixed assets. A stipulated percentage, say 50 percent, of current assets are financed short-term. The exact percentage will depend on the speed of collection of receivables, the turnover of the inventory, and the firm's views toward risk. The remaining current assets and all fixed assets are then financed by long-term sources of funds.

It is quite important for the firm to have some policy on the sources of funds to finance working capital. The problem involves liquidity more than anything else but may have greater impact on profits. If the firm has a permanent need for certain levels of cash, receivables, and inventory, it cannot operate efficiently if it feels pressure to liquidate the assets to pay current liabilities. In the absence of adequate long-term financing, the financial manager will spend excessive time managing the liquidity aspects of current assets rather than focusing on the profits to be made from employing the assets. Thus, whatever guidelines are adopted, the firm should have long-term sources for a major portion of its working capital.

Advantages of Each Financing Source

By financing a portion of current assets with short-term sources, the firm realizes benefits such as

1. **Lower Costs.** If variable working capital is financed on a short-term basis, the firm pays interest on funds only during the period of time they are needed. In addition, accounts payable frequently do not carry any financing costs at all. By making credit purchases and waiting the full time to pay, the firm receives free use of a supplier's capital.

2. **Closer Relations with Financial Institutions.** By borrowing money during peak periods and repaying it promptly when not needed, financial managers work closely with account executives at banks and other financial institutions. These close relations can prove valuable in later, larger dealings with the institution.

By financing the bulk of its current assets and all fixed assets from long-term sources, the firm achieves other benefits, including

1. **Reduction of Risk.** Long-term financing eliminates the need to repay loans at frequent intervals. This reduces the danger that a loan will be due and the firm will lack the funds to pay it.

2. **Provision of Stability.** If assets are financed so they will be available for a long period of time, the financing provides a high degree of stability for the firm's operations. Management does not have to worry about having the ability to purchase enough inventory for production because it can purchase on credit knowing it will have funds to eliminate the payable when it is due.

3. **Increase of Liquidity.** Because long-term debt does not mature in the near future, the firm can tie up current assets as needed to support business activities. Since repayment is not an immediate consideration, long-term financing has the impact of increasing liquidity.

Importance of Working-Capital Strategies

Developing and implementing sound strategies for the management of current assets and the financing of those assets are important parts of the firm's activities. Some of the reasons for this importance are

1. **Significant Resources.** Current assets make up a significant part of the assets employed by most firms. The Federal Trade Commission, Robert Morris Associates, and others publish tables showing the ratio of current assets to total assets for firms in different industries. As a general rule, 40 to 50 percent of total assets consist of cash, receivables, and inventories. Simply on the basis of size, working capital represents important assets with major impact on the ability to conduct business.

2. **Daily Impacts.** When a firm makes investments in capital assets, decisions occur infrequently and with long lead times. Working-capital

management requires day to day attention, lest the firm suddenly be caught short in its business activities. The continuing need to manage current assets and pay bills, with implications if the firm fails, offers major reasons for carefully chosen strategies.

3. **Creditor and Investor Effects.** The firm's creditors regularly read and analyze the balance sheet, reported quarterly or monthly. Decisions on whether to extend credit or lend money to a firm are made within the context of how the firm manages its assets and liabilities. Similarly, investors who might purchase common stock review the same statements and have expectations on good management. Failure to have sound strategies can hurt the firm's ability to borrow or to sell stock.

4. **Ability to Fine Tune Current Assets.** Because cash, receivables, and inventories are in constant motion, the firm has the ability to make changes that increase liquidity and profits. Fixed assets cannot be so managed. Once a factory has been purchased, it cannot easily be modified to achieve short-term goals. Current assets and liabilities can be fine tuned with immediate positive results.

Working-Capital Practices

Within a framework of growing importance for the role of current assets and liabilities, firms make specific decisions to achieve their goals. Some of these decisions are reflected in a survey conducted by Keith V. Smith and S. B. Sell in the late 1970s. The Smith and Sell survey identified the 200 largest and 200 smallest firms in the list of *Fortune* magazine's top 1,000 U.S. industrial corporations. These firms were asked to respond to a questionnaire containing 35 questions on various working capital practices. The results of the full survey can be found in Smith and Sell, *Readings on the Management of Working Capital* (St. Paul, Minn.: West Publishing Co., 1980).

In this section, we will examine some of the findings of this survey and discuss their implications.

Overall Policies

Figure 1-8 shows the responses with respect to the policies followed by the firm. The important findings are

1. **Formal Versus Informal Policies.** Some firms have formal written policies for managing cash, receivables, and inventory. These may be written in an operations manual and often have been approved by the president or even the board of directors. The larger the firm, the more formal the policy. Almost half of the largest firms have formal policies compared to only 18 percent of the smaller firms.

2. **Establishment of Policies.** Working-capital management policies are set at different levels in the firm. Most commonly, the vice-president of finance sets the policies (44 percent). The president establishes policies in one out of five companies. The board sets policies in 14 percent of the cases, and treasurers, controllers, or others formulate policies in the balance of companies.

3. **Periodic Review of Policies.** Approximately half the firms reported that they did not conduct periodic review of the firm's policies on managing working capital. This finding did not differ significantly between the larger or smaller firms. About 30 percent of the firms reviewed such policies at least quarterly.

4. **Philosophy of the Firm.** The surveyed firms were asked to describe their approaches to managing working capital. The most common response was a situational philosophy (46 percent). A cautious or conservative approach was the second most frequent response at 28 percent. An aggressive set of policies was identified by only 22 percent.

Figure 1-8. Working-Capital Policies at Surveyed Firms in the *Fortune 500* (1978).

	200 Largest Firms	200 Smallest Firms	Overall
Does your firm have an overall policy for the management of its working capital?			
Formal Policy	0.48	0.18	0.30
Informal Policy	0.52	0.82	0.70
Who sets the management policy for working capital?			
Board of Directors			0.14
President			0.21
Vice-President, Finance			0.44
Other			0.21
How often is working-capital policy reviewed?			
At Least Quarterly	0.31	0.29	
At Least Once a Year	0.21	0.20	
Whenever Necessary	0.48	0.51	

Which of the following best describes your
policies for managing working capital?

Cautious	0.28
Aggressive	0.22
Situational	0.46
Change Over Time	0.04

Source: Keith V. Smith and S. B. Sell, "Working Capital Management in Practice,"
in *Readings on the Management of Working Capital*, Second Edition, (St.
Paul, Minn.: West Publishing Co., 1980).

Figure 1-9. Credit Policies at Surveyed Firms in the *Fortune 500* (1978).

	Ranking or Relative Importance of Item
Which technique is most important in your decisions on granting credit?	
The "Four C's" of Credit	0.42
Sequential Credit Analysis	0.30
Credit Scoring	0.22
Other	0.06

Which of the following is most important in
setting credit policies for your firm?

Marketing Considerations	0.34
Possible Bad-Debt Losses	0.23
Use of Production Capacity	0.17
Inventory Requirements	0.13
Operating Leverage	0.13

What criteria are used to evaluate
proposed changes in credit terms?

Effect on Firm's Sales	0.27
Effect on Profits	0.26
Effect on Receivables Level	0.24
Effect on Return on Investment	0.23

Source: Smith and Sell, "Working Capital Management in Practice."

Decisions to Extend Credit

An important policy for most firms involves decisions to extend credit to customers and potential customers. Figure 1-9 shows some of the credit policies in the Smith and Sell survey. The percentages do not indicate that a firm uses only one approach. Rather, they give a relative weighting of the importance of each response. Important findings are

1. **Four C's of Credit.** When a firm evaluates a potential customer or a bank reviews a loan application, the four C's of credit refer to (1) character of the borrower, (2) capacity to repay, (3) capital owned by the firm, and (4) conditions in the market and industry. Some classification systems also consider collateral provided for the loan or a sale. The four C's approach is a comprehensive view of the customer and is the most important technique followed by surveyed firms, with a 42 percent weighted response.

2. **Sequential Credit Analysis.** Many firms take a balance sheet and income statement and review financial characteristics using ratios and other analytical tools. This step-by-step approach is important, with 30 percent weighting in the survey.

3. **Credit Scoring.** A formal credit scoring system allocates points mechanically for certain characteristics of a potential customer. The decision to extend credit involves reaching a certain total point level. Such systems are used widely, as shown in the figure.

Framework for Credit Policies

Figure 1-9 contains responses dealing with the framework for making credit decisions. The factors weighted in terms of importance are

1. **Marketing Considerations.** This factor indicates that credit decisions are made in an environment in which the firm is trying to achieve sales. If additional credit is needed to close a sale, such a factor will be given full consideration.

2. **Bad Debt Losses.** Firms do not want to incur excessive exposure to bad debts. This factor is weighted second.

3. **Manufacturing Considerations.** If the firm has excess capacity for producing goods, it may be willing to modify credit policies to achieve greater sales and take advantage of production capabilities. Similarly, if inventories are at undesirably high or low levels, credit policies might be modified to slow down sales or increase them, thus bringing inventories back into line.

4. **Criteria for Changing Policies.** Managers occasionally face the decision as to whether to continue existing credit terms or change them. The figure lists four factors in these decisions, with a relatively even weighting for each factor. It is not surprising that firms consider sales, profits, and return on investment when making such changes. The high weighting for the level of receivables, however, may be something of a surprise.

Inventory Policies

Figure 1-10 presents responses on inventory practices. Some of the key findings areas follows:

1. **Replenishing Inventories.** The most important factor to be considered when ordering new inventory is the need for the materials themselves, generally to facilitate production or to be available in stock to sell. If the supplier offers price discounts, this can also be important. The danger of running out of inventory, as reflected in shortage costs, is listed as well. Credit terms, the effects of anticipated inflation, and other factors also play a role in decisions to replenish inventory.

2. **Factors Influencing Production of Inventories.** At most firms, the production process can be varied so that inventory levels are maintained to match cyclical demand. In making inventory level decisions, we would expect the firm to consider profits, costs, and the level itself to be key factors. The survey shows these considerations to be important, with a relatively even ranking of four factors.

3. **Cost of Trade Credit.** Most firms purchase goods on credit terms, thus paying at a later time for goods received today. Most firms believe that such credit is relatively low cost, as shown by 38 percent of responses indicating a zero cost and another 31 percent responding with a cost of under 6 percent. Some firms receive credit and are willing to sign notes or otherwise pay interest. These are shown in the figure.

Figure 1-10. Inventory Policies at Surveyed Firms in the *Fortune 500* (1978).

	Ranking or Relative Importance of Item
When replenishing inventories, which of the following are the most important?	
Availability of Materials	0.26
Price Discounts Offered	0.22
Shortage Costs	0.18
Credit Terms Offered	0.15
Inflation	0.14
Other	0.04
When producing inventories, which of the following are the most important?	
Effect on Profits	0.26
Effect on Inventory Level	0.25
Effect on Return on Investment	0.24
Effect on Inventory Costs	0.24
What is the estimated annual cost to your firm of the trade credit offered by suppliers of your inventory?	
Zero	0.38
Between 1 and 6 Percent	0.31
Between 6 and 11 Percent	0.27
Above 11 Percent	0.04

Source: Smith and Sell, "Working Capital Management in Practice."

CONCLUSION

Policies on managing working-capital vary considerably because of the many factors identified in this chapter. In the following chapters, we will examine different aspects of working capital management. Such a study begins with an understanding of money and how it flows through an economic system. Dealing with banks and managing cash are major components in working-capital management. Other topics are covered in turn.

II.

The Banking System

2

Understanding the Flow of Money

The appropriate starting point for a book on working–capital management is a macroeconomic view of the flow of money. Without such a foundation, it is difficult to properly develop later concepts. Working–capital management is, after all, little more than collecting money as soon as possible with a minimal amount of risk and using it in a timely way to conduct business and avoid other risks. The ability to perform these tasks is partly dependent on an understanding of the nature of money and the way it moves in an economy around the world.

In this chapter, we will examine the flow of money in the banking system. We begin with the concept of money and the nature of the money supply. The next section examines the banks themselves and some characteristics of commercial banks specifically. Then, the money supply is defined according to different measures used by the Federal Reserve Systems. These discussions set the stage for the creation of money in the banking system and the role of reserves, two concepts tied closely to a bank's ability to lend money.

MONEY AND THE MONEY SUPPLY

The concept of "money" in an economic system is so familiar to most people that they might have difficulty defining the term. Most impromptu definitions would probably identify the term with something spent for goods or services. In fact, the concept deserves a broader viewpoint. We will develop such a viewpoint in this section.

The Nature of Money

A nation's **money supply** may be defined as the total of coins and paper currency in circulation, plus the currency equivalents in bank accounts. Thus, coins, currency, and bank balances constitute a country's **money**. In some economic systems, other items of value have been used as money. As examples, earlier societies have accepted as money such diverse items as silver bars, gems, cattle, tobacco, and sharks' teeth.

However defined, money plays two primary roles in an economic system.

1. **Medium of Exchange**. This is a common measure of value for different products or services. Once we have such a measure, people can trade units of the medium of exchange for products or services.

2. **Store of Value**. This is a vehicle for holding purchasing power over a period of time. If an individual can provide goods or services, payment can be received in money, which can be held until the individual wishes to purchase something. This can be a month or year after the original transaction. Thus, money is a store of value from one period to a later time.

Intrinsic Value of Money

Intrinsic value is defined as the real worth of any product, service, or, in our case, any item used as money. Intrinsic value can be based on many factors but is determined primarily by the willingness of individuals or organizations to acquire and hold the object. An object that is desired will have high value. If no demand exists for an object, it will have low value.
In this context, we can identify two kinds of money.

1. **Full-Bodied Money**. This kind of money has a "real" value because it is desired for itself; that is, it has a value independent of its role as money. Gold or silver are the most widely used examples of full-bodied money. These metals perform a role as a **commodity**, defined as any useful and valuable article of commerce. They are used in jewelry, in alloys for dental applications, and in a variety of cosmetic and industrial activities. Coins made from gold or silver have an intrinsic value based on the amount of precious metal in each coin. If the price of the metal rises, the coins will be worth more than their original value.

2. **Credit Money**. This money has value because a government declares it as **legal tender**, which means that it is legally acceptable to pay debts. A dollar bill is an example of credit money. The actual paper is worth less than a penny, but the bill is accepted at face value by most people because dollars are the legal currency of the United States.

Qualities of Good Money

Some forms of money are better suited to meet the needs of an economic system than are other forms. Good money is:

1. **Highly Liquid**. Good money can be readily transferred from one person to another, either to facilitate the exchange of goods or services or to be held as a store of value.

2. **Stable in Value**. Good money tends to maintain its purchasing power over long periods of time. This makes it a good store of value. In periods when inflation is low, credit money is relatively stable in value. With high rates of inflation, full-bodied money may offer a better store of value.

3. **Easily Divisible**. Good money offers sufficient units so it can be matched against products and services of varying values. Credit money meets this test handily in most cases since governments provide different denominations.

4. **Sufficiently Available**. Good money is available in sufficient quantities to meet the needs of the economic system. If too much is available compared to goods and services, inflation will occur. If inadequate money is found in a system, economic activity will be hampered.

Role of U.S. Currency

In the United States, an important medium of exchange is **currency**, defined as coins and paper money issued by the government. U.S. currency has three characteristics.

1. **Bearer Instrument**. A **bearer** is a person who is holding money. Currency units are bearer instruments; whoever has the currency can pass it on to someone else without the need to verify whether the person has the right to exchange the money. Because currency is exchanged without documentation, it is readily accepted.

2. **Token Value**. U.S. currency is credit money, having only a token value compared to its face value. When coins wear out from usage, they are replaced at a cost to the government that is a fraction of their face value.

3. **Ease of Carriage**. Because currency can be given any face value, it is easy for people to carry it at all times.

Role of Institutional Deposits

Currency is not the major vehicle used in the United States as a medium of exchange. This role is reserved for **institutional deposits**, defined as money balances held by individuals or businesses in banks, thrift institutions, and similar organizations. Money is placed in the institution for the purpose of safeguarding funds, writing orders to transfer funds, or earning interest on it. Until a check or similar instrument is written and cleared or until the money is withdrawn in the form of currency, the financial institution owes the money to the depositor.

Three types of institutions accept deposits.

1. **Commercial Banks.** These institutions receive, hold, and issue money and provide the mechanisms for the transfer of balances among institutions. They facilitate the exchange of funds by handling instruments such as checks, drafts, and notes. In addition, banks lend money to individuals and businesses and provide a variety of related financial services.

2. **Thrift Institutions.** These are the savings and loan associations, mutual savings banks, credit unions, and similar organizations whose original purpose was to encourage individuals to save their money. In recent years, they have taken on many characteristics of commercial banks.

3. **Nonbank Financial Institutions.** In a deregulated banking environment, financial service companies have become major competitors to banks and thrift institutions. Companies such as Merrill Lynch and American Express now perform many of the functions involved with holding and investing money.

Classifications of Deposits

A number of classifications are used to identify deposits in commercial banks and other institutions.

1. **Demand Deposit.** A demand deposit is a deposit in a commercial bank whereby the bank agrees to give cash immediately in return for a check written on an account; that is, the check is **payable on demand**. The demand deposit is a form of money and is counted as such in all definitions of the money supply. A check written against a demand deposit account will transfer the deposit, but the check itself is not a form of money and is not counted in measures of a nation's money supply.

2. **Savings or Time Deposit.** A savings deposit is a deposit at a commercial bank or thrift institution that pays interest or dividends. This kind of deposit is set up under a written contract, allowing the institution to require written notice of the intention to withdraw the funds, frequently with 30 or more days, notice before the actual withdrawal. In many cases, a specific withdrawal date is specified and early withdrawal results in a penalty. At one time, time deposits were differentiated from demand deposits by the interest paid on deposits. This is no longer the case, as institutions now pay interest on many demand deposit balances.

3. **Negotiable Order of Withdrawal (NOW) Account.** A now account is an–interest–bearing deposit allowing the use of negotiable orders of withdrawal, which are similar to checks. These accounts originated in

New England in the 1970s but, effective in 1981, may be offered nationwide by banks and savings and loan associations. In effect, a NOW account is a time deposit that earns interest while allowing the convenience of having funds in a checking account.

4. **Automatic Teller Machines (ATMS),** technological developments have led to the use of computer terminals that accept deposits and payments, and dispense cash and information. Performing most of the same functions as a human teller, ATMs add the convenience of 24–hour service and availability at remote locations.

5. **Certificate of Deposit (CD). Small nonnegotiable certificates of deposit** are a form of time deposit in which a receipt is held by the depositor for funds deposited in a bank or savings and loan for a set period of time and at a set interest rate. The word "small" means $100,000 or less. The interest rate payable on small CDs, like all time deposits, is regulated by Regulation Q of the Federal Reserve System. The amount of interest paid varies with the length of time to maturity for the CD, with higher rates payable for longer maturity CDs. A schedule of maximum interest rates payable on savings deposits is shown in Figure 2-1.

Large negotiable certificates of deposit are issued in denominations of $100,000 or more. The interest rate is set through negotiations, and the certificate can be transferred from one holder to another without the permission of the issuing bank. In 1970, Regulation Q ceilings were lifted from large short-term (30- to 89–day) CDs, and in 1973 Regulation Q ceilings on large long-term CDs were suspended. This action made CDs competitive with treasury issues for corporate funds. CDs are attractive because they are relatively safe, and they offer higher yields than government securities. In addition, they are highly liquid since a large **secondary market** exists in which negotiable CDs can be sold prior to maturity. CDs are sold primarily to business firms and other organizations with sizable amounts of money to invest for short periods of time. Figure 2-2 shows the dollar volume of outstanding large CDs.

Figure 2-1. Maximum Interest Rates Payable on Time and Savings Deposits at Federally Insured Institutions.

Type of Deposit	In Effect 12/31/85
Savings	5 1/4 percent
Negotiable. Order of Withdrawal Accounts.	5 1/4 percent

Money Market Deposit Accounts.

Balance less than $1,000	Account is subject to maximum rate of interest

For NOW accounts.

Balance greater than $1,000	Account is not subject to interest rate restrictions.

Time Accounts

7 to 31 days of less than $1,000	5 1/2 percent
7 to 31 days of $1,000 or more	—
More than 31 days	—

Source: "Domestic Financial Statistics," Table A8, *Federal Reserve Bulletin*, February 1986.

Figure 2-2. Large Certificates of Deposit, 1966-1985.

Year	Amount Outstanding (billions)
1966	$23
1967	31
1968	38
1969	20
1970	45
1971	58
1972	73
1973	111
1974	144
1975	130
1976	118
1977	145
1978	195
1979	219
1980	251
1981	302
1982	328
1983	326
1984	416
1985	427

Source: *Economic Report of the President*, January 1981; *World Financial Markets*, August 1985.

FEATURES OF U.S. COMMERCIAL BANKING

The creation of the Federal Reserve System in 1913 marked the beginning of the modern banking system in the United States. In this section, we examine some of the features and distinctions of that system.

National and State Banks

Under the U.S. dual system of banking, some banks have state charters, whereas others receive their charters from the federal government (see Figure 2-3). In December 1984, the United States had just over 15,000 commercial banks, 10,300 of which were state banks and 4,700 national banks. On the average, national banks are larger than state banks. Although national banks make up only 32 percent of the total number of banks, they hold approximately 58 percent of the total deposits in commercial banks.

Federal Reserve Membership

One distinction among commercial banks involves membership or nonmembership in the Federal Reserve System. A **member bank** is any commercial bank that has been accepted for membership. The law requires all national banks to be members. If state banks meet certain requirements membership is optional. During the 1970s, the Federal Reserve (the Fed) experienced a decline in its membership. Competitive pressures, particularly the high level of reserves required for members of the Fed, encouraged banks to convert national charters to state charters and drop out of the Fed. This situation changed with the passage of the Monetary Control Act of 1980 which required nonmember banks and all nonmember depository financial institutions to conform to the deposit reserve requirements set by the Fed. Through this legislation, the decline in Federal Reserve membership has been reversed.

The Federal Reserve System provides a number of services to member and nonmember banks. The most important ongoing service involves clearing checks. The Federal Reserve District Banks also work with banks to promote stability in the banking system. Figure 2-3 contains some information on the impact of Fed membership in terms of the number of banks and size of deposits.

Figure 2-3. Commercial Banks and Federal Reserve Membership,
December 1984 (dollar amounts in billions).

Category	Number of Banks	Percent	Deposits	Total Percent
U.S. Commercial Banks	15,025	100	1,548,718	100
National Banks	4,753	32	893,757	58
State Banks	102,732	68	654,962	42
Member Banks of Federal Reserve	5,806	39	1,117,595	72
Nonmember Banks	9,219	61	431,123	28

Source: *1985 Annual Report*, Federal Deposit Insurance Corporation, Washington, D.C.

Branch Banking

A **branch** may be defined as a banking outlet other than the main office in which a commercial bank or other financial institution **accepts deposits. Branch banking** exists when a single bank accepts deposits at two or more locations in the same city, county, state, or across state or national lines. This differs from **unit banking** in which where the bank conducts its operations from a single office.

Historically, the U.S. banking system has been dominated by unit banks. The politicians and businesspeople in small communities preferred local control of banking institutions. As a reflection of this preference, federal agencies and state governments restricted branch banking until the 1920s. In 1927, the McFadden Act allowed national banks to open branches within a state if permitted under state laws. Branching did not, however, expand rapidly until after World War II.

The movement toward deregulation of banking activities is rapidly eliminating unit banking. The changing competitive environment for banking services encourages larger institutions that can offer an increasing capability to meet customer needs. Without branching capabilities, banks will experience difficulties competing with nonbank financial institutions that offer services across state and national boundaries.

Bank Holding Companies

A **bank holding company** is a corporation that owns or controls the voting stock of one or more banks. We can identify **one-bank holding companies**, which own or control a single bank, and **multi-bank holding companies**, which own or control two or more separately chartered banks. In many cases, when we think of a bank, we are identifying a bank holding company.

The existence of holding companies facilitates the concentration of assets in a bank structure and allows activities that otherwise might not be possible. There are several major reasons for the establishment of a holding company structure.

1. **Rapid Expansion by Acquisition**. When one bank seeks to purchase another, it may want both banks to operate separately. This is possible in a holding company structure in which each bank has a separate charter, segregated assets, and individual management. Instead of incurring all the problems involved with a merger, both banks continue to operate without interruption.

2. **Operation of Nonbank Activities**. Federal and state laws place tight restrictions on banking activities and the protection of assets for depositors. With a holding company structure, the bank can engage in nonbanking activities that do not jeopardize the assets of depositors, such as offering bookkeeping or data processing services, issuing credit cards, and providing courier services.

3. **Circumvention of Branching Laws**. A holding company structure allows a bank to circumvent laws that prohibit activities in other locations. If branching is forbidden or restricted, a holding company can be used to form separately chartered banks and operate them like a branch structure. Similarly, bank holding companies can conduct subsidiary activities across state lines.

4. **Improved Services and Efficiency**. A holding company structure can provide better services at lower costs to clients. The lead bank in the structure of the holding company can centralize data processing and check clearing, minimize duplication of effort in functions such as purchasing, personnel activities, tax planning, and participation in audits and examinations. At the same time, the larger structure allows the bank to retain specialists who assist customers with their investments, trusts, and financial counseling needs. Generally, a large financial services institution can offer more services at a profit to the bank and reasonable costs to the customer.

Size of Banks

In terms of the size of assets and deposits, commercial banks range from small to enormous. Figure 2-4 shows the size of a sampling from the largest 50 banks and holding companies. If the list continued to the smallest banks, it would show institutions with only a few million dollars in assets, as shown in the aggregate data in Figure 2-5. During the 1980s, we are witnessing a consolidation of financial institutions in the United States. First, the distinctions have blurred among commercial banks, savings banks, and loan associations, and other financial entities. Second, deregulation has produced an environment in which smaller and weaker institutions are combining with larger and stronger institutions. Even stronger institutions are merging to achieve competitive benefits in the increasingly deregulated markets.

Figure 2-4. Size of Selected Banks, December 31, 1984 (millions of dollars).

Rank by Assets	Name of Bank	Assets	Deposits	Outstanding Loans
1	Citicorp (N.Y.)	150,586	90,349	103,624
2	BankAmerica (Calif.)	117,679	94,084	85,046
3	Chase Manhattan (N.Y.)	86,883	59,680	62,003
4	Manufacturers Hanover (N.Y.)	75,714	44,206	58,211
5	Morgan (N.Y.)	64,126	38,760	35,822
7	Security Pacific (Los Angeles)	46,117	31,006	33,011
11	Mellon National (Pittsburgh)	30,603	18,997	19,687
19	Republic Bank (Dallas)	21,595	15,622	14,317
27	PRC Financial (Pittsburgh)	14,870	8,976	8,057
41	Wachovia (Winston-Salem)	8,717	6,381	4,995
46	Ranier Bancorp (Seattle)	7,762	5,471	5,210
50	Maryland National (Baltimore)	7,286	4,374	4,942

Source: *Business Week*, April 8, 1985.

Figure 2-5. Distribution of Commercial Banks by Size of Assets.

Number and Total Assets of FDIC Insured Commercial Banks and Trust Companies, Calendar Year 1984 Banks Grouped by Class and Asset Size (in millions of dollars)

| | TOTAL | Commercial Banks and Trust Companies | | |
		Total	National Charter	Fed Member	State Charter Fed Nonmember
Number of Banks					
Less than 25.0 M	5,564	5,556	1,399	379	3,778
$25 to 50 M	3,768	3,763	1,195	273	2,295
$50 to 100 M	2,797	2,738	1,095	188	1,455
$100 to 300 M	1,796	1,691	784	125	782
$300 to 500 M	301	264	142	23	99
$500 to 1,000 M	244	206	105	26	75
$1 to 3 B	204	176	107	26	43
$3 to 10 B	87	78	60	10	8
$10 B or more	26	24	17	7	0
Total Banks	14,787	14,496	4,904	1,057	8,535
Amount of Assets					
Less than $25.0 M	79,388	79,255	20,727	5,397	53,131
$25 to 50 M	135,348	135,152	43,459	9,819	81,874
$50 to 100 M	194,469	190,038	76,282	13,009	100,747
$100 to 300 M	290,971	271,586	128,425	20,428	122,733
$300 to 500 M	113,875	99,471	53,204	9,108	37,159
$500 to 1,000 M	169,358	142,886	73,871	17,619	51,396
$1 to 3 B	350,476	303,451	177,873	49,462	76,116
$3 to 10 B	465,319	423,371	332,833	58,977	31,561
$10 B or more	889,846	864,789	591,490	273,299	0
Total Assets	2,689,050	2,509,999	1,498,164	457,118	554,717

Source: 1985 *Statistics of Banking*, Federal Deposit Insurance Corporation, Washington, D.C.

MEASURES OF U.S. MONEY SUPPLY

To understand the roles of inflation and the level of interest rates in an economic system, one must recognize the impact of the growth of the money supply. Too much money compared to the available goods and services is a contributing factor to rising prices. A shortage of money to finance investments and business activity can lead to high interest rates and economic stagnation. Economists differ as to which measure best reflects the amount of money available to purchase goods and services and finance economic activity. In order to report monetary data that meet the needs and requests of the major groups of economists, the Federal Reserve System has developed several categories for identifying the money supply.

The Federal Reserve has historically reported different categories of monetary aggregates. Through the 1970s the Fed used five primary categories of the money supply ranging from the most liquid to the least liquid. At different times, the classification scheme has been changed. Two factors affected these changes.

1. **New Monetary Assets.** In the 1970s and 1980s, a variety of new monetary assets appeared as important components of the pool of liquid assets available in the United States. These new forms had to be recognized in measurements of the money supply.

2. **Changing Financial Institutions.** In the 1970s and 1980s, the distinctions among financial institutions changed. Services restricted to commercial banks are now offered by other financial institutions. The increasing similarity among banks, thrift institutions, and financial services institutions has an effect on the money supply that is not reflected in previous monetary categories.

The new definitions of the money supply are also scaled from most liquid to least liquid. In addition, some individual categories of monetary assets are identified. In this section, we examine the current Federal Reserve measures of money in the United States.

Five Official Measures

The Federal Reserve System employs five official measures of the U.S. money supply, with simplified definitions as follows:

1. **M-1.** This measure includes money in circulation plus demand deposits at commercial banks and checkable deposits. **Checkable deposits** include NOW and ATM accounts, demand deposit accounts at mutual savings banks, and credit union share draft accounts. This is the most liquid measure of the money supply.

2. **M-2.** This measure includes M-1 plus the most liquid of the remaining monetary assets. These consist of savings accounts and small time deposit balances, money market mutual fund shares, and overnight repurchase agreements and Eurodollars. (A Eurodollar is a dollar held outside the United States in a foreign branch of a U.S. bank or in foreign bank.) If M-1 is generally viewed as the amount of money readily available for transactions, M-2 is the measure of what could be available almost immediately if needed.

3. **M-3.** This measure includes M-2 plus two large liability items of banking and thrift institutions. The two items are large certificates of deposit and term repurchase agreements. Certificates of deposit under $100,000 and overnight repurchase agreements are already counted in the M-2 definition.

4. **L.** This measure includes M-3 plus a variety of other liquid assets including U.S. savings bonds, short–term government securities, commercial paper, and banker's acceptances.

5. **Debt.** This measure consists of the liabilities of the federal government and private sector, including corporate bonds, mortgages, and consumer credit. It is the least liquid measure of money supply.

Figure 2-6 shows the amounts of "money" in each of the five measures.

Figure 2-6. Money Stock, Liquid Assets, and Debt Measures. (billions)

Item	Dec. 1981	Dec. 1982	Dec. 1983	Dec. 1984	Dec. 1985
M1	441.8	480.8	528.0	558.5	626.3
M2	1,794.4	1,954.9	2,188.8	2,371.7	2,564.1
M3	2,235.8	2,446.8	2,701.8	2,995.0	3,190.9
L	2,596.4	2,854.7	3,168.8	3,541.3	n.a.
Debt	4,255.8	4,649.8	5,177.2	5,927.1	n.a.

Source: "Money Stock, Liquid Assets, and Debt Measures," Table A13, *Federal Reserve Bulletin,* February 1986,

Usefulness of Each Measure

With five different approaches to measuring the money supply, it is natural to discuss the utility of each measure. No one approach can be viewed as the optimal measure of the money supply. To meet the economy's transactions demand for cash, the M-1 or possibly M-2 measures are most useful. These are the most liquid measurements of the amount of money in the United States. To meet precautionary or speculative demands, the M-3 or L measures might be more useful. These contain a variety of liquid funds held by individuals or businesses that could be used if a sufficient opportunity or need arose. We conclude that the appropriate measure of the money supply will depend on the purpose of the economist or analyst. The Federal Reserve publishes different measures to facilitate economic research and analysis of the relationships between money and different kinds of economic activity.

From the viewpoint of working–capital management, an awareness of the money supply is quite important. Because the manager is making decisions on the level of cash, credit policies, and the timing of payment for payables, the activities of the Federal Reserve Board in managing money supply are important. When money supply is tightened, the firm begins to experience liquidity problems that previously did not exist. Interest rates begin to rise, and banks have less funds to lend. Similarly, relaxed money supply policies provide opportunities to use increased liquidity to achieve a number of profit purposes. Policy decisions in working–capital areas should always be made in the context of Federal Reserve policies on managing money supply.

Money Creation

There are two primary methods for creating money in the U.S. economic system.

1. **Printing Currency or Minting Coins.** Since the United States uses credit money as opposed to full-bodied money, money is created whenever the government prints additional paper money or mints new coins and circulates them.

2. **Creation of Deposits.** Whenever a financial institution makes a loan, it participates in the creation of additional deposits in the banking system. Since deposits are counted in the money supply, the lending activity of a bank creates money in the system.

In this section, we examine the deposit creation of financial institutions. We begin with examples of money creation when a loan is made. Then we examine the limit on deposit creation, which is also the limit on money creation. Finally, we develop a money creation formula for the maximum amount of money that can be created as the result of lending.

Figure 2-7. Balance Sheet, Republic Bank and Trust Company.

Assets		Liabilities and Capital	
Vault Cash	$200,000	Demand Deposits	
Due from Banks	500,000	and NOW Accounts	$1,100,000
Investments	1,500,000	Savings Accounts	1,500,000
Loans	3,500,000	Other Time Deposits	2,800,000
Furniture, Fix-tures, Premises	250,000	Bank Capital	550,000
	$5,950,000		$5,950,000

Figure 2-8. Creating Money When a Loan is Deposited Directly to a Borrower's Account.

Republic Bank and Trust Accounts			**Lincoln Bank Accounts**	
Due from Banks	*John Randolph's NOW account*		*Due from Banks*	*Demand Deposits*
500,000	6,350		xxxxxx	xxxxxxxxxxx
	7,500			
10,000	10,000		10,000	10,000
Loans				
3,500,000				
7,500	Loan is made by direct deposit.		Check for $10,000, transfers $2,500 of original $6,350 plus $7,500 new loan. $7,500 is still in banking system as newly created money.	

Three Ways a Bank Loan Creates Money

Whenever a bank or other depository institution makes a loan to a customer, money is created in the economic system. To illustrate this concept, we examine the three ways a loan can be made.

1. **Direct Deposit to Borrower's Account**. The most common lending arrangement is for the bank to credit the money to the account of the borrower. To illustrate this process, begin with the balance sheet for Republic Bank and Trust Company, which is given in Figure 2-7. Assume that John Randolph, a customer of the bank, has a NOW account with a balance of $6,350 in it. Mr. Randolph has approached the bank to borrow $7,500, to finance a new car. The bank has approved the loan request and, after the appropriate papers are signed, the loan is made by depositing the money in Mr. Randolph's NOW account. This is a bookkeeping entry that increases two accounts on the bank's books. Loans is debited $7,500, and demand deposits is credited $7,500. This action increases the level of demand deposits and, thus, increases the money supply.

   The next step is for Mr. Randolph to write a check to purchase his car. When his check clears, the NOW account balance is transferred from Republic Bank to another bank, but it remains in the money supply for the system as a whole. Based on the assumption that the car dealer has an account at Lincoln Bank, Figure 2-8 shows the creation of money as a result of Mr. Randolph borrowing $7,500.

2. **Issuance of Currency.** A borrower may wish to receive the loan proceeds in currency. Even though this is risky when $7,500 is involved, we can follow the effects of the transaction. Currency in the bank's vault is excluded from the money supply. The M1 definition includes only currency that is circulating among individuals and businesses. Therefore, the removal of the currency from the vault increases the money supply. The bank accounts for the loan as follows:

Vault Cash		Loans	
200,000		3,500,000	
	7,500		7,500

The $7,500 removed from the vault becomes currency in Mr. Randolph's wallet and therefore enters the money supply. It stays in the money supply when it is given to the car dealer and deposited in Lincoln Bank.

3. **Issuance of Cashier's Check.** If a borrower does not have an account at the bank or if the borrower desires, the bank will make the loan in the form of a **cashier's check**, which is a check drawn by a bank on its own funds and signed by an officer. The dealer would prefer to receive a cashier's check instead of a personal check because of the reduced chance that the check might not clear. The accounting by Republic Bank would be as follows:

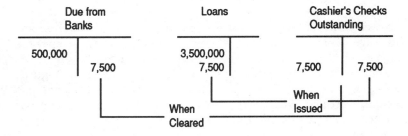

An outstanding cashier's check is classified as a demand deposit. Even though the bank is writing the check on its own funds, giving the check to the customer is the same as putting money in the customer's account. Since cashier's checks count in the money supply as a demand deposit, the loan increases the money supply when made with such a check.

The Role of Reserves

When Republic Bank is establishing its lending policies, it recognizes that it cannot lend all its money. The limits on its ability to lend restricts the banking system's ability to create money. These limits occur because all financial institutions are required to hold a percentage of their deposits in the form of noninterest–bearing assets called **reserves**. Next identify three terms to help understand the limits on a bank's ability to lend.

1. **Legal Reserves**. These are non-interest bearing assets that are held by a financial institution for the purpose of meeting reserve requirements. Depository institutions can hold legal reserves in three forms.

   a. **Vault Cash**. These reserves are the coins and currency held in the vaults, teller's cages, and automatic money machines.

   b. **Deposits with Federal Reserve Banks**. For the purpose of holding legal reserves, both member and nonmember institutions of the Fed establish deposit accounts at Federal Reserve District Banks. Similarly, savings and loan associations and credit unions establish accounts at the Federal Home Loan Bank or National Credit Union Administration's Central Liquidity Facility.

   c. **Deposits with Correspondents**. A **correspondent banking relationship** occurs when two depository institutions agree to work together to provide services from one institution to the other. For example, a large bank may assist a smaller bank in collecting checks, providing credit to customers, offering investment advice, and making available various banking services. One such service is passing legal reserves. One institution can make a deposit with a correspondent who then makes a deposit with the appropriate federal agency. Under this pass-through arrangement, deposits with correspondents count when counting legal reserves.

2. **Required Reserves**. These reserves are the level of reserves a depository institution must hold, as calculated by different percentages applied to each category of deposits. To determine required reserves, we **calculate** them. The level of required reserves is specified under the provisions of the Monetary Control Act of 1980 and the Depository Institutions Act of 1982 for categories of deposits as follows:

   a. **Transactions Accounts**. This catagory includes demand deposits, NOW accounts, ATM accounts, share drafts, accounts subject to telephonic or preauthorized transfers, and other accounts with special arrangements for making payments. Each depository institution is required to maintain as reserves 3 percent of the first $28.9 million, and 12 percent on amounts above this figure as established by the Federal Reserve. The $28.9 million is adjusted each year to reflect growth or contraction in the money supply.

   b. **Personal Time Deposits**. These deposits are savings, certificates of deposit, and similar accounts held by individuals. No reserves are required for these accounts.

    c. **Nonpersonal Time Deposits**. These accounts include Savings accounts and certificates of deposit held by businesses and such depositors. For accounts with original maturities of less than 1 1/2 years, a 3 percent reserve requirement applies.

    d. **Eurocurrency Liabilities**. When a **Eurodollar** is converted into francs, marks, or other currency, it becomes **Eurocurrency**. When a U.S. bank borrows a Eurocurrency from abroad, a 3 percent reserve requirement is applied. The same requirement is imposed when foreign branches of U.S. banks make loans to U.S. residents or when U.S. institutions transfer assets to their foreign offices. The full requirements for reserves are shown in Figure 2-9.

3. **Excess Reserves**. These reserves are the difference between legal reserves and required reserves. As an example, if a bank is required to hold $500,000 in reserves and it has $650,000 in items that count as legal reserves, the bank has $150,000 in excess reserves ($650,000 minus $500,000).

The concept of excess reserves is important in determining the maximum amount of money a bank can lend. The **excess reserve rule** states that a bank or other financial institution can make loans up to the limit of its excess reserves. Stated differently, when legal reserves equal required reserves, the depository institution cannot make additional loans.

Adjusting Reserves in the Fed Funds Market

Federal funds, or Fed funds, are demand deposits of member commercial banks in the Federal Reserve District Bank; that is, the member bank holds reserves at the Fed. If a bank has excess reserves, it may allow another bank to borrow a portion of its deposit at the Fed. The borrowing bank will pay interest on the funds. Such borrowing occurs in the **Fed funds market**, a linkage of commercial banks and security dealers that specialize in Fed funds transactions. If a bank is a borrower of Fed funds, its balance sheet will have a liability account entitled **Fed funds bought**; if it is a lender, it will have an asset account called **Fed funds sold**.

The amount of money a commercial bank may lend to individuals or businesses reflects the liquidity of the bank. If a bank has sizable funds to lend, it is viewed as being highly liquid. If the bank has lent most of its funds, it will not be able to accommodate many additional requests for funds. It is therefore said to be relatively illiquid. The Fed funds market allows a bank to adjust its liquidity to provide earnings of idle assets or to meet the demand of its customers for loans. By borrowing or investing in this market, usually on an overnight basis, a bank can adjust its liquidity position and level of legal reserves. It can invest excess reserves to earn a return on them; similarly, it can borrow so it has sufficient legal reserves to meet the Federal Reserve requirements.

Figure 2-9. **Member Bank Requirements After Implementation of the Monetary Control Act.**

Type of Deposit and Interval	Percent
Net Transactions Accounts	
$0m - $29.8m	3
Over $29.8m	12
Nonpersonal Time Deposits By Original Maturity	
Less than 1 1/2 years	3
1 1/2 years or more	0
Eurocurrency Liabilities	3

Source: "Reserve Requirements of Depository Institutions," Table A7 *Federal Reserve Bulletin*, February 1986.

Primary and Derivative Deposits

A **primary deposit** occurs when money is placed in a financial institution as the result of an independent transaction; that is, the money is derived from a source outside the bank. A **derivative deposit**, on the other hand, is the bank's liability that is created when the bank lends money to a customer and it is redeposited in the bank. If borrowers do not immediately spend the proceeds of loans, a bank will have large derivative deposits. Banks seek derivative deposits because they help it meet its reserve requirements and a portion of the derivative deposits may be lent to other customers.

Limit on Deposit Creation

The process of lending money and derivative deposits in transactions accounts expands the supply of money available in the economic system. How much money is created? The answer depends on the amount of excess reserves that are lent out and the reserve requirement that applies to derivative deposits. To determine the maximum amount of money that can be created, in addition to the level of money that already exists, we can use the formula:

$$\text{Money Created}_{(max)} = \frac{\text{Reserves}_{(excess)}}{\%\text{RES}_{req(deriv)}}$$

where

$\text{Money Created}_{(max)}$ =   the maximum amount of new money that can be created in the economic system

Reserves$_{(excess)}$ = the excess reserves of all financial institutions in the system

%RES$_{req (deriv)}$ = percent of reserve requirement applicable to derivative deposits

Example: Central National Bank has excess reserves of $9 million and a reserve requirement of 12 percent on derivative deposits in transactions accounts. What is the maximum amount of new money that this bank can create in the banking system?

Answer: $75 million, as follows:

$$\text{Money Created}_{(max)} = \frac{9,000,000}{0.12} = 75,000,000$$

CONCLUSION

We have developed the basic framework for examining the movement of cash in an economic system and the extension of credit by commercial banks. A bank's liquidity is dependent on its level of deposits, the size of the nation's money supply, reserve requirements on different forms of deposits, and the philosophy and policies of the bank. We will return to these factors and their roles in cash management in the following chapters.

SETON NATIONAL STATE BANK CASE—
FUNDS AVAILABLE TO LEND

This case provides insight into the bank's development of lending policies. In periods of tight money, a bank is unable to meet all the loan demands from its customers. The bank must calculate the funds it has available to lend within the restrictions of the system of reserve requirements. This case allows the reader to perform such a calculation.

Harold Walters, the president of Seton National State Bank (SNSB), was in the process of conducting his year-end review of the position of the bank. An unaudited balance sheet is attached.

The bank's performance in the past 12 months had not lived up to Harold's expectations. The bank's cost of funds was almost one-half percent higher than the Management Committee's forecast. The bank had experienced difficulties automating portions of its automatic funds transfer (AFT) processes, and this caused a rise in operating expenses. A second problem occurred when a small but significant number of depositors shifted from low–cost accounts to higher yield certificates. These and several minor factors combined to affect the bank's likely earnings for the year.

Harold was determined to improve SNSB's earnings next year. He felt confident that the bank had a firm grasp on its operations and cost of funds as it entered a new year. The trick now, in Harold's mind, was to avoid having idle funds on hand. He wanted to ensure that the bank was lending all of its available funds, either in commercial loans, residential or construction mortgages, or consumer loans. This would be his goal for the next year.

With the Fed funds market offering a device for adjusting the bank's liquidity against loan demand, Harold decided to evaluate his current lending posture. His first question dealt with the bank's level of funds that could be lent. He knew that funds available to lend depend on three factors.

1. **Level of Excess Reserves.** Since the bank must maintain legal reserves equal to the requirements of the Federal Reserve System, it must have excess reserves in order to be able to lend money.

2. **Derivative Deposits.** If borrowers do not immediately spend the proceeds of a loan, the bank will have derivative deposits. Or if a compensating balance is required, derivative deposits will result. A **compensating balance** is a requirement commonly found in a line of credit or other business loan whereby the borrower is required to maintain a certain minimum balance in a transactions account. Such a requirement helps the financial institution meet its reserve requirement.

3. **Reserve Requirements on Derivative Deposits.** When Seton National State Bank receives a derivative deposit from a loan, the money is normally placed in a demand deposit account. A portion of the derivative deposit can be re-lent, depending on the size of the reserve requirement.

The calculation of excess reserves should prove no problem, Harold felt. The schedule of reserve requirements was

0.03 on the first $28.9 million of net transactions accounts

0.12 on remaining net transactions accounts

0.00 on personal time deposits

0.03 on nonpersonal time deposits with maturities under 1 1/2 year

0.00 on remaining nonpersonal time deposits

0.03 on Eurodollar liabilities

Neither would it be a problem to estimate the level of derivative deposits. With a 10–percent compensating balance requirement that was more or less standard, derivative deposits should approximate 14 percent on new business loans. No compensating balances were required on mortgages or other non–business loans. The bank had a policy of maintaining a portfolio in which business loans made up 42 percent, mortgages 35 to 38 percent, and other loans the balance. This would be followed with future lending.

A greater problem occurred in locating a method for calculating the funds available to lend. After some research, Harold structured the problem. The likely derivative deposits and their reserve requirement must be applied to the bank's excess reserves at any moment in time to calculate the funds still available to lend by the bank. To calculate the funds available, he found the following formula:

$$\text{Funds Available to Lend} = \frac{\text{RES}_{legal} - (\text{DEPOSITS})\,(\%\text{RES}_{(req)})}{1 \text{ minus } (\%\text{DEP}_{(deriv)})\,(1 \text{ minus } \%\text{RES}_{req(deriv)})}$$

where

RES_{legal} = legal reserves

$(\text{DEPOSITS})\,\%\text{RES}_{req}$ = sum of each category of deposit times the appropriate reserve requirement for the category

%DEP$_{(deriv)}$ = percentage of the bank's loan-created deposits that it ordinarily retains. As an example, if a customer who borrows $1,000 normally deposits $150 of it in his checking account and leaves it there, this item is 150/1,000 or 15 percent.

%RES$_{req(deriv)}$ = percentage of reserve requirement applicable to derivative deposits

To illustrate the use of this formula, let us consider the following example:

Example: The Neighborhood Bank of Safety Harbor has $8 million in capital and $1.5 million in building, equipment, and related assets. It has individual demand deposits of $9 million and business demand deposits of $17 million. NOW accounts total $11 million, and ATM accounts are $2.5 million. Its passbook accounts total $18 million for individuals and $1.5 million for business corporations and other organizations. Certificates of deposit with maturities of less than 1 1/2 years amount to $6 million for individuals and $7 million for others. Nonpersonal CDs of $200,000 have maturities in excess of 1 1/2 years. The bank has Eurodollar liabilities of $1.5 million. The bank has outstanding loans of $55.2 million and securities investments of $9.5 million. A total of $1.5 million is due from banks, $3 million of Fed funds have been sold, and $9 million is on deposit in a reserve account at the Federal Reserve District Bank. The balance of the bank's funds are in the vault in the form of coin and currency. Derivative deposits from loans average 13 percent, deposited almost entirely in checking and NOW accounts. Prepare a balance sheet for this bank. What are the funds available to lend for the bank?

Answer: If vault cash is used as the balancing item, the balance sheet is as follows:

Balance Sheet
Neighborhood Bank of Safety Harbor (000s)

Vault Cash	$2,000		Transactions Accounts	
Fed Deposits	9,000		Indiv Demand	$9,000
		$11,000	Other Demand	17,000
Due from Banks		1,500	NOW Accounts	11,000
Fed Funds Sold		3,000	ATS Accounts	2,500
				39,500
Investments		9,500	Savings Accounts	
			Individual	18,000
Loans		55,200	Other	1,500
				19,500
Fixed Assets		1,500	Time Deposits	
			Individual	6,000
			Other	7,000
			Maturities–over	
			4 Years	200
				13,200
			Eurodollar liabilities	1,500
			Capital	8,000
TOTAL		$81,700	TOTAL	$81,700

The legal reserves for this bank consist of vault cash and Fed deposits and total $11 million. The required reserves from the schedule are $2,358,000 as follows:

Category of Deposit	Dollar Amount	Reserve Requirement	Required Reserves
Transactions	29,800,000	0.03	894,000
	9,700,000	0.12	1,164,000
Nonpersonal Time	1,500,000	0.03	45,000
	7,000,000	0.03	210,000
Eurocurrency	1,500,000	0.03	45,000
Total			2,358,000

Using a 13 percent derivative deposit, a 12 percent reserve requirement on derivative deposits, and the formula, we find that the funds available to lend would be $9,758,356.

Funds Available to Lend	
Legal Reserves	11,000,000
Sum of Deposits Times Reserve Requirements	2,358,000
Percentage of Derivative Deposits	0.13
Reserve Requirement Percent Applicable	0.12

$$\text{Funds Available to Lend} = \frac{11,000,000 - 2,358,000}{1 - ((0.13) * (1 - 0.12))} = 9,758,356$$

After reviewing the formula and the example of the Safety Harbor Bank, Harold wondered if the formula worked correctly. How could he know? Suddenly, he had a thought. If the formula were correctly formulated, the Safety Harbor Bank would have zero excess reserves if it lent out $9,758,356. Sure enough, excess reserves came out to be zero when he performed the calculation. He began with the original level of legal reserves, and assumed new loans of $9,758,356 and derivative deposits of 13 percent of that amount. Similarly, he began with the original required reserves and assumed a 12 percent reserve requirement on the derivative deposits from the new loans. His calculation was.

Original Legal Reserves	$11,000,000
Less New Loan	(9,758,356)
Plus Derivative Deposits	
(9,758,356) x 0.13	<u>1,268,586</u>
Legal Reserves	2,510,230
Original Required Reserves	2,358,000
Plus New Requirements on	
Derivative Deposits	
1,268,586 times 0.12	<u>152,230</u>
Required Reserves	2,510,230
Excess Reserves	0

At this point, Harold Walters took exception to one point in the formula from the illustration. The Safety Harbor had Fed funds sold as an item on its balance sheet, but this money did not get counted in the funds available to lend. Technically, Harold recognized that this was correct. But, he reasoned, Fed funds could be liquidated quickly and the bank would have more funds to lend. When he did his own calculation, he would assume a liquidation of Seton National's Fed funds sold and would consider them as funds available to lend.

Required: Assuming that Fed funds sold can be immediately converted into demand deposits with the Federal Reserve, what are SNSB's funds available to lend?

What would be the bank's balance sheet if it lent out all available funds?

Seton National State Bank Balance Sheet

Assets		
Coin and Currency Held in Vault		$5,780,000
Deposits, Demand, Federal Reserve		13,651,000
Pass–through Deposits, Correspondent Banks		825,000
Checks in Process of Collection		6,215,000
Holdings of U.S. Treasury/Agency Securities		3,577,000
Holdings of Municipal Securities		1,230,000
Other Securities		215,000
Loans Outstanding		
Business	88,407,000	
Mortgage	78,512,000	
Individual	39,415,000	
Other	2,395,000	208,729,000
Federal Funds Sold		1,600,000
Bank Premises, Fixtures, Miscellaneous		22,590,000
Total Assets		**$264,412,000**

Liabilities and Capital	
Demand Deposits	$99,835,000
NOW Accounts	28,414,000
Time and Savings Deposits,	
Individuals	25,214,000
Other (nonpersonal under 1 1/2 Years)	67,903,000
Deposits of U.S. Government	2,410,000
Deposits of States or Municipalities	710,000
Certified and Cashier's Checks	355,000
Time Deposits, over 1 1/2 Years Maturities	2,200,000
Other Liabilities	
Checks in Process	6,215,000
Large CDs, under 1 Year	5,800,000
Eurodollar Liabilities	100,000
Total Liabilities	239,156,000

Common Stock–Par Value $1	400,000
Surplus	3,200,000
Undivided Profits	21,306,000
Reserve for Contingencies; Other Reserves	350,000
Total Capital	25,256,000
Total Liabilities and Capital	**$264,412,000**

3

Managing Disbursements and Collections

The firm's system of cash management employs a combination of instruments, techniques, and services. The goal is to achieve efficient use of corporate funds. In this sense, banks and company treasurers become partners in the management of money. Disbursement and collection practices recognize the movements of money through the banking system and should be designed to provide the maximum amount of cash at the lowest possible cost.

In this chapter, we will examine the major elements of a cash management system. The specific emphasis is on the twin tasks of managing disbursements and speeding up collections.

CASH MANAGEMENT SYSTEM

In developing its approach to the management of cash, the company's primary goal should be to optimize the availability of funds for use by the treasurer. Achieving this goal involves certain activities in a comprehensive system. In this section, we will identify some of the features of such a system.

Float

Whether disbursing or collecting money, the firm should recognize that money movements involve lags and delays. The term **float** refers to the time periods when cash is not available as a result of lags between the sale of goods or providing of services and the cash on hand in a form that can be disbursed or invested. Four kinds of float can be identified.

1. **Billing Float.** An **invoice** is the formal document requesting payment for goods sold or services provided. It is usually prepared by a seller and sent to the purchaser, at approximately the same time as the goods are delivered or services completed. Sometimes there are delays in creating the invoice. The time between the sale and the mailing of the invoice is the billing float.

2. **Mail Float**. This is the time period when a check is being processed by the post office, messenger service, or other means of delivery.

3. **Check Processing Float**. This is the time required for the seller to sort, record, and deposit the check after it has arrived in the company's mailroom.

4. **Bank Processing Float**. This is the time from the deposit of the check to the crediting of funds in the seller's account.

A major task of cash management is the control of float. It involves a number of activities, including the effective use of information on the status of cash receipts, disbursements, and balances. It requires complete and timely reporting on the varying aspects of the system to allow an up-to-date monitoring of cash requirements. Such a system permits the firm to exploit opportunities that may arise and avoid shortages of funds when needed. This chapter covers several different approaches to controlling the firm's float.

The Kind of Bank

A large corporation should design a cash management system that makes use of cash control features of the banking system. Two distinct categories of banks may be identified.

1. **Depository Bank**. This institution specializes in collecting checks, processing them quickly, and making funds available to the firm. Such a bank offers a range of services designed to speed up collections. Generally, depository banks are located in large cities convenient to airlines and other means of transportation.

2. **Disbursing Bank**. This institution does not specialize in rapidly receiving and processing checks. Since checks are slower to clear, the float is extended for the individual or firm that writes the check. These banks offer services that ensure that checks will be properly covered by funds in the account when presenting for payment. At the same time, it will not be necessary to leave large idle balances on hand prior to presenting of the checks.

The Kind of Account

A cash management system should distinguish among three categories of bank accounts:

1. **Operating Account**. This account is used to pay bills and otherwise conduct the daily activities of the firm. The balance in this account must be sufficient to satisfy the bank's requirements and provide cash as

checks are presented for payment. Usually, the bank does not pay interest on balances in these accounts, and service charges are paid by the company.

2. **Investment Account**. This account is used to hold funds in excess of operating needs. The institution will pay interest on funds held in this account on a daily basis. Funds may be transferred from this account to other forms of liquid investment, such as the purchase of marketable securities.

3. **Lockbox Account**. A lockbox is a post office box under the control of a bank. The bank providing the lockbox service collects the mail and deposits the checks directly into the firm's account. The bank then sends a copy of the checks, along with letters or other materials, to the company's Accounting Department. The lockbox account may be the firm's operating account and may exist at the firm's regular disbursing and depository bank. It may also exist at a bank where the only activity is the receipt of checks into the lockbox account and the transfer of money from that account to another bank.

The Kind of Movement

An important aspect of cash management is the ability to move funds between accounts and banks. If all collections and disbursements occur in accounts at the same bank, this task is straightforward. The bank moves funds using bookkeeping entries in its computer. When different banks are involved, the task becomes more complicated. Three kinds of movements are commonly used.

1. **Paper Transfer with Individual Checks**. The treasurer can always write a check on an account and deposit it in another account. For small dollar amounts or for arrangements that are too costly, this is a slow but effective way to transfer money.

2. **Paper Transfer with Depository Transfer Checks**. A **depository transfer check (DTC)** is a nonnegotiable demand deposit instrument drawn by a bank and payable to a firm or individual. It is used to move money between banks and is generally a faster vehicle for movement than an individual check. The DTC can be written by either the receiving or sending bank. In either case, the movement of funds normally takes only a single day. Thus, a DTC drawn on Tuesday means funds are available in the receiving bank account on Wednesday.

3. **Electronic Transfer. Electronic funds transfer (EFT)** refers to the movement of money in the banking system without the use of paper. This is accomplished under names such as wire transfer, electronic depository transfer checks, and by direct computer transactions where

instructions are typed on a screen and transmitted to banks. Electronic transfers can be accomplished using facilities of the Federal Reserve System or private services offered by large banks. Electronic transfer is the fastest way to move money between banks.

The Need for Information

The correct movement of money cannot take place without knowlege of funds available in different accounts and banks. Thus, timely information must be an element of a cash management system. Three categories of information may be identified.

1. **Periodic Reports.** For most accounts, the bank provides written reports on some periodic basis. For small accounts, a monthly statement is sent to the firm. For larger accounts, it is possible to receive daily reports on transactions and activity. The firm can use these statements to evaluate the collection and disbursement functions in operating and investment accounts.

2. **Telephonic Information.** With large balances of cash, the firm may not wish to wait until a written statement is received. Early each morning, the treasurer may seek a telephonic report of activities and available balances. This allows excess cash to be invested more quickly and problems to be resolved immediately.

3. **Electronic Reporting.** Many banks, particularly the large commercial banks specializing in collections or disbursements, offer direct electronic reporting. This method allows the bank's computer to communicate directly with the computer at the firm. The cash manager reviews the electronic report, either on the screen of the computer terminal or printed on paper, and makes decisions on necessary investing or other actions.

Concentration Banking

A large firm can tie the various features and services offered by banks into an overall approach to cash management. **Concentration banking** refers to a system of centralizing corporate cash with a goal of controlling the movement of funds and minimizing idle cash balances. A **concentration bank** is designated to receive funds from lockboxes or other accounts at depository banks. Electronic or Depository Transfer check movements are made automatically, according to the instructions of the firm. The concentration bank reports available balances daily, so the firm can take maximum advantage of investment opportunities.

Figure 3-1 presents an overview of a concentration banking system.

MANAGING COLLECTIONS

Because most firms make a majority of their sales on credit, the task of collecting funds is an important part of working–capital management. Two processes are involved. One involves the credit decisions that eventually produce payment in the form of a check. The other involves converting the check into cash in the shortest possible time. In this section, we will cover the collection process once a check has been received in the company or at the bank.

Figure 3-1. Schematic of Concentration Banking.

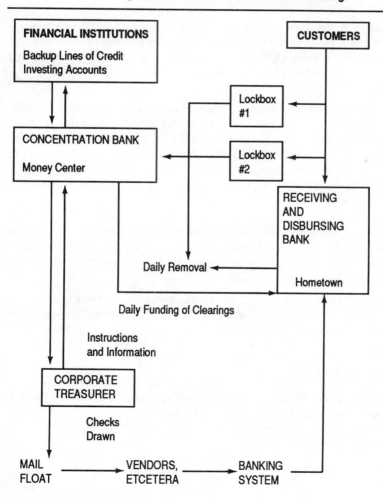

Clearing the Banking System

Clearing refers to the presentation of checks among banks, the offsetting of counterclaims, and the settling of net balances. The term is used to identify local, regional, and national activities when banks exchange checks with a goal of returning them to the banks on which they are drawn.

The process of clearing checks distinguishes between two kinds of instruments.

1. **Cash Item.** This item is accepted by a bank for immediate credit to a depositor's account. Generally, checks and other items payable on demand are cash items. Even though they are cash items, they may not be immediately available to be spent.

2. **Collection Item.** This item is accepted subject to further processing, and the bank must receive actual payment before the proceeds of the collected item will be credited to the depositor's account. Notes and some forms of drafts are collection items.

Because most checks are cash items, the process of converting them to cash involves presenting them at the bank where they are drawn. Once this is done, a bookkeeping entry will remove the cash from the account of the maker of the check and the cash can be made available in the account of the receiver of the check. This is what the banking system does in its clearing process.

When a check is received by a bank, the dollar balance can be represented in two categories.

1. **Ledger Balance.** Also called a book balance, the dollars represented by the check are identified as a deposit in the account of the firm. The bank will report the ledger balance to the firm but might not allow the funds to be removed from the account.

2. **Available Funds.** Also called collected balances or good funds, the dollars in the account can be spent by the firm only when they achieve this status. This usually occurs during a one- to five- day period.

Availability of Funds

To manage the collection of funds properly, the firm should know the bank's policies on converting funds from ledger balances to available funds. Such policies exist within a framework that assists the Federal Reserve in managing the money supply. Three rules apply.

1. **Availability in One Bank Only**. The Federal Reserve allows the banking system to provide availability to one party only. Both the drawee and payee on a check cannot have the funds available in a bank account. The check must clear before funds can be available. Although this is a general rule, the Federal Reserve recognizes that delays in clearing can hamper an effective banking system. Hence, an exception exists to this rule. If clearing cannot take place in two days, the Federal Reserve allows banks to make funds available. Thus, a check deposited on Monday will be available on Wednesday even if the check cannot clear by that day.

2. **Availability by Full Day Only**. Funds are made available on each banking day. Thus, if the depository bank allows the funds to be available on Tuesday, the disbursing bank must not allow the funds to be available the same day.

3. **Banks May Set Their Own Policies**. Once the first two rules are met, banks are allowed to set their own policies. If a bank is concerned that a check will not clear, it may withhold availability until it verifies that the clearing has taken place.

Bank Policies on Availability

Banks follow a variety of different policies on when funds can be converted from ledger balances to available funds. Common policies are as follows:

1. **By Individual Check**. Large banks with computerized clearing schedules are able to determine when individual checks will clear. These banks can record each check and use an availability schedule to convert ledger balances to available funds. Figure 3-2 shows such a schedule for a hypothetical bank and for deposits in its lockboxes. For example, if a check is received from American National Bank by 2:00 A.M., the funds can be disbursed by the close of business that day.

2. **By Average Availability**. Some banks do not have the capability to determine individual check availability. These banks can use an estimate of the average availability. As an example, since most checks clear in one day, the policy can be one day for all checks received before 2:00 P.M.

3. **By Posting Date**. Small banks might not have the capability to distinguish between ledger and available balances. The Federal Reserve allows these banks to post checks and give availability when posted. In effect, this is one–day availability since the posting is done overnight.

Figure 3-2. Chicago National's Availability Schedule for Lockbox Deposits.

Immediate Availability (Funds available on same business day)

Area	Bank

8:00 A.M. Cutoff Time

Chicago
Chicago National
Chicago Federal Reserve Bank, Postal Money Orders, U.S. Treasury Checks

2:00 A.M. Cutoff Time

American National, Central National, Continental Illinois, Drovers National, Exchange National, First Chicago, Harris Bankcorp, Las Salle National, Mercantile National, National Boulevard, Northern Trust

Atlanta, Georgia
Citizens and Southern Georgia Bank, First Atlanta Bank, Fulton National Bank, Trust Company of Georgia

California
BankAmerica, California First Bank, Lloyds Bank, Security Pacific Bank, Union Bank, United California Bank, Wells Fargo Bank

Charlotte, North Carolina
North Carolina National Bank

Cleveland, Ohio
Central National Bank, Cleveland Trust Company, National City Bank

Dallas, Texas
InterFirst Bank, Republic Bank

Denver, Colorado
Colorado National Bank, First National Bank, United Banks of Colorado

Des Moines, Iowa
Bankers Trust Company, Central National Bank

Detroit, Michigan

City National Bank, Manufacturers National Bank, National Bank of Detroit

Houston, Texas

Bank of the Southwest, First City Bancorporation of Texas, Texas Commerce Bankshares

Indianapolis, Indiana

American Fletcher National Bank, Indiana National Bank

Kansas City, Missouri

Commerce Bank, First National Bank, United Missouri Bank

Lansing, Michigan

Michigan National Bank

Milwaukee, Wisconsin

First Wisconsin National Bank, Marine Bank

Minneapolis, Minnesota

First National Bank, Norwest National Bank

New York, New York

Bank of New York, Chase Manhattan Bank, Chemical Bank, Citibank, Irving Trust Company, Manufacturers Hanover, Marine Midland Bank, Morgan Guaranty Trust

Omaha, Nebraska

First National Bank, Omaha National Bank, Provident National Bank

Phoenix, Arizona

Arizona Bank, First National Bank, Valley National Bank

Pittsburgh, Pennsylvania

Mellon National Bank, Pittsburgh National Bank

Portland, Oregon

First National Bank, United States Bancorp

Seattle, Washington

Peoples National Bank, Rainier Bancorporation, Seattle First National Bank

St. Louis, Missouri

Boatmen's Bankshares, First National
Bank, Mercantile Bancorporation

St. Paul, Minnesota

First National Bank

Wichita, Kansas

Fourth National Bank

1:00 A.M. Cutoff Time

Louisville, Kentucky.

Citizens Fidelity Bank, First National Bank

Memphis, Tennessee

First Tennessee National Bank, Union
Planters National Bank

Nashville, Tennessee

First American National Bank, Third
National Bank

New Orleans, Louisiana

First National Bank of Commerce, Hibernia
National Bank, Whitney National Bank

New York, New York

Bankers Trust Company

Tulsa, Oklahoma

Bank of Oklahoma, First National Bank

Next–Day Availability

All Banks in These Cities

9:00 P.M. Cutoff Time

Cincinnati, Ohio; Cleveland, Ohio; Denver,
Colorado; Des Moines, Iowa; Detroit,
Michigan; Indianapolis, Indiana; Kansas
City, Kansas; Kansas City, Missouri;
Louisville, Kentucky; Memphis, Tennessee;

Milwaukee, Wisconsin; Minneapolis, Minnesota; Nashville, Tennessee; Omaha, Nebraska; Salt Lake City, Utah; St. Louis, Missouri; St. Paul, Minnesota

6:00 P.M. Cutoff Time

Atlanta, Georgia; Birmingham, Alabama; Charlotte, North Carolina; Columbia, South Carolina; Dallas, Texas; Houston, Texas; Jacksonville, Florida; New Orleans, Louisiana; New York, New York

Chicago

Regional Check Processing Center (RCPC) Banks

1:00 P.M. Cutoff Time

7th Federal Reserve District

Illinois, Indiana, Iowa, Michigan, Wisconsin

9:00 A.M. Cutoff Time

Federal Reserve Cities (except Helena, Montana)

Helena, Montana

Correspondent Banks in These Federal Reserve Districts

Dallas, Texas; Kansas City, Missouri; Minneapolis, Minnesota; New York, New York; Oklahoma City, Oklahoma; Omaha, Nebraska; Richmond, Virginia; San Antonio, Texas; St. Louis, Missouri

Two–Day Availability

All Other Banks
Canadian Checks
Non par Items

Saturday Availability

Encoded checks deposited Saturday prior to the time below obtain the following availability:

> 7th District Illinois Items Immediate on Monday 8:30 A.M.
>
> All Federal Reserve Cities Immediate on Monday 10:00 A.M..
>
> All RCPCs Immediate on Monday 10:00 A.M.
>
> Correspondent Clearing Points Available Tuesday 10:00 A.M.

Clearing for a Depository Bank

A depository bank that specializes in rapid clearing of checks can speed up availability of funds because availability can be given as soon as an individual check clears. If the bank uses faster means of clearing, it can give earlier availability. To illustrate this process, let us examine the hypothetical availability schedule of Chicago National Bank. The schedule shows the major ways that checks clear in the banking system, namely:

1. **Intrabank.** This clearing occurs when a check is drawn on a bank and deposited in the same bank. In the Figure 3-3, checks drawn on Chicago National and deposited in the bank's lockbox have same-day availability if received by 8:00 A.M. A check that arrives in the lockbox at 7:30 A.M. on Monday will be deducted from the drawee immediately. Availability on Monday will be given to the payee account.

2. **Direct Send.** A **direct send** clearing exists when banks clear checks by messenger. In the schedule, all banks with a 2:00 A.M. deadline have this type of clearing. To illustrate this process, assume that a $25,000 check drawn on Citizens and Southern (C&S) Bank of Atlanta is deposited in Chicago National's lockbox at 8:45 A.M. Figure 3-3 shows how the check might clear the same day. In the figure, the check arrives at Citizens and Southern Bank before 3:00 P.M., where it will be posted immediately and the funds will not be available to C&S on that date. Since this is the case, the funds can be credited for availability in Chicago on the same day.

3. **Regional Check Processing Center (RCPC).** Over 40 RCPCs have been established in urban areas to allow banks to meet at a given time and location for the purpose of clearing checks. On the availability schedule, times are given for "all banks in these cities." This generally indicates that an RCPC, or clearinghouse, exists to assist in clearing checks.

4. **Correspondent Relationships.** If a check is drawn on a bank that is not a member of a clearinghouse, it may clear through a correspondent bank that is a member. In these situations, the correspondent bank

picks up the checks at the clearinghouse and gives them to the drawee bank to post to the depository's account.

5. **Federal Reserve System**. Many checks are cleared using the facilities of the Federal Reserve District Banks. The Federal Reserve charges for these services.

The clearing of checks is a massive business, with billions of checks each month to be physically returned to the drawee bank. An elaborate network of private airlines, commercial airlines, and ground carriers is used to move checks to clearinghouses, correspondent banks, RCPCs, and Federal Reserve District Banks for rapid clearing. Corporate treasurers in large companies take advantage of specialized clearing capabilities by using the services of depository banks.

Figure 3-3. Representative Clearing of Check Deposited in Lockbox.

1:00 A.M.		8:45 A.M.		10:12 A.M.
$25,000 C&S Bank Account 1443	through the mail →	Chicago National Lockbox	Messenger →	Chicago National Operations Center

Messenger ↓

Arrives 1:36 P.M.		Departs 10:56 A.M.		10:22 A.M.
Love Field Atlanta	← Flown to	Delta Flight 963	← Placed aboard	O'Hare Airport

Messenger on route through ↓

Fulton National Bank	Continues through →	First National Bank	Delivers check to →	Citizens and Southern Bank
2:34 p.m.		2:45 p.m.		2:57 p.m.

MANAGING DISBURSEMENTS

A **disbursement** is any expenditure of cash by a firm, whether for the purpose of paying bills, distributing cash dividends, or transferring funds. Efficient disbursing is a key element of total cash management. Most firms want to maintain their reputations and good relations with suppliers, and so pay bills in a timely and accurate fashion. At the same time, a disbursement system should have low operating costs, provide accurate management reports, and extend disbursement float where practical and reasonable. In this section, we will examine disbursement techniques.

Electronic Funds Transfer (EFT)

Increasingly, cash management systems are making use of the electronic movement of funds. Transactions are recorded on magnetic tape or disk storage and cleared directly using automation. The transactions included range from the payment of salaries to employees to the transfer of millions of dollars to retire loans.

Electronic transfers offer a number of benefits. They eliminate the need to print and mail checks, a costly process even when automation is used to minimize delays and errors. Electronic movements eliminate float, since the movement from one computer to another can be virtually instantaneous. They also significantly reduce expenses. Once the calculations are completed, the rest of the process can occur automatically. Electronic processing also improves recordkeeping while minimizing errors. An audit trail is readily available, with fewer activities to be monitored and verified.

Electronic transfers also pose some problems. For one thing, the equipment needed to initiate them is costly and not widely available. Until national systems are in place using the telephone and bank computers, this problem will not easily be surmounted. An even more important problem concerns the reduction of float. Many firms and individuals aggressively take advantage of delays between the writing and clearing of checks. With automation, however, money is invested overnight during the period of the float, thereby eliminating such investing. Thus, there is resistance to fully automated systems of funds transfer.

Zero Balance Account Disbursing

A **zero balance account** is a regular checking account in which the firm is permitted to leave no idle funds on hand. Banks offering this service allow the firm to write checks that will clear against operating accounts containing no funds. The checks clear through normal channels and are presented for collection at the bank in the evening. After processing the checks, the bank automatically transfers funds from the company's concentration or master account to the different operating accounts to return each operating account to a zero balance. The bank charges for this service.

A zero balance account structure is established with a master account and a number of subsidiary accounts. The computer links them in a family of accounts arrangement so that funds in the master account can be used to cover shortages in the operating accounts. An even more sophisticated structure is available when two banks work together to offer zero balance disbursing. A depository bank maintains the master account, and the disbursing bank has the operating accounts. As checks are presented for payment, funds are electronically transferred from the depository bank to cover them.

A zero balance account system offers a number of benefits to the firm. No idle cash balances are maintained in varying disbursing accounts. That is, all excess cash is invested on a daily basis. In addition, the bank normally provides extensive computerized reports to the firm's Accounting Department so that the treasurer can monitor cash balances in considerable detail. This facilitates decisions on allocating cash and choosing the proper investments for short-term funds. Overall, zero balance disbursing offers decentralized disbursements with centralized control.

The only disadvantage of a zero balance system is cost. Because banks are providing a valuable service that involves a large investment in computers and software, they must charge an appropriate fee. With large cash balances, the return on investing excess cash will exceed the fees. With small amounts of cash, the costs would be prohibitive.

Remote Disbursing

Remote disbursing is the practice of using a disbursing bank that is not a member of a clearinghouse and is located outside a major metropolitan area. Checks drawn on such a bank will require more time to clear than checks drawn on money center banks. If a firm writes checks on such a bank, the checks will take more time to clear. The firm will have additional funds to invest.

This practice, also called **controlled disbursing**, can have magnified effects when combined with a zero balance system. As an example, a firm can choose a New York bank as its depository bank and a North Carolina bank as its disbursing bank. To clear, checks must be delivered to North Carolina and be presented to the bank. When this happens, the New York bank will electronically transfer funds to cover the checks. If the North Carolina bank does not receive frequent clearing services from the Federal Reserve System or correspondent banks, disbursement float will be extended.

The Federal Reserve System is concerned about possible abuses connected with remote disbursing and has taken steps to minimize improper practices. The banking system has cooperated with the Federal Reserve to curb misuses and speed up clearing of checks in remote areas. Still, U.S. firms widely practice controlled disbursing.

CASH MANAGEMENT PROBLEMS

To better understand some of the components of check clearing, collections, and disbursements, this section discusses problems dealing with cash management.

A Clearinghouse Problem

A medium-sized midwestern city has a regional check processing center in which all local banks meet at 11:00 A.M. each working day to exchange checks, drafts, and similar items, and to settle resulting balances. First State Bank, Citizens Trust, and Fidelity Bank are members.

On one morning, First State Bank held $1 million of checks drawn on Citizens and $1.5 million drawn on Fidelity. Citizens held $2.5 million drawn on First State Bank and $800,000 drawn on Fidelity. Fidelity Bank held $1.2 million drawn on First State Bank and $1.8 drawn on Citizens.

Prepare a spreadsheet calculation of the clearing that morning.

Solution to Clearinghouse Problem

	Col C	Col D	Col E
Checks Held, Input Screen			
Row	*First State*	*Citizens*	*Fidelity*
9 First State			
10 has checks		1,000,000	1,500,000
12 Citizens			
13 has checks	2,500,000		800,000
15 Fidelity			
16 has checks	1,200,000	1,800,000	
Settlement Balances, Output Screen			
	First State	*Citizens*	*Fidelity*
23 Amount Owed	(3,700,000)	(2,800,000)	(2,300,000)
24 Amount Due	2,500,000	3,300,000	3,000,000
25 Received (Due)	(1,200,000)	500,000	700,000

Formulas

At C23	-@SUM(C10..C16)
At C24	@SUM(C10..E10)
At C25	+C23+C24

An Electronic Transfer Problem

The decision on whether to use a wire or paper depository transfer check to move money between two banks involves a tradeoff between the cost of each service and the rate of return that can be obtained investing money overnight.

At 9:00 A.M. on Tuesday, a firm learns that it has $100,000 in available funds in a lockbox account in Boston. The money must be transferred to a concentration bank in Dallas, where it can be invested overnight at an annual rate of 11 percent. The money can be wired immediately and invested on Tuesday. A paper depository transfer check can be cut that will make the money available in Dallas on Wednesday. The wire transfer will cost $18, while the (DTC) will cost $1.50. Should the money be wired or sent overnight?

Solution to Electronic Transfer Problem

ROW	Financial Data, Input Screen	Col C	Col D
7	Dollar Amount	100,000	
8	Annual Investing Rate	0.11	
9	Days in Year	365	
10	Days to Invest	1	
11	Cost of Electronic Transfer	18.00	
12	Cost of Paper Transfer	1.50	
	Analysis, Output Screen		
19	Dollars	100,000	
20	Daily Rate	0.00030136	
21	Days to Invest	1	
23	Benefit		$30.14
	Cost of Electronic Transfer		
26	Wire Cost	18.00	
27	Paper Cost	-1.50	
28	Net Cost		$16.50
29	Net Benefit(Cost)		$13.64

Formulas

At C19	+C7
At C20	+C8/C9
At D23	+C19*C20*C21

A Lockbox Problem

A firm currently pays $21,000 a year to its bank to cover the service charges on processing deposits and checks drawn against its checking accounts. All activities occur at a hometown bank in Flint, Michigan.

The firm is evaluating a plan to convert its depository functions to a St. Louis bank that specializes in lockbox services. This would save it almost $9,000 in fees in Michigan. The St. Louis bank would operate a lockbox service and wire funds either to an investment account or to operating accounts in Flint.

The benefits to the lockbox system would be a reduction in collection float. At the present time, the firm has a total collection float of $4.6 million. With the system, it would drop to $3.4 million. Since the money could be invested overnight at an estimated 13 percent annual rate, the lockbox would offer a real benefit.

The drawback to the lockbox system is its higher cost. Including fees to process checks and the cost of transfers, the St. Louis bank would collect first-year fees of $26,000.

What is the net cost or benefit to the lockbox system?

Solution to Lockbox Problem

ROW	Financial Data, Input Screen	Col C	Col D
7	Original Float	4,600,000	
8	New Float	3,400,000	
9	Investing Rate	0.13	
11	Original Fees	21,000	
12	New Bank Fees	12,000	
13	Lockbox Fees	26,000	
	Analysis, Output Screen		
17	Savings on Float	1,200,000	
18	Annual Rate	<u>0.13</u>	
20	Benefit		156,000
22	Savings	9,000	
23	New Costs	<u>26,000</u>	
25	Lockbox Costs		<u>17,000</u>
27	Benefits (Costs)		139,000

Formulas

At C17	+C7-C8
At C22	+C11-C12

CHICAGO NATIONAL BANK–LOCKBOX ANALYSIS CASE

Haydon Industries Incorporated is a manufacturer of packaging materials with annual sales of just under $300 million. The firm sells to companies and distributors located in the midwestern, southeastern, and eastern areas of the United States with some sales in the Far West and Canada. The company's primary operations are located in a suburb of Philadelphia, but it has sales offices in seven other cities.

At the present time, the company sells on terms of 2/10 net 30 and requires customers to remit payments to Haydon Industries Inc., ATTN: Accounting Department, at a Philadelphia post office box. Mail is collected by messenger three times a day, sorted in the company's mail room, and all payments are hand carried to the accounts receivable section in the Accounting Department. All payments are recorded on a computer ledger system with multiple terminal access. Invoices are coded and entered, and checks are verified for correct amounts, dates, and signatures before being separated from the invoice copy for deposit at a nearby bank. Deposits are made in the early afternoon, once again by messenger.

The company has recently programmed its ledger system to generate a management report on the differing kinds of "float" in its collection process. Using the postmark on envelopes and other estimates of mailing date, the new program can estimate the **mail float**, or time period when the check is being handled by the post office and messenger. Since checks are logged in upon arrival at the company, the system can also calculate the approximate **check processing float**, or time period needed to sort, record, and deposit the check. The system can also calculate the **bank processing float**, or the time period from the deposit of the check to the crediting of funds in the seller's account.

After running the new program for three months, the company's treasurer determined the following average times and dollars for each type of float:

Type of Float	Average Days	Average Daily Balance
Mail Float	2.80	2,302,000
Check Processing Float	1.40	1,151,000
Bank Processing Float	1.80	1,480,000
Daily Totals	6.00 days	$4,933,000

Shortly after the completion of these calculations, the company was visited by a representative of the Chicago National Bank, one of the major commercial banks that specializes in corporate cash management. The representative told Haydon's treasurer about the Chicago National "Cash Pro" system that offered a variety of cash management services. The basic concept centered around a **lockbox** setup that was no more than a post office box under the control of Chicago National. The bank recommended nine lockbox cities in its network: Boston, New York, Atlanta, Chicago, Kansas City, Dallas, Denver, San Francisco, and Seattle. All these cities have either Federal Reserve District Banks or Federal Reserve District Branch Banks. The representative felt that Haydon Industries could save considerable time in receiving and utilizing incoming funds if it installed a lockbox system. In addition, Chicago National could offer related services at reasonable charges. For example, concentration banking, a system of centralizing corporate cash as a method of controlling the firm's funds and minimizing idle cash balances, was an integral part of the system. Each day, funds would be moved from the lockbox city to a control account at Chicago National, where the company would give instructions to the bank and funds would automatically be processed according to the instructions.

The representative argued that the Chicago National system would speed up collections in a number of ways.

- Lockboxes reduce mail float because the receiving addresses are located closer to the firm's customers.
- Chicago National picks up mail from its lockboxes 16 hours a day, 365 days a year. The mail is sorted using automated, high-speed processors.
- Return-avoidance procedures" are used where appropriate. The bank attempts to verify amounts when the face of the checks has two different figures, seeks authorization when a check is unsigned, and times postdated checks so they clear on the exact date shown. All these procedures are designed to reduce the number of checks that must be returned.

The representative from Chicago National Bank gave the following schedule of charges to the treasurer of Haydon Industries:

Item	Unit Charge
Basic Lockbox Charge	$0.40 per item
Cash Concentration Service	$200.00 per month
Checks Deposited and Credits	$0.08 each
Checks Drawn and Debits	$0.13 each
Debit Reconciliations	$0.05 each
Depository Transfer Checks	$1.25 each
Wire Transfers	$7.50 each
Account Reconciliation Reports	$15.00 each

The cash concentration service is Chicago National's version of concentration banking. The service has several features.

- **Rapid Clearance**. Chicago National goes beyond the facilities of the Federal Reserve System for clearing checks. Every day, checks are sent directly to over 40 Regional Check Processing Centers and 49 major banks to speed up collections. The overnight air transport of these checks means that virtually all of the dollars deposited with Chicago National (99 percent actually) are available to companies within 24 hours for disbursement. This is important, the representative noted, because a deposited check gives book credit but not available funds until the check clears.

- **Automatic Depository Transfer Checks (DTCs)**. A DTC will be drawn on an account any time the balance exceeds a predetermined level. Chicago National draws the check authorizing the movement of funds from the lockbox accounts to Haydon's master account where it can be immediately used by the treasurer. The funds transferred by DTC will be available within 24 hours for disbursement or investment.

- **Wire Transfer**. The **Fed wire** system links all Federal Reserve Member Banks and can be used to immediately transfer funds from one account or bank to another. The **bank wire** system is a private communications network linking major banks throughout the country. Both systems eliminate any "float" resulting from paper processing. Wire transfers are the fastest way to move money between accounts or banks, but, because they are relatively costly, they are usually employed for the transfer of large sums of money. The transfers can be authorized in advance and will occur automatically whenever the prescribed conditions are met.

The availability of funds through the extensive Chicago National system can be seen from Figure 3-2. To achieve these times, the bank uses 6 private airlines, 11 commercial airlines, and 13 ground carriers.

Chicago National Bank also provides a service of reconciling accounts and balances. This service is particularly important if the firm is using the bank for its disbursements. Checks are arranged by check number, amount, and date paid. All disbursements are included in the reconcilement reports.

The treasurer of Haydon Industries figured that idle cash cost his company at the rate of 13 percent annually. He asked the representative of Chicago National for the costs involved in their services other than direct costs. There were none, he was assured, and Haydon could even choose to pay for Chicago National's services by leaving funds on deposit. The bank would give credit for average balances at the rate of the weekly Treasury Bill rate which was running 11 percent and might average this rate over a long period of time.

The treasurer indicated an interest in the service and agreed to turn over the computer tapes that were used in Haydon's own study of float. A few weeks later, the treasurer received the following letter from Chicago National.

We have run your transactions on our computer model and recommend a three-lockbox system with mailing addresses in Chicago, New York, and Atlanta. With such a system, you should be able to cut your float considerably. We suggest that you compare the following figures with your own study. If you are interested in discussing a lockbox system when you finish the analysis, we would be happy to send a team of analysts to Philadelphia to develop the details with members of your staff. We will call you in the near future.

Comparing Philadelphia Only With Three-Lockbox System Developed By Cash Management Section, Chicago National Bank.

Prepared for Haydon Industries, Philadelphia, Pennsylvania.

Percent of Philadelphia Float in Each
Lockbox and Total New Float as a
Percent of Original Level of Float

Type of Float	Philadelphia	Chicago	New York	Atlanta	Total
Mail	$2,302,000	13.02%	28.52%	20.46%	62.00%
Check Processing	1,151,000	16.25%	27.30%	21.45%	65.00%
Bank Processing	1,480,000	13.52%	20.80%	17.68%	52.00%

Attached as an enclosure to the letter from Chicago National Bank was a table of estimated activities in a normal month.

Enclosure: Assumed Activity Under Three-Lockbox System with Haydon Industries Data in Normal or Average Month.

Item	Estimated Volume	
Checks Deposited and Credits	16,581	per month
Checks Drawn and Debits	3,471	per month
Debit Reconciliations	3,471	per month
Depository Transfer Checks	62	per month
Wire Transfers	14	per month
Account Reports, Debits	2	per month
Account Reports, Credits	2	per month

The only additional information needed by the treasurer of Haydon Industries dealt with the split between total checks received and those to be processed through the lockboxes. In the Chicago National Bank study, the bank assumed that 9,200 checks monthly would be run through the lockboxes and the rest would continue to be sent to Philadelphia. This seemed to be a reasonable assumption to be used in the lockbox analysis.

Required: 1.   Prepare the savings summary showing the reduction in float in both dollars and days under the three-lockbox system.

2.   How much is this savings worth at Haydon's cost of money?

3.   How much would the bank charge for one month's activity in the lockbox and cash management system if Haydon accepted all the services outlined above?

4.   What demand deposit balance would be required to cover the cost of the cash management services provided in an average month?

OLEAN NATIONAL CORPORATION–LOCKBOX CASE

Olean National Corporation is a Buffalo–based financial holding company known primarily for its insurance activities. Its largest operating subsidiary is the Olean National Life Insurance Company, a multiline insurer in the life insurance, health and accident insurance, annuity, and reinsurance fields. This subsidiary is the fifth largest stockholder-owned insurer in the United States, and it contributes some 65 percent of the parent company's revenues.

Two principal markets may be identified for Olean National Life: direct sales to individuals or businesses; and reinsurance to other life insurance companies. In addition to its largest subsidiary, Olean National Corporation has other important subsidiaries. Salamanca Title and Trust Company is the second largest U.S. title insurer with a full line of trust services. The Allegany Insurance Companies provide approximately one-fourth of Olean National's revenues, mainly with their property and casualty insurance operations but also through some sales of life insurance. Niagara Life Assurance Company is a Canadian subsidiary that offers life and health insurance throughout Canada, as well as in some parts of the United States.

In January 1990, Olean National Corporation began a major evaluation of its cash management policies. As a company with over $7 billion in assets and $2 billion in revenues, Olean National had to control a sizable volume of cash flowing in and out of its bank accounts on any given day. To ensure that the firm was effectively managing and investing its cash flows, Roger Michaels, president, requested a study of cash management in Olean National Life. Once the study was completed, its findings and lessons would be forwarded to the other operating companies for their consideration.

Olean National Corporation asked representatives of the Bradford Consulting Group to assist the treasurer of Olean National Life (ONL) in conducting a systematic review of two areas. First, a study was made of the cash movements in and out of the different bank accounts maintained by Olean National Life. The treasurer felt that steps should be taken to increase the speed of collection and decrease the time needed to clear checks and drafts. Both steps would have to be taken in a way that would not harm the ONL image.

Second, a study was begun on the nature of cash forecasting as it was historically performed at the company. During the 1980s, future cash flows were estimated using historical relationships between interest rates, available investment opportunities, and the degree of activity of the sales force of the firm. The changing interest rates of the 1980s all but destroyed many of the historical relationships. As a result, ONL's actual monthly cash flows during the winter of 1989-1990 did not resemble the forecast. The same situation was true in the other subsidiaries. The deviation in cash flows caused significant problems for the Investment Committee of the parent corporation. The

Committee traditionally followed a policy of making mortgage commitments up to 18 months in advance. When the cash flow dropped significantly in early 1990, Olean National Corporation had to make adjustments in order to release sufficient funds to meet its commitments. A revised cash forecasting methodology was clearly a high priority to ONC and its subsidiaries.

By April 1990, a cash management task force was actively working on the two projects. Headquartered in the Treasurer's Office of ONL, the group began to outline its activities. The project would begin by examining the geographic patterns of cash flows of the major operating divisions of ONL, a necessary first step in a lockbox analysis. Once sufficient cash flow data were gathered, the task force would evaluate the effectiveness of the current collection and disbursement procedures and prepare a recommendation for the company treasurer.

STRUCTURE OF OLEAN NATIONAL LIFE

In 1989, Olean National Life itself had almost $5 billion of assets to manage and $1.6 billion of cash inflows. The sheer magnitude of the cash flows, combined with the complexity of the accounting process in the life insurance industry, created serious problems for the task force. It decided to develop cash flow patterns along the lines of the major operating divisions in the company: (1) the Individual Division; (2) the Group Division; and (3) the Reinsurance Division. A wholly owned subsidiary, Weston National Pension Company, would be excluded from the initial study.

ANALYZING CASH RECEIPTS

In early June, the cash management task force felt that it had sufficient information to evaluate the installation of a lockbox system. Buffalo Trust had studied Olean National Life's 1989 cash receipts and provided the geographic breakdowns shown in Figure 3-4. Cash was mailed in volume from all areas of the country, with some skewing toward ONL's traditional eastern markets. Over half of the cash inflows were attributed to the Group Division, primarily as a result of the accident and health lines of business.

The Bradford Consulting Group recommended that a four–lockbox network be established for Olean National Life, with Buffalo Trust Company acting as the concentration bank and lockboxes established in Chicago, Atlanta, Dallas, and San Francisco. This system would be initially established for the three operating divisions of ONL, with the possibility of adding Weston National Pension Company after the completion of a separate study. The four–lockbox arrangement would take advantage of shorter mail times between clients and collection sites. A summary of average mail times is given in Figure 3–5.

In addition to a reduction of mail float, the four–lockbox system would speed up the processing and clearing of checks. According to the Bradford Consulting study, ONL currently had to wait 3.2 days on the average for a check to be recorded in the Treasurer's Office and cleared by Olean National Bank. Under the lockbox system, check deposits would be available for disbursement in 1.7 days on the average. Since ONL's management group used 11.5 percent as the before-tax cost of funds, the faster processing was worth considerable money to Olean National.

After pointing out the benefits of the four–lockbox system, Bradford's representatives noted that some additional costs would be incurred. After some negotiations between ONL's treasurer and a vice-president of the bank, an agreement was reached. First, ONL wanted to use the Bradford data to do its own study of the benefits of the lockboxes. If they were beneficial to ONL, another study would be performed for Weston National Pension Company, which was not included in the original analysis. Second, Buffalo Trust would be paid $0.27 a check the first year for processing a minimum of 100,000 checks annually. This would cover all expenses involved with the transfer of funds, the lockbox collections, two monthly reconciliations, and related services. As part of the package, Buffalo agreed to connect ONL's Treasurer's Office with its computer in Buffalo so that daily balances could be read from the ONL terminal by 9:15 A.M. on workdays.

Figure 3-4. Cash Receipts by Geographic Region for Major Activities of Olean National Life (1989 data).

	South-East	East	Upper Midwest	Lower Midwest	Far West	Total
Individual Division						
Life	43,800	34,900	18,350	29,000	79,845	205,895
Accident and Health	3,999	4,275	8,327	1,995	3,500	22,096
Annuities	1,000	1,200	2,500	750	1,345	6,795
Group Division						
Life	7,900	11,450	22,750	12,000	13,000	67,100
Accident and Health	50,000	81,500	145,795	73,450	97,750	448,495
Annuities	1,200	1,700	3,100	1,700	1,600	9,300
Total	107,899	135,025	200,822	118,895	197,040	759,681

Figure 3-5. Input Screen, Type of Float, Four Lockbox System, and Olean.

	South-East	East	Upper Midwest	Lower Midwest	Far West
Average Mail Float					
Olean	2.5	2.0	3.0	3.2	3.6
Lockboxes	1.6	1.5	1.9	2.0	2.2

ONL's representatives were satisfied with these terms. At that time, ONL was paying Olean National Bank $0.11 an item for deposited checks, reports, and reconciliations. This charge would be eliminated for all checks handled in the new system. In addition, ONL expected no problem in reaching the 100,000 minimum volume requirement with Buffalo, even if the system excluded small premium checks. The 1989 volume of checks received was over 3 million items, not counting checks received by Weston National Pension, as shown in Figure 3-6.

At this point, the ONL treasurer felt that the task force had sufficient information to evaluate the lockbox system, as proposed by Bradford Consulting Group. He requested a specific recommendation within 10 days since he had indicated to the Bradford representatives that he would call them within three weeks. The task force members agreed to meet in three days to begin developing the recommendation.

Figure 3-6. Annual Volume of Checks, Three Operating Divisions, 1989.

	Annual Checks Deposited
Individual Division	3,612,000
Group Division	86,000
Reinsurance Division	45,000
Total	3,743,000

Required: Prepare the recommendation for the task force.

4

Commercial Bank Packages
For Cash Management

As a result of the increasing sophistication of mainframe and microcomputer networks, commercial banks and other financial service organizations now offer an impressive range of cash management services. The goals of these services are twofold: (1) to move money; and (2) to provide information on cash balances. The various packages are designed to increase the amount of useful information available to the firm at any moment in time. By providing daily or instantaneous reports, banks assist firms in analyzing needs, balances, and investment opportunities.

Computerized cash management services have reached full maturity in recent years. Computer networks and accompanying software have become more refined, offering increased speed, detail, and accuracy. Contemporary data transmission from the bank's computer to the company computer, and vice versa, can be done easily and quickly. The firm can monitor its cash balances in a variety of accounts at the start of the day. Decisions to transfer funds, either to reduce borrowings or to take advantage of investment opportunities, can be transmitted quickly and accurately to the institutions that can move the monies. Along with current developments, the banks provide information in a variety of formats. Daily, weekly, monthly, and annual reports can be generated in management formats so that idle cash can be identified and more effective systems can be developed.

To understand the kind of services that are available from banks, this chapter offers a representative sampling of marketing materials. The items in this chapter were selected to show a variety of services. Some cash management services offered by large banks allow almost instantaneous monitoring of account activities. Other services provided by regional banks are designed for smaller firms, yet provide cost effective information and the ability to move money quickly.

A CAVEAT

The materials in this chapter represent financial service firms in three geographic areas–New York, Philadelphia, and Chicago. New York's Citibank is one of the largest bank in the world, with a full range of multinational services. Its computer operations are arguably the most sophisticated of any banking institution in the world. It provides networking services to routinely move large cash balances all over the world, while allowing the firm to track and analyze such movements. Philadelphia National Bank concentrates on domestic banking services for its regional market. Although it offers some powerful information and movement capabilities, it represents a different approach to cash management. Phoenix-Hect in Chicago is not a bank at all: it offers analytical services to help firms evaluate their banking system and relationships.

The three organizations whose materials are displayed in this chapter are seriously committed to developing services for businesses and other organizations. Their inclusion here does not constitute an endorsement, nor does it claim that these are the most advanced or most cost effective services for an individual firm. Since the cash management industry is constantly changing and upgrading, these institutions may offer more sophisticated services than are depicted in these materials, which were gathered in 1986. The documents presented should be used only to familiarize the reader with the kinds of services available.

CITICASH MANAGER PACKAGE

The CitiCash Manager Package allows interaction between all Citibank locations throughout the world. At the same time, the system links Citibank accounts with domestic and international banks. Money transfers can be initiated automatically or manually in a complex range of forms and according to specified criteria. Automated recurring transactions, semiautomated transactions, or manual overrides are permitted. The analyst can manage accounts and balances on the screen using predefined report formats tailored to the specific needs of the firm. Figures 4-1 to 4-6 illustrate the CitiCash Electronic Funds Transfer System, and Figure 4-7 illustrates the CitiCash Lockbox Reporting system. By any yardstick, the CitiCash Manager System provides an impressive capability for multinational firms and other large organizations.

Figure 4-1. CitiCash Manager Transfers.

 CitiCash Manager enables you to initiate electronic funds transfers as well as receive detailed and summary information about incoming and outgoing transfers.
The transfers you many initiate are:

Predefined Lines: repetitive, predefined transfers which have been programmed into the CitiCash Manager system. Lines make it easier to initiate a debit from your account at Citibank in New York for credit to an account in any bank. The bank can be domestic or foreign, but the debit will be in U.S. dollars.

Predefined Charge Wires: allow you to request that funds be withdrawn from your account at another bank and credited to your account at Citibank in New York. A charge wire may be processed in either of two ways: through the Federal Reserve system (a Fed drawdown), or through a correspondent relationship.

Free Form Transfers: allow you to transfer funds from your Citibank account when the transfer records have not been previously entered into the system. With this option, you can transfer U.S. dollars to any bank in the world. Due to the power and flexibility of this option, each Free Form transfer requires a second approving user ID and password.

Depository Transfer Checks: preprinted, unsigned, non-negotiable checks that allow you to concentrate funds into your Citibank account. Using predefined instructions to create this option, you can initiate or cancel DTCs with predefined transfers where the records have been programmed into the CitiCash Manager system.

ACH Debits: Predefined Automated Clearing House Debits are repetitive transfers for which records have been programmed into the CitiCash Manager system. They allow you to collect or concentrate funds into your Citibank account. Like most DTCs, and unlike wire transfers, ACH funds have one–day availability. All parties to the transaction will have next day settlement. The ACH Debit subfunction has two options: initiate and cancel.

ACH Credits: Predefined Automated Clearing House Credits, like ACH Debits, are repetitive transfers for which records have been programmed into the CitiCash Manager system. They also have one–day availability and next day settlement. This subfunction also has two options: initiate and cancel.

Figure 4-2. Transfer Initiation Predefined Lines.

This is the main CitiCash Manager menu. Here we've selected the Transfers "module."

Then we've selected the Lines subfunction which allows us to initiate a debit from the Citibank account.

We've chosen to initiate transfers on all the programmed, predefined lines.

Amounts to be debited, for each corresponding line.

```
(1) Inquiries              (2) Transfers           (3) Messages
(4) Security               (5) Lockbox             (7) Trans Entry
(8) Batch Rpt              (9) Deposit Rpt
Enter Option:
>2
Transfer Options:
(1) Lines                  (2) Charge Wires        (3) DTCs
(4) ACH-Debits             (5) ACH-Credits         (6) Free Form
(7) Transfer Inquiry       (8) Approve             (9) Predefines

Enter Option:
>1
Enter Customer Number:
>77022
Enter Processing Date (MMDDYY) or (T) Today:
>T
Enter (A) All or Specific Line # or (S) to Stop:
>A
Line# Debit Acct#          For Credit to:          Credit Bank ABA#
OC1T13                     77030005                XYZ Co                  02600980
Enter Amount:
>7,500
Edited Amount:             7,500.00
Line #                     Debit Acct#             For Credit to           Credit Bank ABA#
OOJB11                     77030005                Noble Cement            02100023
Enter Amount:
>7,234
Edited Amount:             7,234.00
Transfer Items: 2          Dollars: 14,734.00
Correct as Entered? (Y) Yes (D) to Cancel or (C) to Change
>Y
Password:
>*****
Transfer Being Processed for 01/27/86
Line #OC1T13               Debit Acct #77030005    Amount 7,500.00         Req #461
Line #OOJB11               Debit Acct #77030005    Amount 7,234.00         Req #462
```

When the last record has been entered, the number of transfers and the total dollar amount will appear.

This indicates that your transfers have been accepted for processing and the Transfers options menu will appear.

The edited amount will appear automatically.

CitiCash Manager automatically assigns a request number to your transfers for reference purposes.

Figure 4-3. Transfer Initiation-Free Forms.

We've returned to the Transfers Options sub-functions and chosen to initiate a Free Form transfer.

The identifying number and name of the bank to be credited.

The name and account number of the party to be credited.

You have three lines of 36 characters to enter any details of the transaction.

Transfers Options:
(1) Lines   (2) Charge Wires   (3) DTCS
(4) ACH-Debits   (5) ACH-Credits   (6) Free Form
(7) Transfer Inquiry   (8) Approve   (9) Predefines
Enter Option:
>6
Enter Citibank Account Number to Debit:
>77030005
Enter Bank ABA # or CHIPS # or (B) Bank Name (C) City or (U) Unknown
>02100023
Name of Bank to Credit: Sist Trust Co.
Enter Method of Payment (C) CHIPS or (F) FED
>F
Enter Name of Party to Credit:
>Noble Cement
Enter Account Number to Credit:
>77022234
Enter Advice Type (M) Mail (P) Phone or (C) Cable:
>C
Enter Details-1: Advise by cable to C. Jackson, Supv.
Enter Transfer Amount:
>10,000
Enter Processing Date (MMDDYY) or (T) Today:
>T
Transfer Requested by: Andrea Shafto   01/27/86   10:55

Customer ID   77022/Noble Mfg. Concentration
Type of Transfer   Free Form Debit
1)   Account # to Debit   77030005 Citibank, N.A.
        Name of Party to Debit   Noble Mfg. Concentration
Correct as Entered? (Y) Yes (D) to Cancel or (C) to Change:
>Y
Password:
>********
Enter Approving User ID or (D) Delay:
>********
Transfer Req # Being Processed for 01/27/86:

A full re-cap (partially shown) of the requested transaction will then appear on the screen.

For this type of transaction, a second, approving user must type in his or her ID.

When the ID is accepted, this indicates that the transaction is being processed.

Figure 4-4. Transfer Approval Option.

From the main CitiCash Manager menu and from the Transfer Options menu we've chosen to Approve transfers.

This automatically appears if there are pre-defined transfers awaiting your approval. This convenient feature, in effect, monitors your transactions.

Here we've asked to see a detailed report of each transfer to be approved. A summary report would show a one–line summary of all transfers, and allow you to approve them all at once, if desired.

```
**Transfers Awaiting Supervisor Approval**
(1) Inquiries              (2) Transfers              (3) Messages
(4) Security               (5) Lockbox                (7) Trans Entry
(8) Batch Rpt              (9) Deposit Rpt
Enter Option:
>2
Transfer Options:
(1) Lines                  (2) Charge Wires           (3) DTCs
(4) ACH-Debits             (5) ACH-Credits            (6) Free Form
(7) Transfer Inquiry       (8) Approve                (9) Predefines
Enter Option:
>8
Approval Options:
(1) Summary                (2) Detail
Enter Option:
>2
Enter Transfer Request Number to Approve or (A) All:
>A
Transfer Inquiry–Requests
Transfer Request #: 88                    01/27/86         14:59
Fed/CHP/Book Ref #:                       Transfer Type: Line
Date Requested: 01/27/86       14:55      Process Date: 01/27/86
By: Linda Gregg                           Supervisor: Ray Edwards
       Bryson Mfg. Co.
Status                                    Delayed          14:55
Transfer Amount                           847,000.00 Debit
Transfer ID                               103
Account # to Debit                        39081864
Name of Party to Debit                    Bryson Manufacturing Co.
Method of Payment                         CHIPS–Same Day
Credit Bank ABA#                          002 CHIPS#
Name of Bank to Credit                    Sisti Trust Co.
Name of Party to Credit                   Stallworth Mktg. Co.
Account # to Credit                       88540793 Account
Advice Type                               Cable
Details: Invoice #38
Enter Approving User ID or (C) to Cancel (D) to Delay or (S) to Stop
>78451
Password:
>********
```

Each detailed report gives you such information as the date and amount of the request, the parties to be debited and credited, and the person who requested the transfer.

The transfer is approved only by entering your Approving User ID and your password. If there is another transfer awaiting approval, it will automatically appear.

The option to cancel (or delay) a transfer is also available. Again, this is a security feature, and the name of the cancelling party will become part of the audit trail.

Figure 4-5. Transfer Inquiry Detailed Reports.

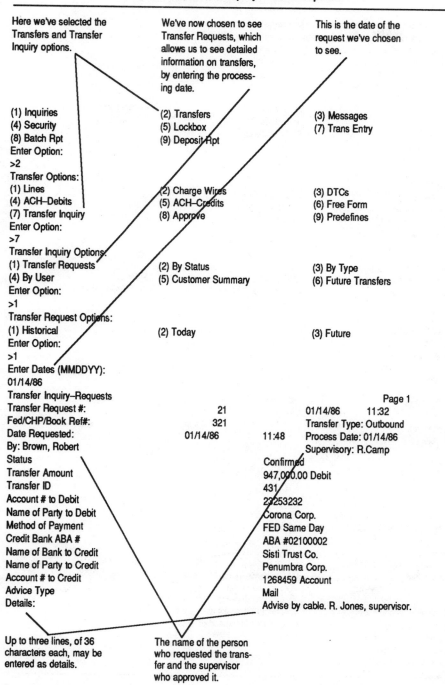

Here we've selected the Transfers and Transfer Inquiry options.

We've now chosen to see Transfer Requests, which allows us to see detailed information on transfers, by entering the processing date.

This is the date of the request we've chosen to see.

(1) Inquiries   (2) Transfers   (3) Messages
(4) Security   (5) Lockbox   (7) Trans Entry
(8) Batch Rpt   (9) Deposit Rpt
Enter Option:
>2
Transfer Options:
(1) Lines   (2) Charge Wires   (3) DTCs
(4) ACH–Debits   (5) ACH–Credits   (6) Free Form
(7) Transfer Inquiry   (8) Approve   (9) Predefines
Enter Option:
>7
Transfer Inquiry Options:
(1) Transfer Requests   (2) By Status   (3) By Type
(4) By User   (5) Customer Summary   (6) Future Transfers
Enter Option:
>1
Transfer Request Options:
(1) Historical   (2) Today   (3) Future
Enter Option:
>1
Enter Dates (MMDDYY):
01/14/86

Transfer Inquiry–Requests		Page 1
Transfer Request #:	21	01/14/86 11:32
Fed/CHP/Book Ref#:	321	Transfer Type: Outbound
Date Requested:	01/14/86 11:48	Process Date: 01/14/86
By: Brown, Robert		Supervisory: R.Camp
Status	Confirmed	
Transfer Amount	947,000.00 Debit	
Transfer ID	431	
Account # to Debit	29253232	
Name of Party to Debit	Corona Corp.	
Method of Payment	FED Same Day	
Credit Bank ABA #	ABA #02100002	
Name of Bank to Credit	Sisti Trust Co.	
Name of Party to Credit	Penumbra Corp.	
Account # to Credit	1268459 Account	
Advice Type	Mail	
Details:	Advise by cable. R. Jones, supervisor.	

Up to three lines, of 36 characters each, may be entered as details.

The name of the person who requested the transfer and the supervisor who approved it.

Figure 4-6. Transfer Inquiry Summary Report.

The Transfer inquiry option provides a file of all transfers initiated within the past 45 business days or for today's or future processing.

Here we've chosen to see a summary of information for all transfers processed on a specified date.

(1) Inquiries
(4) Security
(8) Batch Rpt
Enter Option:
>2

(2) Transfers
(5) Lockbox
(9) Deposit Rpt

(3) Messages
(7) Trans Entry

Transfer Options:
(1) Lines
(4) ACH-Debits
(7) Transfer inquiry
Enter Option:
>7

(2) Charge Wires
(5) ACH-Credits
(8) Approve

(3) DTCs
(6) Free Form
(9) Predefines

Transfer Inquiry Options:
(1) Transfer Requests
(4) By User
Enter Option:
>5
Enter Date (MMDDYY):
01/27/86

(2) By Status
(5) Customer Summary

(3) By Type
(6) Future Transfers

Transfer Inquiry–Customer Summary   01/27/86   14:26
Acme ACH Corporation

Description	Items	$Debit	$Credit
All Transfers	8	500,000.00	800,000.00
Predefined DTC	1	N/A	100,000.00
Predefined ACH	2	1.00	300,000.00
Lockbox DTC	1	N/A	100,000.00
Lockbox ACH	1	N/A	200,000.00
Other Transfers Delayed	1	0.00	100,000.00
Other Transfers Acknowledged	1	300,00.00	0.00
Other Transfers Confirmed	1	1.7,000.00	0.00

Enter
(1) Transfer Requests
(4) By User

(2) By Status
(5) Customer Summary

(3) By Type
(6) Future Transfers

This line represents the total number, debit amount and credit amount of all transfers for the requested date.

This menu will automatically appear at the end of the report.

Figure 4-7. Lockbox Reporting.

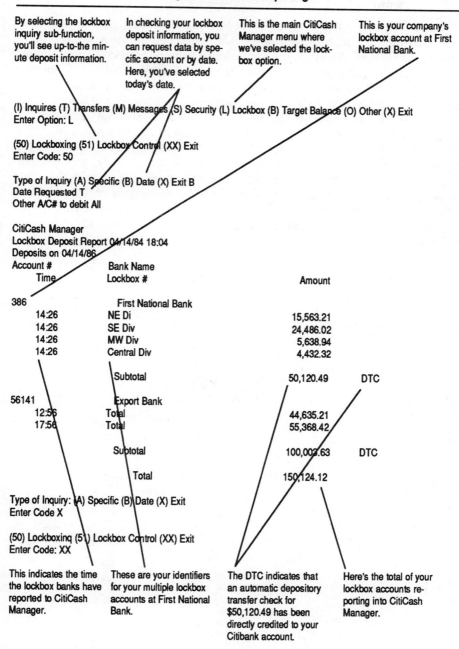

By selecting the lockbox inquiry sub-function, you'll see up-to-the-minute deposit information.

In checking your lockbox deposit information, you can request data by specific account or by date. Here, you've selected today's date.

This is the main CitiCash Manager menu where we've selected the lockbox option.

This is your company's lockbox account at First National Bank.

(I) Inquires (T) Transfers (M) Messages (S) Security (L) Lockbox (B) Target Balance (O) Other (X) Exit
Enter Option: L

(50) Lockboxing (51) Lockbox Control (XX) Exit
Enter Code: 50

Type of Inquiry (A) Specific (B) Date (X) Exit B
Date Requested T
Other A/C# to debit All

CitiCash Manager
Lockbox Deposit Report 04/14/84 18:04
Deposits on 04/14/86

Account # Time	Bank Name Lockbox #	Amount	
386	First National Bank		
14:26	NE Di	15,563.21	
14:26	SE Div	24,486.02	
14:26	MW Div	5,638.94	
14:26	Central Div	4,432.32	
	Subtotal	50,120.49	DTC
56141	Export Bank		
12:56	Total	44,635.21	
17:56	Total	55,368.42	
	Subtotal	100,003.63	DTC
	Total	150,124.12	

Type of Inquiry: (A) Specific (B) Date (X) Exit
Enter Code X

(50) Lockboxing (51) Lockbox Control (XX) Exit
Enter Code: XX

This indicates the time the lockbox banks have reported to CitiCash Manager.

These are your identifiers for your multiple lockbox accounts at First National Bank.

The DTC indicates that an automatic depository transfer check for $50,120.49 has been directly credited to your Citibank account.

Here's the total of your lockbox accounts reporting into CitiCash Manager.

PNB COMPULINK PACKAGE

The Philadelphia National Bank (PNB) is a regional bank that is nationally recognized for the high quality of its cash management services. The Bank made an early commitment to the computer systems needed to offer automated cash transfers and report generation. It has extensive capability to provide information, collection, and disbursement services to medium–sized and large firms. The Bank's CompuLink System allows the customer to choose a range of services tailored to specific needs, either on a regional, national, or international basis. Figures 4-8 and 4-9 are parts of a brochure reporting the PNB Electronic Payments Service. Figure 4-10 outlines PNB's CompuCash 2 System which is an upgraded, video-based, automated lockbox system. Figures 4-11 through 4-19 illustrate the PNB CompuLink Package. This package allows the monitoring of accounts by management by providing balance reports, detailed transaction reports, and lockbox reports. This system also creates movement of funds through wire transfers and depository transfer checks.

Figure 4-8. PNB Electronic Payment Services.

 Philadelphia National Bank

Electronic Payments Service

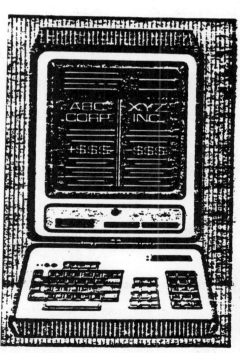

With the Electronic Payments Service your employees, pensioners, stockholders or suppliers are assured of:

- *Accuracy,* since the payments are made according to pre-established instructions.
- *Reliability,* since PNB's system is designed to assure payment on the proper date. If payees are ill, on vacation, or travelling, the deposits are still made on the specified date. In addition, the system is not subject to mail delays.
- *Safety,* since there are no checks to be lost or stolen.
- *Convenience,* since it eliminates the need for a trip to the bank to make a deposit.

Your company is assured of:

- *Cost reductions* in the activities associated with funds disbursement, including check processing and distribution.
- *Security,* since no checks can be lost or stolen; consequently, stop payments and re-issue problems will cease.
- *Control,* because companies with multiple payroll accounts will now only need to fund one account, rather than funding numerous accounts at various banks.
- *Speed,* since the ACH system is designed to assure the availability of funds at the receiving financial institution on the date due.

For further information on PNB's Electronic Payments Service, contact your PNB account manager or the Marketing Services Division, The Philadelphia National Bank, FC 1-4-2, P.O. Box 7618, Philadelphia, PA. 19101, (215) 629-4051.

Figure 4-9. PNB Electronic Payment Services (Continued).

Electronic Payments Service

The Philadelphia National Bank offers corporate customers an innovative paperless payment system which reduces expenses associated with disbursements to employees, pensioners, stockholders or suppliers. As a subscriber to PNB's Electronic Payments Service, your organization benefits from faster payments, fewer errors and greater security. Concurrently, your payees are provided with the safety and convenience of deposits made directly to checking or savings accounts at virtually any financial institution of their choice.

    The Electronic Payments Service is one application of The Philadelphia National Bank's Automated Clearing House (ACH) capabilities. The ACH nationwide network is an independent legal association of financial institutions which maintain a computerized facility that performs the inter-bank clearing of prearranged transactions. As one of the founding members of the Third District Automated Clearing House (3DACH), PNB is actively addressing the development of ACH products which offer our customers a more convenient and efficient means for funds transfer.

How the Electronic Payments Service Works:

PNB's Electronic Payments Service permits funds to move through the banking system via the "Automated Clearing House" (ACH), a computerized facility utilized by banks to transfer funds from bank-to-bank according to pre-established instructions by the payor and payee.

    For example, a typical electronic payroll payment to employees would work as follows:

1. Two days prior to date due, your company provides PNB with payment data in the prescribed format.
2. During the two day period, PNB electronically transfers funds through the ACH to the employee's bank for credit to his/her account.
3. On the pay date, the total amount of the payroll is charged to your corporate PNB account.
4. Your company provides the employee with a payment advice listing gross pay, deductions and net pay.
5. In addition, the payee's monthly bank account statement reflects these electronic payments.

The process for making Electronic Payments to pensioners, stockholders or suppliers works in a similar manner.

Figure 4-10. Eleven Things CompuCash 2 Can Do.

Increase Availability

1
Accelerate cash receipts for better control of corporate funds.

2
Reduce collection float (the costs associated with cash flow delays).

Reduce Internal Processing Costs

3
Eliminate manual processing of receipts.

4
Automatically post receivables information.

Improve Credit Management

5
Provide detailed receivables information to credit managers on a same-day basis, without delaying the deposit of remittance checks.

6
Generate a data base system for accounts receivable information.

Specify Reporting/Output Requirements

7
Choose from a number of flexible reporting options, including electronic transmissions, magnetic tapes, on-line reporting systems, and printed reports.

8
Have checks automatically sorted for special handling according to criteria you establish.

Experience State-of-the-Art Quality and Timeliness

9
Realize greatly improved systems accuracy, speed and efficiency in processing remittance checks from customers.

Achieve Integration

10
Benefit from a service which is readily compatible with your internal processing systems.

11
Benefit from compatible automated banking services, including CompuLink®, an on-line financial reporting system that transfers funds by wire, CompuDraft®, which collects and report international payments, and our Corporate Trade Payment System.

Figure 4-11. PNB-CompuLink, Balance Report, B Function.

```
ENTER FUNCTION?B
ENTER ACCOUNT NUMBER (12 CHAR MAX) OR END?
```

Previous day's
closing balance

PNB Compulink
Based Upon the BankLink Information Service
Balance Information   04/23/79   14:32 EST3
XYZ Widget Corp

Account No. As of DT	Ledger Balance Coll Balance	1 Day Float 2 Day Float	Tot Crd Amt Tot DBT Amt	NO. Crd NO. DBT
0111-2346	12,068,921.13	5,385,200.00	7,956,678.29	5
4/20/79	6,674,421.13	9,300.00	14,474,072.37	5
0123-4562	5,982,400.63	5,152,500.00	7,272,173.82	5
4/20/79	829,900.63	0.00	2,426,678.80	5
LNB 2323232	125,000.00	7,800.00	19,500.00	3
4/20/79	108,700.00	8,500.00	35,600.00	3
Totals	18,176,321.76	10,545,500.00	15,248,352.11	13
	7,613,012.76	17,800.00	16,936,351.17	13

```
ENTER FUNCTION?
```

Ledger balance minus one
and two day float

Figure 4-12. PNB CompuLink, Balance History Report, BHIS Function.

```
ENTER FUNCTION?BHIS
ENTER OPTION?LIST

C        :   CURRENT MONTH
P        :   PREVIOUS MONTH
U        :   UPDATE   ——————  Option to update information
MM/DD/YY :   STARTING DATE ——— Option to specify time period
END      :   END BHIS FUNCTION

ENTER OPTION?04/01/79
ENTER END DATE (MM/DD/YY)?04/05/79
ENTER: ACCOUNT NUMBER OR 'ALL' OR 'END' ? 0123-4562
FULL DETAIL (Y/N) ?Y
```

```
                                 PNB COMPULINK
                 BASED UPON THE BANKLINK INFORMATION SERVICE
                            BALANCE HISTORY REPORT
                              APR 1 TO APR 5
                                                    04/23/79   14:30EST
```

ACCOUNT NO: 0123-4562

DAY	LEDGER	COLLECTED	ID FLOAT	2D FLOAT	DEBITS	CREDITS
1	4,838,853.00	2,078,853.00	2,671,700	88,300	0.00	0.00
2	9,322,544.00	2,242,444.00	6,295,200	784,900	6,027,491.00	10,511,181.00
3	7,461,600.00	2,339,200.00	4,958,400	164,000	6,202,636.00	4,341,692.00
4	6,387,893.00	3,051,793.00	3,234,400	101,700	4,244,202.00	3,180,496.00
5	4,469,885.00	2,161,485.00	2,154,800	153,600	4,128,878.00	2,210,870.00

```
TOTALS FOR APR 1 TO APR 5                               20,603,207.00  20,244,239.00
AVERAGES FOR APR 1 TO APR 5
       6,496,155.00  2,374,755.00   3,862,900   258,500   4,120,641.40   4,048,847.80
```

```
ENTER: ACCOUNT NUMBER OR 'ALL' OR 'END' ?END
ENTER OPTION?END
ENTER FUNCTION?
```

Figure 4-13. PNB CompuLink, Target Projection Report, TP Function.

ENTER FUNCTION?TP CURRENT
ENTER ACCT: OR 'ALL' OR 'END'?
DO YOU WISH BANK SUBTOTALS ONLY (Y/N) &N

PNB COMPULINK

BASED UPON THE BANKLINK INFORMATION SERVICE   04/23/79 14:34 EST
8 TARGET BALANCE INFORMATION

XYZ WIDGET CORP   FISCAL YR ENDS ; 12/31/79

REM DAYS IN MON:
REM DAYS IN YR: 253

ACCOUNT NO / AS OF DT	MTD AVG COL / YTD AVG COL	TARG BAL (M) / TARG BAL (Y)	AVG TARG (M) / AVG TARG (Y)	1 DY BAL (M) / 1 DY BAL (Y)	REV TARG (M) / REV TARG (Y)	DYS (M) / DYS (Y)
0111-2346	3,150,000	3,000,000	3,000,000	-300,000	2,587,500	22
4/20/79	3,800,000	4,000,000	4,000,000	26,400,000	4,088,538	112
0123-4562	900,000	1,000,000	1,000,000	3,200,000	1,275,000	22
4/20/79	1,395,000	1,500,000	1,500,000	13,260,000	1,546,482	112
PNB TOTAL	4,050,000	4,000,000	4,000,000	2,900,000	3,862,500	
	5,195,000	5,500,000	5,500,000	39,660,000	5,635,020	
LNB 2323232	350,000	500,000	500,000	3,800,000	912,500	22
4/20/79	412,000	400,000	400,000	-944,000	394,688	112
TOTALS	4,400,000	4,500,000	4,500,000	6,700,000	4,775,000	
	5,607,000	5,900,000	5,900,000	38,716,000	6,029,708	

ENTER FUNCTION?

Current target balance

Reflects any changes to target balance

Amount needed today to meet month/year average target

Amount needed for each remaining day of month/year to meet set target

No. of days for which this information has been reported

Figure 4-14. PNB CompuLink, Previous Day Credit Report, C Function.

PNB Audit Trail No.
for tracing purposes

```
ENTER FUNCTION?C
ENTER ACCOUNT NUMBER (12 CHAR MAX) OR END
ENTER MINIMUM AMOUNT 00         Items below minimum
                                will be summarized
```

PNB COMPULINK
BASED UPON THE BANKLINK INFORMATION SERVICE

ACCOUNT NO : ALL   PREVIOUS DAY CREDITS   04/23/79 14:36EST

DATE	TRANS CODE	CREDIT AMOUNT	1 DAY FLOAT	2 DAY FLOAT	ITEM NO.
4/20	DEPOSIT	3,530,507.00	0.00	0.00	52590338
4/20	LOCK BOX	1,039,894.00	0.00	0.00	66313185
4/20	DEPOSIT	1,296,135.62	0.00	0.00	43562490
4/20	DOM WIRE	1,057,634.67	0.00	0.00	43562512
4/20	MISC CR	1,032,507.00	0.00	0.00	57531525
0111-2346		7,956,678.29	0.00	0.00	5 TOT ITEMS
4/20	DEPOSIT	1,031,119.24	0.00	0.00	01250000
4/20	DOM WIRE	1,053,552.96	0.00	0.00	35010082
4/20	MISC CR	1,056,998.17	0.00	0.00	35010172
4/20	DOM WIRE	3,095,055.20	0.00	0.00	35010083
4/20	DEPOSIT	1,035,448.25	0.00	0.00	35010084
0123-4562		7,272,173.82	0.00	0.00	5 TOT ITEMS
GRAND TOTAL		15,228,852.11	0.00	0.00	10 ITEMS

ENTER FUNCTION?

Figure 4-15. PNB CompuLink, Previous Day Debit Report, D. Function.

```
ENTER FUNCTION?D
ENTER ACCOUNT NUMBER (12 CHAR MAX) OR END
ENTER MINIMUM AMOUNT 1,000
```

Items below minimum
will be summarized

PNB Audit Trail No.
for tracing purposes

```
                                PNB COMPULINK
               BASED UPON THE BANKLINK INFORMATION SERVICE
              ACCOUNT NO : ALL       PREVIOUS DAY DEBITS        04/23/79  14:38 EST

DATE      TRAN CODE      CHECK NO.      DEBIT AMOUNT      ITEM NO.

4/20      MISC DR                         960,004.80      14740568
4/20      MISC D                          992,671.63      48900008
4/20      CUSTODY                       1,789,342.28      42030602
4/20      CHECK          131312         4,725,356.96      52621345
4/20      DOM WIRE                       6,006,696.70      22090505

ACCOUNT 0111-2346      TOTAL           14,474,072.37                    5 ITEMS

4/20      MISC DR                         183,334.25      49300614
4/20      DOM WIRE                        300,001.50      48682011
4/20      CHECK          131459           583,336.25      40031808
4/20      DOM WIRE                        596,669.65      67101040
4/20      CUSTODY                         763,337.15      67101034

ACCOUNT 0123-4562      TOTAL            2,426,678.80                    5 ITEMS

10 ITEMS              GRAND TOTAL      16,900,751.17

ENTER FUNCTION?
```

Figure 4-16. PNB CompuLink, Lockbox Report, LB Function.

ENTER FUNCTION?LB

Number of deposits received for each box

```
                           PNB COMPULINK
              BASED UPON THE BANKLINK INFORMATION SERVICE
                      LOCK BOX REPORTING      04/23/79    14:33EST
                      XYZ WIDGET CORP

ACCOUNT NUMB   BOX NO   I.D.    DATE           AMOUNT

0111-2346      1234      1     04/23/79       564,327.99
                         2     04/23/79         8,765.45
                         3     04/23/79       987,789.12
               1234                         1,560,882.56

               4321      1     04/23/79        87,234.56
                         2     04/23/79       675,489.99

               4321                           762,724.55

0111-2346                                   2,323,607.11

TOTAL                                       2,323,607.11

ENTER FUNCTION?
```

Figure 4-17. PNB CompuLink, Depository Transfer Check Report, DTC Function.

Report to list all valid DTC locations

Locations which have reported

Locations which have not reported

To override a reported deposit

Company division for which data is being entered

```
ENTER FUNCTION ?DTC
ENTER DTC REQUEST ('HLL', 'IN', 'OUT', OR 'ISSUE') ?ALL
ENTER BANK ID OR 'END'?1
ENTER DIVISION NUMBER OR 'ALL' OR 'END'?
```

```
                                    PNB COMPULINK
                    BASED UPON THE BANKLINK INFORMATION SERVICE
PHIL. NATIONAL BANK    CORP. NUMBER: 1234         DTC REPORT      06/01/79   08:14EDT
                                                 XYZ WIDGET CO
```

Company division available on report

LOCATION NAME		DATE	LOCATION	TIME	ITEMS	AMOUNT
DIVISION: 001 MANUFACTURING						
CROCKER BANK	0020	01/10/79	07:29EDT		1	$15,000.00
EMPIRE TRUST CO.	0030	06/01/79	07:29EDT		1	$35,000.00
SUPER BANK AND TRUST	0040	06/01/79	07:29EDT		1	$55,000.00
MARYLAND NATIONAL	0614	06/01/79	07:29EDT		1	$75,000.00
LAST BANK	0714	06/01/79	07:29EDT		1	$95,000.00
MARYLAND NATIONAL	1614	06/01/79	07:29EDT		1	$115,000.00
		6 LOCATIONS		TOTAL		$390,000.00
DIVISION: 002 DISTRIBUTING						
FIRST NATIONAL BANK	0010	06/01/79	07:29EDT		1	$135,000.00
GOTHAM CITY BANK	0015	06/01/79	07:29EDT		1	$155,000.00
STATE BANK OF IDAHO	0020	06/01/79	07:29EDT		1	$175,000.00
		3 LOCATIONS		TOTAL		$465,000.00
		9 LOCATIONS		GRAND TOTAL		$855,000.00

```
ENTER FUNCTION?BYE
'AT'
```

Figure 4-18. PNB CompuLink, Wire Transfer Report, W Function.

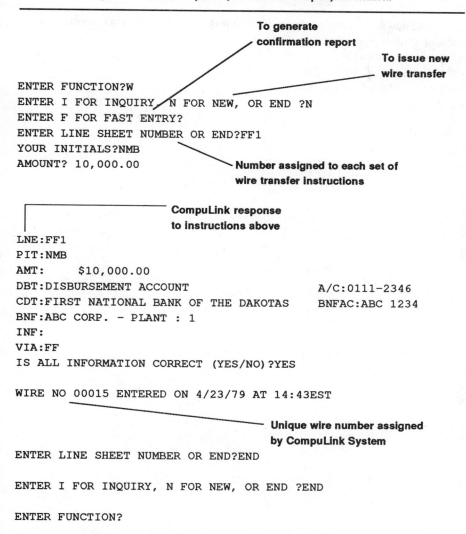

To generate
confirmation report

To issue new
wire transfer

```
ENTER FUNCTION?W
ENTER I FOR INQUIRY, N FOR NEW, OR END ?N
ENTER F FOR FAST ENTRY?
ENTER LINE SHEET NUMBER OR END?FF1
YOUR INITIALS?NMB
AMOUNT? 10,000.00
```

Number assigned to each set of
wire transfer instructions

CompuLink response
to instructions above

```
LNE:FF1
PIT:NMB
AMT:     $10,000.00
DBT:DISBURSEMENT ACCOUNT                    A/C:0111-2346
CDT:FIRST NATIONAL BANK OF THE DAKOTAS      BNFAC:ABC 1234
BNF:ABC CORP. - PLANT : 1
INF:
VIA:FF
IS ALL INFORMATION CORRECT (YES/NO)?YES

WIRE NO 00015 ENTERED ON 4/23/79 AT 14:43EST
```

Unique wire number assigned
by CompuLink System

```
ENTER LINE SHEET NUMBER OR END?END

ENTER I FOR INQUIRY, N FOR NEW, OR END ?END

ENTER FUNCTION?
```

PHOENIX-HECHT SERVICES

Phoenix-Hecht is a pioneer in services dealing with collecting money in a banking system, as shown in Figure 4-19. It was one of the first firms to recognize the importance of mail times in float costs. By analyzing the time it took to mail envelopes from one zip code location to another, the firm focused on the importance of lockboxes. Now, a major Phoenix-Hecht service is a lockbox system for firms. The company has the capability to design a system that minimizes mail float and accelerates the collection of funds into disbursing accounts.

Figure 4-19. Products and Services Offered by Phoenix-Hecht.

PRODUCTS AND SERVICES OFFERED BY
PHOENIX-HECHT

COLLECTIONS

Postal Survey

Measures lockbox mail and availability float twice per year from 110 of the largest business centers to more than 120 remittance processing centers (individual banks, city averages, and networks). The Postal Survey is the most widely used tool in collection system analysis.

Postal Expander

A report on lockbox mail and availability float for 60 regional sending points not included in the standard Postal Survey. Used specifically to expand the scope of collection analysis capability.

Lockbox Evaluator

A set of reports which provides comprehensive statistical analysis of individual bank, city, and regional float times and mail arrival patterns. Marketing section reports rank bank and city performance by local area, geographic regions, and individual sending zip codes. Operations section reports evaluate operational efficiency and the integration of scheduled post office pick-up with availability deadlines.

Evaluator/PC

An IBM PC based model used to analyze the impact of changes to availability and mail pick-up schedules on Postal Survey performance. Also allows you to use current survey data to print out customized marketing reports useful to the sales force.

Lockbox System Analyzer

A study service which utilizes the Lockbox Location System—Release 4.0 mainframe model to evaluate the effectiveness of an existing collection system and to identify optimal collection locations.

Lockbox Micro Model

A user-friendly, accurate, and low-cost lockbox optimization model which runs on an IBM PC. The Micro Model is used for analyzing middle market company collection systems and for demonstrating the benefits of your bank's lockbox.

Customized Postal Survey

An analysis tailored to individual client specifications.

AVAIL SERIES

Cash Letter Manager

An IBM PC based model used to perform cost and profitability analysis of bank cash letters of lockbox accounts. Cash Letter Manager provides display and comparison functions for schedules included in the Phoenix-Hecht Correspondent Availability/Price Data Base.

Endpoint Manager

Current all-items data is summarized and transferred from your mainframe to the IBM PC. All of the AVAIL Series applications are enhanced by the use of live, accurate transaction data.

Transit Manager

Transit Manager performs a cost analysis of your current transit system. then finds the optimal clearing banks by simultaneously analyzing the all-items data for all the time periods in the day. Runs on the IBM PC.

Figure 4-19. Products and Services Offered by Phoenix-Hecht (continued).

PRODUCTS AND SERVICES OFFERED BY
PHOENIX-HECHT
(continued)

DISBURSEMENTS

Clearing Study

Measures presentation times for over 140 drawee bank checks deposited in major lockbox locations. Used to quantify the effects of fluctuating clearing patterns on specific corporate payables systems. Large dollar items are used to measure the effects of the Fed's High Dollar Group Sort Program.

Disbursement System Analyzer

A study service which utilizes the Disbursement Location System—Release 3.0 mainframe model to evaluate the effectiveness of an existing disbursement system and to identify optimal disbursement locations.

Disbursement Micro Model

A user-friendly, accurate, and low-cost disbursement optimization model which runs on an IBM PC.

COMPREHENSIVE NON-CREDIT SERVICES

PRODUCT MANAGER SERIES

Product Line Manager

A competitive analysis tool available to the non-credit services product manager, consisting of three distinct survey sections: disbursements, collections, and electronic delivery products. Allows you to compare your bank's services, pricing, and market share with those of other bank groups.

Disbursement Site Survey

A survey of bank disbursement capabilities and procedures. Used for comparative analysis in bank selection and evaluation.

Collection Site Survey

A survey of bank lockbox collection services. To be used in conjunction with computer model analysis to define non-float characteristics of an identified site.

The Cash Management Service Guide

A two-volume set designed to provide corporations with information about bank non-credit services. Contains the most up-to-date information available for determining which banks have product offerings that best meet a company's needs. Also available on diskette.

ELECTRONIC BANKING

Corporate Electronic Payments Evaluator

An IBM PC based model which analyzes the impact on corporate collection and disbursement if conversion is made from a paper-based system to an electronic system with negotiated settlement dates.

EDUCATION

Programs are designed to meet specific client needs, normally including current product knowledge and environmental analysis.

CONSULTING

The resources of Phoenix-Hecht are available to clients for consultation on an individual basis regarding corporate and bank-related treasury management issues. Assistance involves problem definition, solution design, and implementation advice.

CONCLUSION

Materials are available from other organizations and may be obtained from marketing departments. These materials, along with the sampling in this chapter, show the wide range of capabilities offered on a local, regional, national, and international basis. Firms must analyze their needs, perhaps with the assistance of a financial services firm. Then, a timely, accurate, and cost effective system for cash management can be designed and implemented.

III.

Cash Management

Cash Forecasting

Forecasting the amount of cash that a firm will have and need in future periods is a difficult task. Many factors affect cash flows; some can be identified in advance and some cannot. In this chapter, we will tackle the problem of forecasting the firm's need for cash to support its operations. The chapter begins with some traditional techniques, which are then modified in light of developments associated with the computer and electronic spreadsheet. The strengths and weaknesses of each format for forecasting are analyzed and evaluated. The second half of the chapter covers statistical approaches to increasing the accuracy of forecasts. Probability distributions and linear regression are employed as examples of using statistical tools when forecasting.

TRADITIONAL FORECASTING TECHNIQUES

During the 1950s, controllers, systems analysts, and others developed a number of cash forecasting methods. In this process, three kinds of budgets were distinguished.

1. **Cash Budget**. This type of budget is a formal plan for forecasting future receipts and disbursements of cash. It focuses on cash movements by recognizing the difference between a transaction and the cash that flows from it.

2. **Operating Budget**. This budget is a formal plan that deals with revenues and expenses from operations. It is commonly prepared for the short term, often only a year, and usually does not make sharp distinctions between cash and noncash expenses.

3. **Capital Budget**. This formal plan deals exclusively with major investment proposals and time periods in excess of a year.

Cash Cycle

The cash budget properly focuses on receipts and disbursements of cash. It will reflect the cash cycle of a business enterprise, as shown in Figure 5-1 for a

manufacturing firm. The figure begins with the purchase of raw materials and
ends with the collection of cash from the sale. The figure shows the concept of
a **lag**, in which the transaction occurs on one day while its cash effect occurs
at another time. The same situation exists for a firm providing services rather
than manufacturing goods. The firm may incur salary or other costs while the
service is being provided, and the cash effects will occur at a later date.

Figure 5-1. Cash Cycle for a Manufacturing Firm.

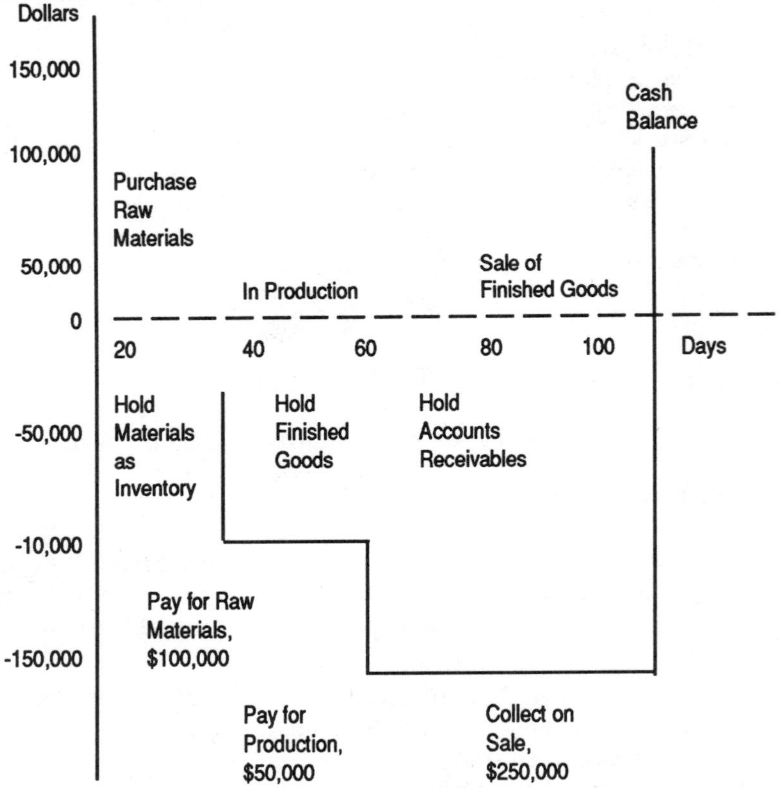

A more detailed representation of the cash cycle is shown in Figure 5-2, in
which a firm is assumed to begin operations on January 1 of a given year. The
transactions and cash effects are displayed for each month, and the firm's net
cash position is summarized in the final column of the figure. The simplified
activities of the firm involve the purchase of materials, labor costs in manufacturing, and credit sales of finished goods. With a one–month lag, payables are
discharged, labor costs are paid, and receivables are collected. Since the firm
started activities on January 1, its net cash position is negative initially.
Collections turn it positive in August.

Figure 5-2. Cash Cycle, One–Year Period (Operations Beginning January 1).

Accounting Activities

Month	Materials Purchased	Labor Costs	Sale of Goods
January	100,000		
February	110,000	63,000	
March	140,000	73,000	240,000
April	120,000	83,000	250,000
May	100,000	93,000	260,000
June	85,000	53,000	270,000
July	95,000	63,000	280,000
August	105,000	73,000	215,000
September	115,000	83,000	225,000
October	125,000	93,000	235,000
November	135,000	103,000	245,000
December	145,000	113,000	255,000

Cash Flows

Month	Paid Payables	Paid Labor	Collected Receivable	Cash Out	Cash In	Net Position
January				0	0	0
February	-100,000			-100,000	0	-100,000
March	-110,000	-63,000		-173,000	0	-273,000
April	-140,000	-73,000	240,000	-213,000	240,000	-246,000
May	-120,000	-83,000	250,000	-203,000	250,000	-199,000
June	-100,000	-93,000	260,000	-193,000	260,000	-132,000
July	-85,000	-53,000	270,000	-138,000	270,000	0
August	-95,000	-63,000	280,000	-158,000	280,000	122,000
September	-105,000	-73,000	215,000	-178,000	215,000	159,000
October	-115,000	-83,000	225,000	-198,000	225,000	186,000
November	-125,000	-93,000	235,000	-218,000	235,000	203,000
December	-135,000	-103,000	245,000	-238,000	245,000	210,000

Note in both figures that the business operations differ markedly from the cash forecast. The impact of the lag is significant and must be recognized to avoid shortages of cash or idle cash balances.

It is one thing to recognize the nature of the cash cycle and lags for a firm. It is another to successfully forecast the different cash effects. Two traditional methods were developed in the 1950s to assist the cash manager in the task of cash forecasting. We will examine both approaches.[1]

Receipts and Disbursements Method

The receipts and disbursement method is the most widely used approach to preparing a cash budget and, even antedates the electronic spreadsheet. It identifies the cash receipts and disbursements by major categories and spreads them in columns over time, normally in periods of one month or one quarter. Using this method, the analyst prepares a **cash forecast**, which is a schedule over time of cash inflows and outlays. Each column represents a time period, and rows represent cash activities. The goal is to identify, by major category, every cash flow that will be incurred during the given time period. The following sections identify some of the important elements that must be included to achieve this goal.

Input Screens and Output Screens

The cash forecast is set up using an electronic spreadsheet. It is important to distinguish between input and output screens. An **input screen** is an area of the spreadsheet that contains at least one direct entry. An **output screen** is an area in which all entries are referenced or calculated from other areas. When seeking variables or assumptions in the forecast, the analyst need only look at input screens. This facilitates the changing of assumptions to see the impact of different variables on the forecast.

When creating input and output screens, the cash manager should follow the principles of spreadsheet design. The most important of these principles are the following:

1. **Identify all areas as input or output screens.** This is done on the first row of the area.

2. **Minimize the number of input screens.** When a forecast model has been completed and is being used to evaluate the effect of changing factors, variables are permitted only in input screens. By keeping the number of such screens to a minimum, we facilitate locating variables.

---

[1] For more details on the techniques covered in this section, the reader is referred to William E. Mitchell, "Cash Forecasting: The Four Methods Compared," **The Controller**, April 1960.

3. **Enter a variable directly only one time**. Any factor that may change should be directly entered only once in the model. Then, it can be varied by going to a single cell and changing it.

4. **Move between input and output screens by reference only**. Assume that cash sales are given at position C45 (which represents the particular column and row whose intersection contains the variable "cash sales"). If it is needed on an output screen at C126, we enter +C45 on the output screen. Thus, if cash sales are changed at C45, they will also be changed at C126.

5. **Never hard code a variable in a formula**. If cash sales represent 90 percent of total sales, we type 0.90 in the input screen. Later on, if we want to change the percentage to 0.85, we find the appropriate cell in the input screen and enter 0.85. We should not have to change the formula in the output screen.

6. **Create screens with parallel structure whenever possible**. In our forecast, column E will represent the month of January. Column F will represent February, and so on, on every screen. This facilitates locating earlier entries and permits powerful use of commands such as copy and move.

A cash forecast can be set up in many formats. It is common to use a single input screen to handle all variables and one or more output screens. A separate input screen can be set up for each debt repayment or depreciation schedule. To illustrate cash forecasting, we will set up a forecast with three components: (1) cash inflows; (2) cash expenses; and (3) summary cash forecast.

Cash Inflows in the Forecast

Figure 5-3 shows the cash inflow portion of the cash forecast using the receipts and disbursements method. Some features of the cash inflow areas are:

1. **Total Sales**. The sales begin in November, even though the forecast is intended for January to December of the next year. The November and December sales are needed because the account receivable is collected in January and February.

2. **Cash and Credit Sales**. The input screen distinguishes the percentage of cash sales in total sales.

3. **Growth Rate of Sales**. The input screen allows sales to grow at a forecasted rate.

4. **Collections Lag**. The firm forecasts either a one– or two–month lag in collections. That is, of the sales made in January, 45 percent will be collected in February and 55 percent will be collected in March.

Figure 5-3. Cash Inflows, Receipts and Disbursements Method.

Input Screen (thousands)

	Nov.	Dec.	Jan.	Feb.	Mar.	Apr.	May	Jun.
Total Sales	3,200	3,210	3,219	3,229	3,239	3,248	3,258	3,268
Cash Sales (pct.)	0.1	0.1	0.1	0.1	0.1	0.1	0.1	0.1
Growth Rate (pct.)	0.003	0.003	0.003	0.003	0.003	0.003	0.003	0.003
Credit Sales	2,880	2,889	2,897	2,906	2,915	2,923	2,932	2,941

Collections

	Nov.	Dec.	Jan.	Feb.	Mar.	Apr.	May	Jun.
Lag 1 Month (pct.)	0.45	0.45	0.45	0.45	0.45	0.45	0.35	0.35
Lag 2 Month, (pct.)	0.55	0.55	0.55	0.55	0.55	0.55	0.65	0.65

Output Screen

	Jan.	Feb.	Mar.	Apr.	May	Jun.
Cash Sales	322	323	324	325	326	327
Collections	2,884	2,893	2,901	2,910	2,919	2,634
Total Cash	3,206	3,216	3,225	3,235	3,245	2,961

Input Screen (continued)

	Jul.	Aug.	Sep.	Oct.	Nov.	Dec.
Total Sales	3,278	3,287	3,297	3,307	3,317	3,327
Cash Sales (pct.)	0.1	0.1	0.1	0.1	0.1	0.1
Growth Rate (pct.)	0.003	0.003	0.003	0.003	0.003	0.003
Credit Sales	2,950	2,959	2,968	2,976	2,985	2,994

Collections

	Jul.	Aug.	Sep.	Oct.	Nov.	Dec.
Lag 1 Month (pct.)	0.25	0.25	0.35	0.35	0.45	0.45
Lag 2 Months (pct.)	0.75	0.75	0.65	0.65	0.55	0.55

Output Screen (continued)

	Jul.	Aug.	Sep.	Oct.	Nov.	Dec.
Cash Sales	328	329	330	331	332	333
Collections	2,935	2,649	2,952	3,258	2,971	3,278
Total Cash	3,263	2,978	3,282	3,558	3,302	3,611

Figure 5-4. Cash Expenses, Receipts and Disbursements Method.

Input Screen (thousands)

	Nov.	Dec.	Jan.	Feb.	Mar.	Apr.	May	Jun.
Total Sales			3,219	3,229	3,239	3,248	3,258	3,268
CofGS (pct. of sales)			0.7	0.7	0.7	0.7	0.7	0.7
CofGS (dollars)			2,253	2,260	2,267	2,274	2,281	2,287
CofGS (pct. cash)			0.9	0.9	0.9	0.9	0.9	0.9
G&A (dollars)			563	565	567	568	570	572
G&A (pct. cash)			0.75	0.75	0.75	0.75	0.75	0.75

Output Screen

	Nov.	Dec.	Jan.	Feb.	Mar.	Apr.	May	Jun.
Cash, CofGS			2,028	2,034	2,040	2,046	2,053	2,058
Cash, G&A			432	424	425	426	427	428
Total Cash Expenses			2,451	2,458	2,465	2,473	2,480	2,488

Input Screen (continued)

	Jul.	Aug.	Sep.	Oct.	Nov.	Dec.
Total Sales	3,278	3,287	3,297	3,307	3,317	3,327
CofGS (pct.of sales)	0.7	0.7	0.7	0.7	0.7	0.7
CofGs, dollars	2294	2301	2308	2315	2,322	2,328
CofGS, pct.cash	0.9	0.9	0.9	0.9	0.9	0.9
G&A (dollars)	574	575	577	579	580	582
G&A (pct. cash)	0.75	0.75	0.75	0.75	0.75	0.75

Output Screen (continued)

	Jul.	Aug.	Sep.	Oct.	Nov.	Dec.
Cash, CofGs	2,065	2,070	2,077	2,084	2,090	2,096
Cash, G&A	430	431	433	434	435	437
Total Cash Expenses	2,495	2,501	2,510	2,518	2,525	2,533

Cash Expenses in the Forecast

Figure 5-4 shows the cash expenses portion of the forecast. Some features of these areas are:

1. **Cost of Goods Sold (CofGS) as a Percent of Sales.** The cost of goods sold number would be expected to vary according to the level of sales. This is reflected on the input screen, since CofGS is shown as a percentage of sales.

2. **Cash Portion of CofGS.** A part of the cost of goods sold reflects depreciation and other noncash expenses. This is reflected on the input screen, where 90 percent of the CofGS represents cash.

3. **General and Administrative Expenses (G & A).** These are given in dollars. Seventy-five percent of G&A is estimated to represent cash expenses.

Summary Cash Forecast

Figure 5-5 shows the summary of the two previous areas.

Figure 5-5. Summary Cash Forecast, Receipts and Disbursements Method.

Input Screen (thousands)

	Nov.	*Dec.*	*Jan.*	*Feb.*	*Mar.*	*Apr.*	*May*	*Jun.*
Beginning Balance			1,200					
Safety Level			900	900	900	900	900	900

Output Screen

			Jan.	*Feb.*	*Mar.*	*Apr.*	*May*	*Jun.*
Beginning Balance			1,200	1,955	2,713	3,472	4,234	4,706
Cash Sales			322	323	324	325	326	327
Collections			2,884	2,893	2,901	2,910	2,626	2,633
Cash Available			4,406	5,171	5,938	6,707	7,186	7,666
Cash, CofGS			2,028	2,034	2,040	2,046	2,053	2,059
Cash, G&A			423	424	425	426	428	429
Cash Outlays			2,451	2,458	2,465	2,473	2,480	2,488
Ending cash balance.			1,955	2,713	3,472	434	4,706	5,179
Safety Level			900	900	900	900	900	900
Surplus/Shortage			1,055	1,813	2,572	3,334	3,806	4,279

Input Screen (continued)

	Jul.	*Aug.*	*Sep.*	*Oct.*	*Nov.*	*Dec.*
Beginning Balance						
Safety Level	900	900	900	900	900	900

Output Screen

	Jul.	*Aug.*	*Sep.*	*Oct.*	*Nov.*	*Dec.*
Beginning Balance	5,179	5,799	6,715	7,783	8,558	9,633
Cash Sales	328	329	330	331	332	333
Collections	2,787	3,090	3,248	2,962	3,268	2,980
Cash Available	8,294	9,218	10,293	11,075	12,158	12,946
Cash, CofGS	2,065	2,071	2,077	2,084	2,090	2,096
Cash, G&A	430	431	433	434	435	437
Cash Outlays	2,495	2,503	2,510	2,518	2,525	2,533
Ending Cash Balance	5,799	6,715	7,783	8,558	9,633	10,413
Safety Level	900	900	900	900	900	900
Surplus/Shortage	4,899	5,815	6,883	7,658	8,733	9,513

Some features of Figure 5.5 are:

1. **Beginning Balance**. A beginning balance of $1,2 million is given, representing cash on hand at the start of the year. After the first month, the beginning balance for each subsequent month is the ending balance of the previous month.

2. **Safety Level**. A **safety level** is the minimum cash on hand that the firm desires to ensure liquidity of day–to–day operations. In many cases, it will be invested in money market or other interest–bearing investments. A safety level of $900,000 has been established by the firm.

3. **Cash Available**. This reflects the sum of the original cash on hand for any month, plus inflows.

4. **Surplus/Shortage**. If the ending cash balance exceeds the safety level, the firm has a **surplus**. If the ending cash balance is below the safety level, the firm has a **shortage**, even though the forecasted cash balance may still be positive.

Utility of Receipts and Disbursements Method

The receipts and disbursements method is widely used because it is straightforward and logical. At the same time, it must be used carefully for several reasons:

1. **Accuracy of Estimates**. The final cash forecast assumptions are usually the work of several departments. This is particularly the case in a manufacturing environment. Although it may be prepared under the direction of the Accounting or Planning Department, serious errors can be made if other groups do not take the time to prepare their inputs. As an example, sales estimates should be developed in consultation with marketing, and production expenses should not be estimated unless operating personnel and cost accountants are included in the discussion.

2. **Noncash Items**. These must be treated correctly. In a complex environment, it is easy to treat prepaid expenses as cash items when, in fact, they bear little relationship to disbursements. Similar problems arise with items carried on the books as work in process, since reported expenses do not match operating costs. In addition, the analyst must beware of noncash items that are offset with credits to various accounts. This might occur in a standard cost system where budgeted labor expenses do not match actual disbursements.

3. **Systematic Data**. Cash forecasting works best when receipts and disbursements are readily identifiable. This method requires a sys-

tematized budget that produces reliable numbers. This can be difficult in a manufacturing environment or when dealing with reports from stand-alone subsidiaries. For example, a firm may plan to purchase a machine and such an expenditure would be listed in the capital budget rather than operating budget. But what happens if the firm's internal engineering shop fabricates a portion of the machine? Will the cash effects be correctly allocated when cash flows are being forecast? This and similar problems can pose difficulties if data are not systematically collected.

Balance Sheet Projection Method

The second approach to cash forecasting deals with the accounts on the firm's balance sheet. The current assets, long-term assets, short-term liabilities, long-term liabilities, and equity sections are sorted into significant groupings. Then, changes in these accounts are forecasted. The difference between the changes on the asset side and liabilities side is the additional cash that will be needed or generated over the course of the year.

This method is usually used in conjunction with the receipts and disbursements method. It is particularly suitable in three situations.

1. **Inability to Identify Receipts and Disbursements.** In complex manufacturing environments, it can be difficult to identify specific receipts and disbursements. As an example, consider the manufacture of electronic products. The components are taken from inventory and have been purchased over a long period of time. The fact that 25,000 completed units were shipped during a single month tells almost nothing about when components were purchased. Instead, the firm can focus on inventory and when it is replenished. The balance sheet method is particularly suited for this purpose.

2. **Control of Independent Operating Units.** The balance sheet method builds on historical data without a detailed understanding of the business activities of a unit. The analyst can see that receivables or inventories change. The analyst does not know what is happening with sales or profits. To control cash flows of independent units and monitor them on a monthly basis, the cash manager can set goals for receivables, inventories, and payables. Thus, cash flows are held within limits without interfering with daily operations.

3. **Allocations to Subsidiaries.** Parent firms may want centralized control over major disbursements and collections of cash. This control can be achieved by providing targets for balance sheet accounts. As long as the subsidiaries remain within the targets, cash flows are being controlled.

An example of a balance sheet projection of cash flows is given in Figure 5-6. The input screen contains the projected balances in different accounts during each of the next six months. The output screen converts those balances into changes in cash flow that must be financed or that will provide funds. By setting up the balance sheet in a spreadsheet model, the cash manager can enter numbers that match the firm's historical or seasonal working–capital patterns. The output screen shows whether cash will be needed or excess funds will be available. This is estimated without the complex task of identifying cash movements in the operating areas. For the amount of time expended, this approach to cash budgeting is cost effective.

*Figure 5-6.*Cash Forecast, Balance Sheet Projection Method.

Input Screen (thousands)

	Nov.	*Dec.*	*Jan.*	*Feb.*	*Mar.*	*Apr.*	*May*	*Jun.*
Accts. Rec.	9,400	9,100	8,700	8,400	8,600	9,100	9,700	10,300
Inventories	12,500	12,300	11,600	12,700	13,500	15,200	14,900	14,700
Other Curr. Assets	325	345	365	400	380	370	350	375
Fixed Assets	43,600	42,500	41,300	40,400	42,500	42,300	41,700	41,400
Wages Payable	140	150	165	150	135	145	160	145
Trade Payables	6,500	6,300	5,500	6,400	7,300	8,800	8,300	7,700
Other S-T	250	250	230	325	325	300	275	280
L-T Debt	19,800	19,600	18,800	17,500	16,800	16,400	17,100	17,100
Equity	39,100	38,600	38,600	39,200	39,400	39,700	39,500	39,200

Output Screen

CHANGES IN BALANCES (+ = cash provided)

Accts. Rec.	300	400	300	-200	-500	-600	-600
Inventories	200	700	-1,100	-800	-1,700	300	200
Other Curr. Assets	-20	-20	-35	20	10	20	-25
Fixed Assets	1,100	1,200	900	-2,100	200	600	300
Wages Payable	10	15	-15	-15	10	15	-15
Trade Payables	-200	-800	900	900	1,500	-500	-600
Other S-T	0	-20	95	0	-25	-25	5
L-T Debt	-200	-800	-1,300	-700	-400	700	0
Equity	-500	0	600	200	300	-200	-300
Cash Flow	690	675	345	-2,695	-605	310	-1,035

With the balance sheet projection method, the analyst has to beware of the same kinds of problems that arise with the receipts and disbursements method. One difficulty occurs when an account changes radically with no warning and no apparent explanation. This will throw off the forecast without a visible reason. There is a disadvantage to using a method that does not identify the details which cause cash changes. At the same time, an offsetting factor is that the analyst will know immediately that the forecast was not accurate. The ability to identify a miss on a forecast is also the ability to respond quickly to see what happened and make corrections, as needed. Since the firm's accounting system reports closing balances each month, it only takes days or weeks to see the missed forecast number. In spite of the lack of detail, many analysts feel that the balance sheet projection method is the best technique for measuring the accuracy of the forecast once the period is over.

A Variation–Modified Income Statement Method

Even though there are two traditional methods of cash forecasting, in the article cited earlier in this chapter, "Cash Forecasting: The Four Methods Compared", William Mitchell identifies two other methods that are variations on the receipts and disbursements method. One of these is the **modified income statement method**, an approach that works from the firm's monthly or quarterly income statement. The analyst begins with sales and adjusts them to reflect collections of cash. Then, each expense item is covered beginning with cost of goods sold and working through general and administrative expenses, interest, and taxes. For each account or category, the cash effect is isolated and recorded. The end result is cash from operations.

A variation on this technique is to assume that the after-tax income is equivalent to cash, with the exception of noncash expenses and certain other adjustments to accrual accounts. This is generally less accurate than the more detailed analysis.

The modified income statement method does not appear to be widely used in cash forecasting at the present time. Although it uses a straightforward and familiar format, many analysts do not trust the method in situations where earnings fluctuate from period to period. A feeling exists that the method may not be sufficiently powerful to catch sudden changes and their impact on cash. The same statement could be made about the receipts and disbursements or projected balance sheet approaches. Still, the income statement appears to be used primarily as a supplemental tool. Once receipts and disbursements are identified, the income statement is prepared and compared with it.

A Second Variation–Working-Capital Extrapolation Method

This approach, whose name was coined in the Mitchell article, is a second variation on receipts and disbursements. The format is that of the flow of funds statement prepared by many firms for their annual reports. By using monthly or quarterly figures, each major category supplying funds or using funds is identified. Once all the sources are listed, total sources for the period are calculated. The total uses are subtracted from this amount. The result is the forecasted change in the firm's cash position during the period.

This method follows a format similar to that of the receipts and disbursements method. Its ability to provide accurate forecasts is dependent on the ability of the analyst to identify factors affecting sources and uses. It also depends on the accuracy of assumptions on the level of sales, expenses, receivables, and other disbursements.

The working capital extrapolation format is not widely used as a primary approach to forecasting cash needs. Like the modified income statement approach, it is often used as a supplemental tool. An exception exists for long–term projections. When the firm is preparing a long–range plan, treasurers and analysts frequently make use of a flow of funds format for projecting cash requirements.

CONCLUSION

Since the 1950s, the traditional methods of cash forecasting have not changed significantly. Many companies follow techniques and formats developed many years ago. A dramatic change has occurred in the preparation of the forecast with the development of the electronic spreadsheet. The ability of the computer to perform lightning fast calculations after assumptions or data have been changed has increased the importance of the preparation of cash budgets. As analysts master the spreadsheets, further sophistication of basic techniques developed in the 1950s and 1960s is likely.

INCREASING THE ACCURACY OF FORECASTS

Most firms experience fluctuating needs for cash on a cyclical, seasonal, or other basis. In many cases, the fluctuations are tied to other factors such as sales, economic conditions, or related industries or products. Such variables define the operating environment for business activity as being filled with uncertainty. Thus, analysts spend a great deal of time attempting to minimize and to anticipate uncertainty and to prepare for unavoidable variations.

Quantitative approaches to preparing for future events have proved to be powerful allies in cash forecasting. In effect, developments in statistics have produced applications to increase the firm's ability to forecast in the face of an uncertain environment. Entire books have been written to explain such techniques. In this section, we will examine a few basic tools to illustrate how statistics can assist in increasing the accuracy of forecasts.

Fluctuating Levels of Cash

A firm's requirements for cash are primarily affected by five factors:

1. **Level of Sales.** This is probably the most important single factor. When a firm increases sales, cash needs rise. When sales decline, less cash is required. Over time, we might expect a firm to maintain a fairly steady relationship between the volume of sales and cash receipts and disbursements.

2. **Seasonal Fluctuations.** The demand for goods and services often fluctuates according to the season of the year. Some products sell better in the summer; others sell better in the winter. As these fluctuations occur, the need for cash will vary.

3. **Cyclical Fluctuations.** Similar variations occur with cyclical changes in economic activity. If the country or worldwide markets for products are experiencing growth, sales will rise and more cash will be needed. With cyclical downturns in business activity, cash needs will decline.

4. **Changes in Technology.** Products are made and services are supplied in a technological framework. If new technologies are introduced, the firm must adjust its cash needs. As an example, when a firm purchases a new machine that processes raw materials at a faster rate than previously, inventory requirements will change. This will also affect cash needs.

5. **Policies of the Firm.** In many ways, the firm determines a large part of its cash needs based on its philosophy and policies. If the firm sells on terms of net 30, it will have one level of receivables. If it changes to 2/10 net 30, a different level will result. If it changes production policies, inventory requirements may be permanently or temporarily altered. Since the need for cash is linked to different policies, a policy change can cause fluctuations in cash levels.

Planning for Cash Needs

For planning purposes, a firm may forecast some optimum level of cash on hand. For a growing firm, the level will slope upward over time. The actual level maintained will fluctuate seasonally or otherwise around the optimum. This is illustrated in Figure 5-7. Two kinds of fluctuations are evident in the figure.

1. **Seasonal Fluctuations**. In the early spring, the actual cash level takes a downturn, probably matching low sales or low production in that period. By late summer, the actual cash level appears to be at a seasonal high.

2. **Random Fluctuations**. The actual cash levels are connected by a jagged line. It appears that changes in cash are not smooth over the course of the year. The random fluctuations occur on a weekly or even daily basis and may be the result of mail delays, the timing of cash disbursements, or other factors that are not included in the planning process. The company treasurer will manage money on a day-to-day basis to minimize the negative impacts of these random movements.

Figure 5-7. Actual and Planning Level of Cash.

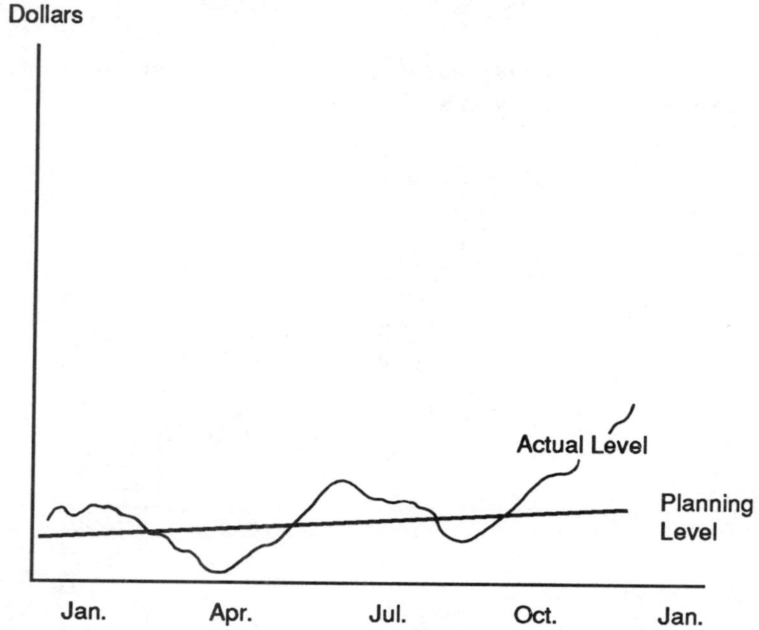

Probability Distributions–A Statistical Tool

One way to manage fluctuations in cash levels is to view them as variables from the beginning. To assist in visualizing this process, we can borrow a statistical tool. A **probability distribution** may be defined as a range of estimates of the likelihood of the occurrence of different future outcomes. For example, consider a firm that expects to receive $100,000 in a lockbox on an average day.

The mean or **expected value** is defined as the most likely or average estimate of the cash inflow. It might be determined by totaling the cash inflows over a period of time and dividing by the number of days in the period.

Let us suppose that the analyst studies prior deposits and develops the likelihood of different levels of deposits. The analysis may reveal the following pattern of deposits:

Approximate Level of Deposits	*Likelihood of Occurrence*
$60,000	0.10
80,000	0.20
100,000	0.40
120,000	0.20
140,000	0.10

A **discrete probability distribution**, defined as having a limited number of identifiable values, can be formed as shown in Figure 5-8.

Figure 5-8. Discrete Probability Distribution.

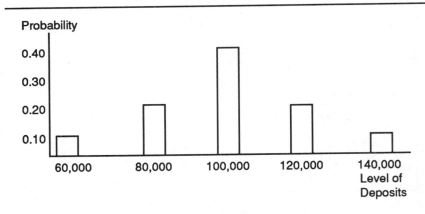

With respect to deposits in a lockbox, it is not likely that five levels would be adequate to describe the daily possible changes. The analyst is dealing with a situation that is better described by a **continuous probability distribution**, defined as a distribution that can take on all possible numerical values over the range between the highest and lowest values. A **normal** or bell-shaped distribution is continuous and has been found to describe accurately many types of frequency data, such as forecasts of dispersion around a central value. It is useful to describe changes in cash balances and the clearing of checks in a banking system.

The probability distribution highlights the fact that a forecasted value is a **point estimate** that is, a single value usually at the center of a possible range of values. The firm may forecast a cash level of $1 million in six months. The actual value may be above or below this point, and it is unlikely to be exactly $1 million. Thus, in forecasting future cash levels we have point estimates and ranges of possible values. This is shown in Figure 5-9, in which future estimates are represented by bell-shaped curves, or normal probability distributions.

Two normal probability distributions are given in the figure. One describes changing cash levels for a firm that mails all its checks on Friday of each week. The other describes a firm whose checks are mailed each working day. By accumulating all payments to a single day of the week, the one firm has larger day–to–day changes in cash levels than the firm that pays its bills on a daily basis.

One importance of the probability distribution is that it highlights the fact that a cash forecast is not a point estimate. That is, it is not a single number that can usually be achieved. Rather, a forecasted number will be the **expected value** or center point of a range of possible cash levels. The exact level will be determined by business actions, the clearing of checks, and a myriad of other factors that influence receipts and disbursements. In stable stituations, a firm will have a more compact probability distribution. In a less stable situation, wide fluctuations are likely. The average or expected value may be the same, but the range of inflows or disbursements may differ significantly in the two situations.

Figure 5-9. Continuous Probability Distribution.

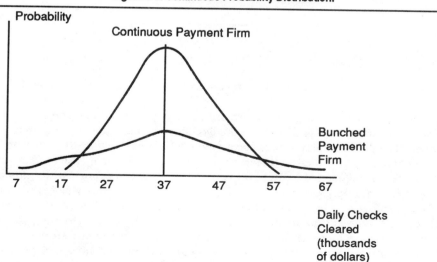

Standard Deviation

We are now ready for a more formal process of measuring variations in cash levels. A **standard deviation** is defined as a measure of the dispersion of values that approximate a normal probability distribution. A small standard deviation indicates a tight distribution and identifies a receiving and disbursing situation with smaller fluctuations than similar situations with large deviations.

The usefulness of the standard deviation as a measure of dispersion may be attributed directly to a single fact: it is an absolute measure of the area under a normal probability curve. Actually, **six standard deviations make up virtually the entire range** of possibilities. Thus, three standard deviations above the expected value will be the highest likely value.

Example: A firm has a subsidiary that controls its own disbursements, but its cash position is managed by the parent company's treasurer. On each working day, the subsidiary will have checks averaging $12,000 clear the parent's master account. The standard deviation of checks clearing is $3,000. What is the entire range of possible clearings?

Answer: $3,000 to $21,000, as follows:

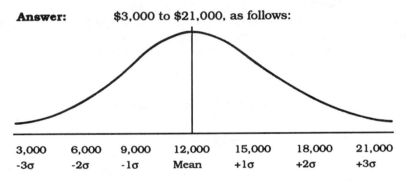

| 3,000 | 6,000 | 9,000 | 12,000 | 15,000 | 18,000 | 21,000 |
| -3σ | -2σ | -1σ | Mean | +1σ | +2σ | +3σ |

where σ = the Greek symbol **sigma** used to represent the standard deviation

In addition to specifying the entire range of possible values, the standard deviation can be used to determine the likelihood of achieving a single value or range of values. This is true because we have tables that provide the percentage of occurrences in different areas under the normal curve. Such data are presented in Figure 5-10 where 68 percent of all values occur within plus or minus one standard deviation from the expected value or mean. Note that half of all possibilities occur above the midpoint and that another 34.13 percent occur within one standard deviation of the mean. Thus, values close to the center point are more likely to occur than values further away. More specifically, 34.13 percent occur between the mean and one sigma; 13.59 percent occur between one and two sigmas; and approximately 2 percent occur beyond two sigmas from the midpoint.

The relationships in the figure can be handled precisely for any range of values by using a standard normal distribution table, such as the one given in Figure 5-11. As an example of the use of such a table, consider a firm that is forecasting average daily cash changes of $66,000 with a standard deviation of $45,000. What is the entire range of possible daily changes? What is the chance of a negative change on any given day?

This problem can be diagrammed as shown in Figure 5-12. The entire range is from a negative $69,000 to a positive $201,000, representing three standard deviations from the expected value. The possibility of a negative value is the possibility of a value that is 1.47 standard deviations from the mean (66,000/45,000 = 1.47). In the standard table, this is nearest 1.5 standard deviations. The chance of a value below 1.5 sigmas is 0.50 - 0.4332, or 6.68 percent. Thus, the chance of a negative change in any given day is relatively small but it will happen about 7 percent of the time.

Figure 5-10. Likelihood of Occurrence of Values by Standard Deviation Groupings.

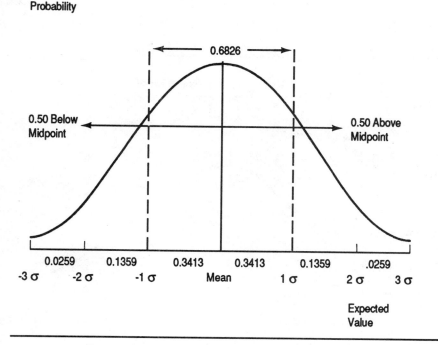

Figure 5-11. Standard Normal Distribution Table.

Number of Standard Deviations from Mean	Percent of Values Between Mean and Given Standard Deviation	Number of Standard Deviations from Mean	Percent of Values Between Mean and Given Standard Deviation
0.1	3.98	1.6	44.52
0.2	7.93	1.7	45.54
0.3	11.79	1.8	46.41
0.4	15.54	1.9	47.13
0.5	19.15	2.0	47.72
0.6	22.57	2.1	48.21
0.7	25.80	2.2	48.61
0.8	28.81	2.3	48.93
0.9	31.59	2.4	49.18
1.0	34.13	2.5	49.38
1.1	36.43	2.6	49.53
1.2	38.49	2.7	49.63
1.3	40.32	2.8	49.74
1.4	41.92	2.9	49.81
1.5	43.32	3.0	49.87

Figure 5-12. Normal Curve for Firm in Example.

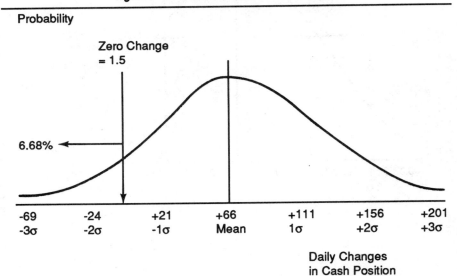

Probability

Zero Change = 1.5

6.68%

-69	-24	+21	+66	+111	+156	+201
-3σ	-2σ	-1σ	Mean	1σ	+2σ	+3σ

Daily Changes in Cash Position

Forecasting Cash as a Probability Distribution

The standard deviation and normal probability distributions are tools to help visualize future cash fluctuations. If we return to our earlier example of planning levels of cash and actual levels, we can see the impact. In Figure 5-13, the actual levels are plotted through a day in July. After this point, the firm has estimated a range of cash levels, as illustrated by probability distributions. Knowing the likely historical fluctuations, the firm can plot expected values and standard deviations, and prepare to meet shortages or invest excess cash.

Linear Regression–A Second Statistical Tool

If the normal probability distribution helps visualize and estimate dispersion, other statistical tools can help increase the accuracy of estimates. This is also done by recognizing the probabilistic nature of the firm's operating environment. The analyst can build on past data that have been collected (systematically we hope), in a form suitable for computer processing. By evaluating relationships among variables in prior periods, the analyst can forecast similar relationships in the future. If, for example, the cash level fluctuates directly with orders processed, the firm can monitor orders and use such data to forecast cash levels.

One specific tool to match two variables is called **linear regression**, a statistical procedure for calculating a straight line to best fit a set of data points. A formula is developed for the straight line that best fits the data, and this formula can be used to express the relationship between the two variables. The most widely used regression technique employs the method of **least squares**, a technique that is programmed into financial calculators and is also available in statistical computer programs. The least squares method, which is described in most basic statistics books, solves for a linear equation of the form:

$$y = a + bx$$

where:

$x =$	the independent variable
$y =$	the dependent variable
$a =$	the intercept of the least squares line with the vertical axis
$b =$	the slope of the line

Figure 5-13. Cash Levels as Probability Distributions.

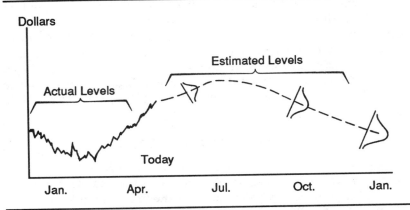

To illustrate forecasting by comparing relationships using a statistical tool, let us consider a firm whose sales fluctuated last year between $250,000 and $700,000 per month. The average weekly cash disbursements varied between $20,000 and $50,000 when analyzed each month. Figure 5-14 shows the data for this firm.

The question to be asked is whether a relationship exists between the monthly sales figures and weekly cash disbursements. The data are sufficiently simple to allow us to determine this relationship either statistically or graphically. Using monthly sales as the independent variable, we can plot the data, as is done in Figure 5-15. In this figure, the data points are scattered in no apparent pattern; therefore, we would conclude that no relationship seems to exist.

As we consider the data in the figure, we might want to check to see if other formulations would produce a relationship. There may be, for example, a leading or lagging effect. That is, the cash disbursements might correlate to the prior or future month's sales pattern. To do so, we determine that the December sales in the prior year were $450,000 (Figure 5-16), and we plot this value next to January. Then, all the sales figures in Figure 5-14 are shifted to produce Figure 5-15. When these values are displayed graphically, we get the pattern shown in Figure 5-17. From this diagram, we conclude that a relationship does exist between one month's sales and the next month's cash disbursements.

We now know that a relationship exists where disbursements rise with increases in the prior month's sales and decline with any decreases in the prior month's sales. With the use of graphing techniques, as soon as a month's sales level is known, we could estimate the next month's cash disbursements. This is useful to illustrate the point in a book but is not practical in actual situations. Instead, we use statistics to test many possible combinations, With the formula for least squares, we would solve for a linear equation

| weekly cash disbursements | = | 5,170 + 0.07 (prior month's sales) |

This means that the firm's pattern of weekly cash disbursements can be approximated by recognizing that $5,170 is disbursed each week independent of any sales activity, and the balance of disbursements is roughly equal to 7 percent of the prior month's sales.

Figure 5-14. Sales and Cash Disbursements Data.

Month	Monthly Sales	Weekly Cash Disbursements
January	$400,000	$30,000
February	350,000	30,000
March	300,000	25,000
April	250,000	22,000
May	500,000	20,000
June	700,000	40,000
July	600,000	50,000
August	300,000	45,000
September	250,000	30,000
October	650,000	25,000
November	550,000	50,000
December	450,000	40,000

Figure 5-15. Pattern of Relationship Between Sales and Cash Disbursements (000s).

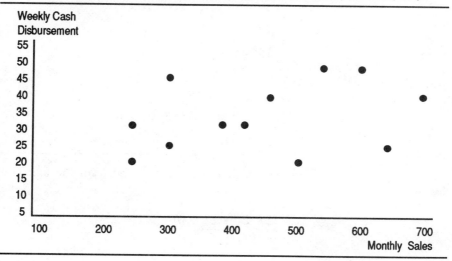

Figure 5-16. Lagged Sales and Disbursement Data.

Month	Prior Month's Sales	Weekly Cash Disbursements
January	$450,000	$30,000
February	400,000	30,000
March	305,000	25,000
April	300,000	22,000
May	250,000	20,000
June	500,000	40,000
July	700,000	50,000
August	600,000	45,000
September	300,000	30,000
October	250,000	25,000
November	650,000	50,000
December	550,000	40,000

Figure 5-17. Pattern of Relationship with Lagged Data.

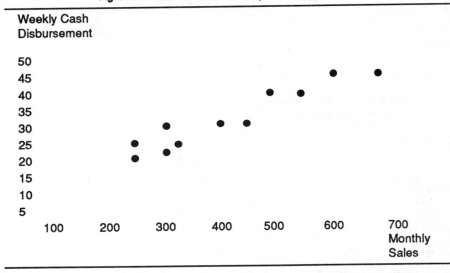

The values of a and b for n data points are calculated from the following formulas:

$$a = \frac{(\Sigma y)(\Sigma x^2) - (\Sigma x)(\Sigma xy)}{(n)(\Sigma x^2) - (\Sigma x)^2}$$

$$b = \frac{(n)\,(\Sigma xy) - (\Sigma x)\,(\Sigma y)}{(n)\,(\Sigma x^2) - (\Sigma x)^2}$$

To develop this line graphically, we need to solve for two points and then connect the points. Let us solve for zero and $700,000 sales in the prior month. The level of disbursements for each would be:

zero
sales $5,170 + 0.07(0) = 5,170$
level

$700,000
sales $5,170 + 0.07(700,000) = 54,170$
level

Connecting the two points gives us the line in Figure 5-18.

Linear regression and other statistical tools can assist the analyst in making more accurate estimates, but they must be used with care for several reasons.

1. **Completeness of the Relationship**. A straight line can be fitted to any data. This does not mean that the results are useful. Some additional statistical techniques are needed to see how well the regression line actually describes the relationship between two variables.

2. **Improper Statistical Tool**. A linear relationship may not be accurate. The real relationship may be curvilinear, and more powerful analytical tools may be needed to express it correctly. Care must be taken to ensure that the statistical evaluation is appropriate given the nature of the data and the correlation between variables.

3. **Changing Relationships**. Still another caution involves the nature of the underlying correlation. In one period, monthly sales and weekly disbursements may have been linked in an independent and dependent variable relationship. This does not mean that the relationship will always hold in the future.

The analyst should evaluate the overall situation to be reasonably sure that the regression analysis or other statistical methodology is providing useful information for forecasting. In spite of the limitations, linear regression and other statistical methodologies can be valuable supplements to assist in forecasting cash needs.

Figure 5-18. Least Squares Line for Lagged Data.

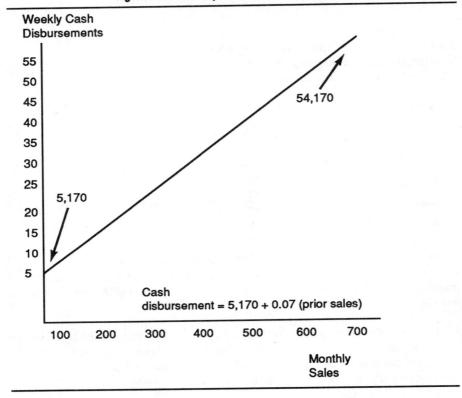

Cash
disbursement = 5,170 + 0.07 (prior sales)

TONNERVAE, INC.—CASH FLOW FORECASTING

Tonnervae, Inc. is a leading distributor of microcomputers. The company, located in an industrial park in a suburb of Bloomington, offers a broad line of electronic instrumentation test equipment to customers in a twelve county area of Indiana and Illinois. The company's business has grown to annual sales near $9 million over the past seven years, partly reflecting the sound management of the firm but also demonstrating the growth of the microcomputer business. Tonnervae has carefully monitored technological improvements in its product lines, so it offers quality products, excellent service, and aggressive marketing in a successful package approach to distribution.

The next 18 months will pose a slightly different picture for the firm. Monica Blong, a financial analyst for the company, has been assigned the task of preparing a monthly cash flow forecast for this period so the firm's management will be prepared to overcome some cash difficulties. The long term prospects are quite good but the firm expects six to nine months of shortages. Monica's task is to develop a picture of those tight months, as well as the strong months afterwards, so the firm can obtain some backup lines of credit from its banks.

Monica is starting with the revenues picture. From marketing, she received the following schedule:

PERIOD	QUARTERLY SALES
1st Quarter	$2,010,000
2nd Quarter	1,800,000
3rd Quarter	2,520,000
4th Quarter	2,220,000
5th Quarter	3,120,000
6th Quarter	3,600,000

The second-quarter weakness is one of the firm's problems. The changeover in suppliers on some product lines coupled with a generally weak economy are expected to cause some headaches for the marketing department. Once the new products are available in the third quarter, a pronounced recovery is likely. These numbers are compatible with the recent sales figures known to Monica. Last month, for example, November's sales were $765,000 with credit sales making up $667,000 of the amount. Preliminary figures for the current month (December) show total sales of $832,000 with credit sales of $720,000.

Once Monica had the sales forecasts, she needed information breaking down cash and credit sales, collection patterns, and bad debts. She discovered from the credit manager, a cyclical pattern with slower collections and slightly higher bad debt losses in the second and third quarters. She summarized the pattern as follows:

ITEM	1st & 4th QUARTERS	2nd & 3rd QUARTERS
Percent cash sales	.18	.18
Collections, percent		
From current month	.21	.16
One month earlier	.50	.46

The collections for two months earlier will fluctuate so as to collect 100% of the outstanding receivables.

An important part of the forecast dealt with the cash spent on the firm's operations. When talking to the Treasurer, Monica discovered some interesting historical patterns. First, the cost of goods sold can be expressed as a percentage of sales, for planning purposes at least. Then, about 86 percent of the cost of goods sold represented cash expenditures. The situation with general and administrative expenses was somewhat different. One portion was roughly a fixed cost; the other varied with sales. Finally, operating expenses in each month were likely to be stable with the exception of the first quarter of the forecast, when nonrecurring expenses must be absorbed. The patterns that Monica decided to use for planning purposes were

ITEM	1ST QUARTER ONLY	REMAINING QUARTERS
CofGS as percent of sales	.75	.65
Cash portion, CofGS	.86	.86
G&A fixed portion (monthly)	170,000	140,000
G&A, percent of current month sales	.05	.05

Monica wanted to pay particular attention to the firm's operating expenses in order to remain above the firm's desired safety level of $350,000. At the start of the forecast period (January 1st), Monica expected the firm to have approximately $135,000 in the operating accounts at each of two banks and $200,000 invested in money market funds. Thus, the firm was starting with cash approximating the safety level without any short term borrowing. Of course, Monica was prepared to back up her cash investments with a line of credit should it be needed.

One of the important elements in the cash flow forecast was the repayment schedule on the firm's existing bank loan. On the first of January, the firm would owe $495,120 on a variable rate loan with American Bank and Trust Company. The firm was paying $15,000 a month on the loan, an amount that would not fluctuate with interest rate changes. Still, the principal repayment portion did change with fluctuations in the prime rate since the interest rate was pegged at 2 percent above prime. Monica's forecast of the prime rate over the 18-month period was

1st six months	.085
2nd six months	.080
3rd six months	.095

The distinction between principal and interest was important in Monica's calculation of the estimated monthly tax payment. For planning purposes, Monica used a 40 percent tax rate on earnings before taxes. The estimated tax payment was one line in the forecast just prior to the total outlays line. When outlays were subtracted from cash available, Monica had an ending cash balance that could be compared to the safety level to see if the firm expected a surplus or shortage at the end of each month.

Required: 1. Prepare the cash flow forecast for the 18 month period beginning January 1.

2. If the firm needs a backup line of credit, prepare your recommendation concerning the amount and time period.

3. Assume that average interest rates would be 2 percent higher than Monica's numbers. How does this affect your recommendation?

MORGAN COMPUTER CORPORATION CASE— LINEAR REGRESSION

Morgan Computer Corporation is a manufacturer of computer peripheral equipment. Located in South Bend, Indiana, the company sells directly to other manufacturers, including a major contract with IBM. Known for product reliability, the company's facilities are utilized for two shifts, six days a week. This reflects a new product line for lap-top computers that will be assembled from components supplied by Mexican and Japanese sources. Distribution contracts have been signed for the first nine months of production.

As a result of the expansion, the firm has stretched its sources of financing. Inventories have grown to support the new product line, and most sales are made on credit terms to large corporations. These firms purchase on terms of net 30 but, for the most part, do not pay on time. The average collection period usually averages more than 45 days and efforts to tighten up collections have proved largely unsuccessful. The firm's management realizes that it has to be prepared to finance large receivables balances.

Patrick Robinson has been assigned the task of forecasting cash needs over the next 12 months. This project involves the preparation of a complete cash forecast that incorporates sensitivities to changes in the operating or economic environment. He has been working on the task for over 6 weeks.

Pat has a theory on the collections of receivables. He suspects that the level of receivables varies with the cost of money. That is, when customers are paying high interest rates for their funds, they are slow to pay Morgan's invoices. If he could prove his hypothesis, he could incorporate the relationship into the cash forecast. Then, if interest rates rise or decline, he could modify expected cash collections.

Pat Robinson formed a specific hypothesis:

> **The firm's average collection period is a dependent variable that is correlated with interest rates in the economy, as measured by the 6 month T-Bill rate.**

To test this hypothesis, he collected the attached data for the past 12 quarters, as given in Figure 1. Even though this was a small sample, it might reveal a relationship that would be useful for forecasting collections.

Since this issue was a relatively small portion of the task of preparing the cash forecast, he did not want to spend a great deal of time on it. Still, he wanted a sound statistical approach. He finally chose three statistical tools described in Figure 2.

Figure 5-19. Data for Past Three Years.

Quarter	Average Collection Period	T-Bill Rate
1	40	11.0%
2	43	11.8
3	46	11.9
4	52	12.1
5	54	12.3
6	49	12.0
7	50	12.1
8	47	11.9
9	44	11.9
10	42	11.5
11	41	11.3
12	39	10.9

In addition to the historical data, Pat Robinson had interest rate forecasts for the next 12 months. He decided to use quarterly data only, with the forecasted T-Bill rates as of the end of March, June, September, and December. The predictions, which reflect a rapid rise in interest rates through most of the year, are:

1st Quarter	11.0%
2nd Quarter	13.0
3rd Quarter	15.0
4th Quarter	13.5

Pat also has the operating and marketing departments' predictions of sales during the next 12 months. The pattern follows the cyclical trend of strong 1st and 4th quarters, with weaker 2nd and 3rd quarters. The quarterly sales numbers in the forecast are:

1st Quarter	$100,000,000
2nd Quarter	90,000,000
3rd Quarter	70,000,000
4th Quarter	105,000,000

With this data, Pat Robinson was ready to forecast the receivables balance for the next 4 quarters.

Required: 1. What is the likely average collection period for each quarter? The likely receivables balance?

2. Using six standard deviations as the entire range, what is the minimum and maximum collection periods? (Hint: Use the built in standard deviation function in the spreadsheet).

Figure 5-20. **Description of Statistical Tools.**

The three statistical tools used in the case are the method of least squares, goodness of fit, and level of significance.

Least Squares Regression Line.

The method of least squares is a mathematical technique used to fit a straight line to numerical data. It solves for the "best" line by minimizing the sum of the squares of the vertical deviations between each data point and the line itself. The line is of the form **y = a +bx** where

y = the dependent variable

x = the independent variable

a = the point where the line crosses the **y** axis

b = the slope of the line

The formula for solving for **a** is:

$$a = \frac{sumY*sumX^2 - sumX*sumXY}{N*sumX^2 - (sumX)^2}$$

The formula to solve for it is:

$$b = \frac{N*sumXY - sumX*sumY}{N*sumX^2 - (sumX)^2}$$

where

N	=	number of data points
sum**Y**	=	the sum of the **Y** values
sum**X**	=	the sum of the **X** values
sum**XY**	=	the total obtained by multiplying each **X** value by each **Y** value and adding the resulting products
sum**X**^{2}	=	the total obtained by squaring each **X** and adding the resulting products
sum**Y**^{2}	=	the same for the **Y** values
(sum**X**)^2	=	the value obtained by adding all the **X** values and squaring the result
(sum**Y**)^2	=	the same for the **Y** values

Coefficient of Correlation.

Fitting the straight line is not sufficient by itself. A line can be fitted to any set of data points. The analyst needs a measure of the **goodness of fit** of the line. This can be found by solving for the coefficient of correlation. If the fit is poor, the coefficient will be near zero. If the fit is positively or negatively strong, the coefficient will be near +1 or -1. The formula for solving for the coefficient of correlation is:

$$r = \frac{N*sumXY - sumX*sumY}{@SQRT(N*sumX^2 - (sumX)^2) * @SQRT(N*sumY^2 - (sumY)^2)}$$

where

@SQRT = a mathematical function built into a spreadsheet to solve for a square root

Level of Significance

A final statistical test deals with the size of the data sample. With many data points, we can have a higher level of confidence in the strength of the relationship. We can use the standard deviation of the correlation coefficient to measure the level of significance. If the standard deviation is large compared to the coefficient, we have less confidence than with a small sigma. The formula is

$$\sigma = 1/@SQRT(N-1)$$

Cash Forecasting:
Advanced Techniques

The traditional methods of cash forecasting, particularly when augmented by statistical techniques to increase accuracy, are satisfactory for many applications. Large companies, on the other hand, are always seeking more sophisticated approaches to the management of cash. In this chapter, we will cover two such areas. The first deals with simulation methods of estimating cash dispersion. The second is an approach to developing the optimal cash balance under conditions of uncertainty.

SIMULATION MODELS

A **simulation model** represents an attempt to capture the external characteristics of a real world situation with a goal of determining likely outcomes based on different conditions. In the case of a cash forecasting model, the factors that affect cash balances are developed as variables and the model is then run on a computer to see the results. A number of complex simulation models can be adapted to the problem of estimating likely changes in cash balances. In this section, we will develop a simple model to illustrate simulation models.

Key Terms and Concepts

In building a simulation model, we can recognize certain key concepts that affect our design:

1. **Discrete Probability Distribution.** A probability distribution has been defined as the likely outcomes associated with different future events. A discrete distribution has a limited number of such outcomes. The input screen for our model will employ a range of values in a discrete distribution.

2. **Normal Probability Distribution.** Also previously defined, this continuous distribution can take on all values from the highest to lowest. This will be used in the output screen.

3. **Standard Deviation**. Defined in the last chapter, this is a measure of dispersion in a normal probability distribution. The output screens will use this measure.

4. **Subjective Probability**. This is a forecast of the likelihood of a future occurrence that cannot be validated externally or verified by other persons. It is usually based on a combination of past data, known relationships, and the past experience of the forecaster. **Bayesian statistics** is the method of using subjective probabilities, which are widely utilized in business decision making. Although simulation models can use historical data as a measure of probabilities, our model will use subjective probabilities.

5. **Random Event**. This is a single action whose outcome cannot be determined in advance. As an example, the tossing of a coin is a random event. Even though we will get heads half the time and tails the other half over the long run, the outcome of a single toss cannot be known in advance. A simulation model can have probabilistic variables–a 50 percent chance of heads and 50 percent of tails–but any individual outcome will be a random event.

The Basic Equation

In the previous chapter, we recognized the fact that cash inflows and outflows are variable in nature. Building on that foundation, we can identify the fundamental relationships between cash and other factors. These are needed to simulate the real world. Once the variables are linked in a model, we can express the relationships using mathematics. Then, we can run simulations of the variables and linkages.

Our model, derived from a classic article by David Hertz[1], it will be based on historical data, a subjective forecast of current expenses, and relationships between receipts and disbursements as percentages of expenses. The model assumes that changes in cash balances in the future are linked to the level of activity of the firm, as measured through cost of goods sold. The task of the forecaster is to build a model based on historical expenses, allowing for variation when predicting future expenses, future cash receipts, and future disbursements. Subjective probabilities are used to forecast future probabilities and the model converts these into changes in cash.

The basic equation will be:

Cash = (CofGS-12) * %CofGSfutr * (%receipts -% disb)

The variables in the formula are

[1] David B. Hertz, "Risk Analysis in Capital Investment," **Harvard Business Review**, January-February 1964.

1. **Change in Cash Balance (Cash).** This variable is the monthly change in cash as a result of the differences between receipts and disbursements. The simulation model will solve for this variable and provide a measure of its dispersion.

2. **Cost of Goods Sold Last Year (CofGS-12).** This variable is the dollar amount of cost of goods sold in the same month one year earlier. If we are forecasting December's cash changes, this variable will be the cost of goods sold in the previous December.

3. **Cost of Goods Sold in Future Month, (CofGSfutr).** This variable is a forecast of cost of goods sold in a future month. It is expressed as a percentage of the year earlier figure, using subjective probabilities. As an example, we may say that next month's CofGS has a one-third chance of being 90 percent of the previous year's level, a one-third chance of matching the prior year, and a one-third chance of being 110 percent of the previous year.

4. **Cash Receipts as a Percentage of CofGS, (%receipts).** When the firm sells goods, it has cash receipts. This variable is expressed as a percentage of cost of goods sold and varies using subjective probabilities. This is actually not as good as using sales data and lagging the collections. Such a model could easily be constructed but would be more complicated than needed to illustrate a simulation model.

5. **Cash Disbursements as a Percentage of CofGS (%disb).** This variable matches disbursements with expenses, once again using subjective probabilities.

The basic equation for our model was developed by the firm after it carefully studied the relationships between its cost of goods sold, cash receipts, and cash disbursements. The first step was to recognize that future CofGS may vary from the same costs in the previous year, even though the firm is cyclical in its production. Receipts and disbursements are also variable, even at a consistent level of CofGS. These variations will be handled by treating the variables as random events with probabilistic outcomes.

Variables and Probabilities

The first step in developing the simulation model is to identify each variable and its associated probabilities. This is done in Figure 6-1. The historical cost of goods sold comes from the actual CofGS 12 months ago, or $715,000. The future CofGS is linked to the historical number, with three possible outcomes

120 percent of last year's CofGS	one-third chance
105 percent	one-third chance
90 percent	one-third chance

144 CHAPTER 6

Thus, the future CofGS will have three possible levels in the model: $858,000 (715,000*1.20), $750,750 (715,000*1.05), and $643,500 (715,000*.90).

Similarly, the figure shows four levels are identified for cash receipts. They are forecast to be 90, 105, 120, or 135 percent of future CofGS, with associated probabilities of 25 percent each. Cash disbursements have four projected levels with probabilities.

One additional item should be noted in Figure 6-1. Each probability has been identified with a capital letter, from A to K, in order to facilitate running the simulation trials. In the David Hertz article already cited, an analogy is drawn to a roulette wheel. Once the probability value has been assigned, the model is run on a computer in a series of simulation trials. The computer creates one random event for each of the three variables. It is like having three roulette wheels in the spreadsheet. One wheel has values (A) to (C), the second has (D) to (G), and the third has (H) to (K). Each capital letter is weighted to reflect the probability associated with it. The theoretical wheel for (A) to (C) is shown in Figure 6-2.

Figure 6-1. Simulation Model, Input Screen.

Variables And Subjective Probabilities, Input Screen

CofGS, One Year Earlier 715,000
CofGS, Future Month COL D COL F

	Event	Percent	Probability
Row 10	A	1.20	0.33
Row 11	B	1.05	0.33
Row 12	C	0.90	0.33

Cash Receipts, Percent of CofGS

	Event	Percent	Probability
Row 17	D	0.90	0.25
Row 18	E	1.05	0.25
Row 19	F	1.20	0.25
Row 20	G	1.35	0.25

Cash Disbursements, Percent of CofGS

	Event	Percent	Probability
Row 25	H	0.75	0.25
Row 26	I	0.90	0.25
Row 27	J	1.05	0.25
Row 28	K	1.20	0.25

Figure 6-2. Theoretical Roulette Wheel for Cost of Goods Sold.

(A)	120 percent
(B)	105 percent
(C)	90 percent

Simulation Trials

The next step in the simulation exercise is to run a number of trials on the computer. As a general rule, 20 or more trials are needed to develop a probability distribution for changes in cash position. We will use the number 20. For each trial, the computer will generate one value from ABC, one value from DEFG, and one value from HIJK. The 20 simulation trials were run on an output screen of a spreadsheet, as shown in Figure 6-3. The key formulas are

1. **Random Number Formula.** The figure shows the output screen for a spreadsheet that contains a random number function "@RAND." It also offers an integer function "@INT" so that only integers are generated. At position C76, the formula is @INT(@RAND*3+1), which generates three random integers beginning at the number 1. This formula is copied down column C, generating either 1, 2, or 3 randomly at each position. Similarly, column D has formulas generating integers of four numbers beginning with 4. Column E generates 4 integers beginning with 8.

2. **Random Event Letter.** The spreadsheet permits IF/THEN statements, using the "@IF" function. These are used in narrowed columns H, I, and J. At H76, for example, the formula checks position C76. If the value is 1, an "A" is displayed. If it is 2, a "B" is displayed. If the value is neither 1 nor 2, a "C" is displayed. A similar formula is entered in each positon in columns H, I, and J.

Figure 6-3. Simulation Trials, Output Screen.

Formulas

At C76:	@INT(@RAND*3+1)
At D76:	@INT(@RAND*4+4)
At E76:	@INT(@RAND*4+8)
At H76:	@IF(C76=1,"A",@IF(C76=2,"B","C"))
At I76:	@IF(D76=4,"D",@IF(D76=5,"E",@IF(D76=6,"F","G")))
At J76:	@IF(E76=8,"H",@IF(E76=9,"I",@IF(E76=10,"J","K")))

	COL B	COL C	COL D	COL E	COLS H	I	J
	Trial Number	CofGS Event	Receipts Event	Disb. Event	RANDOM EVENT		
Row 76	1	2	4	10	B	D	J
Row 77	2	2	4	10	B	D	J
Row 78	3	1	4	9	A	D	I
Row 79	4	3	6	8	C	F	H
Row 80	5	3	7	10	C	G	J
Row 81	6	2	5	9	B	E	I
Row 82	7	1	6	10	A	F	J
Row 83	8	1	6	8	A	F	H
Row 84	9	2	6	10	B	F	J
Row 85	10	1	6	10	A	F	J
Row 86	11	2	7	8	B	G	H
Row 87	12	3	5	9	C	E	I
Row 88	13	1	7	8	A	G	H
Row 89	14	2	6	9	B	F	I
Row 90	15	3	4	10	C	D	J
Row 91	16	3	7	10	C	G	J
Row 92	17	2	4	11	B	D	K
Row 93	18	1	5	10	A	E	J
Row 94	19	2	6	9	B	F	I
Row 95	20	2	4	9	B	D	I

Changes in Cash

Once the 20 trials have been run, their effect is plotted on an output screen that calculates changes in monthly cash balances. This is done in Figure 6-4. Each trial is displayed in the left–hand columns, L, M and N. Then, column O contains the previous year's CofGS, and columns P, Q, and R contain the percentages that match the trials in L, M, and N. Column T contains the cash change that matches each trial. The key formulas are also displayed in the figure.

1. **Matching Percentages with Trials.** IF/THEN formulas are used in columns P, Q, and R to match each trial with an appropriate percentage. At P19, for example, the formula reads positions L19. If "A" is found at L19, the entry at position D10 is entered. This would be 1.20, from

Figure 6-1. When "A" is not found, the formula looks for "B." It found "B" and entered 1.05 taken from position D11 in Figure 6-1.

2. **Cash Changes.** At T19, the cash formula multiplies the previous year's CofGS (O19) by this year's percentage (P19), then by the difference between receipts and disbursements percentages (Q19 - R19). The net cash change is negative 112,613.

3. **Total of the Trials.** Once all 20 simulations are run, the total is displayed at T40. This is simply a summation formula using the built-in function @SUM.

4. **Average Monthly Change.** At T42, the mean or average cash change is calculated. The built-in @AVG function is used for this calculation.

5. **Standard Deviation.** The standard deviation is calculated at T44 using the built-in @STD function.

6. **High and Low Values.** The model displays the full range of a normal probability distribution, three standard deviations above and below the mean. The formula at T48 is three times the standard deviation subtracted from the mean; at T50, three times the standard deviation is added to the mean.

Cash Changes as a Normal Probability Distribution

The purpose of the simulation model was to measure the average monthly change and dispersion of such changes. The simulation exercise gave us a mean of $125,482 and a standard deviation of $189,095. The entire range can be diagrammed, as is done in Figure 6-5. Note that the firm would never expect a negative change in excess of $441,802 nor a positive change greater than $692,767. Some 68 percent of the time, the change will be between -$63,613 and +$314,577.

Figure 6-4. 20 Simulation Trials, Output Screen.

At P19: @IF(L19="A",$D$10,@IF(L19="B",$D$11,$D$12))
At Q19: @IF(M19="D",$D$17,@IF(M19="E",$D$18,@IF(M19="F",$D$19,$D$20)))
At R19: @IF(N19="H",$D$25,@IF(N19="I",$D$26,@IF(N19="J",$D$27,$D$28)))
At T19: +O19*P19*(Q19-R19)
At T40: @SUM(T19..T38)
At T42: @AVG(T19..T38)
At T44: @STD(T19..T38)
At T48: +T42-(3*T44)
At T50: +T42+(3*T44)

COLS L	M	N	COL O Last Yr CofGS	COL P This Yr. Percent	COL Q Receipts Percent	COL R Disb. Percent	COL T Cash Change
Trials							
Row 19 B	D	J	715,000	1.05	0.90	1.05	(112,613)
Row 20 B	D	J	715,000	1.05	0.90	1.05	(112,613)
Row 21 A	D	I	715,000	1.20	0.90	0.90	0
Row 22 C	F	H	715,000	0.90	1.20	0.75	289,575
Row 23 C	G	J	715,000	0.90	1.35	1.05	193,050
Row 24 B	E	I	715,000	1.05	1.05	0.90	112,613
Row 25 A	F	J	715,000	1.20	1.20	1.05	128,700
Row 26 A	F	H	715,000	1.20	1.20	0.75	386,100
Row 27 B	F	J	715,000	1.05	1.20	1.05	112,612
Row 28 A	F	J	715,000	1.20	1.20	1.05	128,700
Row 29 B	G	H	715,000	1.05	1.35	0.75	450,450
Row 30 C	E	I	715,000	0.90	1.05	0.90	96,525
Row 31 A	G	H	715,000	1.20	1.35	0.75	514,800
Row 32 B	F	I	715,000	1.05	1.20	0.90	225,225
Row 33 C	D	J	715,000	0.90	0.90	1.05	(96,525)
Row 34 C	G	J	715,000	0.90	1.35	1.05	193,050
Row 35 B	D	K	715,000	1.05	0.90	1.20	(225,225)
Row 36 A	E	J	715,000	1.20	1.05	1.05	0
Row 37 B	F	I	715,000	1.05	1.20	0.90	225,225
Row 38 B	D	I	715,000	1.05	0.90	0.90	0
Row 39							
Row 40	Total of 20 Trials						2,509,650
Row 42	Average Monthly Cash Change						125,482
Row 44	Standard Deviation of Cash Changes						189,095
Row 46	Entire Range (6 standard deviations)						
Row 48	Low						(441,802)
Row 49	Mean						125,482
Row 50	High						692,767

Figure 6-5. Entire Range of Cash Changes from Simulation Model.

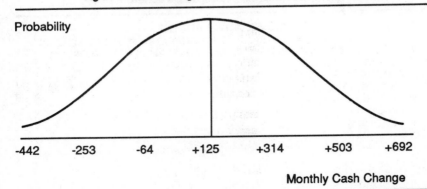

By developing simulation models, the cash manager can test the sensitivity of different courses of action and can measure the level of dispersion in cash flows. Even if the analyst is able to improve his or her forecasting accuracy, cash flows still occur in a probabilistic environment. By running simulation trials, a picture is gained of the possible dispersion under controlled conditions. This facilitates an understanding of what may happen and allows the firm to prepare for the unexpected.

DETERMINING THE OPTIMAL CASH BALANCE

One of the policy decisions a firm must make involves the calculation of cash on hand in highly liquid form to meet daily needs. Such policies should recognize certain key contributions in the financial literature while taking advantage of the capabilities offered by electronic banking. In this section, we will examine the nature of the decision and develop an approach to determining the optimal cash balance to be maintained by a firm.

The Baumol Model

One of the earliest systematic approaches to managing cash was developed by William Baumol in a 1952 article.[2] The model identifies the task of the cash manager as holding some level of cash over a number of time periods. The model uses a sawtooth pattern of cash disbursements, as shown in Figure 6-6. The firm begins at some maximum cash level and disburses funds steadily over time. When it reaches a zero balance or some safety level, it sells marketable securities and replenishes its cash position to the original amount. The amount of replenishment is equal to some **economic order quantity** (EOQ), a concept borrowed from inventory management. Then, the process is completed. On the average, the firm will maintain cash balances equal to one–half of the maximum amount, which is also one–half of the EOQ amount.

The Baumol model makes two major contributions to the literature on cash management.

1. **Goals of Cash Management**. The first contribution is that Baumol correctly identified the twin goals of cash management. The task is to minimize the total cost of holding cash while having sufficient liquidity to achieve the firm's other goals. This process can involve a constant tradeoff between investing cash and having access to cash.

2. **Costs of Cash Management**. The second contribution is that Baumol identified the two costs of cash management. One expense is incurred

---

[2] William J. Baumol, "The Transactions Demand for Cash: An Inventory Theoretic Approach," *Quarterly Journal of Economics*, November 1952.

in transactions, when the firm must move money among accounts. The second expense occurs as a result of **lost opportunity costs**, defined as the loss of income when cash is held idle.

Figure 6-6. Sawtooth Pattern of Cash Disbursements.

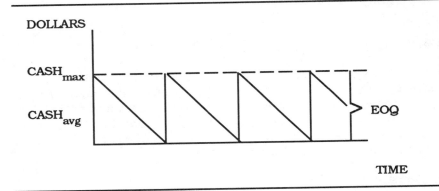

Mechanics of the Baumol Model

The Baumol model develops a mechanism for minimizing the total cost of cash disbursements. The first component deals with transactions costs, which can be calculated by the formula.

Transactions
Costs $\quad = \quad (Cost_{MStoC})(DISB_{annual}) / (Cash_{EOQ})$

where

$Cost_{MStoC}$ $\quad = \quad$ the transactions cost for a single conversion of marketable securities to cash

$DISB_{annual}$ $\quad = \quad$ annual cash disbursements

$Cash_{EOQ}$ $\quad = \quad$ the economic order quantity for replenishing cash

Example: A firm will disburse $3.6, million in the next year. Each time it runs out of cash, it will sell a $100,000 treasury bond, on which a commission of $45 must be paid. What are the annual transactions costs for this firm?

Answer: $1,620, as follows:

Transactions
Costs   = $45(3,600,000) /100,000   =   1,620

The second cost of managing cash was not widely acknowledged in 1952 when the Baumol model appeared. The lost opportunity cost of idle cash will depend on the amount of cash held on the average and the rate of return that could have been earned by investing the cash. The formula is.

$$\text{Lost Opportunity Costs} = (E(Rtn)mktsec) \; \frac{Cash_{EOQ}}{2}$$

where

$E(Rtn)mktsec$ = the annual expected return on marketable securities

In this formula, the firm is assumed to replenish from zero to the maximum cash holding, or the economic order quantity (EOQ). Therefore, it holds half of the EOQ amount on the average. This is the idle cash.

Example: A firm replenishes $150,000 every time it runs out. The current yield on marketable securities is 9.4 percent. What is the lost opportunity cost?

Answer: $7,050 per year, as follows:

                  (0.094)(150,000/2) = 7,050

Limitations on the Baumol Model

Several assumptions limit the utility of the Baumol model in actual situations where the firm is managing cash, including:

1. **Steady Disbursements.** The model follows a sawtooth pattern of steady cash disbursements and eventual replenishment of cash. The actual pattern of cash movement for most firms does not match this assumption.

2. **Absence of Cash Receipts.** The model deals only with disbursements. Yet, the tradeoff of expenses in cash management needs to include the impact of receipts.

3. **High Variable Transactions Costs.** The model measures transactions costs as variable expenses of moving from marketable securities to cash. In fact, transactions costs may be largely fixed, and the movement from securities to cash and vice versa must be covered more comprehensively.

In spite of these limitations, the Baumol model should be viewed in terms of an historic identification of the key costs of cash management.

Miller-Orr Model[3]

A workable cash management model should recognize the fluctuating pattern of cash needs in a probabilistic environment. In 1966, Merton Miller and Daniel Orr developed a classic model that approaches this task . This approach employs a **finite stochastic process**, defined as a series of events that can be analyzed using probabilities. A decision tree is an example. Each event can be followed by a given number of outcomes with given probabilities. The outcome of each event will depend on some chance or stochastic element. We can distinguish two kinds of stochastic processes:

1. **Markov Chain.** In this process, the probability of an outcome depends only on the probability of the preceding outcome. As an example, in a common stock model the probability of reaching a certain price-earnings multiple might be dependent on the multiple that was achieved in the prior period.

2. **Bernoulli Process.** This is a stochastic process in which the probability of an outcome is independent from event to event. As an example, the likelihood of a salesperson making a sale on any one day might be totally independent of whether a sale was made on a prior day.

The Miller-Orr model is a Bernoulli process in which cash receipts and disbursements from period to period are chance or random events. As opposed to the deterministic process of Baumol, the Miller-Orr model uses a stochastic process that more closely resembles the actual changes in a firm's cash position. Unlike Baumol, the model covers both receipts and disbursements. It is assumed that the firm begins at some optimal level of cash. Over time, the balance changes with different daily receipts and disbursements. At some upper level of cash, the firm invests its excess cash, thus returning the checking account to the optimal. At some lower level, the firm replenishes its checking account by selling marketable securities or borrowing. The total process of cash management is to **stay within the boundaries** and **replenish to the optimal level** as needed or **invest the excess cash**. This process is diagrammed in Figure 6-7.

Professors Miller and Orr argued that the critical element was not to correctly and precisely forecast the exact cash level. Rather, the firm works within boundaries and allows cash to fluctuate as it does anyway. The cash account must be backed up so that excess cash can be invested and shortages

---

[3] Merton H. Miller and Daniel Orr, "A Model of the Demand for Money by Firms," *Quarterly Journal of Economics*, August 1966.

can be remedied. This is a different viewpoint from that previously found among cash managers.

If this is a logical way to manage cash in a probabilistic environment, two questions remain. What is the optimal level? Where are the boundaries? Let us examine each in turn under the constraints of the model.

Figure 6-7. Miller-Orr Stochastic Model.

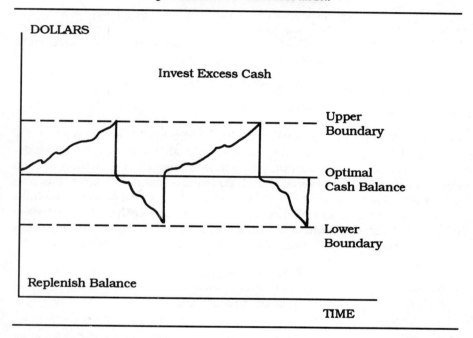

To achieve the optimal cash level, we must consider three variables: (1) transactions costs; (2) lost opportunity costs; and (3) variations in cash flows. The first two of these come from the Baumol model. The third is the contribution of Miller-Orr in an environment in which cash flows fluctuate. The total cash costs come from a formula that is similar to the Baumol formula. We may write it as

$$\text{Total Cash Costs} = (\text{COST}_{\text{Transfer}})(\#\text{Trans}) + (\text{Cost}_{\text{Oppor}})\text{CASH(bal)avg}$$

where

$\text{COST}_{\text{Transfer}}$ = cost of converting cash to marketable securities or vice-versa, or cost of exercising against line of credit or vice-versa

#Trans	=	number of cash transfers in a year
COSToppor	=	lost return on idle cash
CASH(bal)avg	=	average cash balance (also the optimal cash balance)

Example: A firm has determined that its optimal cash balance is $47,000 at a time when its money can be invested at 10.3 percent. The management time and actual fees involved with the investing of cash or borrowing it are estimated at $55 per transaction. In a year, the firm had 23 transactions. What was the total cost of the cash management system?

Answer: $6,106, as follows:

$$\text{Annual Cost} = (55)(23) + (0.103)(47,000) = 6,106$$

How does the firm minimize its total costs under the Miller-Orr model? The answer is that the firm seeks an optimal level of cash that trades off the transfer costs against the lost opportunity cost in a framework of variability of cash flows. A firm with highly variable cash flows must maintain a larger balance; otherwise it will incur excessive transfer costs. A firm with highly predictable cash flows can maintain a smaller balance. The optimal cash balance is derived from an optimization formula in which the standard deviation of cash flows is used as the variability element. The formula is

$$\text{Cash Balance Optimal} = \sqrt[3]{\frac{(3)(\text{COSTtransfer})(\sigma^2)}{(4)(\text{COSToppor})/365 \text{ days}}}$$

This optimization formula is more complicated than the Baumol EOQ formula, but the concept is the same. The cube root requires a logarithmic, calculator, or computer solution, but otherwise is a sound optimization equation. But what does it mean? The answer is that, if the firm holds the balance obtained by the formula and replenishes or invests when it reaches the boundaries, it will incur the lowest possible planning costs for its cash management system. Stated differently, based on the assumed variability as reflected in the standard deviation of cash flows, the optimal cash balance will produce the lowest possible total costs for cash management.

Example: A firm has average daily cash changes of $150,000 with a standard deviation of $110,000. It costs $65 for each transfer of funds, counting both administrative fees and time of personnel. The opportunity cost of funds is 12.3 percent. What is the optimal cash balance for this firm? If the optimal level produces 28 transfers a year, what will be the total cost of the cash management system?

Answer: The optimal balance is $120,517, as follows:

$$\sqrt[3]{\frac{(3)(65)(110,000^2)}{(4)(0.123)/(365)}} = 120,517$$

The total cost for the system for a year will be $16,644, as follows:

$$(65)(28) + (0.123)(120,517) = 16,644$$

The Miller-Orr model is a significant improvement over the less realistic Baumol model. Still, its major value lies in concepts, not applications. Some limitations are

1. **Estimating the Parameters of the Formulas.** One problem is to determine the values to use. As an example, the transfer cost must include both the time and fees inherent in the investment situation. The question may be asked as to whether the time costs are not sunk; that is, the time will pass and be paid for anyway even if no investment or borrowing takes place. The manager is asked to make almost impossible judgments.

2. **Determining of Boundaries.** Another problem involves the points at which cash is invested or secured. According to the original article, the lower boundary is zero and the upper boundary is three times the optimal amount. Two difficulties should be noted. First, if the firm does not have an arrangement with its bank that allows an occasional negative balance for a short period of time, the lower boundary cannot be zero. The firm must leave some funds in the account to avoid a negative balance of collected funds. This is a cost of the system of banking, not of the model. Second, the upper boundary in the Miller-Orr article is given as three times the optimal amount. This is because the article assumes one cost to purchase marketable securities and a similar cost to sell them. Thus, the investment decision involves twice as many costs as the decision to borrow or liquidate securities. This is not realistic. The cost is to buy marketable securities in most cases;therefore, the upper boundary should be twice the optimal cash level.

3. **Making Changes in the Banking System.** Perhaps the most serious limitation on the use of the model has ocurred because of changes in the

way money can be moved. It is no longer necessary to have any level of idle cash beyond that required to maintain banking relations. In addition, transactions costs are often insignificant in situations in which excess cash is automatically swept into overnight investments. In a modern cash management environment, it is difficult to discuss an optimal balance of idle cash because cash virtually never needs to be uninvested.

Conclusion

The Miller-Orr article identified the need to systematically evaluate probabilistic cash flows, along with the costs noted by Baumol. The literature contains occasional articles that use statistical techniques to achieve comprehensive approaches to determining the optimal cash balance.[4] With or without such models, the optimal balance of idle cash is approximately zero for most companies. This fact does not negate the contributions of Baumol, Miller and Orr, and others. The zero balance of idle cash reflects changes in the banking system. The task remains essentially unchanged in theory. The financial manager should recognize the twin costs of transactions and lost opportunities and the probabilistic environment of cash receipts and disbursements. Sufficient liquidity should be maintained to cover operational needs that fluctuate daily. Excess cash should be invested in less liquid securities to achieve higher yields. The optimal cash balance is the level of cash and near cash that meets the needs of liquidity while minimizing lost short-term opportunity costs.

---

[4] See, for example, Gerald A. Payne and Ralph N. Bussard, "A Linear Programming Model for Short Term Financial Planning Under Uncertainty," *Sloan Management Review*, Spring 1972, or Michael D. Carpenter and Jack E. Miller, "A Reliable Framework for Monitoring Accounts Receivable," *Financial Management*, Winter 1979.

SALTLAKE RESOURCES INCORPORATED—
CASH FLOW SIMULATION CASE

Peter Jhenning, president of Saltlake Resources Incorporated, has spent the past five years restructuring the company. The process has not been easy. Since the company was founded in 1911, it has emphasized the construction of railroad cars to move bulk products over long distances. Its main customers have been mining companies in California, Nevada, and Utah. The product destinations have typically been West Coast ports or eastern factories. As part of the restructuring, Jhenning has divested the construction operation and emphasized financial services and the management of bulk storage facilities.

The goal, simply stated, is to take advantage of a strong asset base and match it with opportunities produced by solid cash flows. The company is seeking new investments that can reduce the negative impact of downturns in the business cycle. The firm is willing to borrow to expand. Financial leverage is at an all–time high, even as growth is being achieved in new markets.

Jhenning is considering the problem of borrowing next year versus generating expansion funds from operating cash flows. Two issues arise. First, the level of revenues from operations is not certain. The marketing department estimates that sales may vary from $30 to $45 million in any quarter next year, depending on the price of petroleum products and activity in bulk commodity markets in the United States, Canada, and Southeast Asia. To simplify the analysis, marketing has estimated an equal chance of revenues of $30, $35, $40, or $45 million in any quarter.

The second problem is markup on revenues. This figure varies with fluctuations in the demand for storage facilities and changes in interest rates. The actual analysis is complicated, but the treasurer has made some assumptions on net cash flow from sales after operating expenses are covered. He relayed this to Jhenning as a Markup as a Percent of Sales, an interesting term for cash flows. In any case, he sees an equal chance in any quarter for a 20, 25, or 30 percent markup–that is, net cash flow as a percentage of sales.

Jhenning is always looking for new ways to visualize the impact of uncertainties on Saltlake Resources. Thus, it is not surprising that he decided to use a simulation model to measure the variability of cash flows from operations. He set up the model so that sales was an independent variable that matched the estimates of the marketing department. Then, the markup percentage would be applied to the sales figure to get quarterly cash flow. Using a random number generating feature of his electronic spreadsheet program, Jhenning processed 25 trials for simulating sales and markups, as shown in Figure 6-8. The numbers 1-4 were reserved for sales events, and the numbers 5-7 for markup events. He used the results produced in these 25 trials to calculate 25 quarterly cash flows which formed the basis for the simulation exercise.

Figure 6-8. Simulation Trials, Sales Level and Markups.

Trial Number	Sales Event	Markup Event	Trial Number	Sales Event	Markup Event
1	3	7			
2	4	7	14	2	6
3	1	5	15	2	5
4	3	6	16	3	5
5	2	6	17	4	5
6	4	5	18	2	6
7	3	7	19	1	7
8	1	6	20	3	7
9	2	5	21	2	6
10	4	5	22	4	7
11	3	7	23	3	6
12	4	6	24	2	5
13	3	7	25	1	5

Required: 1. Run the 25 simulation trials in the format:

<u>Trials</u>   <u>Sales Level</u>   <u>Markup Percent</u>   <u>Cash Flow</u>

2. Calculate the average quarterly cash flow.

3. Calculate the standard deviation and entire range of variability using six standard deviations as the full range.

UNION PACKAGING AND PRODUCTS—
CASH MANAGEMENT CASE

This case demonstrates the application of trading off transactions and lost opportunity costs in a probabilistic environment. It should be solved using the approach advocated by Miller and Orr.

Union Packaging and Products (UPP Inc.) is a national distributor of cartons, bags, and related items used by major manufacturers for packaging goods for shipment. The company operates out of an industrial park near St. Louis, Missouri, but has three manufacturing plants in Virginia, Indiana, and Texas. UPP's sales force is widely distributed, and the firm has receivables representing sales in 46 states. At the present time, the firm has annual sales of just over $70 million, with sales being fairly constant throughout the year. Only in January and February are sales noticeably lower than in other periods.

UPP has been working with Chicago National Bank to develop a comprehensive approach to managing its cash inflows and disbursements. The bank has analyzed the firm's pattern of cash receipts and has recommended a three-lockbox system: New York, Chicago, and Los Angeles. The bank will establish a master account with an automatic provision for investment in marketable securities, according to directives from UPP's treasurer. Disbursements will be made from accounts controlled by the manufacturing plants in Virginia, Indiana, and Texas, and funds will not be needed in these zero balance accounts until the checks clear. At this time, the master account will be used to transfer the needed funds into each disbursing account. The entire system will be backed by a line of credit in the amount of $3.5 million, which must be drawn down in units of $200,000 or more for periods of 60 days or more. The line of credit must be cleaned up at least once a year for a period of 30 days.

The treasurer of Union Packaging is concerned about the cost of this system. Since the firm incurs an estimated total transfer cost of $150 every time funds are manually transferred from cash to or from securities or the line of credit, the treasurer wants UPP to hold an optimal balance of funds in the master account. But since the firm has a lost opportunity cost of 11.6 percent on its idle funds, the treasurer does not want excessive balances sitting in the master account.

In May, shortly after the new system was operating, the treasurer sampled his inflows and disbursements over a 21-day period and determined the movements in Figure 6-9.

Figure 6-9. Daily Changes in Cash.

Day	Daily New Funds Available	Checks Cleared	Daily Changes
1	$306,000	$117,000	$189,000
2	161,000	355,000	(194,000)
3	152,000	62,000	90,000
4	58,000	224,000	(166,000)
5	224,000	165,000	59,000
6	165,000	253,000	(88,000)
7	87,000	91,000	(4,000)
8	157,000	212,000	(55,000)
9	212,000	119,000	93,000
10	110,000	172,000	(62,000)
11	274,000	195,000	79,000
12	216,000	115,000	101,000
13	79,000	206,000	(127,000)
14	219,000	241,000	(22,000)
15	141,000	92,000	49,000
16	95,000	135,000	(40,000)
17	291,000	233,000	58,000
18	255,000	82,000	173,000
19	103,000	112,000	(9,000)
20	169,000	45,000	124,000
21	129,000	91,000	38,000
TOTALS	$3,603,000	$3,317,000	$268,000
		MEAN	$13,619
		STANDARD DEVIATION	$102,150

The one–month sample (21 working days) showed a nice match of receipts and disbursements with a sizable daily fluctuation in daily changes, as shown by the $102,150 standard deviation. With such data at an optimal cash balance, the treasurer expected about 30 manual transfers a year. A **manual transfer** is defined as a conscious decision by the treasurer, as opposed to the automatic reconciling of the zero balance account structure. It involves a telephonic message to the bank to transfer cash between the master account and either marketable securities or the line of credit.

Overall, the system could be diagrammed as shown in Figure 6-10.

Required: What is the optimal cash balance, the annual total costs, and the upper boundary?

Figure 6-10. Zero Balance Account System.

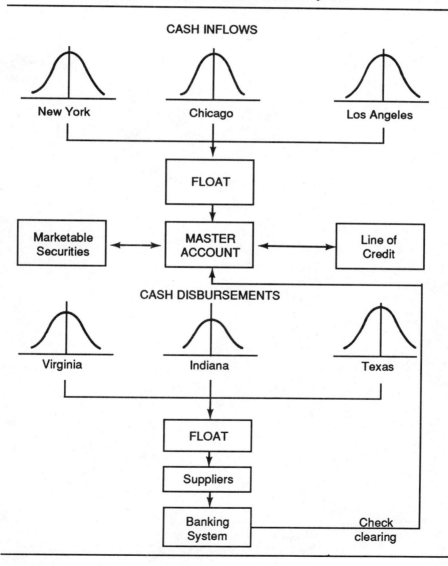

7

Investing Excess Cash—
A Risk Return Framework

Once the firm has developed an efficient system for minimizing idle cash balances, the Treasurer's Office must decide how to invest the excess cash. This task is essentially a dual one of maintaining adequate liquidity while achieving a reasonable return at a level of risk that is acceptable to the firm. In this chapter, we examine a philosophy of investing excess cash. We begin with the methods of calculating rates of return and then develop the concept of risk in cash investments. We then build a philosophy that ties together liquidity, risk, and return in a single investing methodology.

EXPECTED RETURN

The **concept of expected return** from an investment has a number of different meanings. The firm's cash manager tends to seek near-term cash inflows to maintain liquidity and hence gives less value to more distant returns. Some firms have a portion of their assets in long-term securities and seek higher yields and growth of the investments. In either case, the firm must come to grips with the concept of return. To see how the firm does so, let us examine what is really happening.

An investor is like a person who places money on a table where it will not be available as long as it is on the table. Someone else will use it until the investor removes it from the table. Why would the investor do such a thing? The answer is that he or she expects a "meter" to be running the whole time the money is on the table. If, for example, the meter is set at 10 percent, when the money is removed from the table, interest or additional cash will also be paid so the investor earns 10 percent on the money. When the money is completely removed, the meter will be turned off.

This approach, which deals with the amounts of cash and the timing of cash outlays and receipts, is a cash flow concept of rate of return. It focuses solely on money expended and money returned, and compares outlays and inflows by using a cash flow "meter." The meter reading is the rate of return.

In this section, we develop the concept of **expected return**, defined as the annual percentage of likely or forecasted return on an investment calculated on a cash flow basis. Once the approach is developed, it will be applied to a variety of short-term cash investments.

Time Value of Money

The first step in our process is to recognize the essential difference between present and future dollars. If given the choice between having a dollar (or a German mark or a French franc) today or a dollar next year, business firms and individuals alike would choose the dollar today. This is because money has a time value. If the firm had the dollar today, it could invest the dollar and have more than a dollar next year. The amount would depend on the interest received on the investment. If, for example, the interest rate is 9 percent, a dollar today would be worth $1.09 next year.

Once an analyst accepts the fact that money has a time value, it is possible to compare the value of different amounts of money received at different times. As an example, suppose a firm is offered $10,000 today or $11,000 in one year in payment for goods. In this situation, the firm could consider the time value of the two offers. If money had a 10 percent time value, the firm would be indifferent to the two offers. If the $10,000 were accepted, it could be $11,000 in one year. Or, if the $11,000 were accepted, the firm could borrow against it today and receive $10,000. When the money actually arrived, it would repay the loan plus $1,000 interest. This example assumes that the firm's borrowing and lending rates are the same, an assumption that may not be true. But the example shows that, at a 10 percent time value of money, a receipt of $10,000 today is worth exactly the same as a receipt of $11,000 in one year. This may be diagrammed as

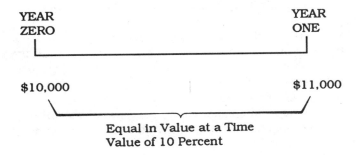

Time Value Calculations

Once the analyst has mastered the concepts of present and compound value, several approaches are available for performing expected return analysis. These are formulas, tables, financial calculators, and electronic spreadsheets.

1. **Formulas**. The return can be computed mathematically using time value formulas.

   For present value:

   $PV = FV/(1 + i)^n$ or $PV = FV/(1 + i)$ ^N

   For future value:

   $FV = PV * (1 + i)^n$ or $FV = PV * (1 + i)$ ^N

2. **Tables**. Many finance books contain time value factors in tables organized in a grid of percentages and periods. When the appropriate factor is multiplied by the dollar amount, a present or future value can be calculated. By finding the factor that links a present and future value, we also find the expected return.

3. **Financial Calculators**. Analysts commonly use time value of money calculators to solve for expected return. Although these are variations in format, such a calculator will generally have five buttons, as follows:

   $\boxed{n}$ $\boxed{i}$ $\boxed{PMT}$ $\boxed{PV}$ $\boxed{FV}$

   where

n	=	the number of periods in a financial transaction
i	=	the interest rate or discount factor per period
PMT	=	payment or receipt amount per period (assumes equal payments and equal time periods between payments)
PV	=	present value or amount of money at the start of the time period
FV	=	future value or amount received or paid at the end of the time period

The formulas for present value and compound value are built in to the calculator, so the analyst can work solely with it. The general rule is that three buttons must be pushed (including either n or i), with values given by the analyst, and the calculator will determine the value of a fourth button.

When using these calculators, several considerations should be noted. First, there are variations in the different calculators available. Some may require that n be entered before i and so forth. In addition, the calculator answers will usually differ slightly from answers achieved using present value or compound value tables. This is true because the calculators carry up to eight or ten decimal places, whereas printed tables have only three to five decimal places. Finally, the machines offer more flexibility than tables. A printed table usually is limited to even or integer percentage, whereas the calculator can handle interest or discount factors with decimal values.

4. **Electronic spreadsheets.** Increasingly, analysts are building models for use in expected return calculations. These models are covered in the next section.

CALCULATING RETURN WITH AN ELECTRONIC SPREADSHEET

The rate of return on a cash investment can be calculated by using models developed on an electronic spreadsheet. In this section, we will discuss two kinds of return. First, we will show the impact of compounding assumptions on the expected return. Second, we will develop two models for calculating expected return.

Compound Interest

Compounding may be described as a situation in which interest earned on a sum of money becomes part of the principal at the end of each period. Thus, interest earned in a period will be calculated on the basis of the original principal plus any interest earned in earlier periods.

Three forms of compounding are commonly encountered, as shown in the cash investment in Figure 7-1.

1. **Daily Compounding.** If an investment assumes daily compounding, the period is expressed in terms of days and a daily interest rate is used. For the 90–day investment in the figure, the time periods are 90 and the rate is 0.0003 (0.12/365). A short-term investment at 12 percent for 90 days with daily compounding produces a maturity value of $618,016.

2. **Periodic Compounding (Days in Year over Days of Investment).** If the investment assumes compounding during a period equal to the investment period, the period is expressed as 1 and a periodic rate is used. The rate is calculated by multiplying the annual rate by the

period, or 0.12 times 90/365. The periodic rate is 0.029589, and the future value is $617,753.

3. **Annual Compounding**. If an investment assumes annual compounding, the period is expressed as a portion of a year and the annual interest rate is used. The time period is 0.246575 (90/365) and the rate is 0.12, producing a maturity value of $617,003.

In Figure 7-1, the highest maturity value occurs with daily compounding and the lowest with annual compounding. This is reasonable. With more frequent compounding, more interest is earned on earlier interest and the maturity value will be higher.

Figure 7-1. Calculating Future Amount with Different Compounding Assumptions.

	Col D	Col E	Col F	Col G	Col H

Data on Cash Invested, Input Screen

ROW	Cash Invested	Annual Rate	No. of Days	Days in Year	
13	600,000	0.12	90	365	

Calculation of Value At Maturity, Output Screen

		Annual Rate	Periods	Rate	Cash Invested	Future Value
20	Daily Compounding	0.12				
21	Data		90	0.0003	600,000	
22	Solution					618,016
24	Periodic Compounding	0.12				
25	Data		1	0.029589		600,000
26	Solution					617,753
28	Annual Compounding	0.12				
29	Data		0.246575	0.12	600,000	
30	Solution					617,003

Formulas:

$$FV = PV * (1 + INT)^N$$

At H22   +G21* (1+F21)^E21

At H26   +G25 * (1+F25)^E25

At H30   +G29 * (1+F29)^E29

Expected Return under Different Compounding Assumptions

The compounding assumption is an important part of the determination of expected return from a short–term investment. When the treasurer is offered an investment and a return is quoted, it is a good idea to check on the expected rate of return using the same approach to all investments. Figure 7-2 provides a model for calculating expected return under varying compounding assumptions.

Figure 7-2. Calculating Expected Return with Different Compounding Assumptions.

	Col D	Col E	Col F	Col G	Col H
Data on Cash Invested, Input Screen					
Row	Cash Invested		No. of Days	Days In Year	Future Value
73	$350,000		60	365	360,000
Calculation of Expected Return, Output Screen					
	Expected Return	Periods	Rate	Cash Invested	Future Value
Daily Compounding					
82 Data		60		350,000	360,000
83 Solution	0.1714				
Periodic Compounding					
86 Data		1		350,000	360,000
87 Solution	0.1738				
Annual Compounding					
90 Data	0.1644			350,000	360,000
91 Solution	0.1869				

Formulas:

Rate = ((FV/PV)^(1/N)-1) * Compounding Factor

At D83   ((H82/G82)^(1/E82)-1) * G73

At D87   ((H86/G86)^(1/E86)-1) * (G73/F73)

At D91   ((H90/G90)^(1/E90)-1) * 1

In the figure, the treasurer is investing $350,000 for 60 days with no intermediate interest and an ending maturity value of $360,000. What is the expected return on this investment? Three answers are given: 17.14 percent, with daily compounding; 17.38 percent, with periodic compounding; and 18.69 percent, with annual compounding.

Most of a company's short-term investing occurs after the treasurer has received some rate information, either telephonically or as a result of looking at rates on a computer screen. In many cases, the treasurer has asked for rates on different items based on morning quotes in the *Wall Street Journal* or similar financial publication. The quoted rate itself is insufficient information for making an investment decision. The compounding assumption must be included. In our example, assume that two brokers quoted a 60–day investment. One quoted 17.38 percent and the other 18.69 percent. Which would be better? With periodic and annual compounding, respectively, the two quotes would produce an identical return of $10,000 on the original $350,000 investment.

In Figure 7-2, the formulas for expected return are identical except for the compounding factor. For daily compounding, the factor is the number of days; for periodic compounding, it is the days in the year divided by the days of the investment; and for annual compounding, the factor is 1.

Expected Return with Fees and Intermediate Cash Interest

Some investments require the payment of a brokerage or other fees at the beginning of the investment. Other investments include the payment of intermediate interest in the form of cash prior to maturity. The expected return under such an arrangement can be calculated using the model shown in Figure 7-3.

In this example, the firm is investing for four months with periodic compounding. Interest is paid each month, and an upfront fee of one half of 1 percent has been charged. What is the expected return on this investment?

In effect, the firm is investing $904,500 to receive three interest payments of $10,125 and a final payment of $910,125 over a period of four months. The periodic return is calculated using a built in formula for the internal rate of return. This is commonly found in electronic spreadsheet software packages. The first variable in the formula at cell position D26 is the quoted interest rate. After the comma, the range of cash flows is stipulated from D24 to H24. The periodic rate is 1 percent. The expected return is 12 percent compounded periodically.

Figure 7-3. Calculating Expected Return with Intermediate Interest.

	Col D	Col E	Col F	Col G	Col H

Data On Cash Invested, Input Screen

Row	Cash Invested	Annual Rate	No. Of Periods	Initial Fee	Periods In Year
12	900,000	0.135	4	0.005	12

Calculation of Value at Maturity, Output Screen

		Period 0	Period 1	Period 2	Period 3	Period 4
19	Cash Invested	(900,000)				
20	Interest Received		10,125	10,125	10,125	10,125
21	Fee	(4,500)				
22	Return of Principal					900,000
23						
24	Cash Flow	(904,500)	10,125	10,125	10,125	910,125
26	Periodic Return	0.010				
28	Annual Return	0.120				

Formulas:

At E20	-D19*E12/H12
AT D26	@IRR(E12,D24..H24)
AT D28	+D26*H12

This model can also be used when no fees are included. Just enter zero for the fees and recalculate the model. It cannot, however, be used when no intermediate interest payments are involved. In this case, the model in Figure 7-2 is applicable.

RISK AND RETURN

A key assumption of investment theory is that the expected return will be linked in a fundamental relationship to the degree of risk posed by an investment. The same is true when the treasurer is investing funds overnight or for a short period of time. In this section, we will develop the framework of risk and return for investing excess cash.

Nature of Risk

Once the cash manager goes beyond government obligations, he or she must recognize that expected returns may or may not be achieved. This adds the element of risk to the management of the firm's liquid assets. **Risk** may be defined as the likelihood that the actual return from an investment will be less than the expected return. Risk arises from two sources

1. **Business Risk**. This risk occurs when an organization does not have the ability to successfully compete with the assets it purchases. As an example, a corporation may not be able to operate its equipment, produce saleable products, sell the products at a profit, or may face other operating or marketing difficulties that cause losses. If such a firm issues bonds, the firm may default on interest or principal payments, a default that arises from business risk.

2. **Financial Risk**. This risk occurs when an organization does not generate sufficient profits to cover interest payments on its debt. The firm may be doing well in the market but the high rates on its sizable debt may cause a default.

Pattern of Risk and Return

The relationship of risk and return can be diagrammed so that risk is the independent variable and expected return is dependent on the risk level. The general pattern is shown in Figure 7-4.

    Once the relationship is recognized, we can develop specific schedules that trade off risk and return, as illustrated in Figure 7-5 in the form of a market line for fixed return bonds. A **market line** is defined as the relationship between risk and return for investments in a specific market. In a number of cases, it has been determined that the tradeoff between risk and return is relatively linear; that is, it can be described fairly well by drawing a straight line. Thus, if the analyst knows any two portfolios in terms of the degree of risk and expected return, a market line can be drawn. This is what has been done in Figure 7-5.

    Once we have an approximation of the market line, we plot individual investments around it. As we will see quickly after plotting, our first approximation of the market line may be off. Who really knows, for example, just what determines the likelihood of default. If we work on it awhile, we may get a line that we are comfortable in using and a diagram that looks something like Figure 7-6.

    A number of key concepts are implied in Figure 7-6, including

1. **Riskless Rate of Return**. This is the return on government securities. It is the minimum expected return on any investment since the firm can

receive some return–Treasury Bills, for example –without taking any risk of default. If a treasurer purchases a Treasury Bill maturing in three days and holds it three days, the expected return is known in advance and is a riskless rate of return.

2. **Market Return.** This is the average return on all instruments in the market. In the figure, it is the average return on all bonds since the market is defined as containing only bonds.

3. **Market Definition.** If the figure contains only bonds, it follows that other investments are found in other markets. The treasurer can define the market for investing excess cash. Many liquid investments are available for inclusion in the defined market.

4. **Level of Efficiency.** Financial securities are bought and sold in a highly competitive environment in which information on likely risks and expected returns is freely available and known to most participants. Thus, most markets will be relatively efficient in pricing investments to give a fair return for the degree of risk. Still, overnight investing does not take place in a totally efficient market. Hence, Figure 7-6 shows investments above and below the market line.

Figure 7-4. General Pattern of Risk and Return.

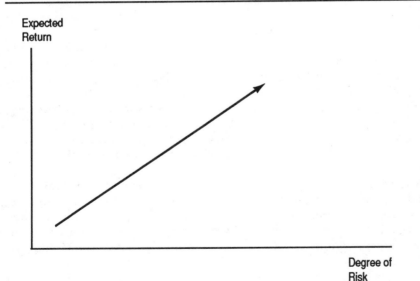

Expected
Return

Degree of
Risk

Figure 7-5. **Market Line for Fixed Return Securities.**

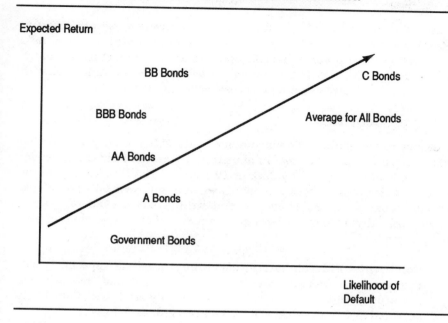

Figure 7-6. **Market Line with Individual Investments.**

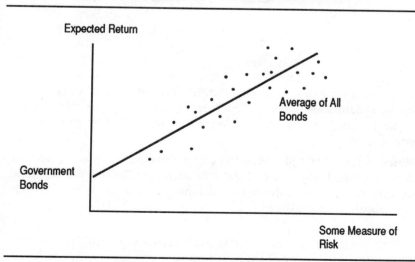

Measuring Risk

Knowing the upward–sloping pattern of risk and return, we are ready to confront specific investment decisions. First, we measure the degree of risk. Then, we choose investments that offer appropriate expected returns to match the firm's risk preferences. In this section, we will discuss measuring risk with popular short-term investments for excess cash.

Treasury Securities

A **Treasury Bill** is an unconditional promise by the U.S. Treasury to pay to the holder of the bill a specified amount at maturity. Treasury Bills are issued for short periods of time, normally 3, 6, or 12 months. The U.S. Treasury sells 91–and 182–day bills at weekly auctions, whereas one-year bills are offered every four weeks. Prospective buyers submit written bids to a Federal Reserve District Bank offering to purchase a given amount of bills. Two types of bids may be submitted

1. **Competitive Bid.** This bid is an offer to buy the bills at a specified yield. For example, a firm may offer to purchase $1 million of Treasury Bills at maturity value for $980,000, with a maturity in 91 days. If the bid is accepted in full, the yield will be 8.44 percent, as follows:

	n	i	PV	FV
Enter	$\frac{91}{365}$		980,000	1,000,000
Solve		[8.44]		

This competitive bid would be submitted on a standard form provided by the Federal Reserve Bank. The Treasury will accept the highest bids, since the higher the bid the lower the interest rate paid by the government.

2. **Non-competitive Bid.** Once the competitive bids are accepted, the noncompetitive bids up to $200,000 each are filled at the weighted average of the competitive bids. If too many bids are received, the bills are prorated among the bidders.

Treasury Bills are the most secure and liquid investment for the firm's excess cash. With respect to security, the U.S. government guarantees their redemption. With respect to liquidity, there is a large active market for the bills. They can be sold quickly and easily prior to maturity if the firm runs short of cash. The large secondary market also allows the firm to purchase bills without submitting a formal bid to the U.S. Treasury. The bills can be bought or sold in denominations of $10,000, $50,000, $100,000, $500,000, or $1 million from securities dealers or commercial banks.

In addition to Treasury Bills, the U.S. government issues interest-bearing securities. A **Treasury Note** is an issue that ranges in maturity from one to seven years, is available in registered or bearer form, and can be purchased in denominations from $1,000 to $1 million. A **Treasury Bond** is similar to the note but may be issued for maturities over seven years. The notes and bonds trade actively in secondary markets with other fixed return securities.

In addition to direct Treasury obligations, a firm may purchase the securities of federal agencies. Over 40 government bodies are empowered to raise money in capital markets, and many of them carry government guarantees or other sponsorship. Two groupings of government entities may be identified. The first group consists of **federal agencies** that issue obligations with a direct government guarantee. Some of these agencies are the Government National Mortgage Association (Ginnie Mae), U.S. Postal Service, Federal Housing Administration (FHA), and Export-Import Bank (Exim Bank). The second group consists of **government–sponsored agencies** which issue securities without an express government guarantee. Generally these agencies are publicly owned and include the Federal National Mortgage Association (Fannie Mae), Federal Home Loan Mortgage Corporation (Freddie Mac), and Federal Land Banks. Government agencies are very active in the money markets, and their securities are regarded almost as highly as direct Treasury securities.

A variety of other interest-bearing bonds are available for purchase by firms with excess cash. These bonds are evaluated with the same techniques as are used for government notes, bonds, and agency obligations.

Treasury securities are viewed as riskless investments because they offer no likelihood of default on the payment of principal and interest. As long as the U.S. government is able to print money, it is unthinkable that the Treasury would ever permit the disruptions to the economy that would accompany a default on a direct government obligation. Much the same situation exists for government agencies, but one can never be sure. Thus, the securities of federal agencies and government–sponsored agencies may offer a slight default risk and actually offer a little higher expected return.

The only exposure on Treasury securities lies in **interest rate risk**, defined as a loss of principal on a fixed return security that must be sold prior to maturity. This exposure results from the fact that the market value of fixed return instruments will fluctuate in the opposite direction of interest rates offered on securities traded in the marketplace. If the firm holds the instrument to maturity, the firm incurs no exposure. But if interest rates rise and the firm must sell the security prior to maturity, the rate of return will be less than was expected when the security was purchased.

To illustrate the process of interest rate risk, let us consider a firm that purchases a $100,000 Treasury Bill with one year to maturity. The bill pays no interest and therefore must be purchased at a discount to afford a return to the investor. Yields on Treasury Bills on an effective basis are currently 9.3 percent annually. How much will the firm pay for the bill?

The answer is $91,491.31, as follows:

n	i	PV	FV
1	9.3	[91,491.31]	100,000

If the firm holds the bill to maturity, the yield will not fluctuate from 9.3 percent. But suppose the company needs the money in four months when yields for eight month bills (the time remaining on the issue) are 10.7 percent. The bill could be sold for $93,447.62, as follows:

n	i	PV	FV
8/12	10.7	[93,447.62]	100,000

If the investing firm holds the bill for four months the equivalent of a 6.55 percent annual return will be earned, as follows:

n	i	PV	FV
4/12	[6.55]	91,491.31	93,447.62

The variation of return from the expected return is a result of the interest rate risk. This risk applies, as in our example, to government securities that offer no dispersion of return when held to maturity.

The exposure on a sale prior to maturity is even greater with longer term instruments. This is true because the degree of interest rate risk is directly related to the length of time to maturity. If a fixed return security is held to maturity and if no default occurs, there can be no dispersion of return. If the time to maturity is fairly short and the security is sold prior to maturity, only a small fluctuation will be experienced. If the term is long and the instrument is sold well in advance of maturity, the fluctuation can be sizable.

Certificate of Deposit (CD)

A **certificate of deposit** is an instrument that evidences a time deposit at a commercial bank or other financial institution. Commercial CDs are generally negotiable, have minimum maturities of at least 30 days, and are sold in denominations of $100,000 or more. The certificates of the nation's largest and strongest banks–the so-called **prime banks**–have been very popular because they are secure investments that offer relatively high yields. In addition, a CD can be sold prior to maturity in a large and well-developed secondary market. The degree of risk offered by a certificate of deposit is related to two factors

1. **Government Insurance.** The federal government agencies insure the first $100,000 of any depositor's funds in insured banks or thrift institutions. If a firm holds a $1 million CD, only the first $100,000 is guaranteed by the government for the payment of principal and interest.

2. **Strength of the Bank.** For the remaining $900,000, the holder of a CD is an unsecured creditor of the bank. If the bank were to collapse, the exposure would be quite real. It could range from a delay in payment of principal or interest to a full loss of both.

For some banks, the risk in CDs may be estimated by examining the credit ratings of its public debt. Figure 7-7 gives the Moody's ratings for corporate debentures, a system that is used to rate bank holding companies that issue debt securities.

As an example of applying the Moody's rating scale to the debentures of bank holding companies, Figure 7-8 shows the ratings of selected issues.

Commercial Paper

Commercial paper is a short-term, unsecured promissory note issued by a large nonfinancial corporation. It is called **finance paper** when issued by a financial corporation. These notes are issued by firms needing cash for periods of 30 days to 1 year, may be sold through dealers or directly to the investing firm, and have historically offered higher yields than other short-term money market instruments. Because a limited secondary market exists for commercial and finance paper, it is generally viewed as being less liquid than many other short-term instruments.

Figure 7-7. Key to Moody's Bond Ratings.

Category	Meaning
Aaa	Bonds that are rated Aaa are judged to be of the best quality. Interest payments are protected by a large or exceptionally stable margin, and principal is secure.
Aa	Bonds that are rated Aa are judged to be of high quality by all standards. They are rated lower

than the best bonds because margins of protection may not be as large as in Aaa securities, or fluctuation of protective elements may be of greater amplitude, or other elements may be present.

A   Bonds that are rated A possess many favorable investment attributes and are to be considered upper medium grade obligations. The designation A1 is used to identify the strongest bonds in the A class.

Baa   Bonds that are rated Baa are considered medium–grade obligations; that is, they are neither highly protected nor poorly secured. Baa1 designates the best bonds in this class.

Ba   Bonds that are rated Ba are judged to have speculative elements; their future cannot be considered as well assured.

B   Bonds that are rated B generally lack the characteristics of the desirable investment.

Caa   Bonds that are rated Caa are of poor standing and may be in default.

Ca   Bonds that are rated Ca represent obligations that are speculative in a high degree.

C   Bonds that are rated C are the lowest rated class.

Note: Beginning May 1982, Moody's began using the numerical modifiers 1, 2, and 3 in each rating classification. These numbers rate securities at the high, middle, and low range of each category.

Commercial paper is an unsecured short–term obligation of the issuer, with full exposure therein. The Moody's ratings of debentures can provide an indication of the risk posed by the corporation. In addition, a separate Moody's rating is often available for the commercial paper of the company. Moody's will use its commercial paper scale to rate selected issues with maturities of less than nine months. The ratings are:

Prime-1	P-1	Highest quality
Prime-2	P-2	Higher quality
Prime-3	P-3	High quality

Figure 7-9 shows the ratings on commercial paper and finance paper for selected organizations.

Identifying the Sources of Risk

The manager investing the firm's excess cash should have the ability to determine the real risk features offered by an investment. We will illustrate this process by comparing certificates of deposit with banker's acceptances.

A **banker's acceptance** is a draft whose payment is guaranteed by a commercial bank or similar entity. The acceptance is used in short-term financing of goods traded by two or more parties. Most acceptances arise from international transactions, but an increasingly large business is being conducted in domestic acceptances.

Two kinds of acceptances are generally identifiable. One finances the fabrication of goods for later shipment, and the second finances the transportation of the goods. Figure 7-10 shows the creation of an acceptance at a time when acceptances yield 9.45 percent to the holder when a 90–day maturity is specified. In this case, a foreign firm has ordered $2 million of goods from a U.S. firm and its bank has sent a letter of credit for the $2 million. The U.S. firm's bank has agreed to provide acceptance financing up to $1.5 million for the purchase of materials and hiring of labor to construct the goods. The firm orders its bank to pay $1.5 million to the bearer of a draft in 90 days, and the bank stamps its approval on it. The draft can now be sold as an acceptance to yield 9.45 percent annually. A treasurer investing excess cash will pay $1,466,518 for the acceptance, as shown in the calculation:

n	i	PV	FV
90/360	9.45	[1,466,518]	1,500,000

Figure 7-8. Ratings of Bank Debentures, 1984.

Rating	Organization	Coupon	Maturity
Aa2	Bankers Trust	8.125%	1999
Aa2	Chemical	8.400	1999
Aa3	BankAmerica	8.350	2007
Aa3	Manufacturers Hanover	8.125	2007
A1	Republic New York	9.000	2001
A1	Wells Fargo	8.600	2002
A2	NCNB	8.375	1999
Baa2	Shawmut	8.625	1999

Figure 7-9. Commercial Paper Ratings, 1986.

Rating	Organization
P-1	American Express Credit Corporation
P-1	Appalachian Power Company
P-1	Bankers Trust Company
P-1	Barclays American Corporation
P-1	Chase Manhattan
P-2	Continental Telecom, Inc.
P-2	Detroit Edison Company
P-2	Firestone Tire and Rubber Company
P-2	GATX Leasing Corporation
P-3	Glenfed Financial Corporation

Figure 7-10. Banker's Acceptance to Finance Construction of Goods.

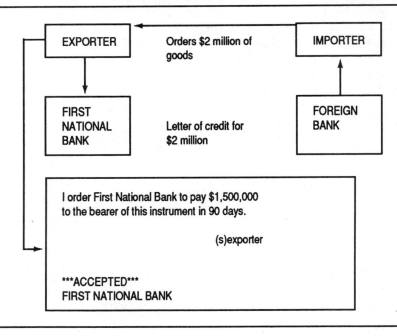

Before beginning the risk analysis of the acceptance, we might examine yields on acceptances and CDs. Figure 7-11 shows the yields for prime banks, as taken from the *Federal Reserve Bulletin*, June 1986. Historically, acceptances have offered a higher yield than CDs by one quarter to one-half percent.

Figure 7-11. Yields on Certificates of Deposit and Banker's Acceptances, Prime Banks, December 1983–March 1986.

		Certificates of Deposit, Secondary Market, 90-Day Maturities	Prime Banker's Acceptances, 90-Day Maturities, Domestic Issues
Dec.	1983	9.07%	8.90%
	1984	10.37	10.14
	1985	8.05	7.92
	1985	7.80	7.65
Mar.	1986	7.24	7.09

What are the sources of risk in each instrument? For both, the primary source of repayment is the bank, and this represents the primary exposure. What would happen if the bank defaulted? For the CD, the government might insure the first $100,000. If the treasurer has no other deposits with the bank, the first $100,000 is safe even if the bank defaults. The balance is at risk. What about the acceptance? It is not insured by the government, but there is a secondary source of payment. The holder can go to the maker of the draft, the exporter in our example above, and demand payment. This alternative provides quite a bit of additional protection. Which is riskier? The analyst can decide after considering these facts and current economic conditions. This is the process of determining the source of risk and then estimating the likelihood of default from each source.

Distinguishing Secondary Risk Sources

A number of investments offer secondary collateral to a primary agreement, as in the case of government insurance backing up a deposit in a bank. One of these investments is a **repurchase agreement**, or repo, an agreement whereby a bank or security dealer sells specific marketable securities to another party and agrees to repurchase the securities at a fixed price on some future date. As an example, $1 million worth of Treasury Bills may be sold on Thursday for $999,764, and the dealer agrees to buy them back on Friday for $1 million. The bank or security dealer uses a repurchase agreement to finance a portion of its securities inventory. This investment is a short-term instrument, most commonly used overnight, over a weekend, or for periods less than a week.

The primary source of repayment on a repurchase agreement is the credit of the bank or dealer. Still, the secondary collateral is deemed as important. If

Treasury or agency securities are used as collateral, the return to the investor will be lower than arrangements wherein municipal bonds are the collateral. In some cases, the spread may be as much as a half percent. Is such a spread justified? Each investor must answer this question individually, but it should be recognized that the marketable securities are the secondary source of risk. The primary analysis should involve the credit of the bank or securities dealer.

Example: A securities dealer agrees to sell a portfolio of corporate bonds for $1,500,000 on Friday and will repurchase them on Monday for $1,501,161. What is the effective return to the investor who holds this instrument?

n	i	PV	FV
3/365	[9.87]	1,500,000	1,501,161

FOREIGN INVESTMENTS

When evaluating investments for the firm's excess cash, the treasurer is not limited to investments in the United States. A number of foreign opportunities can be considered if the firm has funds in excess of $100,000 to be invested at any one time.

Foreign Investments in Dollars

As noted earlier, a **Eurodollar** may be defined as a dollar deposited outside the United States, either in the foreign branch of a U.S. bank or in a foreign bank. The market is quite large, as is shown in Figure 7-12, and provides liquidity to finance world trade as well as offering an investment haven for individuals and companies seeking to hold and invest U.S. dollars.

Figure 7-12. Eurodollar Market Size, (billions of dollars)

Year	Eurodollars
1981	1665
1982	1857
1983	1979
1984	2096
1985	2316
1986	2745
1987	3186

Source: Morgan Guaranty Trust Company of New York, *World Financial Markets.*

Funds may be invested in the Eurodollar market to meet the maturity requirements of the firm's operations. Figure 7-13 shows the yields available, depending on the maturity of the deposit, from 1982 to 1987.

When evaluating Eurodollar deposits, the firm does not face any currency exposure since the funds are held in U.S. dollars. The exposure is the strength of the bank, as with CDs and acceptances. Therefore, the real comparison must deal with yields on competing investments. Suppose, for example, the treasurer has $2 million to invest for 90 days in relatively secure instruments. He or she might compare U.S. Treasury Bills, prime certificates of deposit, and prime bank Eurodollar deposits. Figure 7-14 gives some yields for comparison purposes from 1982 to 1987.

Figure 7-13. Eurodollar Deposit Rates
(prime banks' bid rates in London, at or near end of month).

		Over-night	One Month	Three Months	Six Months	Twelve Months
December	1982	9.25%	9.13%	9.19%	9.50%	9.63%
	1983	9.50	9.69	9.81	10.06	10.38
	1984	8.63	8.38	8.63	9.13	9.81
	1985	12.25	8.00	7.88	7.88	7.94
	1986	6.88	6.81	6.75	6.75	6.81
	1987	6.75	7.06	7.37	7.50	7.81

Source: *World Financial Markets.*

Figure 7-14. Yields on Three 90-Day Investments.

		Treasury Bills	Certificates Of Deposit	Eurodollars Deposits
December	1982	8.15%	8.25%	9.19%
	1983	9.28	9.70	9.81
	1984	7.99	8.35	8.63
	1985	7.25	7.88	7.88
	1986	5.83	6.26	7.31
	1987	5.84	7.10	6.75

Source: *World Financial Markets.*

Foreign Currency Investments

When considering foreign investments, the firm has the opportunity to accept exposure to exchange rate fluctuations. If a firm is holding a currency whose value increases during the holding period, the firm receives both the interest and appreciation in value. On the other hand, a currency that declines in value during the investment period can wipe out the interest and produce a loss of principal. Figure 7-15 shows index numbers when four major currencies were plotted against a weighted average of the currencies of 15 major countries. The period is May 1985 to April 1986, a relatively stable period in terms of currency movements. Still, an investor holding dollars for 30 days could have suffered sizable losses while an investor holding yen could have made sizable gains.

Figure 7-15. Real Effective Exchange Rates, Selected Currencies, May 1985 to April 1986.

		U.S. (Dollar)	Japan (Yen)	U.K. (Pound)	Germany (Mark)
May	1985	126.0	92.4	92.3	94.3
June	1985	124.7	93.1	93.9	94.2
July	1985	120.6	93.6	97.7	94.6
August	1985	118.3	94.1	95.9	96.0
September	1985	117.9	95.5	96.2	96.1
October	1985	114.2	101.3	94.8	96.8
November	1985	112.7	105.6	94.8	97.1
December	1985	111.9	105.1	93.6	97.7
January	1986	110.4	105.7	91.5	98.5
February	1986	105.6	113.0	89.6	99.2
March	1986	101.7	116.4	90.8	98.9
April	1986	100.2	118.6	93.5	96.9
Average		113.7	102.9	93.7	96.9
Standard Deviation		7.99	8.98	2.27	1.76
Maximum Movement in Any Month		-4.8	+7.3	+3.8	+1.4

Source: World Financial Markets, April/May 1986, p. 12.

Note: Index numbers, 1980–1982 average = 100. The index for a currency is a measure against 15 other major currencies.

Once the firm recognizes the possible currency exposure, it can compare yields on different investments to see if they are attractive. The firm's bank can advise on restrictions in foreign investing and facilitate the transfer of funds and make other arrangements. Figure 7-16 shows some representative yields on foreign currency investments in March 1986.

Figure 7-16. Yields on Selected Foreign Currency Investments, March 1986.

Country	Treasury Bills 90 Days	Bond Yields 90 Days	Daily Money Rates	Bank Deposits 90 Days
United States	6.26%	7.34%	7.48%	7.16%
Canada	10.19	10.80	11.10	10.75
Japan	3.90	5.16	5.54	5.32
United Kingdom	11.04	11.06	12.09	11.06
Belgium	9.89	8.52	7.74	9.63
France	8.37	8.52	5.88	
Germany	4.68	4.7	4.15	
Switzerland	4.06	2.25	3.81	

Source: *World Financial Markets*, April/May 1986, pp. 16-18.

A PORTFOLIO APPROACH

Portfolio theory is the body of knowledge that deals with the relationship between risk and return when an investor holds a combination of assets, or a **portfolio.** The goal of portfolio theory is to select optimal combinations of financial or capital assets in order to achieve the highest possible expected return for any level of risk or the lowest possible degree of risk for any level of return. The field of portfolio theory is highly developed, particularly with respect to investment in financial assets. We have already developed some of the theory in our discussion of risk and return. In this section, we will distinguish between holding a single asset and holding a portfolio of assets to reduce risk when investing excess cash.

Portfolio Risk

Security risk is the degree of uncertainty of return inherent in the investment in a single financial asset, such as a certificate of deposit or commercial paper. It can be measured in terms of the dispersion of returns by making use of the standard deviation. **Portfolio risk**, on the other hand, is the degree of uncertainty of return when more than one financial asset is held as part of a group of assets. We are still dealing with a dispersion of return, but portfolio risk can be divided into two components— systematic and unsystematic risk.

Systematic risk is the market-related component of portfolio risk. Interest-rate risk offers an illustration of this concept. Assume that the firm has invested its excess cash in commercial paper of medium-grade firms, with a Moody's rating of P-3. Now let us assume that a number of uncertainties drive up the yields on P-3 paper and the firm must sell its holdings 60 days before maturity. Originally the firm purchased $500,000 of paper to yield 11.4 percent annually in a period of 182 days. Sixty days prior to maturity the yields have risen to 12.8 percent on 60-day paper, and the firm is forced to sell its holdings. Let us see what happens. The firm purchases the paper for $500,000 and will receive $527,653 at maturity, as follows:

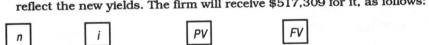

n	i	PV	FV
182/365	11.4	500,000	[527,653]

When it finds a buyer 60 days prior to maturity, the paper will be sold to reflect the new yields. The firm will receive $517,309 for it, as follows:

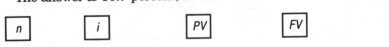

n	i	PV	FV
60/365	12.8	[517,309]	527,653

What has been the yield to the firm for the four months it held the paper? The answer is 10.7 percent, as follows:

n	i	PV	FV
122/365	[10.7]	500,000	517,309

The difference between the expected return of 11.4 and the actual return of 10.7 percent is the result of changes in the rates in the market and affects all fixed return securities. Hence, it reflects systematic risk.

Unsystematic risk is the second component of portfolio risk and represents dispersions of return as a result of random fluctuations in market prices. Sometimes the firm is holding an instrument that no one is interested in buying at the market price. In order to sell it, the price must be dropped. Such an inefficiency is the unsystematic risk from a holding.

Role of Diversification

Diversification is the strategy of investing in more than one financial asset with a goal of reducing risk. Empirical research indicates that the variations of expected return can be significantly reduced when a diversification strategy is followed. In effect, two factors are at work. First, diversification eliminates or minimizes the unsystematic risk in a portfolio. By holding a number of instruments, the firm minimizes the impact of random movements in the return of individual securities. The random pluses for some instruments are offset by the random minuses for others.

The second factor whereby diversification can reduce risk occurs when the firm follows a conscious policy of offsetting the risk of one security with the risk of another security. As an example, let us consider medium-term bonds A and B that have different expected returns in the next year, depending on the level of economic activity and its impact on the bond markets. The likely returns if the four-year bonds are sold in one year have been forecast as follows:

	Bond A Expected Return	Bond B Expected Return
In the event of a recession	0.07	0.10
With normal economic conditions	0.10	0.08
With high economic growth	0.12	0.07

The range of expected returns for bond A is 7 to 12 percent; for B it is 7 to 10 percent. But what would happen if the cash manager held a portfolio with half A and half B? The new expected returns are

Recession $\dfrac{(0.07 + 0.10)}{2} = 0.085$

Normal $\dfrac{(0.10 + 0.08)}{2} = 0.090$

Growth $\dfrac{(0.12 + 0.07)}{2} = 0.095$

With the portfolio, the range of expected returns is 8.5 to 9.5 percent, a smaller range than offered by either individual bond. This is an illustration of offsetting risk when a diversification strategy is followed.

Investing Strategies

Once we recognize the fact that we are dealing with risk and return in a portfolio context, we can develop an investment strategy that is consistent with the firm's viewpoint of risk in its holdings of liquid assets. To clarify the matter of strategy, let us identify three strategies: (A) relatively safe, highly liquid; (B) safe, somewhat less liquid; and (C) some exposure, relatively illiquid. Our first portfolio will be restricted to Treasury issues, bank CDs from highly rated or prime banks, and repurchase agreements with government securities as collateral. Most maturities will be 90 days or less. The second portfolio branches out a bit, with some longer maturities and some less secure investments. The third portfolio accepts longer maturities and the exposure offered by investments in foreign currencies. The three portfolios are given in Figure 7-17.

In a portfolio context, each of the three portfolios offers some diversification. The third portfolio offers the greatest possible dispersion of return but is also the most diversified, thus affording a hedge against risk. As an example, a devaluation of the pound sterling, which would affect the return on U.K. time deposits, could be offset by revaluating one of the other currencies. The willingness of the investing firm to accept some of the risks in portfolio C produces a higher expected return but also offers a wider range of returns than is present in portfolio A or B.

New Opportunities in the Money Markets

In any attempt to determine the appropriate vehicles for investing excess cash, the treasurer must be aware of the constantly changing environment for investments. Throughout recent years, new opportunities and investment variations have been evolving or emerging. Some investments became popular; others receded. But the basic analysis of risk and return did not change.

To illustrate this process, let us consider the advent of money market funds. A **money market fund** is an investment company that pools the money from a group of investors and invests it in a variety of financial instruments. Three characteristics distinguish these funds. First, they make passive investments in securities, not active investments that require them to manage other firms or assets. Second, the investment decisions are made by professional managers hired to make the investment selections in line with the stated policies and goals of the company. Third, they pay no taxes on any income or gains but rather pass these obligations on to the investors.

Although investment companies do not represent a new phenomenon to be investigated by the firm's treasurer, the rules under which they operate and the services they offer do represent such a phenomenon. Many things are possible with such funds. For one, it is difficult to distinguish between some of the funds and ordinary commercial bank services. Money can be withdrawn on demand. Some funds allow checkwriting against balances. Deposits can be made at any time, perhaps with some restrictions. Different rules apply to different funds. Figure 7-18 shows the major features of two such funds, one designed for larger accounts and one for smaller accounts.

Figure 7-17. Three Portfolios Representing Different Investment Strategies.

Percent Invested	Security or Instrument	Yield to Maturity
PORTFOLIO A—Relatively safe, highly liquid		
50%	Overnight Repos (Treasury Bills)	0.1277
10	30-Day Treasury Bills	0.1142
10	30-Day Prime Bank CDs	0.1281
10	90-Day Treasury Bills	0.1220
10	90-Day Prime Bank CDs	0.1302
10	180-Day Treasury Bills	0.1185
	WEIGHTED AVERAGE RETURN. 12.52%	
PORTFOLIO B—Safe, somewhat less liquid		
20%	Overnight Repos (municipals)	0.1305
20	30-Day Repos (corporation bonds)	0.1322
20	30-Day Prime Bank CDs	0.1281
10	90-Day Regional Bank CDs	0.1351
10	180-Day Commercial Paper	0.1322
10	90-Day Eurodollar Time Deposits	0.1444
10	180-Day Japanese Bank Dollar Acceptances	0.1427
	WEIGHTED AVERAGE RETURN 13.36%	
PORTFOLIO C—Some exposure, relatively illiquid		
10%	Overnight Repos (municipals)	0.1305
10	180-Day Regional Bank Acceptances	0.1372
20	180-Day Eurodollar Deposits	0.1456
20	180-Day Commercial Paper	0.1322

10	120-Day Belgium fondes des Rentes certificates	0.1445
10	90-Day New Zealand Commercial Bills	0.1600
10	90-Day Mexican Bank CDs	0.1680
10	90-Day U.K. Bank Time Deposits	0.1681
	WEIGHTED AVERAGE RETURN	14.64%

Figure 7-18. Comparison of Two Money Market Funds.

Fidelity Daily Income Trust	*Fidelity Cash Reserves*
1. $10,000 minimum investment	1. $1,000 minimum investment
2. $500 or more additional investment	2. $250 or more additional investment
3. Checkwriting with $500 minimum	3. Checkwriting with $500 minimum
4. Fixed monthly service charge	4. Fees and transactions charges as incurred

In risk and return terms, the money market funds must be evaluated for the inherent risk they offer. Still, the convenience and yields offered by money market funds make them attractive alternatives for a company's excess cash.

New Opportunities in the Futures Markets

A **financial future** is a contract to buy or sell a financial security at a fixed price for future delivery, most commonly in 30, 60, 90, 180, or 360 days. The development of financial futures markets offers important new opportunities to the cash manager, once again in the overall context of risk and return. An investor, borrower, or lender can use the availability of futures contracts to hedge against interest rate fluctuations.

One of the most important facilities for trading financial futures is the Chicago Mercantile Exchange (CME) where Treasury Bills and other securities are traded. Treasury Bill futures on the CME are traded in volume, and rates and yields are reported widely in the financial press. The Treasury Bill futures can be used to offset part of the effects of interest rate fluctuations, as illustrated in Figure 7-19. In this situation, the Treasury Bill future is used to offset a portion of the loss on a certificate of deposit held for 30 days by the firm.

Figure 7-19. Treasury Bill Future Offsets Loss on Certificate of Deposit.

___

Situation

A firm has purchased a 180-day certificate of deposit with plans to sell it in 30 days for $101,200. This yield is higher than would be available on a 30-day CD. At the same time, the firm has signed a futures contract to sell a 180-day Treasury Bill in 30 days for $96,312.

Development

During the 30 days, yields on all fixed return securities rise. The CD can be sold for only $100,350. At the same time, the 150-day Treasury Bill can be purchased for $95,557 and be delivered against the futures contract.

Results

The firm loses $850 on its CD (101,200 minus 100,350) but makes $755 on the Treasury Bill contract by buying a bill in the open market ($95,557) and selling it for the contract rate ($96,312). NET RESULT: A loss of only $95 (850 minus 755) because of the rise in yields.

___

CONCLUSION

In this chapter, we have examined a risk-return framework for investing the firm's excess cash. In some periods of time, it will seem appropriate to emphasize safety of the liquid portfolio; in other periods, the emphasis will be on securing high returns. Neither approach is conceptually correct. In all periods of time, the treasurer should determine the risk level that is acceptable to the firm and then should find the highest return holdings consistent with this risk level.

The degree of liquidity of the holdings will be determined by the needs of the firm, the volatility of its cash flows, and yields on short-term instruments in the market. During this investing process, the treasurer should always be cognizant of the role played by diversification in reducing the dispersion of return from the firm's marketable security holdings.

Northern Cliffs Manufacturing Case—
Reinvesting Excess Cash

The primary business of Northern Cliffs Manufacturing is the production and distribution of heavy machinery and equipment. With sales in excess of $7 billion, it focuses primarily on seven lines of business in four regions of the world. Its growth overseas, particularly in the Middle East and Pacific run, has been impressive. Relatively high profits have accompanied the successful operations.

To ensure sufficient liquidity, Northern Cliffs maintains a strong cash position, nearing $320 million at the present time. As a general rule, the firm has always invested at least 20 percent but not more than 40 percent of its excess cash in each of three general areas

1. **Liquidity Pool.** This consists of Treasury issues, bank certificates of deposit, and money market instruments, all with maturities under 30 days.

2. **Domestic Pool.** This contains bonds, CDs, acceptances, repurchase agreements, and similar securities of U.S. issuers, with maturities of one day to one year.

3. **International Pool.** This contains time deposits, bonds, and other investments outside the United States, primarily in hard currencies such as the dollar, deutschmark, and yen, and with maturities under one year.

For the past three weeks, the treasurer has been preparing alternative strategies for next year's investment of excess cash. He has identified eight different portfolios in the three general areas. Each portfolio has been assigned a letter from "A" to "H." Using historical data and forecasts by the firm's investment advisers, he has projected a yield and standard deviation for each portfolio, as shown in Figure 7-20. He has also estimated transactions costs for each general area, as a percentage of dollars invested. These are

1. Liquidity Pool   0.0075
2. Domestic Pool   0.0050
3. International Pool   0.0100

After consulting with advisers and members of the firm's executive committee, the treasurer prepared two alternative recommendations for the board of directors. The possible portfolios are

192

Portfolio X   40 percent invested in B

20 percent invested in F

40 percent invested in H

Portfolio Y   40 percent invested in A

30 percent invested in D

30 percent invested in G

Figure 7-20. Risk and Return of Selected Investment Pools.

		Expected Return	*Standard Deviation*
Liquidity Pool	A	0.105	0.015
	B	0.112	0.024
	C	0.098	0.014
Domestic Pool	D	0.120	0.015
	E	0.135	0.025
	F	0.150	0.042
International Pool	G	0.187	0.051
	H	0.205	0.058

Required: Which recommendation should be accepted? Why?

8

International Cash Management

The term **foreign exchange** is commonly used with two distinct meanings, as follows:

1. **Currency of Foreign Nations.** When businesspeople refer to the currencies of other nations, they commonly refer to their need for foreign exchange.

2. **Conversion of Currencies.** Exchanging one national currency for a different national currency at some given or agreed on exchange rate is a foreign exchange transaction.

This chapter deals with the formal markets and mechanisms designed to facilitate the exchanging of national currencies, with an emphasis on identifying and protecting against foreign exchange risks.

FOREIGN EXCHANGE MARKET

The foreign exchange market is a communications network linking a number of participants, including the following:

1. **Commercial Banks.** Many of the leading commercial banks in the United States and abroad provide facilities and services related to foreign exchange. The banks serve individuals and firms seeking to convert currencies or transfer monies from one nation to another.

2. **Brokers and Dealers.** A foreign exchange **broker** brings together buyers and sellers of national currencies. For this service, he or she will receive a commission that varies according to the size of the exchange, the currencies involved, and the terms of the contract. A foreign exchange **dealer** purchases and sells currencies for his or her own account. The dealer makes his or her profit from the spread between what is paid for a currency and what is received for it.

3. **Businesses and Individuals**. The largest group of participants in the foreign exchange market are businesses and individuals requiring currencies of different nations.

Foreign Exchange Transactions

Transactions occur in a communications network linking commercial banks, brokers, and dealers. The network consists of telephones, computer networks, airmail transfers, and drafts.

1. **Telephones**. Most brokers and dealers work out of offices connected by direct telephonic lines to other brokers and to the foreign exchange departments of commercial banks and other institutions. Information is exchanged, and deals are actually consummated over the phone.

2. **Computer Networks**. A common method of conducting foreign exchange transactions is through the use of electronic transmissions. An individual or business will contact a bank and request the delivery of foreign exchange. The bank will send an electronic message to a foreign bank ordering the transaction to occur. As an example, suppose a French importer wants to send dollars to a U.S. exporter in return for goods to be shipped. The importer will ask his Paris bank to electronically transmit the funds to a New York bank, as of a given date and under stipulated conditions, so the dollars can be credited to the exporter's account. Simultaneously, the French bank will withdraw francs from the French importer's account.

3. **Airmail Transfers**. Transactions can be conducted by mail in the same way that electronic and telephone transactions occur. Airmail is cheaper but slower than electronic or telephone transfers.

4. **Drafts**. A **draft** is a written order to a bank used to complete a foreign exchange transaction. Suppose a French importer had funds with the Paris branch office of Citibank. The importer could send a written order directly to the New York Citibank office authorizing dollars to be paid to the U.S. exporter. Upon making the payment, the bank would remove the equivalent amount of funds from the account of the French importer in the Paris branch.

Levels of Transactions

Foreign exchange transactions occur at three different levels:

1. **Commercial Level**. Individuals can convert currencies using the facilities of commercial banks. A bank's international department buys and sells different national currencies. This department may hold

balances of the paper currency of other nations to be purchased by tourists and business travelers.

2. **Wholesale Level.** Larger transactions occur when banks exchange currencies with other banks or with dealers or brokers. Wholesale transactions in the New York money market frequently surpass the equivalent of a $100 billion (U.S. dollars) in a single day.

3. **Central Bank Level.** When a national bank accumulates an excessive amount of the nation's currency and such currency cannot be exchanged with other banks or with dealers, the nation's central bank will intervene to remove the excess currency from the market. Prior to this intervention, exchange rates will fluctuate to reflect supply and demand factors for the different currencies. Central banks also deal with each other to correct imbalances in the foreign currencies available in each nation.

Need for Foreign Exchange

The need for foreign exchange arises from the requirements of a number of customers, and the requirements for transactions such as:

1. **Exports and Imports.** Although domestic business is carried out in a single currency, foreign trade may involve two or more currencies. The importer may wish to pay in one currency whereas the exporter may desire payment in a different currency. The foreign exchange market facilitates the exchange.

2. **Sale of Securities.** When common stock or bonds are purchased by foreign investors, foreign exchange is needed to complete the transaction.

3. **Business Remittances.** The subsidiaries of multinational firms remit funds in various forms to the parent company or, at the parent's direction, to other subsidiaries. Foreign exchange is needed for these transactions.

4. **Tourist Expenditures.** When people travel abroad, they need foreign currencies to purchase goods and services. These transactions are accomplished through the foreign exchange market.

Spot and Forward Exchange Markets

A **spot transaction** involves the immediate purchase of and payment for foreign exchange. The arrangement can be made by telephone, electronically or in person, with the delivery and payment to be accomplished in a day or two. These transactions are said to occur in the **spot market**.

The **forward market** involves foreign exchange transactions in which delivery occurs at a stipulated future date. Two parties agree to the exchange of one currency for another at a specified exchange rate. Because no money is exchanged when the agreement is reached, no money is tied up during the life of the **forward contract**. At delivery in 30, 60, 90, or whatever days stipulated, both parties provide the agreed on amounts of each currency. Sample problems in the forward market are given in Figure 8-1.

PREMIUMS AND DISCOUNTS IN THE FORWARD MARKET

Exchange rates between currencies generally differ in spot and forward markets. A currency trades at a **premium** when it is worth more in the forward market than in the spot market. For example, suppose the exchange rates between dollars and francs are $1/4fr spot and $1/4.1fr one year. One dollar can purchase more francs in the forward market than in the spot market and thus is trading at a premium against the franc.

Similarly, a currency trades at a **discount** against another currency when it is worth less in the forward market than in the spot market. In the example with francs and dollars, the franc trades at a discount against the dollar. Thus, one currency's premium is the other currency's discount.

Figure 8-1. Calculations of Forward Market Transactions.

Data

Exchange Rates, Franc and Krona
Paris Office, Chase Manhattan

	Krona/Franc	Franc/Krona
Spot Market	0.3898	2.5654
30 Days	0.3906	2.5602
90 Days	0.3925	2.5478
190 Days	0.3954	2.5291

1. An importer in France needs 300,000 krona to pay for a purchase. The current date is March 1 but the krona will not be needed until June 1. How many francs will be delivered at maturity?

2. An exporter in France will receive 500,000 krona in payment for goods shipped on March 1. The payment is due to arrive April 1. If the exporter signs a forward contract with Chase Manhattan, how many francs will he receive at delivery?

3. A Swedish exporter is due to receive 120,000 francs in 180 days. If she signs a forward contract, how many krona will she receive at maturity?

Solution

	Using Krona/Franc	Using Franc/Krona
1. Amount (Krona)	300,000	300,000
	divided by	times
Rate	0.3925	2.5478
Units of Currency	764,331	764,340
2. Amount (Krona)	500,000	500,000
	divided by	times
Rate	0.3906	2.5602
Units of Currency	1,280,082	1,280,100
3. Amount (Francs)	120,000	120,000
	times	divided by
Rate	0.3954	2.5291
Units of Currency	47,448	47,448

Example: The exchange rate between the franc and pound sterling is 9.5fr/1 spot and 9.7fr/1 90 days. Which currency is trading at a premium and which is trading at a discount?

Answer: The pound sterling purchases more francs in the forward market and trades at a premium. The franc trades at a discount.

Calculation of Percentage of Premium or Discount

The premium or discount may be calculated for a single unit of a currency using the formula given in Figure 8-2. Basically, the differential between the forward and spot rates is divided by the spot rate. Multiplying this differential by 365 over the days of the contract has the effect of creating an annual rate.

In Figure 8-2, the percentage of the discount is less than the percentage of the premium. This effect is similar to the difference between discounted and nondiscounted loans. For example, suppose we have a 6 percent $1,000 note, and we have a choice of paying interest immediately or at the end of one year.

In one case, the rate is 60/1,000 or 6 percent; in the other case, it is 60/940 or 6.38 percent. The difference in rates is the difference between paying the interest now in one case and paying it later in the other. This same effect occurs in calculating premiums and discounts for currencies.

Figure 8-2. Calculations of Premiums and Discounts.

Formula

$$\% \text{ Premium (Discount)} = \frac{(\text{Forward} - \text{Spot})}{(\text{Spot})} * \frac{(365)}{(\text{Forward Days})}$$

Data

	Franc/Dollar	Dollar/Franc
Spot Market	4.0000	0.2500
90 Days	4.1000	0.2439

Solution

The dollar is at a premium; the franc is at a discount.

	Dollar	Franc
Forward Rate	4.1000	0.2439
Spot Rate	4.0000	0.2500
Forward Days	90	90
Days in Year	365	365
Premium (discount)	0.101	(0.099)

Cause of Premiums and Discounts

A premium or discount is primarily because of two factors:

1. **Interest Rate Differentials.** When national capital markets have different levels of domestic interest rates, the differences are reflected in the forward market for the currencies. Suppose, for example, that the United States and Canada have dollars that are equally strong at the existing exchange rate. Suppose further that the Canadian one-year interest rate on high-grade securities is 11 percent and the U.S. rate is 13 percent. Canadian investors would purchase U.S. dollar securities, hold them for one year, and then guarantee their conversion back into Canadian dollars at a rate fixed under a forward contract. Without

premiums or discounts, the investor would make a 2 percent riskless profit by investing in U.S. dollar securities over comparable securities in Canadian markets. This process of guaranteeing a higher profit at no risk is a form of **arbitrage**. To keep large amounts of Canadian dollars from flowing into the United States, the forward market will have the Canadian dollar at approximately a 2 percent premium against the U.S. dollar. The additional profits from the high U.S. interest rates will be lost when the money is converted back at the forward market's discount rate for the U.S. dollar.

2. **Relative Strengths of Currencies.** The second factor reflected by a premium or discount is the relative strength of the currencies. Investors, including multinational corporations and banks, prefer to hold strong currencies. If they are forced to hold balances of weak currencies, they may execute forward contracts to allow them to get back into strong currencies at the end of a period of time. In return for guaranteeing an individual or firm the right to get out of a weak currency at the end of a period of time, forward contracts will be quoted at exchange rates that put the weak currency at a discount against the strong currency. Similarly, strong currencies will be quoted at a premium against weak currencies.

Both of the above factors are present in any quoting of forward market exchange rates. The effects may be complementary or offsetting. International money managers spend considerable time analyzing interest levels and relative strengths of currencies as they move money between capital markets and take steps to protect the value of their cash holdings.

Bid and Ask Quotes in the Forward Market

Forward exchange contracts are available from the international departments of banks and from foreign exchange dealers. The bank itself may write the contract, or it may be written with the bank acting as a representative for a monetary speculator. If the bank is willing to buy a currency, a **bid** price is quoted. If the bank is willing to sell a currency, an **ask** price is quoted. If the bank is willing to issue a forward contract either to buy or sell a currency, both bid and ask prices are quoted. As an example:

Barclay's Bank, 90–Day Contracts on U.S. Dollars.

	Bid	Ask
Sterling/Dollar	0.4762	0.4831
Franc/Dollar	3.7400	3.7722
Peso/Dollar		9.5000
Krona/Dollar	5.4380	

From these quotes, we can see that the bank (or the speculator it is representing) is willing to make a market for sterling or francs against the dollar, but the bank is only willing to sell dollars for pesos or to buy dollars for krona. Two factors normally account for an unwillingness to provide both bid and ask prices:

1. **Weak Currencies May Not Be Quoted**. The bank does not want to purchase a weak currency if it is not likely to profit from the transaction. In the example of krona, the bank is willing to buy dollars with its own krona but is not willing to sell dollars at a stipulated rate for a future delivery of krona. This may indicate that the krona is fluctuating widely in foreign exchange markets and the bank does not want to undertake the risk of a forward contract to buy it.

2. **The Bank's Position in Currency May be Exposed**. An **exposed foreign exchange position** means that a bank or corporation has greater obligations in one currency with respect to borrowing or holding than it has offsetting obligations. As an example, assume a firm holds $300,000 and owes $530,000 at a time when its native currency, the franc, trades at 4fr/$1 in the spot market. This firm has a borrowing exposure of the difference between the two figures, or $230,000. Valued at the current exchange rate of 4fr/$1, its exposure is 920,000 francs (2,120,000 minus 1,200,000). If, however, the dollar is revalued and the exchange rate increases to 4.2fr/$1, the firm's exposure increases to 966,000 francs (2,226,000 minus 1,260,000). The revaluation of the dollar increases the cash held by 60,000 francs and the money owed by 106,000 francs. Therefore, the debt increases more than the cash held and the firm loses money when it converts its cash and repays its debt.

Example: A U.S. bank is writing 90-day contracts to buy or sell francs. It has contracts totaling 30 million francs to be purchased and 14 million to be sold on March 1. What is the bank's exposure?

Answer: 16 million francs. (30 million minus 14 million)

To reduce its exposure, a bank may halt quotations in a currency on the bid or ask side until the exposure is reduced to an acceptable level.

Example: If the current exchange rate is 3fr/$1, what is the bank's exposure?

Answer: $5,333,333 (10,000,000 minus 4,666,667).

Example: If the exchange rate on March 1 is 2.9fr/$1, what is the bank's exposure?

Answer: $5,517,241 (10,344,827 minus 4,827,586)

Establishing Premiums or Discounts

When banks or monetary speculators quote forward exchange rates, they reflect both interest rate differentials and relative currency strength. Mechanically, they make use of two major elements.

1. **Future Exchange Rate.** This is the analyst's estimate of the spot rate that will exist on the maturity date of the contract. To forecast this rate, factors such as inflation, economic problems, and balance of payments surpluses or deficits must be considered.

2. **Interest Differentials.** This is an evaluation of the yields available on investments in the capital markets of each nation. Because of the variety of securities in mature domestic capital markets, it is difficult to assess the actual differentials. Should the analyst use the spreads on government bonds, institutional rates, private sector lending, or some other measure?

In spite of the difficulties, the bank will finally develop spot and forward quotes that reflect premiums or discounts. The rate to be quoted in the forward market may theoretically be calculated using a formula that includes the likely future exchange rate and an estimate of interest rate differentials. The future exchange rate for currencies A and B may be expressed as

$$FutRate(A)(B)$$

The interest rate differentials for currencies A and B may be expressed as

$$(Int(B)-Int(A))*(Days\ of\ contract/365)$$

The forward contract rate for A and B can be obtained by multiplying the future rate by the difference between one minus the differential.

Example: The spot rate between francs and pesetas is 2.4. The likely future exchange rate is 2.5 in 90 days. The franc can be invested for 90 days at an annual yield of 14 percent and the peseta at 9 percent. What is the forward rate that should be quoted?

Answer: 2.5308 as follows:

FutRate(Fr)(P)	2.5000
Int(Fr)	0.1400
Int(P)	0.0900
Days in Contract	90
Days in Year	365
Future Rate	2.5000
Differential	-0.0123
Forward Rate	2.5000*
	(1-(-0.0123))=2.5308

Bank's Profit on Foreign Exchange Contracts

The bank can cover its costs of writing foreign exchange contracts by adding a service charge to the price of the contract. As a general rule, this charge is reflected as a differential between the bid and the ask price. The rate calculated by the above formula will be bracketed; that is, the bid and ask rates will be quoted so that the bank receives a service charge on any forward contract it writes. The bank will buy currencies at slightly less than the formula rate; it will sell currencies at slightly more.

General Rules for Premiums or Discounts

Two general principles apply to premiums or discounts:

1. **High Yields Produce Discounts in Forward Markets.** If a currency can be invested at a high yield compared to other currencies, the high yield will push the currency toward a discount in forward markets. The high interest rates attract investors who seek forward contracts allowing a return to their own national currency. For the currencies to be in equilibrium, the high yield available when investing one currency must be offset by a discount on that currency in the forward market. For currencies of equal strength, a high yield is usually accompanied by a discount in the forward market.

2. **Currency Weakness Produces Discount in Forward Markets.** An expected decline in the purchasing power of a currency will push that currency toward a discount in forward markets. If interest rates are equal in two national capital markets, the forward market usually offers a discount for the weak currency and a premium for the strong currency.

ARBITRAGE IN FOREIGN EXCHANGE MARKETS

Arbitrage is defined as a situation in which a guaranteed and riskless profit can be made by simultaneously purchasing and selling a currency in one or more foreign exchange markets. Two types of arbitrage are common:

1. **Space Arbitrage.** In this situation, physical distance (space) separates the transactions from which the arbitrage originates. Space arbitrage occurs when a speculator executes simultaneous contracts to buy and sell currencies in two or more capital centers for delivery on the same day. The contracts can be executed in the spot market or forward market, but delivery must occur at the same time.

2. **Time Arbitrage.** This type of arbitrage occurs when an investor makes a riskless profit by executing a spot and forward contract to buy and sell a single currency. The arbitrage arises because the purchased currency is invested at a higher interest rate than is available with the currency that is sold. The forward contract guarantees the investor a return to the original currency. The higher interest provides the arbitrage profit in this kind of transaction.

Figures 8-3 and 8-4 present examples of space and time arbitrage.

WHY DO ARBITRAGE PROFITS OCCUR?

Arbitrage opportunities exist when the forward markets and interest differentials between currencies are in a state of disequilibrium. Figure 8-5 shows the trade off between interest differentials and discounts or premiums in the forward market.

In Figure 8-5, the equilibrium points occur where the interest rate differential is offset by the forward discount or premium. For example, when the dollar can earn 11 percent compared to the franc's 8 percent, equilibrium occurs when the dollar trades at a 3 percent discount in the forward market. If the discount is 2 percent, individuals sell francs for dollars in the spot market and invest the dollars at 11 percent. Simultaneously, they purchase a forward contract, losing 2 percent when they return to francs, but the 3 percent differential provides an arbitrage profit.

In practice, currencies are generally close to the equilibrium points, and limited arbitrage opportunities exist. But exist they do. As a result of inadequate communications, actions by governments to support currencies, and other factors, the fast-moving trader earns a good living on the arbitrage from foreign exchange transactions.

Hedging Foreign Currency Transactions

It is important to know the degree of risk arising from exchange rate fluctuations when dealing in foreign markets. What will be the profit if goods are sold at existing exchange rates? What will happen if exchange rates change between the date of the business contract and the delivery date of a foreign currency? Can the exchange rate risks be avoided at reasonable cost? These issues are covered in this section.

Hedging is the purchase or sale of foreign currencies for the sole purpose of avoiding potential losses stemming from changes in exchange rates. It is the opposite of speculation which involves the purchase or sale of a currency, usually on a forward basis, with the goal of making a profit on changes in rates of exchange.

Figure 8-3. Space Arbitrage.

Data	Zurich	Montreal
Spot Rate, Dollars/Sterling	1.9695	1.9694
90–Day Rate, Dollars/Sterling	1.9477	1.9512

Space Arbitrage Problem

A foreign exchange dealer in Paris is in electronic contact with banks in Zurich and Montreal. He or she executes simultaneous 90–day contracts to buy and sell sterling, purchasing 100,000 pounds in Zurich and selling 100,000 pounds in Montreal. To execute these transactions involves a $35 cost. At the delivery in 90 days, what will be the arbitrage profit?

Amount	100,000
Buy Rate	1.9477
Sell Rate	1.9512
Transactions Cost	35
Dollars to Be Received	195,120
Dollars to Be Delivered	(194,770)
Transactions Cost	(35)
Arbitrage Profit	315

Figure 8-4. Time Arbitrage.

Data	Zurich
Spot Rate, Dollars/Marks	0.3897
90–Day Rate, Dollars/Marks	0.4061

TIME ARBITRAGE PROBLEM

A dealer can borrow or invest dollars or marks at an 8 percent annual yield for a period of 90 days. She executes simultaneous contracts to buy $100,000 worth of marks in the spot market and sell 261,740 marks in the 90–day forward market. The transactions costs are $35. What will be the arbitrage profit?

Spot Amount	100,000
Buy Rate	0.3897
Sell Rate	0.4061
Interest Rate	0.0800
Days to Invest	90
Days in Year	365
Transactions Cost	35
Convert Dollars in Spot Market to Marks	256,608
Interest Received on Investment	5,062
Total Marks at End of Period	261,670
Convert Back to Dollars at End of Period	106,264
Interest on Original Dollar Loan	1,973
Amount Owed on Original Dollar Loan	101,973
Amount Received in Dollars	106,264
Amount Owed in Dollars	(101,973)
Transactions Costs	(35)
Arbitrage Profit	4,256

Figure 8-5. Equilibrium and Disequilibrium Conditions Between Dollars and Francs.

Interest Rates (U.S.)	Interest Rates (France)	Differential in Favor of Dollar	Forward Exchange Discount or Premium on Dollar Expressed as a Percent Per Annum						
			-3%	-2%	-1%	0	+1%	+2%	+3%
11%	8%	+3%	EQ.	$	$	$	$	$	$
10%	8%	+2%	fr.	EQ.	$	$	$	$	$
9%	8%	+1%	fr.	fr.	EQ.	$	$	$	$
8%	8%	0%	fr.	fr.	fr.	EQ.	$	$	$
7%	8%	-1%	fr.	fr.	fr.	fr.	EQ.	$	$
6%	8%	-2%	fr.	fr.	fr.	fr.	fr.	EQ.	$
5%	8%	-3%	fr.	fr.	fr.	fr.	fr.	fr.	EQ.

EQ.	=	equilibrium between dollars and francs.
fr.	=	conditions whereby individuals will convert dollars to francs to take advantage of arbitrage profit.
$	=	conditions whereby individuals will convert francs to dollars to take advantage of arbitrage profit.

The term *cover* is used synonymously with the term *hedge*. When an individual hedges a foreign exchange position, we say she has covered her exposure or that she has a covered position.

The most common method of hedging is to execute a forward contract to buy or sell a currency. This action "locks in" the rate of exchange and eliminates risk from changes in the spot market exchange rate between the two currencies. It is accomplished with a call to the international department of a large bank. Alternatively, a contract can be executed directly through the facilities of a Chicago, New York, or other futures exchange.

A second hedging method avoids the forward market completely. The individual or firm makes an immediate conversion of currencies in the spot market and then holds a currency until the delivery date of the business transaction. The details of the method, called the borrowing alternative, are discussed below.

The Hedging Decision

Two categories of transactions require a decision on hedging:

1. **Future Receipts of Foreign Currency**. When an individual or firm is due to receive a foreign currency at a future time, the firm may want to lock in the value of the receipt in terms of its domestic currency. Hedging allows the firm to do so.

2. **Future Payment of Foreign Currency.** In this reverse situation to future receipts an individual or firm has the obligation to pay a foreign currency at a future time. In order to lock in the amount to be paid in terms of the domestic currency, hedging may be used.

Hedging Alternatives

When an individual or business receives a foreign currency at some future date, three choices are available for dealing with foreign exchange risk:

1. **Full Exposure.** The individual can decide to do nothing until the foreign currency is delivered. At that time, the spot market will determine the value of the foreign currency in terms of the national currency. The individual will benefit if the foreign currency has increased in value since it will purchase more of his national currency. He will lose if the reverse has occurred.

2. **Forward Market Alternative.** The individual can execute a forward contract to sell the foreign currency on the date it is due to be delivered. The forward rate will be fixed and the position is fully covered.

3. **Borrowing Alternative.** The individual can borrow foreign currency today and convert it. The maturity date on the loan will be the same as the delivery date of the currency he is due to receive. When the currency is received in the future, it is used to pay the loan. If the amounts are calculated correctly, no exposure results since the foreign currency borrowed was converted in today's spot market.

If an individual owes a foreign currency to be delivered at some future date, she has three similar choices available. All six alternatives are outlined in Figure 8-6.

Hedging Calculations

The decision on how to deal with foreign exchange risk should be made after the costs of full exposure versus hedging are compared. One example of each situation is given in Figures 8-8 and 8-9.

The amount of the currency to be received or paid is calculated with each alternative shown in Figure 8-7. The firm then selects the largest figure if money is to be received or the smallest figure if it is to be paid.

In calculating the amount received or paid with the borrowing method, it does not matter whether the firm will actually pay or earn interest. The analyst must input a cost to money that is tied up or a return from money that is freed in order to perform a correct analysis.

Figure 8-6. Alternatives for Dealing with Foreign Exchange Risk.

When Receiving a Foreign Currency	*When a Foreign Currency is Owed*
1. Accept full exposure. When a foreign currency is actually received, convert it to the domestic currency in the spot market.	1. Accept full exposure. When the foreign currency is actually due, purchase it in the spot market with the domestic currency.
2. Forward market alternative. Execute contract to sell foreign currency for future delivery.	2. Forward market alternative. Execute contract to buy foreign currency at future date.
3. Borrowing alternative. Borrow foreign currency and convert it today. When foreign currency is received, use it to repay foreign currency loan.	3. Borrowing alternative. Borrow national currency today and convert it to foreign currency. When payment is due, deliver foreign currency.

Figure 8-7. Comparing Costs of Hedging.

Alternatives	*Measuring the Cost*
1. Full exposure	a. Estimate high, most likely, and low exchange rate on delivery date. b. Compare amount received at each rate. Use weighted average technique to determine value of alternative.
2. Forward contract	Calculate amount to be received or paid under terms of contract.
3. Borrowing	Use the following formula:

Amount Received = or Paid	Funds from Conversion at Spot Rate	−	Interest to Be Paid	+	Interest to Be Earned

Figure 8-8. Hedging Future Receipt of Foreign Currency.

Exchange Rates, Dollar/Peso

Spot Market	0.2234
90–day Forward Rate	0.2230
Forecast of Future Spot Rate	0.2294

Interest Rates

Borrow Dollars	0.1200
Invest Dollars	0.0900
Borrow Pesos	0.1600
Invest Pesos	0.1100

Other Data

Days in Period	90
Days in Year	365

FUTURE RECEIPTS PROBLEM

An exporter is due to receive 300,000 pesos in 90 days. An international bank forecasts that a spot rate of $0.2294 will exist in 90 days. Should the exporter hedge this transaction?

Answer: The highest value comes from full exposure. Whether this choice is the best one will depend on the exporter's view of risk. If he desires no risk, the forward market is better than the borrowing alternative.

Full Exposure — Value

Pesos	300,000	
Rate	0.2294	68,820

Forward Market

Pesos	300,000	
Rate	0.2230	66,900

Borrowing

Borrow Pesos today so the exporter will owe 300,000 pesos in 90 Days.

Future Pesos	300,000
Annual Rate	0.1600
Periodic Rate	0.0395
Amount to Borrow	
300,000/(1+.0395)	288,614

Convert in Spot Market

Present Pesos	288,614
Rate	0.2234
Present Dollars	64,476

Investment Value for 90 Days

Current Dollar Value	64,476	
Annual Rate	0.09	
Periodic Rate	0.0222	
Future Dollar Value		
64,476*(1 + .0222)		65,907

Figure 8-9. Hedging Future Delivery of Foreign Currency.

Future Delivery Problem

Using the same data as Figure 8-8, assume the exporter had to make a payment of 500,000 pesos in 90 days. Should the transaction be hedged?

Answer: The lowest cost occurs with the forward market alternative. Since this is better than full exposure, it appears to be the best choice.

Full Exposure		*Value*
Pesos	500,000	
Rate	0.2294	114,700

Forward Market		
Pesos	500,000	
Rate	0.2230	111,500

Borrowing

Borrow dollars today and convert immediately. Invest so 500,000 pesos will be available in 90 days.

Future Pesos	500,000
Investing Rate	0.1100
Periodic Rate	0.0271
Pesos Needed Today	
500,000/(1 + 0.0271)	486,796

Convert in Spot Market

Present Pesos	486,796
Rate	0.2234
Present Dollars	108,750

Cost of Borrowed Dollars

Dollars to Be Borrowed	108,750	
Interest Rate	0.12	
Periodic Rate	0.0296	
Future Value		
108,750*(1 + 0.0296)		111,969

The Hedging Decision—Hemley Shipping

As an example of making a hedging decision, let us consider the situation of Hemley Shipping Company. This firm specializes in exporting and importing for clients, including specialty shops and major department stores. Located in Norfolk, Virginia, the firm receives shipments from abroad and distributes them to U.S. customers. The firm also arranges to export U.S. goods to customers in Europe and North Africa.

One of Hemley's customers has agreed to ship textiles to Austria with 250,000 Austrian schillings as payment to be delivered in 90 days. The schillings will be paid with a draft on an Austrian bank in Vienna. The current exchange rate is $0.05435/Sch 1.

A second hedging alternative is to borrow 250,000 schillings in Vienna for 90 days at 16 percent. This could be arranged through Chase Manhattan at no cost to Hemley. After converting to dollars, the money could be invested in New York to net 12 percent annually for 90 days.

Hemley knows that its customer can also decide to accept full exposure on the money. Hemley's Richmond banker feels that a $0.054/Sch 1 rate is likely in 90 days (a 60 percent chance). He indicates a 10 percent chance of a $0.055/Sch 1 rate and a 30 percent chance of $.0525/Sch 1 rate.

Hemley knows that its customer wants a recommendation on how to handle the expected inflow of schillings. The firm analyzes the situation and forwards the letter reproduced in Figure 8-10 to the customer.

Figure 8-10. Letter from Hemley Shipping Company Evaluating Hedging Alternatives.

HEMLEY SHIPPING COMPANY
12 Orient Way

Norfolk, VA 23506

Cable: HEMCO

Larkin Brothers
2304 Pulaski Road
Baltimore, Maryland 21223

Sirs:

We have evaluated the 250,000 schillings due you in 90 days from Burtshafen A.G. as follows:

Full Exposure:	Using likely exchange rates quoted by our banker, we estimate a value of $13,425 for this alternative:

$$.10 \times \$.055/\text{Sch 1} \quad = \quad .0055$$
$$.60 \times .054/\text{Sch 1} \quad = \quad .0324$$
$$.30 \times .0525/\text{Sch 1} \quad = \quad \underline{.0158}$$
$$\phantom{.30 \times .0525/\text{Sch 1} \quad = \quad} .0537 \text{ weighted exchange rate}$$

.0537 X 250,000 schillings = $13,425

Forward Market:	At the rate quoted by our bank, you will be guaranteed $13,578.

.05431 X 250,000 schillings = $13,578

Borrowing:	We can arrange to borrow schillings in Vienna which can be converted immediately to dollars. When the loan matures in 90 days, we will repay it with the 250,000 schillings. The dollars must be left on deposit in New York at 12 percent as collateral for the loan. The schillings would cost 16 percent. This alternative provides you with $13,458, as follows:

(1) 16 percent annually is .0395 over 90 days. We would borrow 240,500 schillings. In 90 days, we will owe 250,000 and can repay it.
(240,500 principal + 9,500 interest = 250,000)

(2) Convert 240,500 at spot rate
240,500 X .05435 = $13,071

(3) Invest $13,071 at 12 percent for 90 days = $387 interest

(4) Total received = $13,071 + 387 = $13,458

We recommend that you authorize us to arrange a forward contract since the $13,578 from this alternative is the highest value and it is fully protected against foreign exchange loss. Please advise.

Hemley Shipping Company

GUIDELINES ON WHEN TO HEDGE

As the firm considers hedging, some guidelines may prove useful:

1. **Knowledge of Market.** The firm usually has a solid knowledge of the market for its products, but it may not understand the market for foreign exchange. Unless it has excellent knowledge of capital markets, or unless its bank provides such knowledge, the firm generally will seek to hedge its transactions.

2. **Frequency of Hedging the Specific Currency.** Major currencies are involved in frequent hedging and speculating transactions, and the cost of hedging may be nominal. Hedging of weak currencies, however, may not be practical because with high risk few speculators are willing to offer forward contracts. The cost of hedging these currencies may be so high as to offset the return from currency fluctuations. Unless a currency has an active forward market, it will be difficult and costly to hedge it.

3. **Risk Reference.** Every business firm has its own policies toward risk. Some firms are willing to accept foreign exchange exposure, whereas others are not. If a firm is willing to accept this kind of risk, it may profit from doing so. At the same time, it must be prepared to lose if the currencies move the wrong way.

4. **Size of Transactions.** A firm may be willing to remain exposed on relatively small transactions when the risk of loss will not have a serious impact on its resources. Large transactions, on the other hand, may be hedged because a mistake in judgment could prove disastrous.

5. **Number of Transactions.** If a firm conducts many small transactions involving a variety of currencies, it may be willing to ignore hedging techniques. Gains in one currency will be offset by losses in another so the firm is diversifying and thus reducing its risk. If all of a firm's transactions involve the same foreign currency, hedging may be attractive.

HEDGING WITH ORGANIZED EXCHANGES

In addition to hedging in the forward market, investors and speculators have two alternative means that will minimize exposure on foreign exchange transactions. These are foreign exchange futures and currency options, which are futures contracts on organized exchanges. In this section, we will cover hedging with standardized contracts.

Foreign Exchange Futures

A foreign exchange futures contract is a forward market contract executed on an organized exchange. The two largest such exchanges are the International Monetary Market (IMM) in Chicago and the London International Financial Futures Exchange (LIFFE) in England. The primary characteristics of foreign exchange futures contracts are as follows:

1. **Contractual Obligation.** The purchaser agrees to buy or sell a fixed amount of a currency under terms stipulated in a contract, just as in the case of a forward market contract. The obligation under the law is identical for both agreements.

2. **Standard–Sized Contracts.** In the forward market, a party can arrange for a contract of any size. Thus, if an individual is due to receive 300,000 Swiss francs, a contract can be written in this amount. A futures contract, on the other hand, is available only in standardized amounts. As examples, the contract for Swiss francs may be available only in the amount of 125,000 francs. Similarly, the standard contract for yen might be 12.5 million yen.

3. **Limited Range of Currencies.** Futures contracts are available in a limited range of currencies. These are generally the major currencies that are used to finance world trade. The U.S. dollar is the common denominator of most contracts. Commonly quoted currencies are the pound sterling, deutschemark, Japanese yen, and Swiss and French francs.

4. **Standard Delivery Date.** The actual exchange of currencies under a futures contract must take place on a fixed future date that is identical for all contracts expiring in that month. Thus, all October contracts for Swiss francs on the IMM would be terminated on, say, the third Wednesday of October.

5. **Open Trading and Liquidity.** The purchase of a futures contract occurs in a public setting in which transactions are immediately known to interested parties. The public trading also provides liquidity. If an individual no longer wishes to hold a contract, it can be sold prior to maturity on the floor of the appropriate exchange.

6. **Security Deposits.** All organized exchanges require a margin deposit to guarantee performance under the terms of the futures contract. The size of the security deposit is initially set by the exchange. This margin deposit will vary with the degree of volatility of the currency. After the contract is purchased, additional deposits will be required if the currency being sold declines significantly in value. The goal of the exchange is to ensure that all contractual obligations will be met at maturity.

Use of Futures Contract

To illustrate the use of a futures contract, consider an exporter who has sold goods for which he will be paid in francs in December. The amounts are 600,000, 900,000, 700,000, and 800,000 francs. The current spot rate is 3.75fr/$1. A futures contract is available on the IMM to sell 1 million francs on the third Wednesday of December at the current spot rate. No commissions are involved. Assume that the exporter executes three futures contracts total 3 million francs, the amount he is due to receive. If the four transactions occur at a spot rate of 3.8, on the third Wednesday in December, what is the net dollar position of the exporter after all transactions are covered?

The answer will be that the profit on the futures contract will offset the devaluation of francs during the period. The steps are as follows:

1. **Acceptance of Francs in Payment for Goods.** The exporter will receive $789,474 from accepting the francs and converting them in the spot market at 3.80.

FRANCS RECEIVED	SPOT RATE	DOLLARS RECEIVED
600,000	3.80	157,895
900,000	3.80	236,842
700,000	3.80	184,211
800,000	3.80	210,526
	Total	789,474

2. **Execution of the Futures Contracts.** The exporter will execute the three futures contracts and immediately reverse the transactions in the spot market, producing a gain of $10,526.

	Francs	Rate	Dollars
Sell Francs under Contract	3,000,000	3.75	
Dollars Gained			$800,000
Buy Francs in Spot Market			
Dollars Needed			789,474
Profit on Futures Contract			$10,526

The original expectation was 3 million/3.75, or $800,000. The amount received is $789,474 plus $10,526 or $800,000. The profits on the contracts offset the exposure, just as is the case with a forward contract.

This example is highly stylized. It is unlikely that the futures rate would be the same as the spot rate. Still, this shows the goal of using a futures contract to minimize foreign exchange exposure.

Currency Options

A currency option is the right to buy or sell a fixed amount of currency at a stated exchange rate in a given time period. The buyer of the option has the right to make the purchase or sale but is not required to do so.

Currency options are similar in many ways to futures contracts. They are traded on organized exchanges, such as the Philadelphia Stock Exchange, the IMM, and the European Options Exchange (EOE). They trade in standard-sized contracts, such as 62,500 deutschemarks or 125,000 French francs. They have standardized termination dates, such as the last day of a month.

Currency options are available in the major trading currencies and are expressed in terms of puts or calls. A **put** is the right to sell a currency, whereas, a **call** is the right to purchase it. The exchange rate identified in the contract is the exercise price.

A currency option differs from a futures contract in several important ways:

1. **It Costs Money**. The purchaser pays a premium or fee that can be as much as 2 to 4 percent of the face value of the contract. For this fee, the purchaser gets an assurance that the exchange rate is fixed.

2. **It Acts Like an Insurance Policy**. The options contract protects against downside loss. For example, consider a call contract to purchase marks. If marks rise in value, making them more expensive in the spot market, the holder of the option can use it to purchase marks at a lower price.

3. **It Offers Upside Benefits**. An options contract allows the holder to make profits if the currency improves. With the call option to purchase marks, suppose marks decline in value. The individual can purchase the needed marks in the spot market at a lower rate than previously. In this case, the option contract will expire without being exercised.

Currency Option Example–The Put

An exporter will receive 500,000 francs in 90 days. The spot rate is 6fr/$1. A currency option standard contract for 90 days is 125,000 francs. Such a contract is available with an exercise exchange rate of 6/1. The cost is 2 percent of the face value. Assume that the exporter purchases four contracts to sell francs. Further assume that the spot rate in 90 days is (a) 6.2fr/$1, (b) 6.0fr/$1, and (c) 5.8fr/$1. What will happen in each situation?

Answer:　　In each case, the exporter pays a 2 percent premium on the 500,000, or 10,000 francs. Then, in 90 days the following will happen with each spot rate

At 6.2fr/$1:

The exporter will exercise the options, selling 500,000 francs at 6.00 to yield $83,333.

At 6.0fr/$1:

The exporter can go either way. The rate in the spot market is identical to the rate of the option. In either case, the exporter will convert 500,000 francs at 6.00 to yield $83,333.

At 5.8fr/$1:

The exporter will allow the option to expire unexercised. The 500,000 francs will be converted in the spot market at 5.80 to yield $86,207.

Since the 10,000 franc premium has an approximate value of $1,700, in each case the cost should be deducted to arrive at a net profit. Still, if the franc had moved to 6.20, the 500,000 francs would have converted in the spot market at 80,645. With the option, the lowest possible receipt is 83,333 minus 1,700, or 81,633.

Currency Option Example–The Call

An importer must pay 500,000 francs in 90 days. The spot rate is 6fr/$1. A currency option standard contract for 90 days is 125,000 francs. Such a contract is available with an exercise exchange rate of 6/1. The cost is 2 percent of the face value. Assume that the importer purchases four contracts to buy francs. Further assume that the spot rate in 90 days is (a) 6.2fr/$1, (b) 6.0fr/$1, and (c) 5.8fr/$1. What will happen in each situation?

Answer:　　Once again, the purchaser pays a 2 percent premium on the 500,000, or 10,000 francs. Then, in 90 days the importer will do the following, depending on the spot market

At 6.2fr/$1:

The importer will let the options expire. He will purchase 500,000 francs at 6.20, and pay $80,645.

At 6.0fr/$1:

The importer can go either way. The rate in the spot market is identical to the rate of the option. In either case, the importer will purchase 500,000 francs at 6.00 and pay $83,333.

At 5.8fr/$1:

The importer will exercise the option. The 500,000 francs will be purchased at the option price of 6.20 and the importer will pay $80,645.

Since the 10,000 franc premium has an approximate value of $1,700, the net profit in each case should deduct the cost.

Still, if the franc had moved to 5.80, the 500,000 francs would have cost $86,207 in the spot market. With the option, the highest possible payout is ($83,333 + $1,700) or $85,033.

FOREIGN EXCHANGE RESTRICTIONS

All of the aforementioned hedging techniques assume free trade and exchange agreements. However, this situation exists with a minority of the world's nations. The major industrial countries have maintained exchange arrangements under which rates have floated freely according to the market. It is the smaller, developing nations that have tried to protect their economy through tight exchange restrictions. However, in recent years, the trend has been to relax these restrictions. For example, it was not until 1985 that New Zealand, the Dominican Republic, Jamaica, the Philippines, Uganda, and Zaire adopted market-determined floating exchange rates for their currencies. The reason for existing exchange restrictions lies either in the political arena or in the fact that these are poor and underdeveloped countries. For the most part, they owe a substantial debt to the International Monetary Fund (IMF) and the countries that belong to that organization. The IMF provides that fund members have the right to maintain exchange arrangements of their choice. Countries that do not have floating exchange rates usually have their rates **pegged** to another currency or collection of currencies. That is, their rates fluctuate with the currency to which it is pegged.

Some typical trade restrictions concern the amount of money that citizens may take out of a country, money that foreign nationals may transfer from the country, and payments made to nonresidents. Among the industrial countries, France has just recently lifted its ban on residents' use of credit cards abroad. The following is an example of one country's exchange arrangements in the 1980s.

Tunisia

The currency of Tunisia is the Tunisian dinar. The exchange value follows a combination of currencies, and the Central Bank of Tunisia fixes the buying and selling rates of foreign currencies daily. Settlements between Tunisia and foreign countries are made in convertible currencies as quoted by the Central Bank. (The U.S. dollar is an approved currency.)

Tunisia allows foreign accounts in convertible dinars by all nonresidents regardless of nationality. These accounts may be debited freely for any payment within Tunisia. Tunisia allows the transfer of dinars to a foreign account or the purchase of foreign currency without preauthorization. It also allows capital accounts to be opened in the name of any resident. However, nonresidents must get permission from the Central Bank. Only 100 dinars per person may be used per week for living expenses from these accounts, an allocation that cannot exceed 2,000 dinars per year. Nonresident foreign enterprises holding contracts in Tunisia may open, for each contract, a single special account in dinars for deposit of the contract price to cover local expenses. Any transfer from such accounts must be authorized by the Central Bank of Tunisia. Persons who have lived and worked in Tunisia as foreign nationals and left Tunisia permanently after December 1978 are entitled to transfer out only 50 percent of their assets up to a ceiling of 15,000 dinars.

The importance of any regulation concerning a currency to be dealt with should seem apparent. Although this text appears to give the impression of free trade and exchange, in many areas they are not allowed.

TAURUS ASIAN PRODUCTS: HEDGING DECISION CASE

The Taurus Asian Products Company is located in a small set of offices on Broadway in downtown New York City. The company specializes in the marketing and distribution of rubber and rubber-based products on a world-wide basis. It acts in the capacity of either a broker or a dealer in matching demand for these products with available supplies.

The traditional source of supplies for Taurus has been a consortium of plantations in Malaysia which operate out of offices in Singapore. The consortium is controlled largely by several Chinese entrepreneurs who have an excellent record for integrity and reliability. In recent years, Taurus has been diversifying its sources of supply, and it now conducts business with other nations and with major chemical companies that have been developing synthetic-rubber products.

Most of Taurus's customers are located in the United States, Great Britain, and the other Common Market countries. Worldwide communications are maintained through cables and telephone lines. In recent years, the company has been attempting to develop customer relations with the Japanese. John Robertson, vice–president of Taurus Asian Products, recently returned from a visit to Kyoto and Tokyo in an effort to develop some business. While in Kyoto, he successfully negotiated an order for a shipment from Malaysia to Japan. The effective date of the contract was September 9, and the Hibachi Corporation was due to pay Taurus 451.6 million yen 90 days from that date.

By the time Robertson returned from Japan, Taurus had already arranged the shipment of the products from Malaysia to Japan with an approximate arrival date of December 7. Allowing two days for inspection of the product, Taurus would be required to pay the Malaysian/Chinese Consortium Limited 15 million Hong Kong dollars on December 9. This was a new development for Taurus, and Robertson questioned it. Traditionally, payments in Malaysia were made in U.S. dollars. Now, it appears that the Chinese prefer the Hong Kong currency to U.S. dollars, possibly because they feel that the Hong Kong dollar is stronger and possibly because of some local political considerations.

Robertson called in Morrie Sigel, the firm's treasurer, and asked him for a recommendation on the financing for this transaction. As a general guideline, John expressed an interest in hedging the transaction unless a significant profit potential was available from accepting an exposed position.

Sigel began to collect data and he learned the following from a call to Citibank:

1. The spot rate HK/U.S. dollars was 6.8HK/$1.
2. The 90–day forward rate to buy or sell was 6.7HK/$1.

3. The spot rate Japanese yen to U.S. dollars was $1/150.

4. The forward rate 90 days to buy or sell was $1/145.

He also learned that the bank was forecasting a 40 percent chance of a rate of 6.75HK/$1 and a 60 percent chance of 6.7HK/$1. For the Japanese currency, the bank was forecasting a 50 percent chance of $1/155 and a 50 percent chance of $1/140.

Just as he was learning these figures, a member of Sigel's staff brought in some cost data. He told Sigel that Taurus could borrow Hong Kong dollars at an 11 percent annual rate, U.S. dollars at 9 percent, and yen at 7 percent. Similarly, the company could invest Hong Kong dollars at 8 percent, U.S. dollars at 7 percent, and yen at 6 percent.

Required: What course of action should the treasurer recommend to maximize the return on this transaction?

FIELDING OFFSHORE FUNDS CASE—CREDIT SWAPS

Fielding Offshore Funds is a Bahamian company with offices in Nassau and Freeport in the Bahamas. The company was founded by a syndicate of wealthy U.S. investors with a goal of sheltering foreign-source earnings arising from a variety of financing and business transactions. The firm originally employed $400,000 of capital along with $1.3 million of borrowed Eurodollars to finance construction projects in Central America. The results were profitable, as well as satisfactory, to local businesspeople who sought additional and larger financings. Thus, Fielding became a financial "broker" for entrepreneurs seeking funds and investors with excess capital.

In the mid-1970s, Fielding hired Dave Garnett, a former Citibank vice-president, to be its managing director. Garnett began to carve out a role for Fielding in the area of credit swaps and currency exchanges. A **credit swap** is an exchange of currencies between parties in different countries, with the objective of avoiding the purchase of a weak currency with a hard currency. As an example, a German company may need Turkish lira (a weak currency) to finance its operations in Turkey but may not want to pay for them with deutschemarks (a strong currency). A credit swap would be useful in this case. The German company would deposit marks in a European branch of a Turkish bank (or the European office of any bank operating in Turkey). The Turkish bank would lend lira to the local operating unit in Turkey. At the end of the agreed on period, the operating unit would repay the lira with interest and the German firm would take back its marks.

Dave Garnett knew that a credit swap avoided certain foreign exchange risks. For one thing, a devaluation of the weak currency would have minimal impact on the firm. If lira, as an example, are borrowed, lira are repaid, so both the loan and the holding of currency would be devalued simultaneously. If marks had been converted to lira, only the holding would be reduced by the devaluation of the lira. A second advantage to a swap is that currency blockages or restrictions are avoided. If the firm had converted marks and invested them, any later government restrictions on converting lira would have blocked the firm's funds. These dangers are eliminated in a credit swap.

Garnett also knew some of the disadvantages of a credit swap. For one thing, the exchange rate is usually not as good as the spot rate. As an example, the spot rate may be ten units of the local currency to one deutschemark; the swap rate might be eight units to the mark. (This rate will also hold when the currencies are swapped back at the end of the swap period.) Thus, more marks are tied up with a swap than would be the case with a spot conversion. Another disadvantage is the interest that will be charged on the local currency. While the deutschemarks sit idle and earn no interest in most swap arrangements, the lira will require the payment of interest (payable in lira, of course). A third drawback is that the swap only protects the principal; any local currency earnings are not covered.

Garnett utilized his New York City contacts to locate firms with foreign currency excess and shortage positions. He developed a computerbased system of matching companies with apparent needs in different currencies and companies with excess positions in those currencies. A telephone call or cable frequently led to a series of negotiations that produced a credit swap with no Fielding funds involved. As might be expected, Garnett would charge a fee for Fielding's services. In some cases, Fielding would put its own money into the swap and still charge the fee.

It was late autumn in New York when Dave was first approached by Charles Daniels of the Daniels-Wilson Investment Company (DWIC). At infrequent intervals, the **Wall Street Journal** reported DWIC dealings in oil and gas exploration activities in Mexico. Daniels was looking for partners in an absolutely riskless venture involving a loan to Pemex, the state-owned and–operated oil company. The deal was simple. The government was building a facility to capture petroleum and natural gas from a small, new producing oil–field. Permanent financing would be in place in one year. In the meantime, DWIC was seeking 110 million pesos to finance the infrastructure portions of the facility, particularly a loading/unloading dock, supporting warehouses, and hard-surface roadways. The pesos would have to be delivered on December 1 and they would be returned the following November 30th with 24 percent interest. Daniels indicated that DWIC wanted Fielding to handle the details and Garnett would have 10 days to put the deal together.

It took less than two days to find an investor. Information Systems Inc. of Houston, Texas, was looking to place between $5 and $10 million for one year in a high–return foreign investment. Information Systems indicated that a credit swap would be equally acceptable, but it made one point clear. The firm could earn 10 percent on its money in the United States. It would have to do better than this abroad before it would commit any funds. This would be hard to accomplish with a credit swap since the interest on the local currency would be 8 percent. At that point, Dave had an idea. He knew some people at the **National Fananciera** (NAFINSA), the Mexican development bank, and from them he learned that Fielding itself could borrow pesos in Mexico City and invest them in the venture. The money would involve a 20 percent annual interest, but this might be acceptable. Garnett figured his commission at $100,000 (from the profits of Information Systems) if he put the deal together for Information Systems. Perhaps he could do better by investing for Fielding.

Garnett had two concerns. He dealt with the first by checking DWIC's credit. He found no problem there: a double-A rating and an eight-figure line of credit from three New York banks. His second concern was the possibility that the new peso would be devalued. The spot rate was 21P/$1, but many analysts were predicting a move to 24P/$1 by the end of the next year. This forecast reflected a concern with overspending, even as Mexico's longer term prospects looked good. Not all analysts agreed, however, with this estimate. Some were forecasting a stable rate for two years or more. A credit swap could be put together only at a rate of 15P/$1. This was another large burden for the swap arrangement.

Garnett began to analyze three possibilities: an unhedged deal a credit swap or a loan of pesos. Dave decided in advance to take the best deal for Fielding, no matter which one, if a profit could be made.

Required: Analyze the possibilities and prepare a recommendation considering the effects of possible devaluation of the peso.

IV.

Analyzing Working Capital

9

Cash Flow Analysis

FINANCIAL STATEMENTS

In order to understand a firm's cash flow, we must begin with the financial statement. Different statements are prepared to achieve certain goals and provide varied information. An analyst who knows the purposes and characteristics of each kind of statement will be able to use it to gain information concerning the status of a company.

A **financial statement** is a collection of data prepared according to logical and consistent accounting procedures. It is designed to convey information concerning the financial aspects of a business. A statement may show a position at a moment in time, as with a balance sheet. It may show a series of activities over a period of time, as with an income statement. Such statements are employed by firms to present their financial situation to interested parties. Thus, extensive financial statements are included in annual reports, which are widely distributed by the major corporations.

Proper preparation and use of financial statements require an understanding of financial terminology. To avoid misunderstanding in this book, we will define important terms and provide descriptive material with respect to financial statements. In this chapter we focus on three important financial statements: the balance sheet, the income statement, and the flow of funds statement.

Cash Funds and Working–Capital

Terms such as funds and working–capital have many meanings, from the broad to the very restricted. When working with these terms in a business environment, the analyst should ensure that the precise meaning is understood. We will use the following definitions:

1. **Cash**. This term will refer to both cash and near cash items. Examples of near–cash items are monies deposited in checking or savings accounts or in money market funds where the money can be retrieved in less than one day without significant penalties.

2. **Funds.** This will refer to the firm's current assets.

3. **Working–Capital.** This will be synonymous with current assets.

4. **Net Working–Capital.** This will be the excess of current assets over current liabilities. As such, net working–capital will be an important measure of the firm's liquidity.

5. **Assets.** This will refer to the firm's total financial resources; that is, current and long–term assets as reported on a balance sheet.

Income and Profit

Precision is also needed with respect to the terms *income* and *profit*, as follows:

1. **Profit.** This general term indicates that a firm is making more money than it spends. If a firm purchases an item for $10 and sells it for $15, we will say that it made a profit of $5 on the sale.

2. **Income.** This term is used to refer to the firm's profit when such a profit is calculated following accounting procedures. It may be on a before-tax basis, as in the case of earnings before interest and taxes, or it may be on an after–taxes–basis, as in the case of net income.

The distinction between income and working–capital is important to an understanding of working–capital management. A firm cannot pay its bills or repay its loans with income or profit. Cash is needed. A high level of income is important as an indicator that the firm will be able to generate sufficient working–capital for its liquidity needs. At the same time, if the firm invests its cash in new machinery or other fixed assets, it will lack the funds to meet its current obligations. This may be true for a firm that reports high profits. A reverse situation may be true for a firm with a low level of income. Even though it is not profitable, it may be able to acquire funds through borrowing, selling common stock, or selling its fixed assets. Because income and working–capital have different implications for the firm, working–capital management requires an understanding of both liquidity and profitability.

BALANCE SHEET

The **balance sheet** is a financial statement that shows assets, liabilities, and equity for the firm as of a specific date, usually at the close of the last day of a month or fiscal year. It shows how the resources of the firm (assets) are provided by capital from creditors (liabilities) and owners (equity). It is one of the most important financial statements used to evaluate a firm's cash flow.

Balance sheets are written in two columns, illustrating the relationship between the assets and sources of the assets. Assets are displayed in a left–hand column, whereas, liabilities and equity are displayed in a right hand column. In this sense, the assets are balanced by the sources of debt and equity— hence, the term *balance sheet.*

The distinction between resources to conduct business and the historical sources of those assets is important. It should be carefully noted that the liability or equity accounts contain no resources. They show how the firm is able to finance its assets. They do not represent cash or working–capital that the firm can use to conduct operations.

Each of the three major sections on a balance sheet can be divided into subsections. Numerous accounts may be listed, depending on such factors as the nature of the firm's business, the kind of assets it owns, and the sources of its assets. We will cover some important representative accounts.

Current Assets

Current assets are all the resources that will be converted into cash within the current accounting period or within the next year. These include cash, accounts receivables, and inventories:

1. **Cash**. This term has already been defined as cash or near cash items. A worldwide network of banks and currencies dealers is available so that cash may be invested for short periods of time, yet still be ready when needed to finance operations.

2. **Accounts Receivable**. When a firm makes a sale on credit, it collects money from the purchaser at some future date. The right to collect this money is shown on the balance as an account receivable. If the firm has a credit policy that goods must be paid in 30 days from the date of purchase, the bulk of receivables will be converted to cash sometime within the next 30 days. Since few firms use credit terms longer than 60 days, receivables are considered to be highly liquid.

3. **Inventories**. These are the goods held by the firm, either for further processing or for eventual resale. They may consist of raw materials or work in process, which are not yet ready for sale. They may also consist of finished goods that are ready to be sold. Inventories are carried on the balance sheet at their cost, as determined by the purchase price or by cost accounting procedures. Inventories are less liquid than receivables because they are one additional step away from being converted to cash. First, inventories must be sold, which creates a receivable; then, the receivable must be collected.

Fixed Assets

A **fixed asset** consists of resources used to generate revenues. These assets will not be converted into cash in the current accounting period unless they are damaged, become obsolete, or are otherwise replaced. Representative fixed assets include plant and equipment, machinery, real estate, and intangible assets:

When fixed assets are purchased, no expenses are recorded. As an example, the exchange of cash for a piece of machinery is an exchange of one asset for another. In order to receive credit for the wearing out of the asset as it is being used, the firm records depreciation. The sum of such depreciation over the years is recorded in an account called **accumulated depreciation**, which is maintained in the books of the firm. Plant and equipment, machinery, or other assets which may be depreciated will be shown using one of two conventional formats.

1. **Separate Lines**. A first line will show the original cost of the fixed asset as of the day it was purchased. The second line will show the accumulated depreciation recorded against the fixed asset. As an example, consider a firm that has fixed assets that cost $12 million, with accumulated depreciation representing $4 million. The balance entry would be:

Fixed Assets	$12,000,000
Less Accumulated Depreciation	($4,000,000)

2. **Net Book Value**. The second common method of showing assets that have been depreciated is to use a single entry to show the net book value. Fixed assets with an original cost of $12 million and accumulated depreciation of $4 million may be shown:

Fixed Assets	$8,000,000

Separating the original cost and accumulated depreciation offers more information to the user of the balance sheet. By using net book value alone, the firm may retain the outdated plan and equipment. For example, a firm could have $40 million of fixed assets at original cost with $32 million accumulated depreciation. The net book value method would show $8 million. This would be the same as the firm in our example above, even though the two firms would be quite different. The one firm would have a smaller amount of fixed assets, but apparently they would be much newer since they have only been depreciated to two-thirds of their original cost. The other firm's assets have been depreciated to 20 percent of original cost. If the analyst had a need to know the relative age and amount of fixed assets, the first method would be more useful.

Current Liabilities

Current liabilities are the debts of the firm that must be paid during the current accounting period, normally one year. They may consist of money that the firm has actually borrowed for a short period of time. Current liabilities may also consist of certain assets that have been received, even though payment has not yet been made for them. Examples are accounts payable, wages payable, and short–term notes payable:

1. **Accounts Payable**. When a firm makes a purchase on credit, it incurs an obligation to pay for the goods according to the terms given by the seller. Until the cash is paid for the goods the obligation to pay is recorded in accounts payable.

2. **Wages Payable**. If, at the end of an accounting period, the firm owes salaries or wages to any of its employees, the amount is shown in the account.

3. **Short–Term Notes Payable**. Sometimes the firm will borrow money by signing a promise to repay the loan at a future date.

Long–Term Liabilities

Long–term liabilities are debts that are not scheduled to be paid off during the next year. Examples are as follows:

1. **Notes Payable**. These are promissory notes with maturities in excess of one year. When an accounting period closes and the maturity is less than one year, the note will be transferred to current liabilities.

2. **Unsecured Long–Term Debt**. This debt contains general obligations of the firm not secured by a pledge of specific collateral. A common example is a debenture, which is a bond that is generally sold to the general public. The balance sheet may list bonds and other unsecured long–term debt separately by major item or in total.

3. **Secured Long–Term Financing**. When a firm borrows money long–term and pledges real estate or a capital asset as collateral, the debt will be shown in this category. Some secured financings are also called mortgages or secured bonds.

Equity

Equity accounts reflect ownership rights in a company and arise from several sources. Owners purchase stock, either through an initial offering or later sales, and give money to the firm in return for ownership claims. In some cases, the founders retain stock as compensation for opening the business. Once the firm is in operation, profits may be retained and reinvested. These retentions increase the ownership claims of stockholders.

In managing cash flows, it is important to remember that equity does not represent money held by the firm. When looking for cash, we look at the asset side of the balance sheet. When looking for the sources of cash and other assets, we look to liabilities and equity. The equity section shows the portion of assets financed by owners directly and by the retention of profits from prior periods. The balance of the assets are financed by debt.

Some common equity accounts are preferred stock, common stock, and retained earnings:

1. **Preferred Stock**. These shares have been issued with a preference on claims to profits and assets. That is, shareholders of this type of stock receive dividends before common shareholders. In the event of liquidation of the firm, they are paid off before common shareholders. Preferred stock commonly has a par value and a fixed dividend rate. For example, a firm may have 1 million shares of $100 par preferred stock with an indicated dividend of 12 percent. The balance sheet will show $100 million as the value of the stock (1 million shares times $100), and the dividend per share will be $12.

2. **Common Stock**. The primary ownership rights in a corporation accrue to the holders of common stock. Frequently, the balance sheet shows two accounts for capital contributed by common shareholders. The common stock account shows the number of shares times the par value. Par value represents the price at which the stock was issued. Contributed capital in excess of par (also called premium, surplus, and other names) will show any dollars contributed by owners in excess of par values. As an example, if a firm issues 500,000 shares of common stock with a $1 par value and sells it for $10 per share, the accounts will show:

Common stock ($1 par)	500,000
Contributed capital in excess of par	9,500,000

3. **Retained Earnings**. This account shows profits earned in prior periods and not distributed to shareholders as dividends. When the firm reports a net income after taxes that is larger than the period's cash dividends, it increases its retained earnings. As a result, the firm can finance expansion without having to borrow or sell additional stock. For example, if a firm earns $12 million after taxes and declares dividends of $8 million, it will increase its retained earnings by $4 million.

When working with the equity section of a balance sheet, we often refer to the book value per share of common stock. This represents a claim against common stock, contributed capital, and retained earnings, and is an estimate of the equity per share. As an example, consider a firm with the following:

Common Stock ($1 par, 400,000 shares)	400,000
Contributed Capital	2,800,000
Retained Earnings	8,000,000
TOTAL EQUITY	11,200,000

The book value per share would be $28 (11.2 million/400,000).

Account Titles and Arrangements

Individual balance sheets vary a great deal and will show a variety of accounts, including those listed above. Whatever the titles, the analyst must be thoroughly acquainted with the kinds of accounts appearing on the balance sheet. The analyst frequently works with a spreadsheet model that uses a set of titles that do not match the financial statement. The task is to correctly translate the titles into the spreadsheet format. As an example, suppose the spreadsheet model uses the following titles:

Accounts Payable

Other Payables

Short–Term Notes

Accrued Short–Term Liabilities

Current Portion of Long–Term Debt

Suppose the balance sheet shows the following accounts:

Trade Payables	600,000
Taxes Payable	120,000
Wages Payable	75,000
Bank Notes	1,200,000
Finance Company Notes	500,000
Total Current Liabilities	2,495,000

Because the spreadsheet model makes use of different account titles, the analyst must convert the balance sheet accounts. The trade payables are, in fact, accounts payable. The taxes and wages payables are other payables. Bank notes and finance company notes are short–term notes. The balance sheet shows no accrued short–term liabilities or current portion of long–term debt. The spreadsheet entries would be

Accounts Payable	600,000
Other Payables	195,000
Short–Term Notes	1,700,000
Accrued Short–Term Liabilities	0
Current Portion of Long–Term Debt	0

Uses of the Balance Sheet

A major use of the balance sheet is to provide a momentary picture of the firm's financial condition. It shows the balances in permanent accounts and the results of all accounting transactions since the first day of operation. If the company makes money and has retained profits, the balance sheet will show assets financed by equity. If the firm has borrowed to finance expansion, the mixture of debt and equity will reflect the assets financed by debt. If the firm is financing a major portion of its assets with short-term sources of funds, this too will be reflected. In a working-capital context, the balance sheet contains considerable information on the firm's resources and how they are currently financed.

A second use of the balance sheet is to allow comparisons, as follows:

1. **Over Time.** A **comparative balance sheet** displays the current balances and prior year's balances for each account in two columns. An analyst can compare the beginning and end of year positions and measure changes in each account during the year.

2. **Between Firms.** An analyst may want to compare the liquidity, profitability, or sources of financing among two or more firms.

3. **Against Norms.** A <u>norm</u> is a standard or reference that may be used to measure performance. Many financial firms and data services publish financial norms that allow comparisons with other firms. An example might be the average level of working-capital compared to total assets for all firms in an industry. If the firm under study exceeds the average, one conclusion might be drawn. If it is below the average, another conclusion is appropriate.

A third use of the balance sheet is to measure the risk from debt financing. Short-term debt must be paid in the near future and is viewed as being riskier than long-term debt. Equity does not have to be repaid at all, so it offers safer financing than debt. If the firm has a small amount of liquid assets and high current liabilities, it may be in danger of defaulting on its bills. These and similar measures reflect the risk offered by the mix of debt and equity securities on the balance sheet.

As we use the balance sheet, we should recognize some of its limitations. One is that it shows the accounting rather than the market values of assets. A $12 million plant and equipment account on the balance sheet might be worth many times that amount in real value. Or it might be worth a lot less. Although the analyst must be careful, this is not as serious as it might seem in many cases. Most firms follow similar procedures in preparing their financial statements. Once the statements have been audited and certified by a certified public accountant, the analyst knows that the firm is presenting a statement that conforms to generally accepted accounting procedures. The balance sheet cannot be used to learn market values, but many liquidity and other analyses can be made with a reasonable level of confidence.

A second limitation is that the balance sheet does not show the events or activities that resulted in the displayed balances. Nor does it show assumptions. Although many accounting methods are standard, some variance is permitted. One example is depreciation, where the method chosen can greatly change reported asset values. A second example involves reported profits, which affect equity. If a firm overstates profits on the income statement, these will be reflected as increased asset values and equity. Assumptions as to when expense obligations have been incurred or when revenues may be accrued may have marked effects on the final figures.

Despite these limitations, the balance sheet is widely used in many decisions dealing with the management of cash and extension of credit. In this book, we will remember its shortcomings as we use it to make working–capital decisions.

INCOME STATEMENT

The **income statement** is a report of a firm's activities during a given fiscal period. It shows revenues and expenses, the effect of interest and taxes, and the after–tax profit. It may have other titles, such as **profit and loss statement** or **statement of earnings**. It summarizes the profitability of operations and tells shareholders and others whether the firm is making money. It may also be used to identify factors affecting profitability. Once again, when certified by a CPA the income statement has similar strengths and weaknesses as the balance sheet.

The income statement follows a format so that revenues minus expenses and taxes will equal net income. Elements of this format are revenues, operating expenses, financial expenses, income taxes, and net income:

1. **Revenues.** This element reflects money, either in cash or owed by customers, that the firm receives in the conduct of its business. Typical revenue categories are sales, net sales, other income, and income from investments.

2. **Operating Expenses.** These expenses are incurred in support of the activities undertaken to generate revenues. Some expenses are involved directly in the production of goods or provision of services. Other expenses are indirect but support the efforts to achieve sales.

3. **Financial Expenses.** This element is the interest paid on debt. It should be separated from operating expenses in most analyses. The fact that the firm has borrowed money and must pay interest is fundamentally different from the kind of costs required to provide goods and services.

4. **Income Taxes.** These are not an immediate expense but must be shown as a reduction of revenues.

5. **Net Income.** This figure is the residual amount when all expenses and taxes are deducted from revenues.

Three Formats for the Income Statement

For purposes of analysis, three common formats may be used to prepare an income statement:

1. **Management Format.** This format involves separating operating expenses into two categories.

    a. **Cost of Goods Sold (CofGS).** This accounting allocation of the expenses of raw materials, labor, overhead, and other direct expenses can be matched against the goods sold by the firm. It is a mixture of fixed and variable costs. For firms whose primary business does not involve the manufacture of products, it may be called **cost of services**.

    b. **General and Administrative Expenses (G&A).** These costs are incurred in support of nonproduction activities, including marketing expenses, salaries of corporate staff, and general overhead. These costs also represent a mixture of fixed and variable costs.

2. **Marginal Analysis Format.** This format involves separating operating expenses into two different categories:

    a. **Variable Costs.** These expenses change in direct proportion to changes in the volume of sales. Most variable costs are reflected in cost of goods sold, but some are contained in general and administrative expenses.

    b. **Fixed Costs.** These charges are constant and are incurred independently of production levels. The salary of the company president is an example.

3. **Cash Expenses Format.** This format involves separating operating expenses into yet another set of two categories:

    a. **Cash Expenses.** These operating expenses are paid in cash within the next accounting period.

    b. **Noncash Expenses.** These operating expenses do not involve outlays of money. Depreciation is an example.

Problem   A firm has total revenues of $5 million, operating expenses of $3.2 million, financial expenses of $700,000, and paid

$450,000 in income taxes. Its cost of goods sold are 60 percent of operating expenses. Variable costs are 45 percent of operating expenses. Cash expenses are 78 percent of operating expenses. Create a spreadsheet model that generates income statements in three formats: (a) management format; (b) marginal analysis format; and (c) cash expenses format.

Solution

B	C	D	E	F
2	INPUT SCREEN			
3	Revenues		5,000,000	
4	Operating Expenses		3,200,000	
5	CofGS		0.60	
6	Variable Costs		0.45	
7	Cash Expenses		0.78	
8	Financial Expenses		700,000	
9	Taxes		450,000	
10				

B	C	D	E	F
11	OUTPUT SCREEN, Income Statement, Management Format			
12				
13	Total Revenues		5,000,000	
14	Cost of Goods Sold		1,920,000	
15			– – – –	
16	Gross Margin		3,080,000	
17	Administrative Expense		1,280,000	

18		- - - -
19	Operating Income	1,800,000
20	Financial Expenses	700,000
21		- - - -
22	Earnings Before Taxes	1,100,000
23	Income Taxes	450,000
24		- - - -
25	Net Income	650,000
26		==========
27		
28	OUTPUT SCREEN, Income Statement, Marginal Analysis Format	
29	Total Revenues	5,000,000
30	Variable Costs	1,440,000
31		- - - - -
32	Marginal Contribution	3,560,000
33	Fixed Costs	1,760,000
34		- - - - -
35	Operating Income	1,800,000
36	Financial Expenses	700,000
37		- - - - -
38	Earnings Before Taxes	1,100,000
39	Income Taxes	450,000
40		- - - - -
41	Net Income	650,000
42		==========

43

44   OUTPUT SCREEN, Income Statement, Cash Expenses
      Format

45   Total Revenues   5,000,000

46   Cash Expenses   2,496,000

47   Noncash Expenses   704,000

48   — — — — —

49   Operating Income   1,800,000

50   Financial Expenses   700,000

51   — — — — —

52   Earnings Before Taxes   1,100,000

53   Income Taxes   450,000

54   — — — — —

55   Net Income   650,000

56   ==========

The relevant formulas used in the problem are:

At D14: +D4*D5
At D17: +D4-D14
At D30: +D4*D6
At D33: +D4-D30
At D46: +D4*D7
At D47: +D4-D46

Five Measures of Profit

The different approaches to preparing income statements make use of five
important profit measures:

1. **Gross Margin.** This is the amount of profit realized as a result of the difference between cost of goods sold (direct production expenses) and revenues, and is found on the management format.

2. **Marginal Contribution.** The difference between revenues and variable costs, marginal contribution is the profit available to cover fixed costs, interest, and taxes, and to provide a profit after taxes. It may be calculated in total, as on the income statement, or on a per unit basis. This profit measure is found on the marginal analysis format.

3. **Operating Income** (also called **earnings before interest and taxes,** or **EBIT**). In this before–tax measure, total operating expenses are deducted from total revenues.

4. **Earnings Before Taxes (EBT).** This measure is the difference between all operating and financial expenses and revenues.

5. **Net Income** (also called **net income after taxes,** or **NIAT**). This is the measure of profits after all expenses and taxes have been deducted from revenues. It is the "bottom line" of the income statement.

FLOW OF FUNDS STATEMENT

A third important financial statement is the **flow of funds** or **sources and uses of funds** statement, which shows the movements that affect net working–capital. It shows the flow of funds into current asset accounts from external sources such as stockholders, creditors, and customers. It also displays outflows to pay bills, repay principal and interest on debt, retire stock, or pay dividends. The movements are shown for a specific period of time, normally the same as the income statement.

To understand flow of funds, we must recognize the **working–capital pool,** defined as all current accounts on the balance sheet. In a sense, the pool is a measure of net working–capital. If a transaction increases a current asset without increasing a current liability, it raises both net working–capital and the working–capital pool. If, on the other hand, inventories are increased along with accounts payable, neither the working–capital pool nor net working–capital increases. Only transactions that affect a current account and either a noncurrent or income statement account will show up on a flow of funds statement. Figure 9-1 shows flows of funds in the working–capital pool.

Example: A firm uses $100,000 to buy a machine and $70,000 to retire a short–term bank note. Does either transaction reflect a flow of funds?

Answer: Buying a machine affects a current account (cash) and noncurrent account (plant and equipment). It shows a flow of funds from the working–capital pool. Retiring the note affects two current accounts (cash and short–term notes). It is a movement in the working–capital pool and does not reflect a flow of funds.

Figure 9-1. Flow of Funds and the Working–Capital Pool.

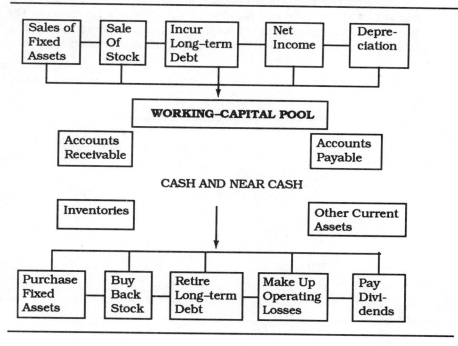

Funds from Operations

The term **funds from operations** is defined as the cash and collections on receivables that are obtained as a result of the business activity conducted by the firm. That is, they occur from everyday operations. Over a period of time, this is the most important source of funds. If the firm is not profitable on a cash flow basis, it will not be able to conduct its business. These funds may be calculated two ways:

1. **Cash Basis, Revenues Minus Cash Expenses.** The originating source of all operating funds is revenues. The firm must make a sale to receive money or the right to collect receivables. The firm also has cash expenses for operations, payment of interest on debt, and income taxes. The difference between revenues and cash expenses including taxes is a change in the working–capital pool and a method of calculating funds from operations.

2. **Accounting Basis, Net Income Plus Noncash Expenses**. Funds from operations may also be calculated by adding back noncash expenses, such as depreciation, to the reported after–tax income. This correctly reflects the fact that depreciation and other noncash expenses shield a portion of the firm's sales. They appear on the income statement as expenses and they reduce net income, but no money is paid. The funds are used when a machine is purchased, not when it is depreciated. The purchase is treated as a use of funds; the depreciation is not. Thus, if we add noncash expenses to net income, we get funds from operations.

Figure 9-2 compares the two methods of calculating funds from operations.

Figure 9-2. Determining Funds from Operations.

	Cash Basis	Accounting Basis
Sales	$100,000	$100,000
Cash Operating Expenses	-60,000	-60,000
Noncash Expenses (depreciation		-8,000
Operating Income (EBIT)		32,000
Cash Remaining	40,000	
Interest on Debt	-10,000	-10,000
Federal Income Taxes	-8,000	-8,000
Net Income		14,000
Cash Remaining	22,000	
Plus Noncash Expenses		8,000
Funds from Operations	$22,000	$22,000

Other Sources of Funds

Three other sources of funds are important in the development of a flow of funds statement. These are sale of stock, long–term borrowing, and sale of fixed assets:

1. **Sale of Stock**. When a firm issues additional shares of preferred or common stock, it receives funds. The receipts are recorded in the cash

account, and the source is shown in equity accounts under contributed capital.

2. **Long-term Borrowing**. When a firm borrows through the use of bonds, mortgages, or other obligations with maturities in excess of a year, the sources are reflected in long-term liabilities.

3. **Sale of Fixed Assets**. If the firm sells a portion of its equipment or other assets used to conduct business, it is exchanging a fixed asset for a current asset. These funds are not revenues but are treated as a flow from the sale of fixed assets.

Uses of Funds

A firm may use funds for a variety of purposes, some voluntary and others involuntary. The common uses are as follows:

1. **To Make Up Losses from Operations**. Just as funds from operations is a source, the firm can lose money on its operations. If the net loss exceeds the amount of noncash expenses, the flow of funds statement will show a loss from operations as a use of funds.

2. **To Purchase Fixed Assets**. As has already been noted, a purchase of plant, equipment, or other fixed assets is a use of funds. The recording of depreciation is not.

3. **To Repay Long-Term Debt**. When long-term debt reaches maturity, it must be repaid. This is a use of funds.

4. **To Retire Outstanding Stock**. If the firm wishes to eliminate outstanding preferred stock or reduce the number of shares of common stock trading in the market, it can use funds for these purposes.

5. **To Declare Cash Dividends**. If the firm is profitable and pays dividends to its shareholders, the declaration of dividends is a use of funds. The actual payment of the dividends occurs later and is not a use of funds in a strict technical sense. When dividends are declared, the retained earnings account is reduced and a current liability account dividends payable is created. This is the use of funds since it affects one current and one noncurrent account. When the cash is actually paid, cash is credited and dividends payable are debited. This transaction affects two current accounts and is not a use of funds. In spite of the technical distinction, a flow of funds statement might state that the payment of cash dividends is a use of funds.

Format of the Flow of Funds Statement

Three formats are commonly used in creating flow of funds statements:

1. **Measuring Changes in Net Working–Capital**. This approach displays sources, uses, and changes in net working–capital. It offers the best measure of liquidity because it shows changes in all current accounts—those that soon will be cash and those that soon will be obligations.

2. **Balancing Sources and Uses**. This approach displays sources and uses only, with sources equaling uses. It is difficult to use this format to measure liquidity because changes in current accounts are included in the sources and uses. The rules are:

   a. **Current Account Sources**. When a current asset is decreased, a source is displayed. The same is true when a current liability is increased.

   b. **Current Account Uses**. These occur when a current asset is increased or current liability is decreased.

   For accounting purposes, balancing sources and uses has merit; for analyzing liquidity, it does not. For example, an increase in receivables is viewed as a use of funds. The rationale is that the firm has used its cash to finance more receivables. This is true in an accounting sense, but it is not a full reflection of liquidity, which is more clearly seen through changes in net working–capital.

3. **Measuring Changes in Cash**. This approach displays sources, uses, and changes in the cash balance during the period. It is useful for focusing on the most liquid of current assets—the cash account. It is not as useful a measure of liquidity as the statement showing changes in net working–capital.

Problem   A firm has a net income of $593,048. Its noncash expenses, including depreciation, were $429,194. During the year, it took out a long–term loan of $370,484 but paid off $118,912 of secured–long–term debt. It sold common stock worth $8,448 but repurchased $133,900 of common stock outstanding. It purchased fixed assets of $938,044 and sold other fixed assets for $24,404. It declared cash dividends of $203,696. The firm's receivables decreased by $20,000, inventories increased by $45,000, and cash increased by $78,026. Its total current liabilities increased by $72,000.

Create a spreadsheet model that calculates the change in the firm's cash balance and then displays flow of funds statements in three formats: (1) net working–capital format; (2) balancing sources and uses format; and (3) measuring changes in cash format.

Solution

		B	C	D	E
2	INPUT SCREEN				
3	Net Income			593,048	
4	Noncash Expenses			429,194	
5	Long–Term Borrowing			370,484	
6	Retire Long–Term Debt			118,912	
7	Sale of Common Stock			8,448	
8	Retire Common Stock			133,900	
9	Purchase Fixed Assets			938,044	
10	Sale of Fixed Assets			24,404	
11	Declaration of Dividends			203,696	
12	Decrease in Receivables			20,000	
13	Increase in Inventories			45,000	
14	Increase in Current Assets			78,026	
15	Increase in Current Liabilities			72,000	
16					
17	OUTPUT SCREEN, Flows of Funds, Net Working–Capital Format				
18	Sources				
19	Net Income			593,048	
20	Noncash Expenses			429,194	
21				— — — —	
22	Funds from Operations			1,022,242	
23	Long-Term Borrowing			370,484	
24	Sale of Common Stock			8,448	

25	Sale of Fixed Assets	24,404
26		$----$
27	Total Sources	1,425,578
28		
29	Uses	
30	Retire Long–term Debt	118,912
31	Retire Common Stock	133,900
32	Purchase Fixed Assets	938,044
33	Declare Cash Dividends	203,696
34		$----$
35	Total uses	1,394,552
36		
37	Change in Net Working–Capital	31,026
38		==========
39	OUTPUT SCREEN, Flows of Funds, Balancing Sources and Uses Format	
40	Sources	
41	Net Income	593,048
42	Noncash Expenses	429,194
43		$----$
44	Funds from Operations	1,022,242
45	Long-Term Borrowing	370,484
46	Sale of Common Stock	8,448
47	Sale of Fixed Assets	24,404
48	Decrease in Receivables	20,000
49	Increase in Current Liabilities	72,000

50		− − − − −
51	Total Sources	1,517,578
52		
53	Uses	
54	Retire Long–Term Debt	118,912
55	Retire Common Stock	133,900
56	Purchase Fixed Assets	938,044
57	Declaration of Dividends	203,696
58	Increase in Inventories	45,000
59	Increase in Current Assets	78,026
60		− − − − −
61	Total Uses	1,517,578
62		==========
63	OUTPUT SCREEN, Flows of Funds, Measuring Changes in Cash Format	
64	Sources	
65	Net Income	593,048
66	Noncash Expenses	429,194
67		− − − − −
68	Funds from Operations	1,022,242
69	Long–Term Borrowing	370,484
70	Sale of Common Stock	8,448
71	Sale of Fixed Assets	24,404
72	Decrease in Receivables	20,000
73	Increase in Current Liabilities	72,000
74		− − − − −

75	Total Sources	1,517,578
76		
77	Uses	
78	Retire Long–Term Debt	118,912
79	Retire Common Stock	133,900
80	Purchase Fixed Assets	938,044
81	Declare Dividends	203,696
82	Increase in Inventories	45,000
83		– – – – –
84	Total Uses	1,439,552
85		
86	Change in Cash	78,026
87		==========

Visualizing the Flow of Funds

The three financial statements discussed in this chapter can be used together to understand what is happening as funds are used to pursue the firm's business goals. They offer valuable insights into liquidity, profitability, and the relationship among sources and resources. Two techniques are particularly valuable in visualizing fund flow from a working–capital management perspective: historical trends and future indicators.

1. **Historical Trends.** When compiled over a number of years, financial statements show which major factors influence the growth and current status of the firm. Inflows from earlier periods provide the financing for present assets.

2. **Future Indicators.** A **pro forma** financial statement is prepared for a future period of time. It is a forecast of the financial performance of the firm. The impact of today's decisions is used to generate the flow of funds and profits, and future financial relationships can be evaluated in advance.

Whether historical or pro forma, the flow of funds through the firm is a critical element in managing resources properly. In most firms, funds are in constant motion, and the task of the manager is to monitor and control them to achieve specific objectives. A graphic view of the internal and external fund flow is provided in Figure 9-3.

Figure 9-3. Flow of Funds in a Firm.

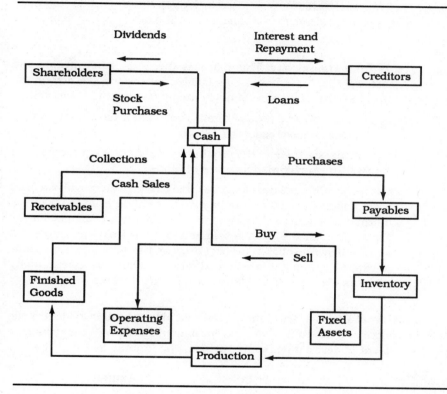

ELLIOT COMPANY CASE

When doing an external analysis of a firm, the analyst frequently does not have access to the firm's internal records. Thus, he or she must develop a flow of funds statement from the firm's balance sheet and income statement.

Techniques

A number of financial techniques are used to develop a flow of funds statement from a balance sheet and income statement data. The most important ones are as follows:

1. **Funds from Operations**. This figure is the total of net income and noncash expenses. It should be available on the income statement, perhaps with the assistance of notes accompanying the statement.

2. **Changes in Plant and Equipment**. These changes involve both a source and use in most cases, as follows:

   a. **Purchases Are Uses**. If the firm buys new plant or equipment, the expenditure is recorded as a use of funds.

   b. **Net Writeoffs Are Sources**. A **net writeoff** is the removal of a fixed asset and associated accumulated depreciation from the books of a firm. It is a source of funds since the firm receives money for the asset. Whether the asset is sold at a profit or loss, the source still equals the write–off. This is true because the gain or loss on a sale of capital equipment is recorded on the income statement, along with tax effects, and will be reflected in net income.

From an external analysis viewpoint, we may not always be able to identify the separate source and use from plant and equipment changes. We may have to take a short–cut to derive a net source or use. The formula is

$$\text{Net Use (Source)} = \text{Increase in Net Book Value} + \text{Annual Depreciation}$$

As an example, assume the following:

	1987	1988
Plant and Equipment	700,000	850,000
Accumulated Depreciation	(450,000)	(525,000)
Net Book Value	250,000	325,000

252

Annual Depreciation, 1988   125,000

The net use or source of funds would be:

$$\text{Net Use} = 325{,}000 - 250{,}000 + 125{,}000 = 200{,}000$$

Example: A firm has a decrease in net book value of plant and equipment of $1.8 million and annual depreciation of $1.5 million. What is the net source?

Answer: Net source of $300,000 = (-1.8 + 1.5)

3. **Changes in Long–Term Liabilities.** When the firm increases its long–term liabilities, it has borrowed money and is provided with funds. Paying off long–term debt is a use of funds.

4. **Changes in Contributed Capital.** The common stock and contributed capital in excess of par accounts represent capital provided by owners. An increase in these accounts is a source of funds, a decrease is a use.

5. **Changes in Retained Earnings.** This account is affected by two major items. If the firm reports a net income, retained earnings will increase by the amount of that income when the books are closed at the end of the period. A loss after taxes will decrease retained earnings. This account is also affected by the declaration of cash dividends, which decreases retained earnings.

Example: A firm has a retained earnings balance of $6 million at the start of a year and a balance of $5.5 million at the end. It declared dividends of $200,000 during the year. What was its net income?

Answer: A loss of $300,000. The decrease of $500,000 in retained earnings can be explained by the $300,000 loss and $200,000 dividends.

A Solved Problem

To illustrate the creation of a flow of funds statement from other financial data, consider the balance sheet and income statement for the sample problem, given in Figure 9.4. The major flow of funds items are as follows:

1. **Funds from Operations.** The net loss of $600,000 and depreciation of $800,000 produce a funds from operations of $200,000 (-600,000 + 800,000).

2. **Changes in Plant and Equipment.** The change in net book value is a $2.5 million increase. Adding this figure to the $800,000 depreciation, we get a net use of funds of $3.3 million.

3. **Changes in Long-Term Liabilities.** The $100,000 in funds are used to retire secured debt while a $1.3 million borrowing is a source of funds from unsecured debt.

4. **Changes in Contributed Capital.** The firm increased outstanding common stock by $1.2 million, a source.

5. **Changes in Retained Earnings.** The firm had a decrease in retained earnings of $1 million. Since $600,000 is explained by the net loss, the balance probably reflects $400,000 of dividends.

The flow of funds statement shows a decrease in net working-capital of $1.1 million, as follows:

Sources of Funds	
Net Loss	$(600,000)
Depreciation	800,000
Funds from Operations	200,000
Increase in Unsecured Debt	1,300,000
Sale of Stock	1,200,000
Total Sources	2,700,000
Uses of Funds	
Net Additions to Plant	3,300,000
Retire Secured Debt	100,000
Cash Dividends	400,000
Total Uses	3,800,000
Change in Net Working-Capital	$(1,100,000)

In this case, a flow of funds statement was created with a limited amount of information. To increase its accuracy, the analyst can work with footnotes and other information, seeking more information or adjustments for past periods that affect different accounts. In spite of shortcomings, the above technique is reasonably accurate in providing a view of fund flow for a firm.

Elliot Company Data

Using the techniques developed above and applied to the sample problem, we are now ready to develop a spreadsheet model for the Elliot Company. Figure 9.5 shows the format of the structure to be followed. Five input screens will be created for income statement data, starting balance sheet, flow of funds data, sale of fixed assets calculations, and working–capital change data. Four output screens will be created, including one that uses cash as the balancing account when computing the other financial statements.

Berry Ltd. is a growing sporting goods manufacturer located on the outskirts of Toronto, Canada. The company was founded 14 years ago by Lawrence Berry after he left his position as a track coach on the Canadian Olympic team to enter private business. Over the years, Berry expanded the firm's activities into the manufacture of custom-made uniforms, as well as a diverse line of sporting goods. In January 1987, the firm had a number of large contracts to supply college and professional teams in eastern Canada and the northeastern United States with athletic equipment and uniforms.

Figure 9.4. Sample Problem Financial Data

Balance Sheet

	Start of Year	End of Year
Cash	$1,700,000	$600,000
Receivables	1,400,000	1,500,000
Inventories	2,500,000	3,000,000
Plant and Equipment	6,000,000	9,000,000
Less Accumulated Depreciation	(2,000,000)	(2,500,000)
Real Estate	3,800,000	3,800,000
Total Assets	$13,400,000	$15,400,000
Payables	$600,000	$1,200,000
Long–Term Secured Debt	1,300,000	1,200,000
Long–Term Unsecured Debt	2,200,000	3,500,000
Contributed Capital	2,000,000	3,200,000
Retained Earnings	7,300,000	6,300,000
Liabilities and Equity	$13,400,000	$15,400,000

Income Statement

Revenues	$7,520,000
Production Costs	4,700,000
Depreciation	800,000
General Expenses	2,340,000
Interest	280,000
Net Income	(600,000)

Berry Ltd. did well in 1988. The firm reported a net income of $4.5 million, and Lawrence Berry felt that the firm was positioned for a period of steady growth. The firm had approximately $32 million in assets, a strong equity position, and the prospects to sign several sizable contracts with colleges and school systems. Berry's strong competitive position encouraged the Elliot Company to propose a joint venture. Rick Sinck, Elliot Company's president, presented a proposal for the two firms to work together on a line of football helmets that would reduce the frequency and severity of head injuries. Sinck presented some figures that were very attractive and indicated considerable growth and profit prospects for both firms in the U.S. and Canadian markets. Berry expressed an interest in pursuing the proposal and told Sinck that he would send him additional information on Berry Ltd.

Figure 9-5. Worksheet Structure Financial Model

Row				
	A	K	U	AE
1	Income Statement			
10	Input Screen			
20	Starting Balance Sheet			
30	Input Screen			
40	Flow of Funds			
50	Input Screen			
60	Sale of Fixed Assets			
70	Input Screen			
80	Changes in Working–Capital			
90	Input Screen			
100	Pro Forma Income Statement		Preparing the	
110	Output Screen		Balance Sheet Output Screen	
120	Pro Forma			
130	Flow of Funds			
140	Output Screen			
150	Comparative Balance Sheet Output Screen			

After Sinck left, Berry called in Frank Collanzo, a planning analyst in the Accounting Department. "Frank," he said, "we're giving serious thought to a venture with Elliot Company. Send them some information on our company; you know, a balance sheet and income statement. I expect they will be sending us the same information on their company. Here's what I would like to do. Run some figures on the expected performance of Elliot Company for 1989. I need to know what you think they will do. As a matter of fact, put it in the form of a balance sheet, income statement, and flow of funds statement. They know we're doing this analysis and will cooperate fully."

Collanzo returned to his office and began the process of checking up on the Elliot Company. He booted up an analysis that was in a data base maintained by an investment service and learned that the company was forecasting 1989 sales of $215 million. It was obviously a big operation. If historical trends continued, Elliot would probably have total operating expenses of $150 million in 1989 including about $22 million in depreciation. After reviewing these numbers, Collanzo called Elliot's Accounting Department. After a few calls, he learned that the company had plans to purchase $35 million of new manufacturing equipment in 1989. This would partly be financed by the sale of a warehouse. The cost accountant at Elliot estimated that the warehouse could be sold for $33 million. It was started on the books at $45 million original cost and had $20 million of accumulated depreciation charged to it. Another item of information was that the firm would probably have 1989 interest charges of $11 million on its interest-bearing debt.

After gathering some related information, Frank made a call directly to Rick Sinck's office. Sinck assured him that Elliot had no plans to change from the level of its 1988 dividend payment, which was $20 million. Sinck also pointed out that Elliot would pay off $8 million in unsecured debt during 1989. This would be more than offset by an increase in secured financing and a sale of common stock.

Secured debt would probably rise by $15 million, and Elliot hoped to sell 200,000 shares of common stock to net $60 a share. The proceeds of these new financings would be used to purchase $6 million of real estate and a $21 million manufacturing facility on the land.

Collanzo needed just a little more information on the Elliot Company's liquidity. He called a staff accountant at Elliot and got several estimates for 1989: inventory would increase by $7 million; accounts payable by $9 million; and the current portion of long–term debt by $3 million. The accounts receivable would decline by $4 million. The accountant also sent Collanzo a 1988 balance sheet, which arrived in three days. The company had a tax rate of 40 percent on its earnings before taxes.

Frank was now ready to set up the problem on his electronic spreadsheet. He selected five input and four output screens as his design for the model, as shown in Figure 9-5. The design uses cash as the balancing account on the balance sheet. In order to follow the top to bottom processing logic of the spreadsheet, he identified one screen for preparing the balance sheet. He did not intend to print this screen, and so he placed it to the right of the other screens. Otherwise, the logic proceeds from top to bottom.

Required: Prepare the financial model for Elliot Company.

Position Statement
Elliot Company
December 31, 1988
(preliminary in thousands)

Cash and Short– Term Holdings	$8,000	Trade and Accounts Payable	$10,000
Accounts Receivable	30,000	Current Portion of Long–Term Debt	11,000
Inventories	55,000		
Plant and Equipment (basis: orig- inal cost or market, which- ever lower)	200,000	Mortgages and Secured Borrowing	35,000
		Bonds and Long– Term Unsecured Debt	22,000
		Common Stock ($1 par)	5,000
Less Accumulated Depreciation	(125,000)	Additional Paid-in Capital	40,000
Land and Real Estate	15,000	Retained Earnings	60,000
	$183,000		$ 183,000

Working-Capital Adequacy

Decisions on the appropriate level of working-capital must deal with the issue of adequacy. Does the firm have sufficient current assets to conduct its business? Are the assets properly distributed among cash, receivables, inventories, and other current assets? Is the level of current liabilities excessive compared to other factors? Answering these and similar questions becomes the task of the financial manager.

In this chapter, we will use the techniques of financial analysis to address issues of working-capital adequacy. Guidelines will be developed on methods of evaluating cash, current assets, quick assets, current liabilities, and overall adequacy. An electronic spreadsheet model will be created to bring all the measures together and will allow the analyst to compare the firm's ratios with norms taken from similar firms. Then, a statistical tool will be used to suggest a method of determining norms for working-capital balances.

NATURE OF FINANCIAL ANALYSIS

Financial analysis is the process of determining the significant operating and financial characteristics of a firm from accounting data. It makes use of the balance sheet and income statement to gain insights into operating and financial problems. In this process, care must be taken to distinguish between causes and symptoms of problems. A **cause** is a situation that produces a result or effect; in financial analysis, the result would be a problem. A **symptom** is a visible indicator that a problem exists. The firm may observe symptoms, such as a low level of profits, but it must deal with the causes of problems, such as high costs. If it does not deal with the cause, the firm will probably not be able to correct the difficulty.

It is important to distinguish between techniques of internal and external analysis.

1. **External Analysis.** This technique is performed by outsiders to the firm, such as creditors, stockholders, or investment analysts. It makes use of existing financial statements and involves limited access to confidential information.

2. **Internal Analysis.** This technique is performed by the Finance and Accounting departments and is more detailed than external analysis. These departments can obtain extensive records and more current information than is available to outsiders. In preparing pro forma, or future, statements, inside analysts can produce more accurate and timely analyses of a firm's strengths and weaknesses.

From both points of view, the analyst can identify symptoms and the likely causes of problems. Then, solutions can be evaluated. Figure 10-1 shows two examples of this process.

Financial Ratios

A **ratio** is a fixed relationship in degree or number between two numbers. In finance, ratios are used to point out relationships that are not obvious from the raw data. Some uses of ratios are

1. **To Compare Different Companies in the Same Industry.** Ratios can highlight the factors associated with successful and unsuccessful firms. They can reveal strong and weak firms, overvalued and undervalued firms. Comparing different firms in the same time period is an example of **cross-sectional analysis**.

2. **To Compare Different Industries.** Every industry has its own unique set of operating and financial characteristics. They can be identified with the aid of ratios. This is also known as cross-sectional analysis.

3. **To Compare Performance in Different Time Periods.** Over a period of years, a firm or industry will develop certain norms that may indicate future success or failure. If relationships in a firm's data change over time, the ratios may provide clues on trends and future problems. Measuring performance over a period of time is an example of **time series analysis**.

From the financial accounts on the balance sheet, income statement, and flow of funds statement, it is possible to formulate countless ratios. To be successful in financial analysis, the manager must select only those ratios that provide significant information about the topic under review. In this chapter, we will focus on working-capital ratios.

Users of Ratios

Different analysts will desire different kinds of ratios, depending largely on the goal of the evaluation and the personal preferences of the evaluator. Some users of ratios are short-term creditors, long-term creditors, stockholders, and internal analysts.

Figure 10-1. Symptoms, Causes, and Solutions for Problems Revealed by Financial Ratios.

Symptom	Problem	Solution
Abnormal Liquidity Ratio	Inadequate Cash	Raise additional funds
"	Excessive Receivables	Restrict terms of trade; institute a more aggressive collection policy
"	Excessive Inventory	Improve inventory management
"	Excessive Current Liabilities	Obtain additional long-term financing
Abnormal Profitability Ratio	High Production Costs	Institute cost-cutting measures
"	Idle Assets	Sell excess or obsolete assets
"	Inadequate Sales	Increase size and quality of sales force; improve advertising
"	Inadequate Selling Price	Raise it
"	High Administrative Expenses	Reduce them
"	Excessive Interest Payments	Seek lower cost debt financing; seek equity financing

1. **Short-term Creditors.** These persons hold obligations that will soon mature. They are concerned with the firm's ability to pay bills promptly. In the short run, the amount of liquid assets determines the ability to pay bills and other current liabilities. These individuals generally use working-capital ratios.

2. **Long-Term Creditors**. These individuals hold bonds, mortgages, or unsecured debt and are interested in current payments of interest and eventual repayment of principal. The firm must have sufficient liquidity in the short-term to cover these payments when due. Thus, long-term creditors are interested in working-capital adequacy.

3. **Stockholders**. Without liquidity, the firm could not pay cash dividends. Profits are also needed to support the value of common stock. Adequate working-capital is needed for both purposes.

4. **Internal Analysts**. A major group of users are the analysts and managers who work in the firm. Once these individuals identify problems, they can take or recommend steps to make corrections.

Comparative Ratios

Ratios are used most effectively when comparisons are made between firm and industry averages or norms for the category of firm. A **comparative ratio** is defined as a fixed relationship between numbers that is derived from data that can provide a benchmark or norm for evaluating an individual firm. As an example, if an industry average shows a ratio of 1/1 and an individual firm has a ratio of 2/1, we can say that, on a comparative basis, the firm exceeds the industry average.

Comparative ratios are provided by a number of organizations, including

1. **Dun and Bradstreet's Key Business Ratios**. Dun and Bradstreet (D&B) publishes comparative ratios for hundreds of businesses. Ratios are provided for the upper and lower quartiles, as well as the median for each line of business activity. Because they represent a large sample of companies, they are widely used as norms for adequacy of working-capital.

2. **Standard and Poor's Compustat Data**. A variety of balance sheet and income statement data is available in electronic formats from Standard and Poor's Corporation.

3. **Robert Morris Associates**. Comparative ratios are available by industry category and size of firm within the category from Robert Morris Associates, the national association of bank lending officers.

4. **Government Agencies**. The Bureau of the Census, Small Business Administration, Department of Commerce, Federal Trade Commission, and Securities and Exchange Commission all provide data and ratios that can be used for comparative purposes.

5. **Miscellaneous Sources**. Trade associations, large banks, private publishers, and others provide financial data in varied forms that can be used to establish norms for working-capital ratios.

Kinds of Ratios

Financial ratios may be classified a number of ways. One classification scheme uses three major categories.

1. **Liquidity Ratios.** These examine the adequacy of funds, the solvency of the firm, and the firm's ability to pay its obligations when due.

2. **Profitability Ratios.** These measure the efficiency of the firm's activities and its ability to generate profits.

3. **Other Ratios.** These are generally linked directly or indirectly to liquidity or profitability but measure other dimensions of the firm's activities.

From the point of view of working-capital adequacy, the analyst must be more creative than the standard ratios reported in these categories. Although some liquidity ratios may be used directly, the analyst may have to develop ratios that are not commonly reported. Then, comparative norms must be derived from the balance sheet and income statement data provided by the organizations that offer comparative data. In the next section, we will develop an approach to categorizing ratios that measure the adequacy of working-capital.

WORKING-CAPITAL RATIOS

The firm's level of working-capital bears a relationship to a variety of operating and financial activities. Without adequate working-capital, the firm's primary lines of business may be jeopardized. With excess working-capital, the firm is bearing unneeded costs. In this section, we will examine some categories by identifying problems in each category.

Adequacy of Cash

Most firms maintain the smallest possible cash balances in checking accounts but keep near-cash reserves invested in overnight and other short-term holdings. Such items should be included in ratios that measure the adequacy of cash. Three ratios are particularly helpful in this analysis.

1. **Cash/Current Liabilities.** Cash must be available to pay bills that will be due in the next weeks or months. A measure of the adequacy of such cash can be made by taking the ratio of cash to current liabilities.

2. **Cash/Total Assets.** The level of cash as a component in the firm's overall mixture of assets reflects management's view of the importance of liquidity versus the desire to tie up funds in fixed, income-producing assets. This can be measured by the ratio of cash to total assets.

3. **Cash/Revenues**. As a firm increases its sales, its cash needs also rise. When a firm maintains inadequate cash balances compared to sales activity, it places constraints on its operations. Eventually, such constraints can be expected to affect profits. A measure of cash needs compared to operations can be obtained using the ratio of cash to revenues.

Adequacy of Current Assets

The firm's current assets represent the broadest measure of liquid funds that may soon become cash and be available to pay bills. Just as cash is compared to current liabilities, total assets, and revenues, a similar comparison can be made to current assets. The ratios are as follows:

1. **Current Assets/Current Liabilities**. Called the **current ratio**, this ratio is widely used as a measure of the pool of liquid funds available to pay near-term obligations. A low ratio is an indicator that a firm may not be able to pay its future bills on time, particularly if conditions change causing a slowdown in cash collections. A high ratio may indicate an excessive amount of current assets, a failure to properly utilize the firm's resources.

2. **Current Assets/Total Assets**. A properly managed firm will use its funds to finance adequate cash, receivables, and inventory in the mix of total assets. A low ratio might reveal inadequate attention to extending credit on sales (low receivables) or failure to support production with proper inventories. A high ratio may indicate poor collection policies (excessive receivables) or sluggish inventories.

3. **Current Assets/Revenues**. When a firm generates sales, it has bills to pay, receivables to finance, and inventories to support sales efforts. The level of these assets should be adequate to pay bills on time, permit rapid deliveries of promised goods, and allow the sales force to extend credit on competitive terms for the industry. Thus, current assets should grow proportionally with sales or decline when sales are reduced.

Adequacy of Quick Assets

Quick assets consist of cash and receivables, the most liquid items on the balance sheet. Cash is immediately available to pay bills; receivables will be collected in the next 60 or so days. Together, they offer a more precise measure of liquidity than current assets by excluding inventories which are the least liquid of current assets. Inventories require a three-step process to convert them to cash. They must be sold, converted into receivables (with a markup), and collected.

Quick assets may be used in three ratios.

1. **Quick Assets/Current Liabilities**. Called the **acid test** or **quick ratio**, this ratio is widely used to measure the most liquid assets against current obligations. It shows the ability of the firm to pay its bills without relying on the sale of its inventories and collection of the resulting receivables.

2. **Quick Assets/Total Assets**. The firm needs a proper level of highly liquid assets as part of its total asset mix. With the ratio of current assets to total assets, excessive inventories would mask an inadequacy of cash and receivables. This ratio highlights cash and receivables in the asset mix.

3. **Quick Assets/Revenues**. Proper levels of cash and receivables are also needed to support sales. Once again, this ratio offers a view of their adequacy as sales rise. It also points out excessive cash and receivables if sales decline.

Cash Flows from Inventory

The cash, current assets, and quick assets ratios measure the pools of liquidity held by the firm. It is equally important that the firm have adequate cash flows from its business operations. These cash flows are measured in terms of receivables and inventory. If the firm does not sell its inventory, it will have no receivables. If it does not collect its receivables, it will have no cash. Four ratios are useful to measure the funds flowing from the firm's operations. The first two deal with inventory:

1. **Revenues/Inventory**. Also called **Inventory Turnover in Cash**, this ratio measures the number of times a year the firm will generate revenues equal to the balance of its inventory. A turnover of 12 to 1 means that one month's sales will be equal to the inventory balance. Stated differently, the firm will generate a dollar volume of sales each month that equals the dollar volume of its inventory.

2. **Cost of Goods Sold/Inventory**. Also called **Inventory Turnover in Units**, this ratio approximates the physical turnover of the inventory. Because both inventories and cost of goods sold are both measured at cost, this ratio contains no markup. A turnover of 6 to 1 means that the inventory is physically turned over every two months.

The two inventory turnover ratios measure different aspects of inventory liquidity. Three factors are reflected in these ratios:

1. **High Markup Means More Liquidity.** The ratio that uses revenues emphasizes the importance of the markup in a firm's liquidity. A firm with a high selling price compared to its costs will be more liquid than a firm with a lower markup.

Example: Firms A and B each sell 1,000 units of a product during a one-year period. Firm A has a selling price of $100 and Firm B has a price of $80. The cost of each unit is $60. Both firms maintain an inventory of 100 units. What are the inventory turnovers in cash and units? Which firm is more liquid?

Answer: The turnovers are:

	Firm A	Firm B
Units Sold	1,000	1,000
Selling Price	100	80
Cost per Unit	60	60
Inventory in Units	100	100
Annual Revenues	100,000	80,000
Cost of Goods Sold	60,000	60,000
Dollar Value of Inventory	6,000	6,000
Turnover in Cash	16.7	13.3
Turnover in Units	10.0	10.0

Firm A is more liquid. It generates cash equal to its $6,000 inventory balance 16.7 times a year compared to Firm B's 13.3 times. This is the case even though both firms have equal physical turnover of the inventory.

2. **Running Out of Goods Is Risky.** In some industries, customers place orders and are willing to wait for production and delivery of the goods. In many industries, however, running out of stock means a loss of sales. When a customer needs an item immediately and it is not in stock, it will be purchased from another firm. When this happens, the firm will suffer a loss of profit. The ratio that uses cost of goods sold measures the physical availability of products to sell. A high turnover may indicate inadequate inventories to support the firm's business.

3. **Carrying Charges Can be Costly.** Maintaining inventory requires that the firm make expenditures for storing the goods, protecting them from theft of breakage, and handling them. If the firm maintains unneeded inventory, it is paying for unnecessary warehouse space, insuring goods that it does not have to hold, and incurring other costs that can be a

financial burden. The ratio that uses cost of goods sold can measure the sluggishness of inventory turnover and reflect excessive carrying charges.

Because the manager must compromise between running out of goods to sell and investing in excessive inventory, either a high or low ratio may be an indication of poor management. A high turnover may indicate future shortages of goods to sell; a low turnover may indicate overstocking of inventories. The interpretation that the turnover is high or low should, of course, be made on a comparative basis with other firms in the industry and with historical inventory levels.

Cash Flows from Receivables

Two ratios are generally used to measure the cash flows from a firm's receivables.

1. **Credit Sales/Receivables**. Called the **accounts receivable turnover**, this ratio compares the volume of sales with uncollected bills owed by customers. If the firm is having difficulty collecting its money, it will have a large receivables balance and a low ratio. If it has a strict credit policy and aggressive collection procedures, it will have a low receivables balance and a high ratio.

2. **Receivables/Daily Credit Sales**. Called the **average collection period**, this ratio compares the receivables balance with the sales required to produce the balance. If the firm has $10,000 of sales each day and a receivables balance of $500,000, we might say it took 50 days to accumulate the receivables. More importantly in a liquidity sense, if neither sales nor receivables change, it will take the firm 50 days to collect dollars equal to the $500,000 currently held as receivables. The 50 days is, of course, the average collection period.

These two ratios offer alternative measures of the same receivables cash flow. If the turnover is 12 to 1, the collection period is approximately 30 days (365 days/12). Similarly, a 60-day collection period reflects a turnover of 6 to 1 (365/60).

Several techniques are available to help the manager analyze the significance of the cash flows from receivables.

1. **Comparisons with Other Firms**. Because conditions concerning the terms of trade and selling practices are often standardized throughout an industry, this comparison can indicate whether a firm is lax or strict in its collection and sales policies.

2. **Comparisons with the Terms of Trade**. Credit terms are an important factor in evaluating receivables. A firm that offers extended terms will have a lower turnover and longer collection period than a firm with more restricted credit policies. To illustrate, consider firms A and B, each with average collection periods of 44 days. Firm A sells on terms of 2/10 net 30, indicating that the firm gives a 2 percent discount for payment in 10 days and the net amount is due in 30 days. For this firm, a collection period of 44 days means that a number of dollars are uncollected after the net period.

   Firm B has terms of 2/10 net 60. For this firm, a period of 44 days means that collections are probably well within the 60-day time period. Without further information, we could conclude that Firm B is doing a better job of collecting its receivables than is Firm A.

3. **Avoidance of Cyclical Distortions**. The analyst must always beware of applying ratio analysis to firms operating in industries with cyclical sales. The busy season will distort the ratios in one direction; the quiet season in the other. Even the average of the busy and quiet periods might not be useful. To avoid distortions from cyclical sales, the analyst may have to use ratios in different quarters or months.

Exposure from Current Liabilities

Capital structure is the composition of debt and equity funds that comprise a firm's asset financing. In managing its capital structure, the firm makes conscious choices between short-term and long-term debt. Long-term debt does not require payments of principal within the next months or year, as does short-term debt. Hence, the lower the levels of short-term debt, the lower the exposure that bills or debts will not be paid on time. Four ratios can help measure the risk from current liabilities.

1. **Total Assets/Current Liabilities**. This ratio measures the portion of assets financed by short-term debt and payables. A large ratio indicates that adequate long-term funds, either debt or equity, are used to finance assets. A low ratio reveals a high level of current obligations in the capital structure.

2. **Total Equity/Current Liabilities**. This ratio measures the commitment of the owners compared to the exposure from liquid obligations. A high ratio indicates that the shareholders have a stake in the business. A low ratio indicates that the firm is minimizing possible losses for the owners by financing a larger portion of its assets from short-term sources.

3. **Funds Flow/Current Liabilities**. This ratio compares net income plus revenues shielded by depreciation and noncash expenses to the level of near-term debt. A high ratio indicates liquidity. A low ratio may indicate working-capital inadequacy.

4. **Cost of Goods Sold/Accounts Payable**. This ratio provides a completely different view of the exposure from a current liability. To maintain its credit rating, a firm must pay its bills in some reasonable time period. If it allows its payables to rise excessively, it may run into difficulty with its suppliers. One way to examine the level of payables is to compare them to the level of business activity. This is done using cost of goods sold. A high ratio indicates the firm is not relying on payables financing excessively. A low ratio may indicate problems.

Overall Adequacy of Working-Capital

Net working-capital, the difference between current assets and current liabilities, is a primary measure of the liquidity of the firm. It can be used in three ratios to evaluate the overall adequacy of working-capital.

1. **Total Assets/Net Working-capital**. This ratio compares the excess of liquid assets over current obligations to the size of the firm. A high ratio indicates a low level of liquidity; a low ratio reveals high liquidity.

2. **Current Liabilities/Net Working-capital**. This ratio is an alternate expression of the current ratio. If the current ratio is low, this ratio will be high, indicating low liquidity. If this ratio is low, the current ratio will be high, indicating high liquidity. Some analysts are able to view liquidity more clearly by comparing current obligations to net working capital rather than current assets.

3. **Revenues/Net Working-capital**. This ratio is a measure of business activity to the excess of current assets over current liabilities. A high ratio indicates low liquidity to support operations; a low ratio reveals high liquidity.

CONCLUSION

The 20 working-capital ratios described in this chapter are not all needed to evaluate the adequacy of working-capital. Used in the seven groupings above, they offer a fairly comprehensive picture of liquidity from different viewpoints. A firm that scores well on the majority of ratios, including some in each grouping, is likely to be highly liquid. A firm that scores well in some categories but poorly in others may need to examine its policies. A firm that scores poorly in most ratios is likely to have liquidity problems.

A SPREADSHEET MODEL OF WORKING-CAPITAL ADEQUACY

Using the working-capital framework just defined, we can develop a model that requires minimal data entry and generates financial ratios. In this section, we will develop such a model.

Data Entry, Input Screen

The 20 ratios measuring working-capital adequacy require the inputs identified in Figure 10-2. Thirteen of these inputs must be entered directly. Three of them—current assets, current liabilities, and total equity—can be calculated from the other entries. In order to use the ratios on a comparative basis, three years of data are provided. We will use these numbers in our model.

Financial Norms, Input Screen

The adequacy of working-capital ratios should be compared to some norm for each item. These items should be included in the model on an input screen, such as is displayed in Figure 10-3. The source of these norms will be determined by the analyst. Not all of the ratios will be available from Standard and Poor's, Robert Morris Associates, and other bodies that provide comparative data. The analyst may have to develop norms based on reasoning and common sense. Our model will use the norms displayed in the figure.

Financial Ratios, Output Screen

The calculation of the 20 ratios is performed in an output screen, as shown in Figure 10-4. Our model displays the ratios for the three year period, as well as the norms from Figure 10-3. The ratios are grouped by category according to the purpose of each ratio.

Figure 10-2. Inputs to Model of Working-Capital Adequacy.

		D	E	F
10		Three	Two	
11		Years	Years	Last
12	INPUT DATA	Ago	Ago	Year
13				
14	Cash and Near Cash	13,400	16,100	15,130
15	Accounts Receivable	5,810	6,630	5,610
16	Inventory	4,970	5,480	6,400
17	Other Current Assets	1,170	870	920
18	Total Current Assets	25,350	29,080	28,060
19	Total Assets	101,200	103,680	110,550
20				
21	Accounts payable	11,600	14,850	17,330
22	Other Payables	4,100	3,710	4,740
23	Short-Term Debt	15,670	15,870	17,990
24	Total Current Liabilities	31,370	34,430	40,060
25	Total Liabilities	55,280	57,440	58,680
26	Total Equity	45,920	46,240	51,870
27				
28	Revenues	230,660	255,340	265,640
29	Cost of Goods Sold	203,680	247,540	260,230
30	Net Income	4,210	5,070	3,890
31	Depreciation	9,040	8,760	7,310

Figure 10-3. Comparative Ratios, Input Screen.

	D	E	F	G
34	Purpose	Ratio		Norm
35				
36	Measure of	Cash/Current Liabilities		0.240
37	Adequacy			
38	of Cash	Cash/Total Assets		0.051
39				
40		Cash/Revenues		0.021
41				
42	Measure of	Current Assets/Current Liabilities		1.180
43	Adequacy			
44	of Current	Current Assets/Total Assets		0.300
45	Assets			
46		Current Assets/Revenues		0.170
47				
48	Measure of	Quick Assets/Current Liabilities		1.100
49	Adequacy			
50	of Quick	Quick Assets/Total Assets		0.180
51	Assets			
52		Quick Assets/Revenues		0.070
53				
54	Measure of	Revenues/Inventory		8.000
55	Flows from			
56	Inventory	Cofgs/Inventory		7.000
57				
58	Measure of	Revenues/Receivables		8.200
59	Flows from			
60	Receivables	Average Collection Period		44.512
61				
62	Measure of	Total Assets/Current Liabilities		8.200
63	Exposure			
64	from	Total Equity/Current Liabilities		3.400
65	Current			
66	Liabilities	Funds Flow/Current Liabilities		1.850
67				
68		Cofgs/Accounts Payable		23.500
69				
70	Measure of	Total Assets/Net Working Capital		5.500
71	Overall			
72	Adequacy	Current Liabilities/Net Working Capital		1.400
73	of Working			
74	Capital	Revenues/Net Working Capital		11.400

Figure 10-4. Working-Capital Adequacy, Ratios Output Screen.

A	B	C	D	E	F	G
76			Three	Two		
77			Years	Years		Last
78		*Ratio Data*	Ago	Ago	*Year*	*Norm*
79						
80	**Cash Adequacy**					
81	Cash/Current Liabilities		0.427	0.468	0.378	0.240
82	Cash/Total Assets		0.132	0.155	0.137	0.051
83	Cash/Revenues		0.058	0.063	0.057	0.021
84						
85	**Current Asset Adequacy**					
86	Current Assets/Current Liabilities		0.808	0.845	0.700	1.180
87	Current Assets/Total Assets		0.250	0.280	0.254	0.300
88	Current Assets/Revenues		0.110	0.114	0.106	0.170
89						
90	**Quick Asset Adequacy**					
91	Quick Assets/Current Liabilities		0.612	0.660	0.518	1.100
92	Quick Assets/Total Assets		0.190	0.219	0.188	0.180
93	Quick Assets/Revenues		0.083	0.089	0.078	0.070
94						
95	**Flows from Inventories**					
96	Revenues/Inventory		46.410	46.595	41.506	8.000
97	Cofgs/Inventory		40.982	45.172	40.661	7.000
98						
99	**Flows from Receivables**					
100	Revenues/Receivables		39.701	38.513	47.351	8.200
101	Average Collection Period		9.194	9.477	7.708	44.512
102						
103	**Current Liability Exposure**					
104	Total Assets/Current Liabilities		3.226	3.011	2.760	8.200
105	Total Equity/Current Liabilities		1.464	1.343	1.295	3.400
106	Funds Flow/Current Liabilities		0.422	0.402	0.280	1.850
107	Cofgs/Accounts Payable		17.559	16.669	15.016	23.500
108						
109	**Overall Adequacy of Net Working Capital**					
110	Total Assets/Net Working Capital		-16.811	-19.379	-9.213	5.500
111	Current Liabilities/					
	NetWorking Capital		-5.211	-6.436	-3.338	1.400
112	Revenues/Net Working Capital		-38.316	-47.727	-22.137	11.400

Working-Capital Trends, Output Screen

Once the ratios have been developed, the analyst can use the model to make comparisons. In Figure 10-5, two views are taken.

1. **Secular Trend.** The model examines the annual percentage change each year. If the ratio is increasing, a positive value is displayed. If it is declining, a negative percentage is shown.

2. **Comparison with Norm.** The third and fourth columns of Figure 10-5 compare the past two years' data with the norm for each ratio. A plus

indicates that the firm's ratio exceeds the norm in a positive direction. This does not always indicate increasing liquidity. The analyst must check each ratio to see whether the change is an increase or a decrease in liquidity.

Figure 10-5. Working-Capital Adequacy, Trends and Comparisons.

		D	E	F	G
114		*Percent of*		*Percent Above*	
115		*Annual Change*		*or Below Norm*	
116					
117		Last 2	Past	2 yrs	Last
118		Years	Year	Ago	Year
119	**Cash Adequacy**				
120	Cash/Current Liabilities	0.095	-0.192	0.948	0.574
121	Cash/Total Assets	0.173	-0.119	2.045	1.684
122	Cash/Revenues	0.085	-0.097	2.003	1.712
123					
124	**Current Asset Adequacy**				
125	Current Assets/Current Liabilities	0.045	-0.171	-0.284	-0.406
126	Current Assets/Total Assets	0.120	-0.095	-0.065	-0.154
127	Current Assets/Revenues	0.036	-0.072	-0.330	-0.379
128					
129	**Quick Asset Adequacy**				
130	Quick Assets/Current Liabilities	0.078	-0.216	-0.400	-0.529
131	Quick Assets/Total Assets	0.155	-0.144	0.218	0.042
132	Quick Assets/Revenues	0.069	-0.123	0.272	0.115
133					
134	**Flows from Inventories**				
135	Revenues/Inventory	0.004	-0.109	4.824	4.188
136	Cofgs/Inventory	0.102	-0.100	5.453	4.809
137					
138	**Flows from Receivables**				
139	Revenues/Receivables	-0.030	0.229	3.697	4.775
140	Average Collection Period	0.031	-0.187	-0.787	-0.827
141					
142	**Current Liabiabilities Exposure**				
143	Total Assets/Current Liabilities	-0.066	-0.084	-0.633	-0.663
144	Total Equity/Current Liabilities	-0.082	-0.036	-0.605	-0.619
145	Funds Flow/Current Liabilities	-0.049	-0.304	-0.783	-0.849
146	Cofgs/Accounts Payable	-0.051	-0.099	-0.291	-0.361
147					
148	**Overall Adequacy of Net Working Capital**				
149	Total Assets/Net Working Capital	0.153	-0.525	-4.524	-2.675
150	Current Liabilities/ Net Working Capital	0.235	-0.481	-5.597	-3.385
151	Revenues/Net Working Capital	0.246	-0.536	-5.187	-2.942

Exceptions Report, Output Screen

The analyst may not be interested in examining every one of the 20 ratios in each of the four columns. The analyst may want to see only those ratios with significant changes in percentages from one year to the next. Figure 10-6 shows an exceptions report with 2 categories:

1. **Annual Changes Greater than a Given Percentage**. The first two columns display only the changes greater than plus or minus 0.15 percent. This percentage is entered as a variable in the heading of the columns. The formulas in each cell use if/then statements, as shown below the report. The first displayed formula uses what is called a **nested if/then statement**. If D160 is greater than or equal to D155, then display D160. Otherwise, use a second if/then statement. If D160 is less than or equal to minus D155, then display D160. Otherwise, display NA. This formula compares the ratio value in Figure 10-5 with the 15 percent value displayed in the heading of the column. If the value in Figure 10-5 is greater than plus or minus 0.15, then value will be displayed. Otherwise, NA will be displayed.

2. **Deviations from Norm by Greater Than a Given Percentage**. The second two columns display only changes greater than plus or minus 100 percent from the norms. The same nested if/then statement approach is used, as shown by the formula for cash to total assets where 2.045 is displayed.

Figure 10-6. Working-Capital Adequacy, Exceptions Report.

		D	E	F	G
153		*Annual Changes*		*Deviations*	
154		*in Ratios by*		*from Norms by*	
155		*0.150 or More*		*1.000 or More*	
156					
157		*Last 2*	*Past*	*2 Yrs*	*Last*
158		*Years*	*Year*	*Ago*	*Year*
159	**Cash Adequacy**				
160	Cash/Current Liabilities	NA	-0.192	NA	NA
161	Cash/Current Liabilities	0.173	NA	2.045	1.684
162	Cash/Revenues	NA	NA	2.003	1.712
163					
164	**Current Asset Adequacy**				
165	Current Assets/Current Liabilities	NA	-0.171	NA	NA
166	Current Assets/Total Assets	NA	NA	NA	NA
167	Current Assets/Revenues	NA	NA	NA	NA
168					
169	**Quick Asset Adequacy**				
170	Quick Assets/Current Liabilities	NA	-0.216	NA	NA
171	Quick Assets/Total Assets	0.155	NA	NA	NA
172	Quick Assets/Revenues	NA	NA	NA	NA
173					
174	**Flows from Inventories**				
175	Revenues/Inventory	NA	NA	4.824	4.188
176	COFGS/Inventory	NA	NA	5.453	4.809
177					
178	**Flows from Receivables**				
179	Revenues/Receivables	NA	0.229	3.697	4.775
180	Average Payment Period	NA	-0.187	NA	NA
181					
182	**Current Liabilities Exposure**				
183	Total Assets/Current Liabilities	NA	NA	NA	NA
184	Total Equity/Current Liabilities	NA	NA	NA	NA
185	Funds Flow/Current Liabilities	NA	-0.304	NA	NA
186	COFGS/Accounts Payable	NA	NA	NA	NA
187					
188	**Overall Adequacy of Net Working Capital**				
189	Total Assets/Net Working	0.153	-0.525	-4.524	-2.675
190	Current Liabilities/ Net Working Capital	0.235	-0.481	-5.597	-3.385
191	Revenues/Net Working Capital	0.246	-0.536	-5.187	-2.942

Formulas:

D160: @IF(D120>=D155,D120,@IF(D120<=-D155,D120,@NA))

F160: @IF(F120>=F155,F120,@IF(F120<=-F155,F120,@NA))

Interpretation

Having completed the model and running it for a sample firm, we can interpret the results.

1. **Adequacy of Cash.** The ratios indicate declining cash adequacy in the past year but the firm is still more liquid than the norms.

2. **Adequacy of Current Assets.** We have declining ratios once again and below the norms.

3. **Adequacy of Quick Assets.** Mixed signals are given here. Possible problems compared to current liabilities.

4. **Flows from Inventories.** These are very high.

5. **Flows from Receivables.** These too are very high.

6. **Current Liability Exposure.** Ratios reflect rising current liabilities and possible liquidity problems.

7. **Overall Adequacy.** Negative net working-capital is displayed in the three ratios. This is not a good sign.

From these profiles of working-capital adequacy, it appears that this firm should examine some of its policies. It may be that the high cash flows from inventory and receivables turnovers offset the low level of current assets compared to current liabilities. Still, some changes might be in order. We need more information to interpret the significance of the liquidity problems.

Conclusion

In this section, we have developed a model to view the adequacy of working-capital and possible exposures from a lack of liquidity. Other outputs could be developed from the basic input data to provide cross-sectional or time series analysis of a firm's working-capital situation. This model shows both, with changes for two years and comparisons to norms.

WALLACE PRODUCTS CASE—
ANALYZING FINANCIAL STATEMENTS

On June 6, 1987, Carl Phelps, a loan officer at the Equitable Savings Bank, was sitting in the office of Bob Smith, the bank's vice-president in charge of commercial lending. Mr. Smith handed Phelps a folder marked "Wallace Products" and began to discuss the contents therein.

Mr. Smith explained that the Wallace Products Company was a long-time customer of the bank. The firm had recently asked that its unsecured line of credit be extended from $7 million to $11 million to allow the firm to raise its notes payable to the bank from the current level of $6.4 million. In his discussions with the president of Wallace Products, Inc., Bob Smith learned that the firm planned to request a first mortgage on a new building that it would use as a combination office and warehouse. The architect's plan for the building indicated that it would cost $18 million and Wallace Products would request an 85 percent mortgage. Naturally, Equitable Savings Bank would be the lead bank in providing the mortgage financing. The construction was scheduled to begin in six months.

Mr. Smith explained some of his background on Wallace Products and its relationship with the bank. The firm was founded in 1965 by Arnold Wallace and has been a successful manufacturer of sporting goods since that time. The firm's product line originally consisted of tennis accessories with first-year sales of just over $65,000. Sales grew markedly to over $48 million to 1986. The firm's after-tax profits have also risen rapidly and are expected to reach $3 million in the next year or two. Over this period of time, Equitable Savings Bank has had excellent relations with Wallace Products and would like to continue to work with the firm as it finances its expansion and growth. Before increasing the line of credit or making a mortgage loan, the bank plans to thoroughly investigate the firm's plans and financial position. Mr. Smith indicated that he would visit the Wallace Products offices the following week to discuss the request.

"Carl," said Mr. Smith, "In that folder on your lap I have put the balance sheets, income statements, and some other information on Wallace Products and the sporting goods industry. I would appreciate if you would analyze those papers and give me a report on the financial status of the company. I'll need the information before I go see Arnold Wallace next Thursday."

Back in his office, Phelps reviewed the contents of the folder. He saw the comparative balance sheets and income statements for 1984 to 1986. He also noted the table of ratios for the sporting goods industry. He decided to use these items to prepare a flow of funds statement for 1986, as well as to develop liquidity and profitability ratios for the firm. He would then take his data and compare them against the industry standards and use the results to prepare his report.

Required:	1. Develop the financial statements and ratios for 1986.
	2. What recommendation would you make to Mr. Smith with respect to the credit capacity of Wallace Products?

Figure 10-7. Wallace Products, Inc. Balance Sheet (000s)

	1986	1985	1984
Cash	$2,800	$2,700	$9,900
Accounts Receivable	5,700	4,200	3,900
Inventories	10,220	7,500	6,600
Plant and Equipment (at cost)	61,100	55,500	45,000
Less Accumulated Depreciation	(29,400)	(25,800)	(22,800)
Total Assets	$50,420	$44,100	$42,600
Accounts Payable	$2,400	$1,900	$1,800
Notes payable—bank	1,400	900	600
Other Current Liabilities	1,900	1,600	1,400
Mortgage (8.5%)	11,400	11,600	11,700
Common Stock	26,120	22,000	22,100
Retained Earnings	7,200	6,100	5,000
Total Liabilities and Equity	$50,420	$44,100	$42,600

Figure 10-8. Wallace Products, Inc. Income Statement (000s)

	1986	1985	1984
Net Sales	$48,600	$42,300	$37,800
Cost of Goods Sold	37,800	33,300	30,300
Gross Margin	10,800	9,000	7,500
General and Administrative Expenses	4,200	3,900	3,600
Earnings Before Interest and Taxes	6,600	5,100	3,900
Interest Expenses	1,400	1,100	1,000
Earnings Before Taxes	5,200	4,000	2,900
Federal Income Taxes	1,500	1,200	800
Net Income After Taxes	$3,700	$2,800	$2,100
Dividends Declared and Paid	$1,500	$1,700	$1,200

LOPEZ AND LOPEZ, INC. CASE—CREDIT CAPACITY

Lopez and Lopez, Inc. is a manufacturer of electronic components located in El Paso, Texas. Its two manufacturing facilities are situated in El Paso itself and three miles across the border in Juarez, Mexico. Over 300 technicians produce the 100 different items in the firm's product line. These consist primarily of fabricated components for computers, telephones, and antennas. After the individual products have passed rigorous quality control tests, they are shipped to assembly points owned by firms such as IBM and Harris Corporation. Then, in locations such as Florida, Texas, Mexico, and Singapore, the components are installed in finished goods.

The firm was founded in the early 1980s by Carlos and Roberto Lopez. Using an economic development grant, Small Business Administration Loan, and personal savings, the two brothers opened a facility in El Paso. Two years later, they moved a portion of their operations to Mexico where they qualified for a Mexican Opportunities Loan. The firm has steadily repaid each loan, all of which are subsidized as compared to market interest rates.

Carlos and Roberto Lopez have recently obtained a contract to manufacture disk drives for personal computers. The initial run of 700,000 units over three years represents a major change in operations for the firm. Since Carlos is a former employee of Salomon Brothers in New York, he has retained this firm to assist in financing the new operation. It should be on line in the next 12 to 18 months, with primary manufacturing taking place in Hong Kong. All projections indicate that the operation will be profitable after the first year.

All of the above information is of interest to Liu Fangtian, the president of New China Industries. Mr. Liu is the largest single supplier to Lopez and Lopez, with outstanding receivables that reached $2.4 million in the last six months of 1988. In November 1988, $1.4 million was converted into short-term, interest-bearing notes, but almost $1 million remained as an account payable on the books of Lopez and Lopez.

Mr. Liu has requested a copy of the Lopez and Lopez financial statements. He also has the Prentice-Hall book of industry averages for the electronics industry, which are displayed in Figure 10-3. He is concerned about the credit capacity of Lopez and Lopez as it begins its expansion.

Figure 10-9. Lopez and Lopez, Inc. Balance Sheet (000s)

	1988	1987
Cash	$4,000	$2,000
Short-Term Investments	4,000	5,000
Accounts Receivable	13,300	7,500
Inventories	20,200	10,000
Total Current Assets	$41,500	$24,500
Plant Equipment		
(less accumulated depreciation)	53,000	33,000
Properties, nondepreciable	27,400	40,500
Total Fixed Assets	$80,400	$73,500
Total Assets	$121,900	$98,000
Accounts Payable	32,000	18,000
Notes Payable	34,000	24,000
Accrued Liabilities	10,000	7,000
Total Current Liabilities	76,000	49,000
Economic Development Grant	16,000	14,000
Small Business Administration Loan	0	6,000
Mexican Opportunity Notes	9,500	11,000
Total Long-Term Liabilities	25,500	31,000
Common Stock ($1 par)	7,000	7,000
Capital to Excess of Par	4,000	4,000
Retained Earnings	9,400	7,000
Total Equity	20,400	18,000
Total Liabilities and Equity	$121,900	$98,000

Figure 10-10. Lopez and Lopez, Inc. Income Statement (000s)

	1988	1987
Sales	$89,800	$87,800
Income from Investments	200	200
Total Revenues	$90,000	$88,000
Beginning Inventory	13,000	14,000
Total Manufacturing Costs	72,000	65,000
Less Ending Inventory	(26,200)	(23,000)
Cost of Goods Sold	58,800	56,000
Gross Profit	$31,200	$32,000
General and Administrative Expenses	9,500	8,000
Operating Income	$21,700	$24,000
Interest Expenses	7,400	6,500
Earnings Before Taxes	$14,300	$17,500
Federal Income Taxes	5,500	6,600
Net Income After Taxes	$8,800	$10,900
Dividends Declared and Paid		$5,000

Required: 1. Develop the financial statements and ratios for 1988.

2. What recommendation would you make to Mr. Liu with respect to the credit capacity of Lopez and Lopez, Inc.?

Economics of Short-Term Financing

In order to finance its cash, receivables, and inventories, the firm secures both long-and short-term financing. Funds are provided by suppliers, creditors, owners, and customers. Some funds involve direct costs, as when a loan is taken out at a bank. Others entail indirect costs, as with capital supplied by shareholders who expect a return on their investment. Still others involve no cost at all, as when the firm delays payment to a supplier who does not charge interest or a late fee.

This chapter is divided into two major sections. In the first, we will concentrate on current liabilities created by suppliers and financial institutions. We will examine funds supplied for relatively short periods of time, with an emphasis on interest-bearing sources, such as those used to finance seasonal working-capital needs. In the second part, we will cover a variety of financing techniques in the area of economics of credit. Specifically, we will discuss the impact of arranging installment financing for customers and the effective cost of specific credit actions, such as not taking discounts or delaying payment beyond the terms of trade.

SHORT-TERM FINANCING

A stable and profitable firm can finance a portion of its working-capital needs from short-term sources. In this section, we will examine these alternatives and evaluate their cost to the business.

Goals of Short-Term Financing

The firm's current liabilities can be used to achieve a variety of goals, including

1. **Flexibility.** Many firms have seasonal or cyclical needs for working-capital. During a period of maximum production, the firm may need to finance large inventories. Then, during the time of peak sales, the firm will have large receivables. Once the sales period is over and receivables have been collected, the firm may have excessive funds on hand. Short-term financing provides flexibility in matching funds against needs over an annual, seasonal, or cyclical period.

283

2. **Low Cost**. Short-term funds may be the most economical alternative available for financing a portion of working-capital. The firm may be unwilling to sell common stock at depressed prices or to borrow long-term if the funds are not needed on a permanent basis. In many cases, the interest charged on short-term financing will be lower than comparable long-term financing. Careful use of short-term liabilities can lower the firm's cost of financing its current assets.

3. **Increased Borrowing Capacity**. In many cases, a firm will be unable to raise money in bond markets or from other long-term sources. Short-term financing may be the only way to raise additional funds to finance inventories or receivables during a peak period.

Characteristics of Short-Term Financing

In evaluating the various opportunities presented by the use of current liabilities, a number of characteristics should be noted:

1. **High Risk**. The use of current liabilities implies repayment in a year or less. If the firm is unable to replace the funding in its mix of financing, it faces the possibility of near-term default. Short-term funds pose a distinct liquidity risk compared to long-term funds.

2. **Unpredictable Cost**. Short-term financing can provide both the highest and lowest cost funds in the capital mix. Some sources are more costly than intermediate or long-term debt. Others may have no interest cost at all. The problem is that these obligations mature in the near future and must be replaced on a regular basis. What will be the cost of these replacements? Will interest rates rise sharply? Will the money supply tighten, eliminating existing low-cost funds and leaving only expensive alternatives? These problems occur less often with long-term financing.

3. **Rollover Effect**. Even though short-term financing must, by definition, be repaid in less than one year, some sources provide funds that are continuously replaced. The funds provided by payables, for example, may remain relatively constant because, as some accounts are paid, other accounts are created. Rollover effect refers to the continual refinancing of short-term liabilities from period to period.

4. **Cleanup**. This occurs when commercial banks or other lenders require the firm to pay off its short-term debt for a given period in an annual cycle. Just as some sources are rolled over, some must be reduced to zero. This is commonly required where the cleanup offers proof that the short-term loan is being used to meet short-term or cyclical needs only.

Sources of Short-Term Financing

The firm's current liabilities are derived from a variety of sources, including

1. **Accounts Payable.** These payables are created when a firm purchases inventories, supplies, or other assets on credit without signing a formal note or loan agreement. A payable represents an unsecured debt obligation, since no specific assets are pledged as collateral for the liability. Payables represent an interest-free source of funds, for no interest is charged as long as the account is not overdue.

2. **Accruals.** These liabilities occur when the firm has received services but has not made payment. Typical accruals are wages payable or taxes payable. Employees may work for up to one month prior to being paid. Taxes may be owed for several weeks or more before a check is mailed to the state or federal government. In each case, the firm has use of money until payment is made and the check clears. Like payables, accruals are interest free.

3. **Unsecured Loans.** Banks and other financial institutions lend money to assist organizations in meeting short-term or cyclical needs. These loans are commonly unsecured because no assets are identified as collateral for repayment of the loan. These loan agreements require the payment of interest and may contain other provisions that increase the effective cost of the loan.

Unsecured Short-Term Loans

Three forms of short-term liabilities are commonly created as a result of lending arrangements by banks and financial institutions. These are the single payment note, the line of credit, and the revolving credit agreement.

1. **Single Payment Note.** This liability exists when a loan is repayable with interest at a specified time and maturity, often within 30 to 90 days. A **note** is a legal instrument that is signed by the borrower as proof of the existence of a debt. The money is provided when the note is signed, often by deposit into the borrower's account and the note is destroyed when repayment has been made. If the note is paid off before or after maturity, adjustments may be made to the interest owed.

2. **Line of Credit.** In this agreement between a commercial bank and a firm, the bank agrees to make available upon demand up to a stipulated amount of unsecured short-term funds, if the bank has the funds available. A line may be established to finance inventory, receivables, or some other short-term need of the firm. This is the most important factor in determining the maximum amount of the line. If the firm's inventory

rises by $1 million in April through June and its receivables rise by $1.5 million in June through September, a line of credit in the range of $2.5 to $3 million can cover the peak needs in this seasonal fluctuation. A line of credit is also commonly used to provide contingency funds or to meet unplanned needs. Thus, the firm may have a need for $2.5 million but may seek a $3 million line. The additional $500,000 will be used only as backup financing.

A standby line of credit exists when the entire request is approved for contingency purposes only. A line of credit is normally established for one year, and the stipulated interest rate is pegged to some financial indicator. The **prime rate** is a widely used measure of interest rates charged by banks. The **London Interbank Offered Rate (LIBOR)** is another indicator used for the cost of money in international financing. The interest rate on the line of credit may be expressed as prime or LIBOR plus some fixed percentage. Banks extend lines of credit in order to avoid the need to reexamine the creditworthiness of a customer each time a small loan is requested.

3. **Revolving Credit Agreement**. This agreement is, in effect, a line of credit with two modifications:

   a. **Guaranteed Availability**. Under most such agreements, the bank or financial institution guarantees the availability of funds regardless of how tight money might be. This is particularly important to the firm that makes a commitment based on receipt of the funds.

   b. **Conversion to Term Loan**. Once the firm draws against the revolving credit agreement, it may be converted to a term loan. Instead of repayment in a single amount or an annual cleanup, the agreement may become a multiple-year loan with steady monthly or quarterly payments. This might be the case when such financing is used for the purchase of a capital asset. Once such a purchase takes place, the agreement becomes an intermediate-term rather than a short-term source of funds.

The line of credit and the revolving credit agreement are used for different purposes. A line of credit normally finances seasonal or cyclical needs, where the asset financed is also the source of repayment. This is known as a self-liquidating loan. If inventory is financed, the sale of the inventory becomes the source of funds to pay the interest and repay the principal. A revolving credit agreement normally finances a capital asset that will be used to earn funds to repay the loan. The role of guaranteed availability becomes important in this context. Suppose, for example, that the firm wishes to order a large metal stamping machine that will require nine months to fabricate. Once it has the approved credit agreement, the firm can order the customized asset. When it is delivered, the firm knows it will have the funds to pay for the asset as a result of the guarantee from the bank. Without the guarantee, the firm would experience difficulty living up to its contract if the bank suddenly notified it that the funds would not be available. The revolving credit agreement is generally convertible to a term loan once the firm has requested a drawdown of funds. This allows the firm to pay off the loan in a series of monthly or quarterly payments spread over a period of time. If the agreement were designed to purchase a delivery truck, monthly payments spread over two to four years might be arranged after the firm made a 25 percent downpayment from other sources.

Effective Cost of Revolving Credit Agreement

To illustrate the effective cost of a revolving credit agreement, consider a firm with a $3 million approval. Six months prior to the expiration of the line, $1.7 million is likely to be borrowed. On the last day of the agreement, another $800,000 is expected to be used.

The terms of the agreement call for conversion to a term loan, with quarterly payments over a 27-month period. The first payment is scheduled to be made three months after the last day of the agreement when the $800,000 is used. During the period of the agreement, interest payments are required quarterly.

The interest rate on the loan is prime plus 2, compounded quarterly. During the agreement period, the prime rate is expected to be 12 percent. During the first nine months of the term loan, it should average 10.5 . For the next nine months, it should be 11.5, and then 13 percent for the last nine months.

What is the amortization schedule for the loan? The cash flow stream? The effective cost?

Figure 11-1 shows the effective cost of the agreement. The first nine months are identified as periods -2 to 0. The two borrowings are shown. The amortization schedule contains interest for only two quarters, and then nine payments that reduce the principal to zero.

The cash flows show the borrowings less interest for periods -2 to 0. Then, they represent the payments for nine periods. The effective cost is calculated using the internal rate of return formula built in to the spreadsheet program.

Figure 11-1. Effective Cost, Revolving Credit Agreement Converted to Term Loan.

Row		Col C Period -2	Col D Period -1	Col E Period 0	Col F Period 1	Col G Period 2	Col H Period 3
	Loan Data						
10	Borrowings	1,700,000		800,000			
11	Periods Left				9	8	7
12	Periods in Year	4					
13	Annual Rate		0.140	0.140	0.125	0.125	0.125
14							
15	AMORTIZATION SCHEDULE						
16							
17	Payment				322,959	322,959	322,959
18	Interest Portion		59,500	59,500	78,125	70,474	62,584
19	Principal Portion				244,834	252,485	260,375
20	Ending Balance	1,700,000	1,700,000	2,500,000	2,255,166	2,002,681	1,742,306
21							
22	Cash Flows	1,700,000	-59,500	740,500	-322,959	-322,959	-322,959
23							
24	Effective Cost			0.133			

At D18   +C20*D13/$C$12
At F17   @PMT(E20,F13/$C$12,F11)
At F19   +F17-F18
At F20   +E20-F19

Row		Col I Period 4	Col J Period 5	Col K Period 6	Col L Period 7	Col M Period 8	Col N Period 9
	Loan Data						
10	Borrowings						
11	Periods Left	6	5	4	3	2	1
12	Periods in Year						
13	Annual Rate	0.135	0.135	0.135	0.150	0.150	0.150
14							
15	AMORTIZATION SCHEDULE						
16							
17	Payment	325,634	325,634	325,634	327,973	327,973	327,973
18	Interest Portion	58,803	49,797	40,488	34,293	23,280	11,584
19	Principal Portion	266,831	275,837	285,146	293,680	304,693	316,119
20	Ending Balance	1,475,475	1,199,638	914,492	620,812	316,119	0
21							
22	Cash Flows	-325,634	-325,634	-325,634	-327,973	-327,973	-327,973
23							

Characteristics of Short-Term Loans

A number of characteristics are commonly found in agreements for short-term financing from financial institutions, namely:

1. **Maximum Amount Borrowed.** The bank will closely monitor the amount of the note or balance outstanding against the line of credit. Without proper controls, the bank will not allow the customer to exceed the maximum approved credit limit. It is technically possible to borrow more than the maximum on a line of credit in a series of borrowings, as long as the outstanding obligation at any one time does not exceed the credit limit. See Figure 11-2.

2. **Fees.** A bank loan may contain fees that are paid when the loan is approved or on the date when funds are first borrowed against a line of credit. Two types are common approval fee and availability fees.

    a. **Approval Fee.** The bank incurs costs evaluating the credit standing of the borrower and completing the paperwork for the loan. Depending on the size of the loan and conditions in the market, the bank may charge a fee of 1/8th of a percent to a full percent to cover its costs in approving the loan.

    b. **Availability Fee.** The bank incurs risks when it guarantees the availability of money. If the Federal Reserve severely restricts the money supply, the bank may have difficulty raising the funds it needs to meet its commitments. When the bank guarantees to provide the funds under any economic conditions, it may charge a fee of 1/2 to 1 percent for this service.

3. **Compensating Balance.** The bank may require that the firm maintain a stipulated portion of the borrowed funds in a demand deposit account at the lending bank. This regulation forces the borrower to be a customer of the bank and also raises the effective cost of the loan. The ability of the bank to require such balances will vary with competitive conditions in the marketplace. When such a requirement exists, it will normally range from 5 to 20 percent of the outstanding loan balance.

4. **Restrictive Covenants.** Banks commonly include certain requirements or restrictions as part of the loan agreement. One example would be operating restrictions to limit the firm's ability to change its activities or structure without bank approval. A loan agreement, for example, may give the bank the right to veto significant changes in a product mix if such changes weaken the firm's ability to pay its short-term obligations. Or the loan agreement may restrict the payment of cash dividends until certain conditions are met. These and similar requirements are **covenants** in the loan agreement.

Figure 11-2. Maximum Amount Borrowed Example.

Example:		A firm has a $2,400,000 line of credit with a large commercial bank. The following transactions occurred during the year. Did the firm exceed its maximum amount allowed by the bank? (Interest not shown in schedule).	

Date	Borrowed	Repaid	Loan Balance
January 12	$1,300,000		$1,300,000
March 9	600,000		1,900,000
April 9		400,000	1,500,000
June 6	800,000		2,300,000
August 27		600,000	1,700,000
October 15		700,000	1,000,000
November 10		400,000	600,000
December 7		600,000	0
	$2,700,000	$2,700,000	

Answer:	No. although the firm borrowed a total of $2.7 million during the year, the outstanding loan balance never exceeded the $2.4 million line of credit.

THE ECONOMICS OF SHORT-TERM LOANS

The decision to borrow money for a short period of time involves the ability to calculate **effective cost**, defined as the actual or real interest rate paid on a loan. Such cost consists of two factors.

1. **Interest Rate.** This figure is expressed in annual terms, even though the loan may be for a day or a month.
2. **Compounding Assumption. Compounding** takes place when calculating a future value of a payment or receipt of money. For example, when money is deposited in an interest-earning account and the interest is compounded, interest is earned on both the principal and on prior interest.

To state the effective cost correctly, the analyst must identify both the interest rate and the compounding assumption. As an example, we might say that the cost of a loan is 12 percent compounded monthly. In this section, we will examine the economics of short-term borrowing using the concept of effective cost.

Compounding Assumptions

The compounding assumption is a critical variable that affects the effective cost of short-term financing. Three assumptions are common:

1. **Annual Compounding.** This expresses the annual interest in the absence of compounding during the year.
2. **Periodic Compounding.** This is the days in a year divided by the days of the loan. For a 60 day loan with periodic compounding, the interest is compounded every 60-days, or 360/60 times a year.
3. **Daily Compounding.** This occurs when the interest is calculated each day and credited to the loan. The next day's interest will then be paid on both the principal and the accrued interest from the previous days.

The impact of compounding assumptions on a loan can be seen in Figure 11-3, where the input screen shows an $850,000 loan for 90 days at 12 percent interest. To calculate the amount due, we use the formula:

$$FV = PV * (1+INT)^N$$

where FV = amount owed at maturity, PV = amount of the loan, INT = the annual rate of interest, and N = the number of periods. The amount due ranges from $874,427 with annual compounding to $875,882 with daily compounding.

Similar results are obtained with financial calculators. For annual compounding, the calculation would be

N	=	0.25
I	=	12
PV	=	850,000
FV	=	874,427

For periodic compounding, the calculation would be

N	=	1
I	=	12 * (90/360)
PV	=	850,000
FV	=	875,500

For daily compounding, the calculation would be

N	=	90
I	=	12/360
PV	=	850,000
FV	=	875,882

Effective Cost, Single Payment Note

The actual or effective cost of a short-term loan may be calculated by the formula:

Annual Rate = $((FV/PV)^{(1/N)}-1) * $ (Periods in Year)

Figure 11-3. Solving Amount Due on Single Payment Note.

	Col D	Col E	Col F	Col G	Col H
Loan Data, Input Screen					
Row	Amount of Loan	Days of Loan	Days in Year	Annual Rate	Amount Due
11	850,000	90	360	0.12	NA
Output Screen					
	Annual Rate	Periods	Rate	Amount of loan	Amount Due
Annual Compounding					
17 Data	0.12	0.25	0.12	850,000	
18 Solution					874,427
Compounding By (Days in Year/Days of Loan)					
21 Data	0.12	1	0.03	850,000	
22 Solution				875,500	
Daily Compounding					
25 Data	0.12	9ø	0.0003	850,000	
26 Solution				875,882	

Formulas

$$FV = PV * (1+INT)^\wedge N$$

At H18	+G17 * (1 + F17)^E17
At F21	+F17 * $_E$11/F11
At H22	+G21 * (1 +F21)^E21
At F25	+F17/F11
At H26	+G25 * (1 + F25)^E25

This formula correctly handles compounding. With annual compounding, there is only one period in a year. With periodic compounding, the periods in a year are 360 days divided by the days of the loan. For daily compounding, the periods in a year are 360.

Figure 11-4 shows the effective cost of a loan under three compounding assumptions. The input screen shows a $700,000 loan for 60 days, with an amount of $718,000 due at maturity. The effective cost of the loan ranges from 16.46 percent with annual compounding to 15.24 percent with daily compounding.

Once again, we get the same results using a financial calculator. For annual compounding, the effective cost would be

N	=	60/360
I	=	16.46
PV	=	700,000
FV	=	718,000

For periodic compounding, the calculation would be

N	=	1
I	=	2.57
PV	=	700,000
FV	=	718,000

This represents a periodic rate. To obtain the annual rate, we multiply 2.57 percent times 360/60 and get 15.43 percent.

For daily compounding, the calculation would be

N	=	60
I	=	0.0423
PV	=	700,000
FV	=	718,000

This represents a daily rate. To obtain the annual rate, we multiply 0.0423 percent times 360 and get 15.24 percent.

Figure 11-4. Solving for Effective Cost, Single Payment Note.

	Col D	Col E	Col F	Col G	Col H
Loan Data, Input Screen					
Row	Amount of Loan	Days of loan	Days In Year	Annual Rate	Amount Due
10	700,000	60	360	NA	718,000
Output Screen					
	Effective Cost	Periods	Rate	Amount of Loan	Amount Due
Annual Compounding					
17 Data		0.1667		700,000	718,000
18 Solution	0.1646				
Compounding By (Days in Year/Days of Loan)					
21 Data		1		700,000	718,000
22 Solution	0.1543				
Daily Compounding					
25 Data		60		700,000	718,000
26 Solution	0.1524				

Formulas

Rate =	$((FV/PV)^{(1/N)}-1) *$ Compounding Factor
At D18	$(H17/G17)^{(1/E17)}-1$
At D22	$((H21/G21)^{(1/E21)}-1) * (F10/E10)$
At D26	$((H25/G25)^{(1/E25)}-1) * F10$

Effective Cost with Fees and Compensating Balance

If a loan requires the payment of upfront fees or involves a compensating balance, the effective cost of the loan is raised. This is illustrated in Figure 11-5 where our loan has a one-half percent immediate fee and a 10 percent compensating balance. Because the fee is deducted in advance and the compensating balance cannot be used, the actual available cash is $626,500. At maturity in 60 days, the firm must repay $648,000 and the bank will return the compensating balance. The effective cost of having $626,500 for 60 days and repaying $648,000 is between 20.25 and 22.44 percent, depending on the compounding assumption.

The same results occur with financial calculators for annual compounding:

Compounding:

N	=	60/360
I	=	22.44
PV	=	626,500
FV	=	648,000

For periodic compounding:

N	=	1
I	=	3.43
PV	=	626,500
FV	=	648,000

The annual rate compounded periodically is 20.59 percent 3.43*(360/60).
   For daily compounding:

N	=	60
I	=	.0563
PV	=	628,500
FV	=	648,000

The annual rate compounded daily is 20.25 percent .0563*360.

Figure 11-5. Solving for Effective Cost with Fees and Balances.

	Col D	Col E	Col F	Col G	Col H	
Loan Data, Input Screen						
Row		Amount	Days of	Days in	Annual	Amount
Fees	Balance, Percent	of Loan	Loan	Year	Rate	Due
10 0.005	0.1	700,000	60	360	NA	718,000
12 Less Fees		(3,500)				
13 Less Balances		(70,000)				(70,000)
15 NET CASH		626,500				648,000
Output Screen						
		Effective Cost	Periods	Rate	Amount of Loan	Amount Due
Annual Compounding						
24 Data			0.1667		626,500	648,000
25 Solution		0.2244				
Compounding By (Days in Year/Days of Loan)						
28 Data			1		626,500	648,000
29 Solution		0.2059				
Daily Compounding						
32 Data			60		626,500	648,000
33 Solution		0.2025				

Formulas

At D25	(H24/G24)^(1/E24)-1
At D29	((H28/G28)^(1/E28)-1)*F10/E10
At D33	((E32/G32)^(1/E32)-1)*F10

Effective Cost, Standby Financing

With a line of credit, the firm is not expected to use all the proceeds of the loan for a full year. In addition, the firm may seek approval for a larger loan amount than it is likely to need even at the peak period. This provides a margin of flexibility. As a result, the effective cost calculation must use the average loan balance less fees and compensating balances (See Figure 11-6).

In the figure, it is assumed that the compensating balance is required on the full approved amount-that is, exercised and unexercised portions. It is further assumed that, on the average, $400,000 will be borrowed during the 60 days. The effective cost rises dramatically because of the large compensating balance relative to the funds used.

CONCLUSION

The cost of short-term financing is a function of the cash received, the cash repaid, and the compounding assumption as shown by the techniques in this section. Considerable skill and flexibility are needed to evaluate all the options and determine the real charges for the funds. The firm should develop a set of policies and procedures so that it can choose cost effective funding of its working-capital needs, particularly taking advantage of competitive short-term bank financing when it is available.

EFFECTIVE COST OF WORKING CAPITAL

To minimize the amount of short-term financing needed, the firm can pay careful attention to managing cash, receivables, and inventory. It can also make optimal use of payables and accruals, two interest-free sources of funds. The firm should be seeking to measure the benefit or effective cost of different working-capital policies. In this context, **effective cost** (or **net benefit**) is defined as the actual gain or loss to each party in a transaction as a result of the time value of money or of administrative expenses. It is possible to devise many examples of the impact of gains or losses when dealing with current assets and current liabilities. Several have been selected and will be used in this section to illustrate the effective cost of working-capital decisions.

Figure 11-6. Solving for Effective Cost, Standby Financing.

		Col D	Col E	Col F	Col G	Col H
Loan Data, Input Screen						
Row Fees	Balance, Percent	Amount of Loan	Days of Loan	Days In Year	Annual Rate	Amount Due
10 0.005	0.1	700,000	60	360	NA	718,000
12 Less Fees		(3,500)				
13 Less Balances		(70,000)				(70,000)
14 Less Unused Part		(300,000)				(300,000)
16 NET CASH		326,500				348,000

Output Screen

		Effective Cost	Periods	Rate	Amount Of Loan	Amount Due
Annual Compounding						
24 Data			0.1667		326,500	348,000
25 Solution		0.4661				
Compounding By (Days in Year/Days of Loan)						
28 Data			1		326,500	348,000
29 Solution		0.3951				
Daily Compounding						
32 Data			60		326,500	348,000
33 Solution		0.3828				

Formulas

At D25	(H24/G24)^(1/E24)-1
At D29	((H28/G28)^(1/E28)-1)*F10/E10
At D33	((H32/G32)^(1/E32)-1)*F10

Effect of Delayed Payments

When a firm makes sales on credit terms, it may not receive cash for 30 or more days. Conversely, when it purchases inventory on credit, it does not immediately pay for the goods. In either situation, two possible costs exist:

1. **Funds Tied Up**. When a check has been mailed late, one party has the use of the money until it clears. The other party is providing financing, which can be measured as a lost opportunity cost. For each day that the funds are not available, the receiving firm loses an opportunity to invest the money or to pay off a short-term loan.

2. **Late Fees or Collection Costs**. Some suppliers charge late fees when customers are slow to pay, and the supplier may incur collection costs with customers who need to be reminded frequently about their obligations. These administrative charges or costs affect the impact of delayed payments.

Figure 11-7 shows the effect of two delayed payments in the following examples.

Figure 11-7. Effect of Delayed Payment.

	Col D		Col G
Input Screen			
ROW			
7 Dollar Amount	$5,000	Dollar Amount	$20,000
8 Cost of Money	0.18	Cost of Money	0.15
9 Days Late	38	Financing Period	127
10 Days in Year	360	Days in Year	360
12 Administrative Costs	$10	Bank Wire	$(12)
Output Screen			
16 Cost of Funds Tied Up	$95	Savings	$1,058
17 Administrative Costs	10	Less Bank Wire	(12)
19 Effective Cost	$105	Net Benefit	$1,046

Formulas

At D16   +D7*D9/D10*D8

At G16   +G7*G9/G10*G8

Example: A clothing supplier is entitled to receive $5,000 in payment for goods shipped. The customer pays the bill 38 days late at a time when money has an 18 percent annual cost. In addition, a reminder had to be sent, costing $10. What was the effective cost of this late payment?

Answer: $105, as shown in Column D in the Figure. $95 of the cost is the result of the lost opportunity cost on the funds; $10 is the administrative cost. This can be done on a financial calculator as follows:

N   =   1

I   =   18*38/360

PV   =   5000

Solve for FV of $5,095 and subtract the original $5,000 to get the $95 cost of funds.

Example: A firm must purchase goods worth $20,000 and has two suppliers who are bidding for the purchase. Although both quote the same price, one supplier offers extended financing by allowing the invoice to be paid 127 days late at no financing fee or penalty. This is significant because the firm can avoid financing the purchase at a 15 percent annual rate. On the 128th day, the supplier does require the money to be wired to his bank. This costs $12. If the firm accepts the extended terms, what is the net benefit?

Answer: $1,046, as shown in Column G in the figure. The savings of $1,058 in financing charges is reduced by the $12 to pay for the bank wire. This can be done on a financial calculator as follows:

N   =   1

I   =   15*127/360

PV   =   20000

Solve for FV of $21,058 and subtract the $20,000 price to get the $1,058 time value of money benefit.

Installment Financing for Customers

When goods are sold on extended credit terms, the firm has the opportunity to subsidize the sale and to provide installment financing for its customers. Or it can assist in financing the sale at a net profit to the firm. In either case, the firm can use working-capital financing to increase sales. The following example illustrates the net benefit when a firm charges a customer 15 percent for installment financing and then sells the customer's note to a financial institution at a slightly lower discount rate.

Example: A truck dealer offers financing on a new vehicle to a local business. The truck costs $55,000 and the customer signs a note for that amount payable in equal monthly install-ments over 36 months. The interest rate is 15 percent compounded monthly. The dealer then sells the note without recourse to a local bank at a discount rate of 14.6 percent, also compounded monthly. This allows the dealer to collect the money immediately instead of waiting the one month (terms of net 30) that is normally required with truck sales. What is the monthly payment on the note? Its net value when sold to the bank? The benefit to the dealer from this financing?

Answer: Net benefit is $973, as shown in Figure 11-8. Through use of the @PMT function built in to the spreadsheet, the monthly payment is computed to be $1,907. When a note for this amount is taken to the bank and discounted at 14.6 percent, it has a present value of $55,312. Having 30 days to collect the $55,000 is like having a present value of $54,339 at 14.6 percent cost of money. Thus, the firm assists in financing the transaction and earns a benefit of $973 for doing so. This can also be calculated on a financial calculator, as follows:

N = 36

I = 15/12

PV = 55000

Solve for PMT of $1,907. Then, discount this payment as follows:

N = 36

I = 14.6/12

PMT = 1907

Solve for PV of $55,312. Then, discount the original $55,000 back one month to a present value as follows:

N = 1

I = 14.6/12

FV = 55000

Solve for PV of $54,339. Then, subtract the $54,339 from the $55,312 to get the net benefit of $973.

Figure 11-8. Net Benefits When Providing Installment Financing.

	Col D
Input Screen	
Row	
7 Face Amount	55,000
8 Annual Interest	0.150
9 Number of Periods	36
10 Periods in Year	12
11 Net Terms in Months	1
12 Discount Rate at Bank	0.146
Output Screen	
16 Periodic Payment	1,907
18 Net Value of Note	55,312
19 Net Value of Credit Sale	<u>54,339</u>
20 Benefit from Financing	973

Formulas

At D16	@PMT(D7,D8/D10,D9)
At D18	@PV(D16,D12/D10,D9)
At D19	@PV(D7,D12/D10,D11)

HARPER COMPANY—ECONOMICS OF CREDIT

Each year, Ed Johnson selects one area of Harper Company for detailed review. This review generally occurs in the late spring, when production activities enter the pre-summer lull. This year, he has become concerned about his staff's knowledge of the fundamental economics of credit. He recently attended a seminar in which a speaker advocated greater understanding of the real cost of certain working-capital decisions. The speaker, a vice-president of a large California bank, claimed that "most firms can easily reduce their short term borrowings by simple steps of reviewing current liabilities and making proper decisions on the extension of credit."

One day, during a routine meeting with Anita Castro, his account representative at City Central Bank, Johnson mentioned the seminar. Anita Castro agreed that a basic knowledge of working-capital costs was an essential part of good bank relations. After some discussion, she agreed to raise some questions on Harper and send them to Johnson so he could use them with his staff.

Two weeks later, Johnson sent the following memorandum to his department heads:

TO: Department Heads

FROM: Edward Johnson

SUBJECT: Executive Development

We are a sufficiently large company that all managers should know about borrowing money and making credit decisions.

The attached questions have been raised by City Central State Bank. They can be solved using electronic spreadsheet software. I request each department head to individually answer each question at our spring program for management development.

Please send me a copy of your printout.

1.   Harper currently has a 120 day loan, interest only, with an industrial finance corporation. The effective cost of that loan is 17.5 percent with periodic compounding. City Central State Bank is willing to pay off that loan, which has an outstanding balance of $3,400,000. The principal and interest would be paid in a single payment in 120 days, such payment calculated at 12 percent interest, monthly compounding. An upfront fee of .005 would be charged and a 2 percent compensating balance would also be required. What is the effective cost with periodic compounding of the bank's proposal if the firm must net $3,400,000 from the borrowing? At what final payment would the 2 sources of financing have the same effective cost?

302

2. The firm has an unsecured line of credit with Manufacturers Hanover Trust Company in the amount of $1,400,000. In the next 150 days, the average usage on the line will be $1,000,000. To obtain this amount, Harper's Treasurer must pay an upfront fee of 1/2 percent on the entire line. Also, the line requires a compensating balance of 10 percent on the exercised portion only. The interest rate is prime plus 2. Although the current prime rate is only 12 percent, the Treasurer expects an average prime rate of 13 percent during the 150 days. What is the effective cost of this loan under periodic compounding?

3. Simpson Industries has billed Harper Company for $325,000 for raw materials. The firm has offered terms of net 75 if the funds are wired on the 75th day. This check would clear on the 76th day and involves a cost of $15. Alternatively, Harper could pay by wire in 10 days and take a 1.5 percent discount. A final possibility is to mail a check for the net amount on the 45th day. This check would clear on the 50th day. Harper's short term cost of money is 13 percent. Which method of payment should be selected by the firm?

4. Harper has completed a sale for $175,000 to a client on terms of net 30. Based on past experience, the company's check will not clear until the 45th day. The company has requested assistance in financing the purchase. Harper's Treasurer has offered 2 year financing at 16.5 percent, with a signed note indicating quarterly payments and compounding. City Central State Bank has reviewed the customer's credit and will accept the note without recourse discounted at 15.5 percent. What is the quarterly payment on this note? The benefit to Harper from the financing?

5. Harper has a loan agreement in the amount of $4.6 million with Chase Manhattan Bank. The period is 45 days and the amount due at maturity is $4,678,629. The loan agreement states that the annual interest cost is 13.75 percent. What is the compounding assumption in this agreement?

6. Harper prepares a monthly payroll at present. The average monthly payroll has been $1.5 million. The Controller has suggested changing the system so payday occurs every other Friday. The firm's cost of funds is 13 percent. The cost of preparing a single payroll is $600. What would be the annual net increase in cost if the firm were to change its payroll system?

7. Harper's current policy is to offer terms of trade of 2/10 net 30. The average customer accepting the discount has a check that clears in 21 days. The average customer who passes up the discount sends a check that clears in 60 days. What is the effective cost of offering discounts if the firm's cost of short term funds is 13 percent?

12

Sources of Near-Term Financing

Short and intermediate-term financing are of primary importance to the firm's efforts to secure adequate funds for the conduct of its business. The proper use of these sources provides flexibility to match cyclical and seasonal variations in operational needs. For many firms it also offers an increase in total borrowing capacity. In identifying such sources, the firm has a variety of alternatives with different benefits, costs, and restrictions.

In this chapter, we will identify different sources of short-term and intermediate-term financing and discuss their characteristics. The line of credit and revolving credit agreement were discussed in Chapter 11. In this chapter we will examine miscellaneous financings, and we will cover receivables financing, including pledging and factoring.

MISCELLANEOUS SHORT-TERM CREDIT

In addition to the conventional line of credit and revolving credit agreement, the firm has several other choices of short-term financing. Some of the sources are banks or financial institutions; some are not. In this section, we will describe some miscellaneous short-term borrowings available to the firm.

Commercial Paper

The term *commercial paper* refers to short-term unsecured promissory notes issued by large nonfinancial corporations. *Finance paper* refers to similar notes from finance companies. These notes are issued by firms that need cash for periods of 3 to 270 days. This kind of paper is often issued in multiples of $100,000 and can be used only by large, well-known corporations because they are unsecured obligations of the firm.

Commercial paper is purchased by other firms with excess cash who desire to earn a higher yield than is available on treasury securities. In return for the higher yield, the investor accepts slightly greater risk and less liquidity.

Commercial paper is normally purchased through a bank or securities dealer, whereas the bulk of finance paper is purchased directly from finance companies. In both cases, the paper is usually held to maturity, since no active secondary market exists to transfer paper. In some cases, firms or finance companies will honor requests to buy back their paper, usually charging a fee for this service.

Commercial and finance paper have grown in importance over the years. At one time, conservative managers insisted that treasurers limit short-term investments to secured assets. The excellent repayment record and higher yields of paper from large stable companies, however, have encouraged firms to become more active in the paper market.

From the point of view of the issuing firm, commercial paper is an attractive approach to raising short-term funds. Although yields to investors are high, the cost of such financing is low compared to direct borrowing from banks. When Treasury securities yield 11 percent, the bank prime rate might be 14 percent. Commercial paper financing is in the middle, perhaps 12 to 13 percent. The yield to investors is above Treasury securities; the cost of financing is below the prime rate. As long as the issuing firm is strong, both sides benefit.

Private Loans

Whereas large firms can use commercial paper, smaller firms can arrange creative private financing. A short-term unsecured loan may be obtainable from a wealthy shareholder, a major supplier, or other party interested in assisting the firm through a short-term difficulty. This kind of arrangement generally occurs when a temporary liquidity problem endangers the firm's operations. In this case, bank financing becomes unlikely. Borrowing from nonbank financial institutions may be prohibitively costly and may contain unacceptable restrictions. In such a case, a shareholder, creditor, or supplier might feel that its existing stake in the company is in jeopardy. A short-term private loan can help the firm get through the liquidity problem and return to normal operations.

Advances from Customers

A customer may pay for all or a portion of future purchases in advance of receiving the goods. This form of unsecured financing provides funds to purchase the raw materials and produce the final goods. In most cases, this form of financing is a special arrangement for expensive or custom-made items that would strain the financial resources of the manufacturing company.

Advances may also be used when a large order involves extensive startup costs. As an example, suppose a customer ordered 300,000 units of a product over a 14-month period. Furthermore, the firm had to create an assembly line to build the product. Over the period of the 14 months, the contract could be quite profitable. The difficulty arises because of the high initial expenses. These could be covered by an advance from the customer.

Secured Short-Term Sources

Commercial paper, private loans, and customer advances are usually unsecured borrowings. A **secured loan** occurs when the borrower pledges a specific asset to back up a loan. The lender is given a claim to the collateral through the signing of an agreement that may be filed in a public office, such as a county or state agency.

Collateral is defined as any asset with a market value that can be pledged with a creditor as security for a debt. It can take a variety of forms. Securities are probably the most desirable collateral, particularly the stock or bonds of companies that are well known or traded publicly. If the firm defaults on the terms of the loan, the securities can be liquidated quickly and without high fees. Receivables are also popular as collateral. Since the sale has already been made, the collateral is self-liquidating as the checks are received to pay for the goods sold on credit. Inventory is also commonly used, even though it is less liquid than receivables or securities. Capital assets, such as equipment, are the least desirable because of difficulties in converting them into cash.

A **security agreement** spells out the terms of the loan, the assets that are pledged as collateral, and the provisions affecting the safeguarding of the collateral. This document may be filed with a public agency. By such filing, the borrower is legally establishing the lender's first claim on the assets in the event of default. The filing also places future prospective lenders on notice that certain assets are not available to back additional loans.

Warehouse Receipt Loan

A common secured source of funds is a **warehouse receipt loan**, a short-term borrowing secured by a pledge of inventory controlled by the lender. The bank, financial institution, or other lender selects the inventory that is acceptable as collateral. A warehousing company then takes physical possession of the inventory in one of two ways.

1. **Field Warehouse**. Under this arrangement, a warehousing company establishes a field warehouse on the premises of the borrower. The pledged goods are isolated from other inventory, counted and listed on a warehouse receipt, and placed in the possession of a guard or warehouseperson who is not allowed to release the goods without authorization from the lender. The warehouse receipt, which itemizes the goods along with an estimated value for each item, becomes, in effect, the title for the goods. By holding the warehouse receipt, the lender has complete control over the inventory and the first claim to it over other creditors in the event of default or bankruptcy.

2. **Terminal Warehouse**. Under this arrangement, a central warehouse near the borrower is used to store the inventory. This arrangement generally occurs when goods are easily and inexpensively transportable.

The goods are checked in upon arrival at the warehouse, and a warehouse receipt is issued. Once again, the public warehouse keeps the collateral under a 24-hour guard, and only the lender can authorize release of the inventory.

Warehouse receipt loans are generally more costly than unsecured short-term financing. In addition to the financing charges, the borrower must pay the warehousing costs and insurance on the goods. It is not uncommon for warehouse receipt loans to run 3 to 7 percent above prime, a rate that is usually in excess of unsecured commercial bank loans.

Trust Receipt Loan

A **trust receipt loan** is secured by specific and easily identified collateral that remains in the control or physical possession of the borrower. Pledges of inventories or receivables are common. When automobile dealers use this kind of financing for the cars in their showrooms or in stock, it is called **floor planning**.

As implied by their name, this kind of loan requires a considerable degree of **trust** in the honesty and integrity of the borrower. As soon as the item of inventory is sold or the receivable is collected, payment must be remitted to the lender. If this is not done, the loan is said to be secured by **bogus collateral** and the loan is technically in default.

Trust receipt loans are common when the collateral is easily identified by description or serial number and when each item of collateral has a relatively large dollar value. For automobiles or appliances, it is fairly easy for a lender to make spot checks by visiting the borrower's facilities to confirm that the collateral has not been liquidated. This kind of control would not be feasible for loans secured by numerous small items without distinguishing characteristics.

Floating Lien Loan

A **lien** is a claim by a lender on the property of a borrower as security or collateral for a debt or obligation. A **floating lien loan** is secured by a group of assets that are not specifically identified by individual items. For example, a loan that is secured by "the hard cover books physically on the premises" would be a floating lien loan. Some books would be sold and some purchased on a continuing basis, but the existing inventory at any one time is the collateral for the borrowing.

From the lender's viewpoint, the floating lien loan is less satisfactory than the trust receipt loan. Thus, floating lien loans typically are made as a lower percentage of value than trust receipt loans. For example, a bank may lend 80 percent of the value of an automobile but only 40 percent of the value of hardcover books. In the event of default, the automobile can be sold quickly and easily at a high percent of its value; it is far more costly to liquidate hundreds or thousands of hardcover books that may have to be sold for only a fraction of their value.

RECEIVABLES FINANCING

Accounts receivable commonly represent a sizable liquidity problem for the firm. Although highly liquid compared to other assets, they are not, in fact, cash. When a sale is made, the firm may already have expended considerable cash for inventory and manufacturing expenses and the goods are gone, but cash has not been received and will not be available for 30 to 90 days after the sale.

Because of the attractiveness of receivables as collateral and the large volume of receivables that may be outstanding at any one time, many firms use them to generate short-term funds. Two techniques that are commonly employed will be discussed in this section.

Pledging Receivables

An **assignment** is a transfer of a claim or right in an asset from one party to another. By pledging or assigning an account receivable, a firm gives up the rights to the cash collected on that account. Because receivables are normally quite liquid, they are attractive as collateral to commercial banks or finance companies.

The pledging of accounts receivable as collateral for short-term financing involves four steps.

1. **Selecting the Accounts**. The firm can pledge some or all of its accounts. Usually, accounts are pledged on a **selective basis,** which means that the lender analyzes the past payment records of each customer and lends money only against the accounts that represent good credit risks. With careful selection, a lender may be willing to lend as much as 90 percent of the face value of the receivable. If weak accounts were included, the lender might not be willing to lend more than 50 percent of the face value.

2. **Adjusting the Face Value**. Each account receivable will have a face value on the books of the borrowing company, but some goods may be returned after being inspected. This will lower the value of the receivable. To allow for returns and to reflect the customers who will take cash discounts for early payment, the lender will adjust the face value of the receivable downward. Thus, a $1,000 receivable may be viewed to be worth $950.

3. **Determining the Percentage.** Next, the lender must determine the percentage of the face value that will be lent. For a strong credit risk, the lender may be willing to advance 90 percent. On a $950 receivable, the loan would be 90 percent of $950 or $855.

4. **Collecting the Payments.** When the customer pays his or her obligation that created the receivable, the bank or finance company gets its money. This can happen in two ways:

   a. **Nonnotification Basis.** In most cases, the customer whose account has been pledged is not notified of the pledging. The customer remits payment directly to the firm as though the account had not been pledged as collateral for a loan. As soon as the firm collects payment, it must immediately notify the bank or finance company and pay off its loan. On a nonnotification basis, the firm's obligation is a form of trust receipt loan.

   b. **Notification Basis.** In these cases, the customer is directed to remit payment directly to the lender. This arrangement is safer from the point of view of the lender. It is less satisfactory to the borrower since the customer may interpret the pledging as a sign that the firm is in financial trouble.

Schedule of Receivables, Simonson Company

Account	Amount	Days Outstanding	Average Payment Period Historically in Days
74	25,000	15	20
91	9,000	45	60
107	11,500	22	24
108	2,300	9	10
114	18,000	50	45
116	29,000	16	10
123	14,000	27	48
	108,800		

Example: Republic National Bank is analyzing the receivables of Simonson Company in order to identify acceptable collateral for a short-term loan. The company's credit policy is 2/10 net 30. The bank lends 80 percent on accounts where customers are not currently overdue and where the average payment period does not exceed 10 days past the net period. A schedule of Simonson's receivables has been prepared. How much will the bank lend on a pledge of receivables if the bank uses a 10 percent allowance for cash discounts and returns?

Answer: $48,816, as follows:

1. **Select Accounts**. The bank requires that no selected accounts be overdue. Since 30 days is the net period, accounts 91 and 114 are overdue. Eliminate them. The bank requires that the average payment be less than 10 days longer than the net period, or 40 days. Eliminate 123. The selected accounts are 74, 107, 108, and 116.

2. **Adjust Face Values and Determine Percentage of Loan**. The bank uses 10 percent adjustment for cash discounts and returns; it lends at 90 percent of adjusted face value. The loan is calculated as follows

Account	Original Value	90 Percent of Original	80 Percent of Adjusted
74	25,000	22,500	18,000
107	11,500	10,350	8,280
108	2,300	2,070	1,656
116	29,000	26,100	20,880
			$48,816 Loan Value

Factoring Receivables

A **factor** is an individual or a financial institution that purchases accounts receivable from business firms. Factoring receivables is the outright sale of the accounts receivable to a factor who generally accepts all the credit risks associated with collection of the accounts. Since the accounts are sold, a factoring arrangement does not involve a loan unless the firm takes an advance against the funds.

A factoring agreement will normally specify the charges and procedures for the sale of the receivables. Most factoring arrangements are continuing; that is, the firm's receivables are sold as they are created. This places the full credit and collection burden on the factor. Some of the key elements of a factoring arrangement are as follows:

1. **Selection of Accounts**. As with pledging, the factor selects the accounts that he or she will purchase. If the factor is accepting all the firm's receivables, the factor then becomes responsible for making the firm's credit decisions. This role of the factor is widely used in the garment and textile industries.

2. **Collection of Accounts.** The factor becomes responsible for the collection of receivables. Normally, the customers are notified and instructed to send their payments directly to the factor. In cases where the firm desires to keep the presence of a factoring agreement secret, the customer is simply informed to send his or her payment to a new address. At this new address, the factor receives the payment directly even though the customer may not be aware of the factoring agreement.

3. **No Recourse on Bad Debts. Recourse** is the right of one party to demand payment from a second party if a third party fails to pay an obligation. Most factoring is done without recourse, that is, without the factor having the right to demand payment from the firm if the customer does not pay his or her bills. In some rare situations, usually with a particularly weak credit, the agreement may be made with recourse.

4. **Date of Payment.** The agreement normally stipulates that the firm will be paid when the factor collects the account or on the last day of the net credit period, whichever occurs first. When the date of payment is also the date of collection, no credit is being granted by the factor.

5. **Advances.** A factor will establish an account for the firm that is similar to a bank account. Payments are made by depositing money in the account. The firm can withdraw the money as needed. The secured short-term credit arises when the factor makes an advance against uncollected and not due accounts. An **advance** is a payment prior to the due date or collection of a receivable. To get an advance, the firm simply overdraws the account set up with the factor. Interest is charged on any advances.

6. **Surpluses.** The firm does not have to withdraw funds from the account as they are deposited by the factor. A **surplus** is any money that is left in the account, and this will draw interest.

7. **Factor's Reserves.** As part of the factoring agreement, a certain percentage of the face value of the receivables is set aside as **reserves** to protect against returns or cash discounts. The reserves are particularly important when the firm draws advances against accounts that have not yet been collected. If the factor made an advance and then the goods were returned because they were damaged, the factor would, in effect, be extending a partially unsecured loan. The reserve of 5 to 10 percent on all the accounts will protect against the possibility of a return producing an unsecured advance. Once the customer has paid the factor, the amount of the reserve is returned to the firm if an advance has been taken against an uncollected receivable.

Factoring Costs

Three kinds of calculations must be considered to measure the cost of factoring:

1. **Factoring Commissions.** These are payments to the factor to cover the administrative costs of verifying credit ratings and collecting receivables. These commissions also cover the risk when accounts are purchased without recourse. As a general rule, the factoring commissions will run between 2 and 4 percent of the face value of factored accounts.

2. **Interest on Advances.** The factor will charge between 2 and 5 percent above the prime rate as the annual interest rate on advances. It is paid in advance, as in the case of a discount, and thus raises the effective borrowing costs as compared to paying interest at the end of the period.

3. **Interest on Surpluses.** The factor will pay a much lower interest on surpluses not withdrawn by the firm. The interest will be close to similar short-term investments, such as certificates of deposit.

The factoring reserves do not represent a cost of factoring. The reserve is no more than a percentage of the account that will not be included in an advance. The advance is made for, say, 90 percent of the receivable, and, upon collection or the date of payment, the factor will forward the remaining 10 percent.

Example: Pierson Associated Milling has sold four accounts that are due for collection on November 30 to Houston National Bank, which is acting as a factor. The bank charges a 4 percent commission. The accounts are given with their status on November 30. How much does Houston National Bank deposit in the Pierson factoring account on November 30?

Account	Face Value	Status on November 30
23	120,000	Collected on Nov. 30
32	70,000	Collected on Nov. 10
35	67,500	Not yet collected
41	47,000	Collected on Nov. 30

Answer: $225,120. Account number 32 was collected on November 10 and the $70,000 has already been deposited. Of the remaining $234,500, the 4 percent commission is deducted and $225,120 is deposited. The fact that account number 35 has not yet been collected does not matter. The factor is liable for the loss if he or she is unable to collect the $67,500.

Example: A factor has accepted an account with a $140,000 face value due on March 30. The factoring agreement requires a 3 percent commission and a 10 percent reserve. The factor charges 15 percent on advances. A maximum advance is given on March 10, and the account is collected on April 10. How much was the advance? What was the total amount of money received by the firm?

Answer: The advance was $121,202, as follows: 97 percent of $140,000 is $135,800, of which 90 percent can be given as an advance since the remaining 10 percent is held as a reserve; 90 percent of $135,800 is $122,220, but 15 percent interest is deducted in advance.

$122,200 x 0.15 x 20/360 = $1,019 interest

$122,220 - 1,019 = $121,202 advance

$134,782 was the total received by the firm,

$121,202 as the advance and 10 percent of

$135,800 or $13,580 on March 30.

Benefits of Pledging and Factoring

Pledging and factoring receivables offer a number of advantages to the firm, including

1. **Flexibility**. Receivables financing is an additional source of funds that can be called on as needed. It also is a rising source of financing as the firm grows since higher levels of sales produce more receivables to sell or pledge.

2. **Assistance in Credit Decisions**. Receivables financing gives outside help to the firm in analyzing customers who desire credit. With factoring, the outside factor makes the complete decision; in pledging, the outside party comments on the relative strength and weakness of customers by selecting only strong customers as collateral.

3. **Cost Savings**. By reducing or eliminating the Credit Department, the firm saves money. With factoring, the collection responsibility is gone, which represents an additional saving. The factor, commercial bank, or finance company charges for providing these services, of course, but the commissions paid may be less than the total of collection and credit

costs, delinquency costs, and default costs. As a general rule, it does cost more to use receivables financing, but it may be close to other financing costs, as shown in Figure 12-1.

Disadvantages of Receivables Financing

Two primary disadvantages are commonly associated with receivables financing:

1. **High Cost.** Even though receivables financing can be comparable to unsecured financing in some cases, as shown in Figure 12-1, in most cases it is more costly. A large firm with established credit procedures for its customers and continuing contacts with its banks can generally locate less costly financing.

2. **Implication of Weakness.** Receivables are a highly liquid current asset that will provide next period's available cash. A firm's customers or creditors may view the receivables financing as harmful to next period's cash and may feel that the firm must be experiencing financial difficulties if it has to give up future cash and resort to the higher cost receivables financing. Today, pledging or factoring receivables is less widely viewed as a sign of weakness, particularly in the garment and textile industries where it has been common for many years.

Figure 12-1. Comparison of Total Costs for Factoring, Pledging Receivables, and Unsecured Short-Term Financing.

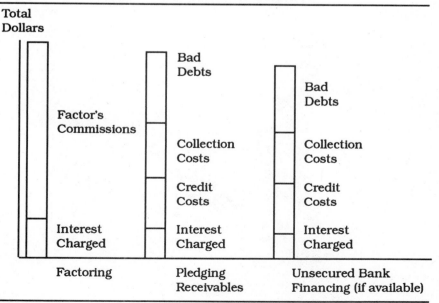

CONCLUSION

The firm has a variety of short-term sources of funds to provide financing for its working-capital needs. Each source has its own advantages and disadvantages. In most cases, the firm is trading off the cost of such financing for the flexibility provided. Unsecured financing offers the greatest latitude but involves the highest cost. Secured financing has a lower cost but will require greater participation in management by the lender. To choose the appropriate mix, the analyst should be aware of the strengths and weaknesses of each source and be able to calculate the effective cost therein.

MADISON MANUFACTURING CASE—FACTORING DECISION

The Madison Manufacturing Company produces a wide variety of display items for the home and office. The firm sells picture frames, trophy cases, gun racks, and related items to department stores throughout the country. In addition, the firm has sales to some 200 independent distributors or sales representatives who make sales to variety stores, furniture stores, and gift shops. The size of Madison's accounts receivable range from $200, which represents the minimum order that it will accept, to $25,000 to $30,000 for its five largest distributors and 10 to 15 of its large department store accounts.

The president of Madison Manufacturing Company is Ed Madison, the youngest son of the firm's founder. The company is privately owned, with the majority of the shares held by members of the Madison family and former employees of the firm. Madison follows the firm's traditional policy of what his father used to describe as "a sound product line and a sound balance sheet." By stressing new technology and a complete product line, the firm has shown strong profits with minimum cyclical downturns. By emphasizing a sound balance sheet, the firm has avoided borrowing to finance capital purchases. The firm has retained a portion of its earnings each year to finance expansion. Last year, as an example, the firm retained almost $100,000 after declaring a dividend of $530 a share. The firm's most recent balance sheet and income statement are attached.

Madison typically selects one area of the company for detailed review each spring. This year he has chosen the firm's credit policy and has begun to collect information so that it may be evaluated. The firm's selling terms are 1/10 net 30, and he does not plan to change them because of competitive factors. But he does want to pay particular attention to bad–debt losses, which seem typically to run some $40,000 to $50,000 a year.

At the beginning of the review, Madison called Anita Castro, his account representative at City Central Bank. She arranged the $245,000 bank note financing that Madison uses to help finance the company's inventory. The total line of credit is $350,000 at prime plus 2.8, and the firm finished the year with $245,000 exercised against it. Castro has pointed out the bank's wishes that the line be "cleaned up" by May 4 of the current year, and she indicated a willingness to work with Madison on the review of the firm's credit policy.

During the early steps of the review, Anita suggested that Madison consider allowing City Central Bank to factor the company's receivables. Factoring receivables, she explained, is the outright sale of the receivables to a factor, who accepts all the credit risks of collecting the accounts. City Central Bank has been in the factoring business for many years and could be very helpful to Madison Manufacturing. When Madison indicated interest, Castro explained the process the bank would follow. First, the bank would select the accounts that would be purchased. Customers who were excessively slow to pay or who had poor credit records would not be acceptable to the bank. Then all customers would be instructed to send their remittances to Madison Manufacturing Company at a new post office box, the box maintained by the bank's Factoring Department. The customers would not know that the receivables had been factored. On the date the bank collects the account or on the last day of the 30-day net period, whichever occurs first, Madison's account at City Central would be credited with a deposit for the amount collected on the face amount of the receivables, less any reserves. A reserve is an amount set aside by the bank to protect against returns, cash discounts, or other adjustments.

Madison had some questions on this procedure. First, would the reserve cover bad-debt losses? The answer was no. The accounts would be purchased by the bank without recourse, that is, without the bank having the right to demand payment from the company if the customer did not remit payment. In special cases, the bank would be willing to purchase individual accounts—those with a weak credit rating—with recourse, that is, with Madison accepting the risk of nonpayment.

A second question was, who would be responsible for collecting overdue accounts? Castro pointed out that this was the bank's responsibility. Madison would get its money at the latest on the last day of the net period.

Madison's final question got to the root of the issue. "How much would it cost?" Castro replied with an example, "Suppose," she said, "the bank purchases a $1,000 receivable on terms of 1/10 net 30 with an invoice dated October 1. On October 30, payment has not arrived at the bank. We deduct our 3.2 percent commission and credit your account with $968 on the 30th." At that point, Madison responded, "Isn't a 3.2 percent commission rather steep?" Castro replied that it was needed to cover the administrative costs of verifying credit ratings, collecting the receivables, and accepting the risk of bad-debt losses.

As Madison thought over the proposal, Castro pointed out the benefits of the program. The company would get its money faster—within 30 days at the maximum—and this would reduce its needs for other financing. In addition, the firm would no longer have to perform the different credit functions. It could reorganize its Accounting Department and cancel its membership in Dun and Bradstreet's rating service. The headaches of collections would be passed on to the bank. The session concluded with Madison expressing a willingness to investigate the matter further.

Madison made an estimate of the possible savings with a factoring arrangement. The Accounting Department had a manager and three clerical accounting personnel. The department's salaries and fringe benefits totaled $46,400, and related expenses were $16,000 last year. These numbers included the direct collection costs of $6,450 (long-distance calls and other out-of-pocket expenses). If Madison turned over the credit function to a factor, he would be able to transfer one of the clerical accounting people, at an annual savings of roughly $9,600. This too was attractive.

Another attractive feature would be the reduction in the firm's average collection period (ACP), or days sales outstanding. Last year, the ACP was almost 53 days; under the factoring arrangement, it would drop to about 25 days according to Madison's calculations of customers who take the firm's discounts.

One thing that did not interest Madison was borrowing against the receivables. Castro had explained that the bank would advance funds against the receivables purchased. Madison felt that his firm's credit standing at the bank would be hurt over the long term if the bank viewed Madison Manufacturing as a secured borrower. He wanted to continue the existing line of credit arrangement independently of any factoring arrangement.

Madison pursued this matter at his next meeting with Castro. She agreed that the bank would probably accept virtually all of Madison's current accounts without recourse at a 3.2 percent factoring commission. Madison then indicated that he would analyze his situation and give her a firm answer in a few weeks. He said, "I consider our normal borrowing cost to be about 9 percent. By collecting our receivables more quickly, we can reduce this financing cost. I can also cut down my Accounting Department, and I do need another clerk in shipping, so this may be very workable. Let me run the numbers and we'll talk again."

Required: Is factoring economically justified for Madison Manufacturing?

Madison Manufacturing Company—Balance Sheet

Cash (1st Nat. account)	$22,441	Payables	
Treasury Bills (April 4		Trade	$144,009
maturity)	25,000	Other	7,272
Receivables		Notes (1st Nat. 9.75%	
Distributors and Representatives	132,415	May 4 maturity)	245,000
Others	232,778	Mortgage (9.25%)	51,738
Inventories		Common Stock (no par,	
Metals and Wood	43,694	520 shares issued)	520
In Process	157,910	Retained Earnings	830,167
Finished	113,124		
Prepaid Items	3,251		
Physical Facilities			
Plant	154,117		
Equipment	318,776		
Land	75,200		
Total assets	$1,278,706	Total liabilities & equity	$1,278,706

Madison Manufacturing Company–Income Statement
(Year Ending Dec. 31)

Cash Sales	$23,551		
Credit Sales	2,633,187		
Less Returns and Discounts	(114,663)		
Net Sales			$2,542,075
Cost of Sales			
Purchases and Materials		$475,631	
Direct Salaries and Wages		515,359	
Overhead and Fixed Costs		229,765	
Selling Expenses			1,220,755
Sales Force Salaries		283,774	
Exhibitions and Shows		43,560	
Administrative and Overhead		109,738	437,072
Management and Administrative Expenses			
Data Processing		55,766	
Salaries and Office		214,047	
Other		33,609	303,422
Earnings Before Taxes			580,826
Reserve for Federal Taxes (40%)			232,330
Earnings After Taxes			$348,496

Notes

1. Depreciation and Noncash Expenses:
   Depreciation   = $47,850
   Noncash Expenses   =   4,784

2. Financing Charges   = $29,853 in Other Management and Administrative Expenses

V.

Credit and Collections

Analyzing the Credit Capacity
of Customers

The decision to extend credit affects every area of a firm's operations. If credit terms are too tight, products cannot be sold by even the most creative sales force. If credit terms are lax, sales may not result in collections. Or, during periods of high interest rates, the firm may be squandering its profits because of excessive financing costs as customers are slow to pay.

The decision to extend credit should always begin with an analysis of the soundness of the potential purchaser. The credit manager is, in effect, determining credit capacity. Is the potential purchaser sufficiently liquid so as to have cash when the invoice is due? Is the customer profitable, so that such liquidity will continue into the distant future? Does the customer have a capital and operating structure that reveals a reasonable approach to the conduct of business?

In this chapter, we will develop a ratio analysis approach to evaluating the fundamental soundness of purchasers. We will begin with an overview of the elements of credit capacity and then briefly review the liquidity aspects that were covered in detail in Chapter 10. Next, we will evaluate the firm's profit picture. Finally, we will examine some miscellaneous ratios that complete the view of credit capacity.

ELEMENTS OF CREDIT CAPACITY

The determination of credit capacity involves the firm in a risk and return analysis. Given the risk of selling on credit, what will be the likely return? If the customer is highly creditworthy, it is likely that the receivable will be collected and profits will be made. If the customer lacks credit capacity but a firm approves the credit sale anyway, the firm takes greater risks.

Credit capacity has financial and nonfinancial components. A traditional way to evaluate both components makes use of the five C's of credit: character, capacity, conditions, collateral, and credit norms. Using this framework, we will examine the elements of credit capacity.

Character

Bank lending officers often observe that a bank does not lend to financial statements; it lends to people. Thus, the quality of management is a critical variable in creditworthiness and a measurement of credit capacity. **Character** is commonly the first, and some say the most important, of the five C's of credit. It reflects an assessment of the willingness of the borrower or customer to repay a loan or to pay on time for products purchased or services rendered.

Some companies take pride in proper business practices, including the payment of bills on a timely basis. Other firms feel little pressure to meet their obligations. Some consider it a challenge to delay payments or extend the terms of trade, with or without the supplier's permission. A reputable firm is always a better credit risk than a firm that is evasive or dishonest in its business dealings. Even though the analyst relies heavily on financial data in making credit decisions, the character of the potential purchaser, if known, should be incorporated into the evaluation of credit capacity.

Capacity

Capacity refers to the ability of the borrower or purchaser to repay the loan or to pay the invoice when due. This term deals with the financial position of the firm and may be divided into two components.

1. **Liquidity**. Does the firm maintain sufficient cash balances to pay its bills? Does it collect its receivables and monitor the level of inventory? Does it avoid excessive short-term borrowing? These are the elements of liquidity that should be considered in financial capacity.

2. **Profitability**. Is the firm making money on the products it sells or the services it provides? Is it able to convert operating profits into after-tax profits? Are profits stable and likely to continue for a reasonable period of time? These are some questions that must be answered to measure the financial prospects of the potential purchaser.

Capital

In a credit sense, the term **capital** has two meanings: the total assets or the total equity of the firm. If the dollar amount of the account payable is small compared to the total value of assets, risk is lower than when the firm has fewer assets. Similarly, if the purchaser's equity as a percentage of total assets is high, this provides a margin of safety to any supplier extending credit. Ratios that measure capital, in terms of both equity and assets, offer a valuable view of credit capacity.

Conditions

A nonfinancial indicator is reflected in **conditions,** which refers to environmental factors that may have an impact on a potential customer. As an example, if the economy is entering a period of economic stagnation, it will be difficult to sell products and maintain historical profits. Such a factor will have more impact on a weak customer than on a strong customer but might affect both. Or, if interest rates are rising rapidly, a firm may experience difficulties paying interest on its debt. In order to maintain relations with the bank, it may be forced to delay payments to suppliers. These and other external factors can have major effects on credit capacity.

Collateral

The term **collateral** refers to assets pledged as security to back up a credit sale or lending arrangement. Collateral is particularly important when a financial institution is making a loan. The existence of identifiable assets that can be recovered and sold to pay off a loan adds a major measure of protection for the loan. It is less important in decisions to sell on open account. When a credit decision involves goods, these can be viewed as collateral. If the customer does not pay, the goods will be retrieved by the seller. In practice, retrieval can be quite difficult. If the goods represent raw materials in a production process, they may be incorporated in work in process or finished goods. How can they be claimed? Or, if they are mixed with other items, can they be identified? If identified, will other creditors recognize the claim without extensive documentation that would be costly to create? The situation is worse when services are provided because no collateral is created by the business activity. Because of the difficulties in matching assets to credit sales, the analyst should not rely primarily on collateral in the evaluation of the credit decision.

Credit Norms

One of the most difficult aspects of credit analysis involves establishing appropriate norms for judging credit capacity. At least five guidelines may be used

1. **Industry Norms.** The firm makes its decisions in a specific industry in which some common operating and financial characteristics should be present. The firm sells to textile manufacturers or service organizations. It may be possible to use industry averages as norms. Usually, this is only partially satisfactory. One problem occurs because a firm may sell across industry lines. A firm that sells desks to large and small businesses, manufacturers, and banks will have difficulty establishing industry norms. Even when all sales are made to firms in the same industry, financial relationships will vary widely from the strongest to

the weakest firm. If the industry average is used as a norm, it may mask important factors that should be considered in the evaluation. In spite of the difficulties, some value may be obtained from industry norms. If a potential customer ranks second in profit in an industry with ten firms, the analyst can at least conclude that it is relatively profitable.

2. **Similar Firms**. If the analyst seeks firms in other industries that have similar operating or financial environments, an insight can be gained into relative strength and credit capacity. For example, if the customer is a rapidly growing firm in a stagnant industry, it may make sense to compare it to other growing firms in similar industries.

3. **Historical Trends**. The analyst can compare a firm with itself, that is, with its own performance over a period of time. It is a good sign if the firm is maintaining or increasing its profits, a bad sign if its liquidity is declining, and so forth. This procedure can be very useful, and is easy to carry out since only historical numbers on one firm are needed. At the same time, it poses some risks. The trend line should be compared with the overall economy and other firms, if possible, to provide a framework for improvements or declines in ratios. In addition, the past is not necessarily the best indicator of the future. A firm that succeeded under one set of circumstances may experience problems when conditions change.

4. **Future Expectations**. Economists and analysts make efforts to forecast conditions in future periods. These expectations can be used as norms to compare firms today. For example, an analyst may expect a surge in oil prices in two to four years. This price increase would affect some firms positively and others negatively. The analyst would view current ratios in terms of how the increase would affect future ratios.

5. **Common Sense**. This is the catch-all guideline that separates the professional from the novice. Experienced credit analysts often use subjective judgments and reason. Do the numbers make sense? As an example, an industry average for a return on investment might be 3 percent. This could never be a norm for rational investors because it is too low. Similarly, the average might be 60 percent. This is not reasonable because it cannot be sustained for very long. Common sense would tell the analyst that, say, 20 percent would be more reasonable than either of these industry averages.

External Analysis

In Chapter 10, we defined financial analysis as the process of determining the significant operating and financial characteristics of a firm from accounting data. For credit reviews, the analyst employs external analysis, defined as a viewpoint from outside the firm. In this chapter, we will recognize two limitations as we develop our approach to external analysis.

1. **Limited Information.** We will assume that the credit manager is restricted with respect to access to confidential information. Instead, he or she relies on annual reports, detailed statements filed with the Securities and Exchange Commission (10-K Reports), financial service reports such as those provided by Dun and Bradstreet, and other public information. These data may be supplemented by current financial statements provided directly by the applicant, but the analyst will have little ability to go beyond the printed numbers and evaluate the customer's accounting and financial records.

2. **Time and Cost Restraints.** The analyst may receive a large volume of credit requests on a typical day. Some will be for large dollar amounts; others will be relatively small. All must be evaluated on a timely basis. The techniques in this chapter will reflect the need for quick decisions within tight time constraints. The external analysis will use a limited number of financial data items and incorporate them in a model that reflects major aspects of credit capacity for a firm.

Contribution of External Analysis

Having covered the limitations of external analysis, we should also note its contribution in the decision to extend credit. The analysis of liquidity, profitability, and capital provides a list of symptoms that may indicate problems. The analyst does not know the source of those problems when the analysis is completed. Nor is it known for certain whether problems really exist. The credit manager completes the analysis either by reaching a conclusion that the financial data support the decision to extend credit or by developing a list of questions to be asked. If the answers seem reasonable, the credit may be awarded. If the answers make no sense, the credit may be denied.

To demonstrate the use of external analysis for measuring credit capacity, we will use the Benton Incorporated balance sheets and income statements provided in Figures 13-1 and 13-2. The ratios derived from these financial statements will be compared to the industry guidelines provided in Figure 13-3.

LIQUIDITY INDICATORS

A firm's ability to pay its debt is measured partly through the use of liquidity ratios. The ratios that are selected reflect the goal of the analysis. In Chapter 10, we examined the full range of working-capital management ratios and used a large number of them. For the purpose of evaluating credit capacity, fewer ratios are needed. In this section, we will select four ratios from Chapter 10 and review them briefly in a credit framework.

Figure 13-1. Benton Incorporated Income Statement (thousands).

	Year 1	Year 2	Year 3	Year 4
Revenues	370,000	495,000	551,000	466,800
Cost of Goods Sold	155,400	198,000	253,460	228,732
Gross Margin	214,600	297,000	297,540	238,068
General and Administrative	27,898	32,670	47,606	45,233
Operating Income	186,702	264,330	249,934	192,835
Less Interest	20,537	27,226	22,494	13,498
Earnings Before Taxes	166,165	237,104	227,440	179,337
Less Federal Income Tax	47,357	63,307	67,777	54,877
Net Income	118,808	173,797	159,663	124,460

Figure 13-2. Benton Incorporated Balance Sheet (thousands).

	Year 1	Year 2	Year 3	Year 4
Cash	10,000	7,000	7,800	6,400
Marketable Securities	23,000	21,000	14,500	12,300
Accounts Receivable	45,000	60,000	71,500	76,200
Inventories	62,000	75,000	87,230	64,300
Other Current Assets	0	0	2,030	3,300
Equipment (Net)	75,000	80,000	84,200	77,400
Physical Assets (Net)	110,000	166,000	189,340	137,700
Land and Real Estate	60,000	60,000	66,400	66,400
TOTAL ASSETS	385,000	469,000	523,000	444,000
Payables	21,000	39,000	49,200	51,400
Short-Term Secured Debt	8,500	19,500	17,400	15,200
Other Current Liabilities	2,500	8,500	9,500	9,700
Secured Long-Term Debt	75,000	70,000	63,000	47,000
Unsecured Long-Term Debt	90,000	80,000	93,450	11,340
Common Stock ($1 Par)	25,000	25,000	26,500	26,500
Additional Paid-in Capital	80,000	80,000	91,400	91,400
Retained Earnings	83,000	147,000	172,550	191,460
TOTAL LIABILITES & EQUITY	385,000	469,000	523,000	444,000

Figure 13-3. Guidelines to Be Used as Financial Norms.

	Guideline
Liquidity Ratios	
Current Ratio	1.80
Acid Test	1.10
Receivables Turnover	7.00
Inventory Turnover (Sales)	5.00
Profitability Ratios	
Gross Profit Margin	0.25
Profit Margin	0.15
Asset Turnover	1.20
Return on Investment	0.20
Return on Equity	0.09
Earning Power	0.11
Times Interest Earned	6.00
Captial Ratios	
Earnings per Share	NA
Price Earnings Ratio	8.00
Debt Equity Ratio	0.50
Dividend Payout	0.40

Magnitude of Liquidity

Liquidity can be divided into two categories conceptually. The **magnitude of liquidity** refers to an absolute quantity on hand—that is, the excess of liquid assets over short-term liabilities. In effect, we are discussing net working-capital but we must tie it in to the size of near-term obligations.

To illustrate this concept, consider firms A and B. Firm A has net working-capital of $100,000; Firm B has $1 million. Which is more liquid? The answer depends on the size of current liabilities. Suppose the full data were as follows:

	Firm A	Firm B
Current Assets	$300,000	$40,000,000
Current Liabilities	200,000	39,000,000
Net Working-Capital	$100,000	$1,000,000

With these details, we can see that Firm A has a much higher magnitude of liquidity than Firm B. Thus, any ratios must tie in the relationship of current assets to current debt in order to reveal an accurate picture of liquidity.

Two ratios are widely used to reflect the absolute level of liquidity at a moment in time: current ratio and acid test.

1. **Current Ratio**. Defined in Chapter 10, this ratio measures the full current asset level to current liabilities. The strong point of this ratio is that it recognizes inventory as a near-term liquidity source. Goods can be sold, and these will produce cash after an intermediate step of receivables. The weakness is that inventory is markedly less liquid than cash or receivables. At least, receivables can be sold off to raise cash at ninety cents on the dollar. Inventory is often impossible to liquidate quickly if funds are needed.

2. **Acid Test**. Also defined in Chapter 10, this ratio measures the most liquid current assets against current liabilities. In a sense, it is a more precise measure of the magnitude of funds that could be available on short notice to pay debts.

Flow of Liquidity

The second category deals with the **flow of liquidity**, referring to the rate at which operational funds enter the firm's cash account. A firm can be liquid, after all, because it has a large sum of cash and few debts. On the other hand, it can be liquid because it sells a large volume of products or services and collects quickly on the sales.

Two ratios are widely used to measure flows of liquidity:

1. **Receivables Turnover**. Defined in Chapter 10, this ratio measures the speed of converting accounts receivable into cash. Firms with strict credit policies and sound collection procedures will collect cash equal to the receivables balance more often than less aggressive firms.

2. **Inventory Turnover**. This ratio reflects the speed of converting the current inventory balance into an equal amount of cash. For credit purposes, the ratio of sales to inventory is more appropriate than cost of goods sold to inventory. The credit manager is interested in dollars generated by sales, not units, and therefore should include the markup on the goods. This is done if the ratio uses sales rather than cost of goods sold.

Liquidity Guidelines

Once the analyst has identified the four ratios to be used to evaluate credit capacity, guidelines are needed. These may be obtained from a variety of sources, as were listed above. At some point, a single listing is needed, either for all applicants or for separate categories of applicants. For the Benton analysis, we will use the guidelines in Figure 13-3. Some comments on these liquidity guidelines might be

1. **Current Ratio.** This guideline expects current assets to exceed current liabilities by 1.8 to 1. Many firms have traditionally used 2 to 1 as a guideline, with the implied assumption that inventories would comprise one-half of current assets. The 1.8 guideline seems reasonable in light of historical wisdom.

2. **Acid Test.** This guideline shows cash and receivables slightly higher than current debt. This also seems reasonable compared to conventional wisdom that the acid test should be 1.

3. **Receivables Turnover.** A guideline of 7 means that receivables should be collected 7 times a year, or once every 52 days. When a firm sells on terms of net 30, it will commonly have an average collection period of 45 to 55 days. This guideline is practical in light of collection practices in the real world.

4. **Inventory Turnover.** A guideline of 5 means cash is generated equal to inventories every 73 days. If the goods are purchased for $1 and sold for $2 then the physical turnover of inventory is 2.5 times a year. This seems sluggish from a point of view of managing inventory but is not critical from the point of view of the credit manager. The guideline might be tightened somewhat, but it is not unreasonable.

Once the firm institutes reasonable guidelines, it can use them to evaluate customers quickly and consistently.

Profitability Indicators

Perhaps the most important element of credit capacity is related to the profits of the potential customer. Once a credit decision is made, sales are likely to continue to the purchaser as long as bills are paid in a responsible manner. If the purchasing firm is not profitable, its ability to pay bills will decline over time. Assets will be eroded, and liquidity will evaporate. Thus, the credit manager should always evaluate profitability when making a credit decision.

In this section, we will examine two major categories of profitability ratios

1. **Profits in Relation to Sales.** The firm must be able to generate adequate profits on each unit of sales. If sales lack a sufficient margin of profit, it is difficult for the firm to cover overhead charges and fixed charges on debt, and to earn a profit for shareholders. As it runs into difficulties, it also becomes difficult to pay bills.

2. **Profits in Relation to Assets.** It is important that profit be compared to the capital invested by owners and creditors. If the customer cannot produce a satisfactory return on its asset base, it may be misusing

assets. If the return is not adequate on the assets financed by equity, the owners may not remain committed to continuing in the business. In either case, suppliers to the firm might experience difficulties in collecting on their receivables.

In addition to these two categories, the analyst links the profit ratios through a ratio of sales to assets. An important factor in the firm's ability to produce profits is the relationship between the level of sales and the level of assets required to attain the sales. The relationship among sales, assets, and profits will be examined as profitability ratios.

Sources of Profit Problems

Ratios can be used in external analysis to identify symptoms of problems. Once they have been identified, the analyst can go directly to financial statements to reveal more detail. In conducting this evaluation of profitability, six areas can contribute to profit problems:

1. **Cost of Goods Sold.** When providing goods or services, the direct cost of sales affects all measures of profit. A low cost of goods or services sold can produce strong profit indicators. High production costs have the reverse effect.

2. **Overhead Expenses.** General and administrative expenses must bear a proper relationship to sales level. Excessive overhead costs can cut or eliminate operating profits.

3. **Selling Price.** The selling price on individual products usually reflects competitive factors in the marketplace. If the firm's product line is properly positioned, the selling prices of different items should be adequate to provide profits. With weak products or intense competition, the unit prices may be inadequate to achieve adequate profit levels.

4. **Unit Sales.** The volume of sales in units must be sufficient to cover fixed costs, overhead, and financial expenses, and to provide a profit to shareholders. Even if the firm makes a large profit on a single product or service, it must have an adequate total volume.

5. **Total Assets.** A firm must employ its plant, equipment, and other assets in an efficient manner. If many capital assets are idle or if cash on hand, receivables, and inventory are excessive, the return on investment may be inadequate, even if all other operating activities are competitive.

6. **Financial Expenses.** The interest paid on the firm's debt will reflect general interest rates and the amount of debt. If these charges are high, they can erode operating profits. If they are low, the effect of operating profits can be magnified in the after-tax profit indicators.

Once the analyst has used ratios to reveal symptoms, the financial statements can provide further information on the likely sources of problems. The analyst still might not know the precise cause of difficulty. If the customer has requested a large credit approval, it may be worth the time to develop questions to discover more accurately the meaning of inadequate or weak ratios. For smaller orders, the firm may make its decisions without additional information.

In the next sections, we will define and discuss the ratios that can be used to reveal symptoms of profit problems.

Profit Margin

The first ratio for measuring profitability is the profit margin, calculated as

$$\text{Profit Margin} = \frac{\text{Operating Income (EBIT)}}{\text{Revenues from Operations}}$$

With external analysis, operating income and revenues are taken from the income statement. This ratio helps measure the relationship between sales and operating profits. If the margin of profit is inadequate, the firm will not be able to achieve satisfactory returns for its investors.

In the formula, operating income is defined as earnings before interest and taxes (EBIT). If it is not displayed separately on an income statement, it can be calculated by subtracting costs of goods sold and general and administrative expenses from sales.

The profit margin is an indicator of the customer's ability to withstand adverse conditions that may arise from various sources, such as

1. **Falling Prices**. If the general price level in the marketplace experiences a decline, does the firm have a sufficient markup to drop its price and still show a profit on sales?

2. **Rising Costs**. If the firm is caught in a period of rising costs when it cannot compensate by raising prices, will the business continue to be profitable?

3. **Declining Sales**. With a large profit margin, fixed operating costs are covered with room to spare. This is not the case if the profit margin is small. Thus, the profit margin helps show whether the firm can withstand an unexpected decline in sales and still show a profit.

Similarly, the profit margin may be used as an indicator of possible success under favorable conditions. As an example, if the firm is able to raise its prices, how quickly will profits rise? Or, if supplies and materials decline in price, what profits can be expected? Finally, if the firm is able to gain large increases in sales without adverse price or cost effects, what will be the profit forecast? These questions reflect the upside potential that is reflected in the profit margin.

Gross Margin

A second ratio that links sales and profits is the gross margin, calculated as:

$$\text{Gross Margin} = \frac{\text{Sales minus Cost of Goods Sold}}{\text{Sales}}$$

where sales is defined as revenues from operations. This ratio shows the profits relative to sales after the direct production costs are deducted. For a service firm, cost of goods sold is replaced by cost of services. Gross margin, also called gross profit margin, may be used as an indicator of operational efficiency. Is the firm able to achieve an adequate margin between the selling price and the cost of bringing products or services to the marketplace?

The difference between the profit margin and the gross margin lies in the breadth of measuring profits. Although both are concerned with operating profits, general and administrative expenses are not included in the gross margin. Since they are included in the profit margin, it provides a view of the total operations results. Gross margin is the more narrow view of production only.

Asset Turnover

A different view of profit is achieved by using the asset turnover.

$$\text{Asset Turnover} = \frac{\text{Sales}}{\text{Operating Assets}}$$

This ratio highlights the amount of assets needed by the firm to achieve its operating revenues level. The ability to produce a large volume of sales on a small asset base is an important part of the firm's profit picture. Idle or improperly used assets increase the firm's need for costly financing and the expenses for maintenance and upkeep. By achieving a high asset turnover, a firm reduces costs and increases eventual profit.

When performing external analysis, we must be careful to be consistent in the definition of operating assets. These assets may be calculated in three ways:

1. **Total Assets**. This is the most common approach when performing external analysis. The total assets on the balance sheet are assumed to be largely operating assets. For ease of calculation and simplicity, no adjustments are made.

2. **Operating Assets.** A more accurate measure of the assets used to generate a given volume of sales is the concept of **operating assets**, defined as total assets less idle capital assets, marketable securities, and similar paper investments. In effect, the analyst uses the footnotes in the annual report to eliminate assets not used to produce the reported operating income. This increases the sharpness of asset turnover as a measure of efficiency. As an example, if a firm is constructing a $40 million factory, this fact may be noted in the annual report. When completed, it will create new products and increase goods available for sale and future sales. Since it does not contribute to current income, it should not be included in the current calculation of asset turnover.

3. **Total Assets Plus Estimated Value of Leased Assets.** When a firm leases capital equipment, it is earning a return on an asset not shown on the balance sheet. To measure profitability on a comparative basis, the value of leased assets should be included. For example, if two airlines have similar profits and the same number of planes but one leases half its fleet, it will appear to be more profitable because fewer assets are shown on the balance sheet. If it leases planes worth $100 million, these can be incorporated in the calculation of asset turnover.

As a general rule, total assets is the practical measure for most applications. When a customer requests an unusually large credit sale or when problems appear to exist with the financial statements, the amount of idle assets should be considered.

Return on Investment

When considered individually, profit margin and asset turnover have certain weaknesses. The profit margin ignores the money invested by owners and creditors and does not acknowledge their commitment of assets to pursue profits. The asset turnover considers the level of assets but does not offer a measure of profits. To overcome the individual weaknesses, the two ratios are combined to form a new profit measure, return on investment (ROI).

The before-tax return on investment may be calculated in two ways. The first is

Return on Investment = Operating Income/Operating Assets

In this formulation, the return on investment is seen as a measure of profits from the firm's operations compared to the assets used to earn the profit.

The second calculation is

Return on Investment = Asset Turnover x Profit Margin

$$= \frac{\text{Sales}}{\text{Operating Assets}} \quad \text{x} \quad \frac{\text{Operating Income}}{\text{Revenues from Operations}}$$

where ROI is viewed as a function of the margin of profit on sales and the volume of sales generated on the asset bases. When the multiplication is performed, the sales in the denominator of profit margin and numerator of asset turnover cancel out, leaving operating income over operating assets, as follows:

$$\text{Return on Investment} = \frac{\text{Sales}}{\text{Operating Assets}} \quad \text{x} \quad \frac{\text{Operating income}}{\text{Revenues from Operations}}$$

Before tax return on investment is the most important single indicator of operating profits. It matches the before—tax income with assets available to earn a return. Efficient firms will use their assets well and have a relatively high return. Firms experiencing difficulties in the markets or with management will normally report a lower return. If the analyst is evaluating a firm that does not have a reasonable return on investment, profit margin and asset turnover should be examined first to determine the root cause of the problem. Decisions to sell to customers who are struggling with operating problems should be made with a great deal of care.

Return on Equity

The return on equity is an after-tax measure of profit that may be calculated as

$$\text{Return on Equity} = \frac{\text{Net Income - Dividends, Preferred Stock}}{\text{Common Stockholders' Equity}}$$

where after-tax income is matched with shareholders of common stock. This is done by subtracting dividends that accrue to holders of preferred stock. The numerator is also known as earnings available to the common shareholder.

This ratio is used to measure the after-tax profits that accrue to the owners of the business. Just as a firm must earn adequate operating profits on its assets, it must also be able to convert those profits into a satisfactory return to owners. If it does not, the owners may eventually abandon the business or otherwise create problems for its creditors. A firm with low interest and taxes will have a high return on equity. A firm that pays high interest and taxes will show a poor return.

Earning Power

Earning power is a second after-tax measure of profits, calculated as

$$\text{Earning Power} = \frac{\text{Net Income minus Dividends, Preferred Stock}}{\text{Total Assets}}$$

This ratio measures the after-tax return achieved by a firm versus the resources available for the conduct of business. If a firm is using assets efficiently, it will have high earning power.

This ratio is often called the after-tax return on investment. For clarity, the analyst should always ensure that comparative ratio norms define after tax profit as net income less dividends on preferred stock.

Times Interest Earned

A useful measure of profit that does not link return to resources is the times interest earned ratio, calculated as

$$\text{Times Interest Earned} = \frac{\text{Operating Income}}{\text{Annual Interest on Debt}}$$

This ratio relates operating profits to the fixed financial obligation created by borrowing money.

The ratio offers a view of the level of financial risk assumed by the potential customer. It shows the margin of safety between profits and fixed charges on debt. A firm may have operating profits but may experience difficulty in covering large interest payments. Or, if it is confronted by a drop in operating profits, it may be unable to meet its financial requirements without holding up payments to suppliers. If the times interest earned ratio is high, the firm has a large margin of protection on paying its debt charges. A low ratio indicates possible problems.

Example: A firm has a times interest earned ratio of 4 to 1. What percentage drop can it sustain in operating income and still meet its interest payments?

Answer: 75 percent. The operating income can decrease to 25 percent of its current level before the firm has a negative earnings before taxes.

Figure 13-4. **Factors Affecting Profitability.**

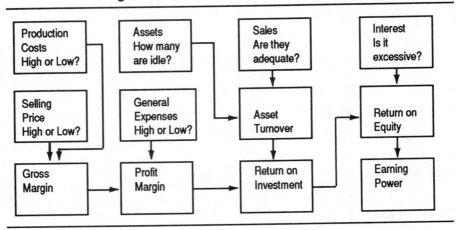

Profitability Relationships

While the analyst calculates individual ratios to evaluate profitability, they are tied together in a total profit picture, (as shown in Figure 13-4). The relationships between sources of profitability and different ratios are diagrammed in the figure. Production costs and selling price determine gross margin, which determines profit margin when general and administrative expenses are considered. The level of assets and sales volume produce asset turnover, which explains return on investment when viewed with profit margin. (The addition of interest expenses brings return on equity and earning power into focus.) The figure shows the cumulative effect, as each individual factor affects earning power even though none leads to it directly.

CAPITAL INDICATORS

Some ratios do not directly measure liquidity or profitability but have definite impacts on a firm's credit capacity. They provide a context for the evaluation of the other ratios. The common thread of these indicators is that they reflect decisions on capital investments, either indirectly in terms of earnings or dividends, or directly through debt and equity components. In this section, we will examine capital indicators as components of credit capacity.

Earnings Per Share (EPS)

The EPS ratio is calculated by dividing net income by the number of shares of common stock outstanding. Shares authorized but not issued, or authorized, issued, and repurchased (treasury stock), are omitted from the calculation.

Similarly, if a firm has preferred stock, earnings available to the common shareholder are used in the calculation. Thus, preferred dividends are deducted from net income.

Earnings per share is an important indicator of the firm's ability to add to contributed capital. If earnings are stable or growing, the firm has the ability to retain capital and grow stronger. Erratic earnings on a per share basis indicate instability, particularly when the EPS report is negative.

A year by year comparison of earnings per share can be informative when evaluating credit capacity. As an example, consider firms A and B that both have recent EPS of $2.45. A four year picture reveals the following:

	1986	1987	1988	1989
EPS, Firm A	1.27	1.65	2.10	2.45
EPS, Firm B	2.75	(0.90)	(1.55)	2.45

The two trends are quite different. Firm A began with a low EPS but has steadily progressed and has almost doubled EPS in three years. Firm B has two negative earnings years in between two profitable years. The greater stability offered by Firm A appears to indicate greater credit capacity.

Price Earnings Multiple

The price earnings ratio is calculated by dividing earnings per share into the market price of the stock. It is the most important measure of value used by investors in the marketplace. Many investors consider few other factors before making purchases of common stock.

A high price earnings multiple, when accompanied by a normal level of EPS, indicates investors' confidence in the firm. If the market has bid up the price of the common stock, as reflected in a high multiple, it is an indicator that investors see future strength. This is a good sign for credit capacity. If the multiple is low, investor confidence may be low. This is a sign of possible problems.

The credit analyst should use the price earnings multiple only when earnings per share are also evaluated. A high ratio occurs when EPS drops unexpectedly and the market sustains the price level for speculative reasons. Care must be taken when evaluating price earnings multiples as part of external analysis.

Debt-Equity Ratio

The debt-equity ratio is a ratio of total debt to total equity. It offers a view of the risk in the capital structure of a firm. If a firm has excessive debt, it will experience difficulty in locating additional debt or equity financing. When it does borrow, funds will be available only at high interest rates. If problems arise, the firm may be forced to slow payments to suppliers. Or the firm may raise funds by creating excessive payables. Both of these alternatives affect credit capacity.

As a general guideline, debt should not exceed 60 percent of the total sources of funds for a customer. In other words, a debt-equity ratio should not be greater than 1.5; that is, 60 percent debt and 40 percent equity. This guideline may be waived for organizations with highly stable earnings or regulated industries, such as public utilities.

Dividend Payout

The dividend payout is a ratio of dividends per share to earnings per share (DPS/EPS). It shows the percentage of earnings being distributed to shareholders in the form of cash dividends. The portion not paid out is retained for the firm's future needs.

Creditors are concerned about the portion of dividends being paid out, particularly for small or family-held companies. If the dividend payout is excessive, the firm is not retaining funds for growth or other needs. A firm that retains a large portion of earnings is becoming more stable as equity capital increases in the capital structure. Once again, this cannot be viewed in isolation; rather the debt-equity trend must also be evaluated. If the firm is retaining earnings but increasing debt more rapidly, a low dividend payout may not be an adequate indicator.

Guidelines for this ratio vary widely. Firms often attempt to pay approximately 50 percent of their earnings as dividends. If the customer is growing rapidly, a higher percentage may be an appropriate norm. If it has little opportunity to invest funds directly, a higher percentage may be in order.

Analyzing Credit Capacity

We are now ready to evaluate the credit capacity of Benton Incorporated, using the numbers and norms in Figures 13-1 to 13-3. The data in these figures have been summarized in the financial data section of a spreadsheet model, displayed in Figure 13-5. The liquidity, profitability, and capital indicators are shown for four years; industry norms are also shown. We assume that all sales are made on credit.

With respect to liquidity, the magnitude of available funds to pay near-term bills exceeds the norms. The analyst might note a declining trend in current ratio and acid test over the 4 years. The flow of liquidity is also solid, as reflected in the receivables and inventory turnovers.

With respect to profitability, the level of absolute profits is maintained for all four years using all the ratios. The norms are exceeded in all cases. On the other hand, the profit trend also shows a decline, but it is not steep and does not appear to pose a problem.

Figure 13-5. Analyzing Credit Capacity, Benton Incorporated.

Financial Data

	Year 1	Year 2	Year 3	Year 4
Revenues	370,000	495,000	551,000	466,800
Cost of Goods Sold	155,400	198,000	253,460	228,732
General and Administrative	27,898	32,670	47,606	45,233
Interest	20,537	27,226	22,494	13,498
Taxes	47,357	63,307	67,777	54,877
Operating Income	186,702	264,330	249,934	192,835
Net Income	118,808	173,797	159,663	124,460
Cash	10,000	7,000	7,800	6,400
Marketable Securities	23,000	21,000	14,500	12,300
Receivables	45,000	60,000	71,500	76,200
Inventories	62,000	75,000	87,230	64,300
Other Current Assets	0	0	2,030	3,300
Fixed and Long-Term Assets	245,000	306,000	339,940	281,500
Current Liabilities	32,000	67,000	76,100	76,300
Long-Term Debt	165,000	150,000	156,450	58,340
Equity	188,000	252,000	290,450	309,360
Shares Outstanding	25,000	25,000	26,500	26,500
Dividends, Preferred Stock	0	0	0	0
Dividends, Common Stock	75,000	109,797	134,113	105,550
Ending Market Price	$36	$46	$48	$39

Liquidity Ratios	Norm	Year 1	Year 2	Year 3	Year 4
Current Ratio	1.80	4.40	2.40	2.40	2.10
Acid Test	1.10	2.40	1.30	1.30	1.30
Receivables Turnover	7.00	8.20	8.30	7.70	6.10
Investment Turnover	5.00	6.00	6.60	6.30	7.30

Profitability Ratios					
Gross Margin	0.25	0.58	0.60	0.54	0.51
Profit Margin	0.15	0.50	0.53	0.45	0.41
Asset Turnover	1.20	1.02	1.10	1.09	1.09
Return on Investment	0.20	0.52	0.59	0.49	0.45
Return on Equity	0.09	0.63	0.69	0.55	0.40
Earning Power	0.11	0.31	0.37	0.31	0.28
Times Interest Earned	6.00	9.09	9.71	11.11	14.29

Capital Indicators

Earnings per Share	NA	4.75	6.95	6.03	4.70
Price Earnings	8.00	7.60	6.60	8.00	8.30
Debt Equity	0.50	1.00	0.90	0.80	0.40
Dividend Payout	0.40	0.63	0.63	0.84	0.85

With respect to capital indicators, once again a strong picture is in evidence. The earnings per share rose in the middle years and then returned to the year 1 level. Throughout the changes in earnings, the price earnings multiple was reasonably steady. The debt to equity ratio shows significant improvements over the four years; only the increase in dividend payout is a negative. Still, since the firm is retiring debt even as its dividend payout rises, no problems seem to exist. The analyst would see no surprises from the interpretation of the capital ratios.

Overall, Benton Incorporated appears to have significant credit capacity, as measured by the liquidity, profitability, and capital ratios. It is likely that credit would be extended without much further investigation. This is risky, of course, since the numbers may have been provided by the firm and conditions do change. Still, this appears to be a strong firm with a solid four year track record. It has demonstrated an historical credit capacity and, in the absence of other factors, should qualify for credit easily.

CONCLUSION

In this chapter, we have examined liquidity, profitability, and capital indicators of credit capacity from the view of an external analyst. Such a review is realistic for customers who seek relatively large credit limits. At the same time, it is not overly burdensome. If problems are indicated by the ratios, further investigation can be undertaken. In addition, it is a straightforward task to conduct this evaluation annually to see if any deterioration has taken place in the firm's ability to pay its bills. If problems are indicated, the firm can review the credit limits and make adjustments as appropriate.

PIZZA KING INCORPORATED–FINANCIAL ANALYSIS

Pizza King Incorporated operates a chain of fast-food restaurants and steak houses out of an office in Pittsburgh, Pennsylvania. At the end of 1987, the firm had 520 fast-service, limited-menu pizza parlors in 21 states and the District of Columbia. The primarily East Coast operation also contained 26 restaurants with a basic menu of hamburgers, cheeseburgers, fried chicken, fish sandwiches, and related items such as salads, french fries, pies, and soft drinks. In addition, the firm operated 14 steak houses and 7 seafood and beef restaurants. The company employed between 10,000 and 20,000 persons, depending on the season, and had regional offices and training centers in various major East Coast cities.

Approximately two-thirds of the company's revenues occur through its pizza outlets. These restaurants compete against national chains such as Pizza Hut; competition demands that the firm be able to respond aggressively and positively to changing consumer preferences. In 1986, the firm had to expand its menu by adding fish and self-serve salad bars in many units. By the end of 1988, all the restaurants will have some additions to the food line; the firm's management has high expectations for the enlarged menu available at most restaurants. These actions were taken to reverse a competitive decline that occurred in 1986 and 1987 as McDonald's and Burger King escalated their advertising in a miniwar in the fast-food business.

The firm's steak houses and seafood and beef restaurants showed a sales growth from $76 to $84 million between 1986 and 1987. Aggressive advertising and menu innovations, including a roast prime rib dinner and a steak and king crab leg entree, were key factors in this growth. The steak house division, which operated both kinds of restaurants, believes that variety is an important factor in the decision to dine away from home. Accordingly it will continue to offer variety in its menus.

Some of the problems that have been facing Pizza King Incorporated are reflected in the financial statements published at the end of 1987. Earnings per share dropped from a high of $1.63 in 1985 to $0.91 in 1987. Sales were up slightly over this period. The firm's net working capital decreased in both 1986 and 1987, and the firm does not pay any dividends. At the present time, management has announced no plans to begin declaring dividends, preferring to retain earnings to finance continued growth.

Required: Analyze the liquidity, profitability, and related factors for Pizza King and indicate whether you would extend unsecured credit for perishable food supplies purchased by Pizza King.

Pizza King Incorporated Consolidated Statements of Income and Retained Earnings Years Ended December 31, 1987 and 1986
(in thousands of dollars)

Consolidated Statement of Income	1987	1986
Sales	$265,639	$255,343
Deductions		
Cost of Sales	110,326	103,580
Operating Expenses	109,049	102,981
Rent	21,928	21,313
Depreciation and Amortization	7,008	6,631
Interest and Debt Expenses	2,858	3,284
Administrative and General Expenses	9,065	9,750
Total Deductions	260,234	247,539
Operating Income	5,405	7,804
Other Income and Expenses, Net	1,774	1,741
Income Before Federal and State Income Taxes	7,179	9,545
Federal & State Income Taxes	2,887	4,478
Net Income	$4,292	$5,067
Net Income Per Common and Common Equivalent Share	$0.87	$1.03

Consolidated Statement of Retained Earnings	1987	1986
Beginning of Year	$45,648	$40,581
Net Income	4,292	5,067
End of Year	$49,940	$45,648

Pizza King Incorporated Consolidated Balance Sheet
Years Ended December 31, 1987 and 1986
(In thousands of dollars)

Assets	1987	1986
Current Assets		
Cash	$5,631	$6,126
Cash Equivalents, Interest Bearing	9,500	10,000
Accounts Receivable	316	514
Notes Receivable	5	340
Advances for New Restaurants	127	605
Inventories	6,115	5,157

Real Estate and Restaurant Equipment		
Held for Sale	3,160	1,613
Income Taxes Receivable	921	——
Prepaid and Other Expenses	2,072	2,934
Total Current Assets	27,847	27,289
Property, Plant, and Equipment, Net	77,697	71,530
Real Estate Held for Development	1,278	1,287
Other Assets and Deferred Charges	3,697	3,519
Total Assets	$110,519	$103,625

Liabilities and Stockholders' Equity

Current Liabilities		
Current Maturities of Long-Term Debt,		
Less Unamortized Discount	$5,425	$5,387
Accounts Payable	13,330	10,850
Accrued Salaries and Wages	1,236	1,223
Income Taxes	——	461
Accrued Expenses	4,723	3,777
Current Portion of Reserve for Loss		
on Closed Restaurant Units	315	370
Deferred Income	174	201
Deferred Income Taxes	——	12
Total Current Liabilities	25,203	22,281
Long-Term Debt, Less Current Maturities		
and Unamortized Discount	28,787	29,985
Reserve for Loss on Closed Restaurants	1,164	670
Deferred Income	12	158
Deferred Income Taxes	4,197	3,667
Stockholders' Equity		
Common Stock Subscription Warrants,		
Issued 150,000	644	644
Common stock, no Par Value		
Authorized–6,000,000 Shares, Issued		
4,921,227 Shares in 1987 and 1986	3,701	3,701
Retained Earnings	49,940	45,648
54,285	49,993	
Less 181,000 Shares of Common Stock		
Reacquired at Cost	3,129	3,129
Total Stockholders' Equity	51,156	46,864
Total Liabilities and Stockholders' Equity	$110,519	$103,625

Pizza King Inc. Consolidated Statement of Changes in Financial Position Years Ended December 31, 1987 and 1986 (in thousands of dollars)

	1987	1986
Sources of Working Capital:		
Net Income	$4,292	$5,067
Add Charges (Deduct Credits) Against Earnings not Affecting Working Capital:		
Depreciation and Amortization	6,932	6,414
Reserve for Closed Restaurant Units	494	280
Deferred Income Taxes	530	(16)
Other	86	33
Working Capital Provided from Operations	12,334	11,778
Decrease in Notes Receivable		682
Carrying Value of Fixed Assets Sold, Reclassified or Retired	389	1,362
Decrease in Real Estate Held for Development		278
Capitalized Lease Obligations	3,168	
Restaurant Equipment Financing	1,182	
Increase in Deferred Income Taxes		504
Sale of Common Stock from Exercise of Options		35
Total Working Capital Provided	17,073	14,639
Uses of Working Capital:		
Additions to Property, Plant, and Equipment	13,625	11,985
Property, Plant, and Equipment Transferred from Current Assets		3,228
Increase (decrease) in Other Assets and Deferred Charges	223	(345)
Decrease in Deferred Income	146	83
Retirement of Long-Term Debt	5,443	5,486
Total Working Capital Used	19,437	20,437
(Decrease) in Working Capital	$(2,364)	$(5,798)

	1987	1986
Increase (Decrease) in Working Capital Consisted of:		
Cash and Cash Equivalents	$(995)	$4,504
Notes and Accounts Receivable	(533)	(83)
Advances for New Restaurants	(478)	470
Inventories	958	84
Real Estate and Restaurant Equipment Held up for Sale	1,547	(11,263)

Income Taxes Receivable	921	—
Prepaid and Other Expenses	(862)	253
Current Maturities of Long-Term Debt	(38)	(2,828)
Accounts Payable	(2,480)	(2,609)
Income Taxes and Other Accrued Expenses	(498)	5,362
Loss Reserve–Closed Restaurants Units	55	(55)
Deferred Income	27	101
Deferred Income Taxes	12	266
(Decrease) in Working Capital	$(2,364)	$(5,798)

Notes to Financial Statements

1. **Summary of Accounting Policies**

    a. **Principles of Consolidation.** The consolidated financial statements include those of the company and all its subsidiaries, each of which is wholly owned.

    b. **Inventories.** Inventories are valued at the lower of cost, determined by the first-in, first-out method, or market.

    c. **Capitalized Interest.** The cost of land and buildings acquired and constructed for new restaurants includes the capitalization of interest costs.

    d. **Property, Plant, and Equipment.** Property, plant, and equipment are carried at cost. Depreciation and amortization are computed using the straight-line method based on the shorter of the lease term or estimated useful lives of the assets. When assets are retired or otherwise disposed of, the cost and related accumulated depreciation are removed from the accounts and any resulting gain or loss is reflected in income for the period. The cost of maintenance and repairs is charged to income as incurred; significant renewals and betterments are capitalized.

    e. **Deferred Charges.** Deferred charges represent the noncurrent portion of lease acquisition costs, financing costs, and other prepayments that are being rateably amortized to operations over the term of the debt and lease instruments. Building design costs are being amortized over five years.

    f. **Intangible Assets.** The excess of cost over the book value of subsidiaries acquired relates primarily to goodwill purchased prior to November 1, 1980, which is being amortized on a straight-line basis over a period of 11 years.

    g. **Deferred Income Taxes.** Deferred income taxes are provided to reflect the tax effect of timing differences between financial and tax reporting, principally related to depreciation, provision for loss on closed restaurant units, prepayments, and certain capitalized interest and site location costs.

h. **Investment Tax Credits**. Investment tax credits have been recorded as a direct reduction of the income tax expenses.

i. **Per Share Earnings**. Net income per common share and per common equivalent share was computed by dividing net income by the weighted average number of shares of common stock and common stock equivalents outstanding during the period. The number of common shares was increased by the number of shares issuable on the exercise of certain employee stock options when the market price of the common stock exceeded the exercise price of the options. This increase in the number of shares was reduced by the number of shares assumed to have been purchased with the proceeds from the exercise of the options, which purchases were assumed to have been made at the average price of the stock during the year. The numbers of shares used in the calculation of per share earnings for 1987 and 1986 were 4,740,609 and 4,775,292, respectively.

2. **Advances for New Restaurants**

Advances for new restaurants consist of construction costs advanced for the account of lessors to be reimbursed to the company by the lessors under lease agreements during or upon completion of the restaurant construction.

3. **Inventories**

Inventories, computed on the first-in, first-out method, including those used in computing costs of sales, were:

	1987	1986	1985
Food	$4,024	$3,513	$3,524
Paper	642	587	567
Used in Computing of Sales	4,666	4,100	4,091
Uniforms and Utensils	1,002	699	648
Supplies	447	358	334
Inventories	$6,115	$5,157	$5,073

4. **Real Estate and Restaurant Equipment Held for Sale**

Real estate and restaurant equipment held for sale consist largely of land, buildings, and restaurant equipment completed or under construction for operating units. Historically, the company has financed the acquisition of its operating properties by purchase and sale and leaseback transactions with investors. The company has classified as a current asset that portion of the real estate and equipment held for sale which it believes will be sold during the succeeding year. In addition, pending sale of these properties and equipment, the company has charged $76,000 and $226,000 of amortization to income in 1987 and 1986, respectively, for the period that these assets were utilized in operations.

5. **Property Plant and Equipment**

In accordance with Financial Accounting Standards, property, plant, and equipment include $3,178,000 of land and buildings leased subsequent to December 31, 1986. Amortization charges of $7,000 related to these capital leases have been included in depreciation and amortization expense.

Depreciation in the amount of $6,932,000 and $6,405,000 has been charged to income for the years ended December 31, 1987 and 1986, respectively.

(in thousands of dollars)

	1987	1986	Estimated useful lives in years
Land	$4,925	$4,869	–
Buildings 23,517	19,552		20 to 45
Machinery and Equipment	43,096	37,405	5 to 10
Leasehold Improvements	38,990	36,224	Shorter of lease term or useful life
	____	____	
Accumulated Depreciation and Amortization	32,831	26,520	
Property, Plant, and Equipment.	$77,697	$71,530	

6. **Income Taxes**

The provision for income taxes for the years ended December 31, 1987 and 1986 includes deferred taxes of $518,000 (federal $421,000 and state $97,000) and $222,000 (federal $133,000 and state $89,000), respectively. Investment tax credits have been used to reduce current and deferred income taxes for the years ended December 31, 1987 and 1986, in the amounts of $771,000 (current $741,000 and deferred $30,000) and $686,000 (current $716,000 less reversal of deferred, ($30,000,) respectively.

Deferred tax expense for the years 1987 and 1986 results from timing differences in the recognition of income and expense for tax and financial statement purposes. The sources of these differences in 1987 and 1986 and the tax effect of each were as follows:

(in thousands of dollars)

	1987	1986
Excess of Tax over Book Depreciation	$861	$576
Capitalized Costs		
Interest	(17)	(37)
Site Location	(30)	(23)
Advances on Adv. Promotion	(11)	229
Deferred Manager Training Costs	(4)	(121)
Investment Tax Credits Used to		
Reduce Deferred Tax	(30)	30
Provision for Loss on Closed		
Restaurant Units	(229)	(353)
Miscellaneous	(22)	(79)
Deferred Tax Expense	$518	$222

7. Interest and Debt Expense

Interest and debt expense consists of

(in thousands of dollars)

	1987	1986
Interest on Long-Term Debt	$2,869	$3,260
Amortization of Debt Discount		
and Expense	45	46
Other Interest	9	9
	2,923	3,315
Less Interest Capitalized	65	31
Interest and Debt Expense	$2,858	$3,284

The company generally finances the acquisition of its operating properties by purchase, construction, and sale and leaseback transactions with its investors. The cost of financing during the period of procurement and construction is capitalized as an additional cost of these properties. The effect on net income of capitalizing such interest was approximately $32,000 in 1987 and $14,000 in 1986.

8. **Pension Plan**

The company and its subsidiaries fund pension costs accrued for its noncontributory pension plan for the benefit of eligible employees. Prior service cost is amortized over 40 years with an unfunded balance of $2,285,000 as of January 1, 1987. The aggregate cost charged to operations was approximately $560,000 in 1987 and $467,000 in 1986.

The actuarially computed value of vested pensions exceeded the market value of pension fund assets by $129,000 as of January 1, 1987.

9. **Leases**

Most of the company's subsidiaries lease appropriate property for their operations. The majority of leases require the company to pay all real estate taxes and personal property taxes and to maintain adequate insurance coverage in addition to other terms that vary with the individual leases. In addition to minimum annual rentals, there may be additional percentage rent if sales exceed a stipulated amount, less certain expenses. Real estate taxes and additional percentage rents were $3,101,000 and $729,000, respectively, for 1987 and $3,004,000 and $823,000, respectively, for 1986. Minimum annual rentals paid under operating leases for the years ended December 31, 1987 and 1986, were $17,745,000 and $17,030,000, respectively. Minimum future annual rentals of subsequent years based on leases as of December 31, 1987, are:

(In thousands of dollars)

	Realty	Equipment	Other
1988	$14,408	$2,921	$268
1989	14,305	2,288	254
1990	14,225	2,261	249
1991	14,064	2,261	229
1992	13,840	2,128	155
Thereafter	159,291	3,177	434

The company accounts for all lease agreements consummated or committed prior to January 1, 1987, in accordance with generally accepted accounting principles.

10. **Contingent Liabilities**

In 1985 an action was brought by RST Produce, Incorporated ("RST"), a former supplier, against the company's claim of $2 million in damages arising out of the company's termination of its business relations with the supplier. The company denies liability and has counterclaimed for

1984 inventory shortages and duplicate payments for certain goods. Discovery is proceeding in the action. Four other related actions have been brought against RST in which the company has been joined. Based on investigation to date and preliminary settlement discussions, it is management's opinion that there are only remote prospects that the supplier's claims or any other actions will, in the aggregate, have a material effect on the company's financial condition.

11. **Long-Term Debt**

The summary of long-term debt is presented as follows:

(In thousands of dollars)

	1987	1986
Revolving Credit and Term Loan Agreement, 11 3/4%'* (The revolving credit loan was converted to a five-year term loan on September 1, 1986 due quarterly beginning December 1, 1986 with interest 1% above prime) *At December 31, 1987.	$15,000	$19,000
Senior Notes		
11.5% to 2,000—Payable Annually, Less unamortized Discount ($413,000 and $445,000)		
10.75% to 1992—Payable Annually	10,420	11,222
10.75% to 1992—Payable Annually	340	340
Secured by Realty Mortgages		
10 3/4%-11 1/4%—Payable Quarterly	3,003	3,157
9%-10 3/4% to 1987-1995—Payable Monthly	539	605
Secured by Chattel Mortgages		
8% to 14% to 1995—Payable Monthly and Quarterly	1,299	464
Other	70	70
Lease Obligations Capitalized		
11.3% to 14.8% to 2012—Payable Monthly and Quarterly	3,541	514
	34,212	35,372
Less Current Maturities, Net of Unamortized Discount	5,425	5,387
Long-Term Debt	$28,787	$29,985

The following is a schedule, by years, of future minimum lease payments under capital leases together with the obligations under capital leases, (present value of future minimum rentals) as of December 31, 1987:

Year Ended December 31   *(in thousands of dollars)*

1988	$460
1989	460
1990	460
1991	460
1992	460
Thereafter	6,226
Total Minimum Lease Payments	8,526
Less: Amount Representing Interest	4,985
Total Obligations Under Capital Leases	3,541
Less: Current Portion of Obligations Under Capital Leases	97
Long-Term Obligations Under Capital leases	$3,444

The aggregate amount of maturities of long-term debt and lease obligations capitalized each year through December 31, 1992, are:

(in thousands of dollars)

December 31, 1988	$5,425
December 31, 1989	5,303
December 31, 1990	5,344
December 31, 1991	4,391
December 31, 1992	1,447

Property, plant, and equipment with a net book value of approximately $9.8 million have been pledged to secure certain of the above indebtedness.

The amended note covenants, and waivers as presently in effect, provide that (a) the earnings coverage test for the incurrence of additional indebtedness or for sale-leaseback financing is 1.75:1 (previous 12 months pre-tax earnings plus interest and rental expense as compared to interest and rental expense for the succeeding 12 months); 25 Pizza King units may be constructed through July 31, 1989, without regard to the earnings coverage test; (b) new units (other than the 25 Pizza King units mentioned above) may be constructed only if and when the company meets the earnings coverage test; (c) working capital must be maintained at the greater of $5 million (excluding the current portion of the term notes payable) or an amount equal to at least 20 percent of consolidated unsecured funded debt (including within the definition of working capital certain properties and equipment constructed or purchased in previous years); and (d) no dividends may be paid except out of 50 percent of the excess of earnings accumulated subsequent to December 31, 1986, over the aggregate payments made on account of funded debt after that date, or in an amount greater than indebtedness that could be incurred under the debt to equity ratio or earnings coverage tests. The earnings accumulation and earnings coverage tests did not allow any amounts to be available for dividend payments as of December 31, 1987.

The company has extended to the holders of its 11.5 percent Senior Notes due 2000 the right to exchange such notes for new notes, which provide for accelerated principal payments beginning December 1, 1991 to 1993. As a condition of such an exchange (which may be made in early 1988), the noteholders must surrender a proportionate amount of the common stock warrants (with a warrant price of $35.40 per share expiring in 1990) which were issued with the 11.5 percent Senior Notes.

The company has guaranteed secured mortgage notes of a subsidiary, the balance of which was $3,003,000 and $3,157,000 as of December 21, 1987 and 1986, respectively.

There were no short-term borrowings in 1987 or 1986.

Compensating balances of 10 percent of the average loans outstanding are required under the term loan agreement. Balances of $3 million were required as of December 31, 1987 and 1986, respectively.

12. **Stock Options**

As of December 31, 1987 and 1986, 18,900 and 308,000 shares, respectively, were reserved for options under Qualified Stock Option Plan II (QSOPII), which expired in February 1987. Qualified Stock Option Plan III, adopted in April 1986, covers 250,000 shares, which have been reserved. No options have been granted under this plan. A total of 150,000 shares are reserved for warrants.

Under QSOP II (covering 436,000 shares) options for 146,900 shares (net of cancellations) had been granted, and 128,000 shares had been exercised as of December 31, 1987. Options, for the most part, are exercisable after two years but not later than five years from the grant date.

Information with respect to stock options as of each balance sheet date is as follows:

(in thousands of dollars)

	Number of shares	Option Price			Market Value		
		Per share		Total	Per share		Total
Shares under option at December 31, 1987	18,900	$9.50 to 20.38		$306	$9.50 to 20.38(a)		$306
1986	147,600	6.50 to 20.38		1,852	6.50 to 20.38(a)		1,852
Options which became exercisable during 1985	9,500(d)	14.00 to 20.38		$187	$7.00 to 7.39(b)		$67
1986	9,400(d)	9.50 to 13.50		119 14.88(b)	11.13	to	132
1987	None (d)						
Options exercised during 1985	None						
1986	3,700	$9.63		$35	11.88 to 14.88(c)		$50
1987	None						

Outstanding options as of December 31, 1987, expire in 1988 (9,500) and 1989 (9,400):

a. At the dates options were granted.

b. At the dates options became exercisable.

c. At the dates options were exercised.

d. Excludes options canceled during 1987.

Proceeds obtained upon the exercise of options are credited to the capital stock account.

As of December 31, 1987, options covering 18,900 shares were outstanding. During the year, options totaling 128,700 shares under QSOP II were relinquished to the company.

13. Common Stock

Analysis of the changes of the common stock account during the years 1987 and 1986 is as follows:

(in thousands of dollars)

	1987 Number of shares	Amount	1986 Number of shares	Amount
Common Stock				
Beginning of Year	4,921,227	$3,701	4,917,527	$3,666
Issued During Year	—	—	3,700	35
End of Year	4,921,227	$3,701	4,921,227	$3,701

There have been no changes in Treasury stock or stock subscription warrants.

14. Other

a. The company operates a chain of fast—food restaurants, which constitutes its only line of business.

b. For 1987 and 1986, approximately 30 percent and 32 percent, respectively, of cost of sales represent purchases from one supplier. These purchases represent a material percentage of that supplier's business.

15. Quarterly Results of Operations (Unaudited)

The following represents the unaudited quarterly results of operations for the years ended December 31, 1987 and 1986.

(in thousands of dollars)
Four Months Ended

	March 31 1987	1986	June 30 1987	1986
Sales	$53,502	$56,323	$67,850	$67,502
Gross Profit	31,439	33,914	39,935	40,148
Net Income (Loss)	(1,198)	646	1,975	2,018
Net Income (Loss) per common and Common Equivalent Share	$(0.25)	$0.13	$0.41	$0.43

	September 30		December 31	
	_1987_	_1986_	_1987_	_1986_
	$75,320	$70,341	$68,967	$61,177
	43,852	42,211	40,087	36,490
	2,356	1,836	1,159	567
	$0.50	$0.38	$0.25	$0.12

16. General Description of the Impact of Inflation (Unaudited)

Menu price increases in the past have been used to partially offset increased costs and expenses caused by inflation. The ability of the company to offset future cost increases depends principally on competition and economic conditions.

Form 10K contains information reflecting quantitative data with regard to the estimated replacement cost of inventories and property, plant, and equipment as of December 31, 1987 and 1986, and the related estimated effect of such costs on cost of sales and depreciation and amortization expense for the years then ended.

ACCOUNTANTS' OPINION

The Stockholders and the Board of Directors
Pizza King, Inc.
Pittsburgh, Pennsylvania

We have examined the consolidated balance sheet of Pizza King Inc. and subsidiaries as of December 31, 1987 and 1986, and the related consolidated statements of income, retained earnings and changes in financial position for the years then ended. Our examinations were made in accordance with generally accepted auditing standards, and accordingly included such tests of the accounting records and such other auditing procedures as we considered necessary in the circumstances.

In our opinion, such financial statements present fairly the financial position of Pizza King Inc. and subsidiaries at December 31, 1987 and 1986, and the results of their operations and the changes in their financial position for the years then ended, in conformity with generally accepted accounting principles applied on a consistent basis.

Robins, Freeman, and Barwick
Certified Public Accountants
Baltimore, Maryland
January 30, 1988
(except as to Note 11 which is as of February 25, 1988)

14

Developing Credit Policies

The decision to extend credit has two aspects. First, the credit capacity of customers must be evaluated, particularly in cases in which large amounts of credit will be approved. Second, the firm must operate within sound credit policies.

In this chapter, we will examine the conceptual framework for making credit decisions, and we will cover the development of policies for managing accounts receivable. Next, we will discuss a specific technique for tying receivables to the firm's profits. Then, we will examine the conceptual framework for making credit decisions. We will cover the development of policies for managing accounts receivable and the effects of the policies on the firm's profits. We will conclude with the establishment of credit limits for large and small customers.

RECEIVABLES POLICIES

Receivables are assets representing amounts owed to the firm as a result of the sale of goods or services in the ordinary course of business. The value of these claims will be carried on the balance sheet under titles such as accounts receivable, trade receivables, or customer receivables. Whatever the title, they play a major role in the conduct of business for most firms. The great majority of companies do not demand immediate cash payment when goods are sold to regular, creditworthy customers. This is true for firms engaging in retail trade and firms that sell primarily to other businesses. Because of decisions to extend credit, most sales require the firm to carry a receivable for a period of 10 to 60 days.

In this section, we will examine factors that influence the policies that may be established for managing receivables. In addition, some techniques for evaluating the size and mix of receivables will be evaluated.

Purpose of Receivables

Every commitment of financial resources in a firm should be expected to contribute to the goal of maximizing the current value of the firm's common stock and contributing to its long–term survival. The tying up of resources in receivables is no exception. In support of these objectives, we can identify three goals of maintaining receivables.

1. **To Achieve Growth in Sales.** If a firm permits sales on credit, it is usually able to sell more goods than if it insists on immediate cash payment. Many customers are not prepared to pay cash when they purchase. For retail sales, individuals may prefer to write a check at a later time rather than carry a checkbook with them. For business purchases, the firm may want all invoices to be sent to the Accounting Department where standard policies are followed for disbursing cash. In many cases, purchase orders may be transmitted over the phone with instructions to ship the goods and bill for later payment. Finally, many firms do not have cash available to make immediate payment when goods are ordered. They may need 30 or so days to resell the goods before they have funds to pay for them. For these and similar reasons, fewer sales would be expected if a firm eliminated credit for its customers.

2. **To Increase Profits.** Since one possible result of maintaining receivables is a growth in revenues, an indirect result will be additional profits derived from additional sales. This is the case when the marginal contribution or gross margin is greater than the additional costs associated with administering the credit and collection activities. If a firm will not realize higher profits from offering credit, it should consider an all-cash sales program.

3. **To Meet Competition.** As a defensive measure, most firms establish credit terms similar to those of competitors. It is a common practice in American business for the terms of trade to be identical throughout an industry, with wide variances in practices from one industry to another. For example, in the same area, textiles may be purchased on terms of 2/10 EOM (a 2 percent discount if payment is made by the tenth day after the end of the month), whereas stationary supplies carry terms of net 30. By adapting its terms of trade to the industry norms, a firm will avoid the loss of sales from customers who would buy elsewhere if they did not receive the expected credit.

Cost of Maintaining Receivables

As with all assets and operations, the willingness to allow credit sales involves certain costs, specifically:

1. **Costs of Financing the Receivables.** The decision to extend credit delays the receipt of cash, thus tying up a portion of financial resources.

These resources must be financed from three sources: (1) past profits retained in the business; (2) contributed capital from owners; or (3) debt provided by creditors. Whatever the source, the firm incurs a cost for the use of the funds.

2. **Administrative Expenses.** The bookkeeping for credit sales and payments involves out-of-pocket expenses. The firm may employ accountants and bookkeepers, provide computer terminals and supplies, and allocate office space for a work area and storage of records. In addition, most firms conduct investigations of potential credit customers to determine their creditworthiness. These and other expenses, such as telephone charges and postage, comprise the administrative costs of maintaining receivables.

3. **Collection Costs.** When an individual or firm does not pay its bills on time, creditors must take steps to increase the chance for eventual payment. Such actions require a firm to incur collection costs. Initially, money will be spent to prepare and mail reminders that the payment is overdue. If such efforts are not successful, the firm may hire personnel or collection agencies to visit the delinquent customer and demand payment.

4. **Bad-Debt Losses.** After making serious efforts to collect on overdue accounts, the firm may be forced to give up. If a customer declares bankruptcy, no payment may be forthcoming. If the customer leaves the city or state, it may be too costly to trace him or her to demand payment. In such cases, the firm is forced to accept a bad-debt loss on the account. Most firms anticipate that bad-debt losses will be incurred in the normal course of business. High-risk customers may be the major source of these losses, but occasionally a sound firm will run into liquidity problems unexpectedly and eventually enter bankruptcy. Bad-debt losses are properly viewed as a cost of administering a credit policy.

Size of Receivables Balances

The size of accounts receivable is determined by a number of factors, including.

1. **Level of Sales.** The most important factor is the level of credit sales. Since the terms of trade are similar in most industries, firms with a large volume of sales will also have large receivables balances. The sales forecast can be used to predict the future volume of receivables. As an example, if the Marketing Department is planning for an increase of 20 percent in the dollar amount of credit sales, the firm should also plan to finance an additional 20 percent in receivables.

2. **Credit Philosophy**. A firm generally tries to develop a cohesive approach to credit management. In effect, it is determining the amount of risk it is willing to take when making credit sales. This risk is viewed in the context of the overall profit available from higher volumes of sales, and may be seen on a continuum from highly restrictive to relatively lax.

   a. **Strict Credit Policies**. When a firm sells only to highly creditworthy customers, it can expect few bad debts, a small volume of receivables, and a low level of collection costs. At the same time, sales volume will not be high. If the firm has a high gross margin per unit of sales, tight credit policies hurt profits. If the margin of profit is small, tight policies may maximize profits.

   b. **Lax Credit Policies**. These policies produce a large volume of receivables, along with higher financing costs. Two explanations can be offered for the higher volume. First, strong customers will be less careful to pay on time. A lax policy encourages all firms to settle their accounts slowly. Companies that otherwise pay bills on time will not be overly concerned if they are a few days late when sending checks to a firm that accepts slow payments as normal. Second, weak customers will default in larger numbers. With pressure to pay, weak firms are more prompt. In the absence of pressure, they will pay even more slowly than usual. During the extra delay, a number of firms may declare bankruptcy, resulting in bad-debt losses.

   When establishing its credit policies, the firm attempts to find a satisfactory middle ground that will maximize its long-term business success. Thus, it avoids a highly aggressive policy that hurts sales and produces high collection costs. Similarly, the firm avoids a lax policy, with excessive defaults and bad debts. These decisions play an important role in determining the size of the firm's receivables.

3. **Terms of Trade**. Even though the terms of trade are usually standardized in an industry, they must be identified as an important factor in determining the size of receivables. If, for example, the firm changes its terms from net 15 to net 30—a 100 percent increase—it can expect a 100 percent increase in the size of receivables. Conversely, if the firm changed from net 30 to 2/10 net 30, many customers will take the discount. The firm will lose revenue but will experience a decline in the volume of receivables.

Symptoms of Problems

The credit manager should routinely evaluate the firm's credit approvals to ensure that an appropriate policy is being followed. Two tools are helpful for identifying symptoms of problems.

1. **Ratio Analysis**. The most common approach is to use ratios, such as those covered in earlier chapters. As an example, the firm can compare its receivables turnover with its past history, industry averages, or other norms. If the ratios differ from norms, it may be a sign of possible problems and further investigation should be undertaken.

2. **Aging of Receivables**. An **aging schedule** is a tabular classification of receivables by the length of time the accounts have been outstanding. The table may be presented in terms of dollar amounts, percentage breakdown, or both, as shown in Figure 14-1. The figure shows a firm that has a $600,000 balance of receivables on January 1. By checking the electronic ledger balances, the analyst has sorted the accounts. As can be seen, $300,000 represents sales made in December, $150,000 sales in November, $100,000 in October, $20,000 in September, and $30,000 earlier than September. With $600,000 used as 100 percent, the aging schedule displays the dollar amounts outstanding by month of sale and percentage.

To use this schedule properly, we must know the terms of trade. If the firm offered credit terms of 2/10 net 30, 50 percent of the receivables would be current, 25 percent would be up to one month overdue, 17 percent up to two months overdue, and 8 percent more than two months overdue. With 50 percent overdue, it would appear that the firm might be lax in collections. If, on the other hand, the terms of trade were net 60, only 25 percent would be overdue—those from October and earlier. This is better but the firm might still want to conduct a review of its credit policies.

Risk-Class Approach

One common approach to establishing a policy framework for credit decisions uses a risk-class approach. A **risk-class** is a grouping of credit customers based on their operating stability and financial strength. With a risk-class approach, the firm identifies a number of categories ranging from strongest to weakest. A separate credit policy is defined for each class. When a customer first applies for credit, an investigation is initiated and the customer is placed in one of the classes. This eliminates the need to make a separate decision on extending credit each time the customer places an order. Figure 14-2 presents risk-classes, a description of the type of firm in each class, and a brief statement of the applicable credit policy.

Figure 14-1. Aging Schedule, Accounts Receivable.

Accounts Receivable, Input Screen

	July	Aug.	Sept.	Oct.	Nov.	Dec.
Acme Products				45,000		
Acme Products						65,000
Acme Products	15,000					
Acme Products					20,000	
Narvin						45,000
Narvin				35,000		
GTR Inc.			20,000			
GTR Inc.						
Echo Systems		15,000				
Echo Systems						60,000
Echo Systems					55,000	
Lodi						30,000
Wuhan						40,000
DDCP					75,000	
DDCP						60,000
Terman Gp				20,000		

Aging Schedule, Output Screen

Representing Sales Made in

	July	Aug	Sept	Oct	Nov	Dec	Total
Dollar Amount	15,000	15,000	20,000	100,000	150,000	300,000	600,000
Percentage	0.025	0.025	0.033	0.167	0.250	0.500	1.00

Figure 14-2. Risk-Class Approach to Receivables Management.

Risk Class	Description of Firm	Credit Policy
1	Large firms whose financial position and past record indicate virtually no risk	Open credit up to certain limit without approval required.
2	Financially sound firms not supported by a detailed past record	Open credit with approval for purchases in excess of certain amounts up to a specified limit.
3	Solid firms with past records that indicate some risk	Limited credit line with frequent checks.

| 4 | Not-too-solid firms that require close watching | Restricted credit. |
| 5 | High-risk, weak firms | No credit. |

As an example of using this approach, consider a firm with a customer named Acme Company. This customer is a relatively new business and was placed in risk-class 2 after a complete credit check. The credit limit for individual orders from Acme has been set at $70,000, and the outstanding receivables balance at any one time is limited to $225,000. The ledger balances for Acme are given in Figure 14-3. On January 30, a purchase order is received from Acme for goods totaling $80,000. What does the firm do with this request?

Figure 14-3. Acme Company-Accounts Receivable.

Date	Item	Charges	Payments	Balance Due
Jan. 20	Invoice 963522	$45,000		$140,000
Jan. 23	Invoice 963641	50,000		190,000
Jan. 25	Invoice 963698	12,000		202,000
Jan. 25			$30,000	172,000
Jan. 28	Invoice 963811	40,000		212,000

The accounts receivable clerk will compare the order with the file on Acme and discover that the order exceeds the $70,000 single-purchase authorization for the firm. The order also places the total outstanding receivables above the $225,000 limit. This order would be brought to the credit manager who can take several actions, including.

1. **Raise the limit**. The manager may decide that Acme is entitled to higher limits. Since the original credit decisions were made, Acme may have demonstrated that it pays its bills promptly. The firm could be moved to risk-class 1 or have its dollar limits raised in risk-class 2.

2. **Investigate further**. The manager may suggest that it be divided into two separate orders and be resubmitted after the outstanding balance is reduced.

COST-VOLUME-PROFIT APPROACH TO CREDIT

When evaluating different proposals for credit or receivables policies, the goal is to provide a high level of stable earnings. This approach is built on the volume of sales, the costs of achieving the sales level, and the profits that accrue to the firm. In effect, the firm is preparing a pro forma income statement for each policy proposal.

A firm can use a cost-volume-profit approach to setting its terms of trade, as will be illustrated in this section. We will assume that a firm seeks to evaluate five possible credit policies: net 30, no credit, 2/10 net 30, 2/10 net 60, and net 60. The firm's current terms of trade are net 30, and we will assume no significant industry norms that would restrict the firm's ability to change its terms. Although this is not a realistic assumption in most situations, it assists us in analyzing the impact of changing the terms of trade using profit analysis.

A number of steps are required in the cost-volume-profit approach to making credit decisions. These include preparing a sales forecast, determining cost of goods sold and administrative overhead, assessing collection costs and bad-debt losses, and measuring the cost of tying up funds in accounts receivables. Each of the major steps will be covered in turn.

Forecasting Sales

The sales forecast is the first step in preparing a pro forma income statement. It is also the most difficult part of evaluating varying terms of trade. In our example, we can work with the Marketing Department on a forecast of revenues with net 30, the current terms of trade. It is far more difficult to evaluate the changing sales level with different terms. If, for example, a 2 percent discount is given, what will be the response of customers? Would they change suppliers to take advantage of the discount? Or would the firm's competitors match the discount? If they did, it would eliminate any incentive to switch and the sales forecast would not be accurate.

In spite of the difficulties, the firm must make its best estimate of future sales under each policy. This task is usually undertaken as a joint effort of the Marketing and Finance Departments, perhaps with the assistance of other members of the top management team.

Determining Cost of Goods Sold

Once sales estimates have been made, the firm can forecast costs involved with producing goods or providing services. This prediction is usually made by assuming cost of goods sold will be a percentage of sales. This is an acceptable assumption because certain fixed costs, such as depreciation, have already been covered and only variable costs are incurred as sales rise.

The best technique for determining cost of goods sold is to divide it into two components—fixed and variable costs. The fixed costs can be expressed as a percentage of revenues. As an example, for a specific firm the cost of goods sold may be viewed as $1.2 million of fixed costs plus 20 percent of revenues.

Forecasting Administrative Costs

The firm's general and administrative costs may also have fixed and variable components tied to the sales level. If this is the case, these expenses could be, as an example, $600,000 plus 10 percent of revenues.

In addition to the basic general and administrative expenses, two items vary directly with changes in the terms of trade. These two, which must be handled separately, are collection costs and bad-debt losses.

1. **Collection Costs.** The costs of collecting delinquent accounts will usually be a fairly constant percentage of the total receivables. If receivables change by a fixed percent, collection costs should change by a similar percent. For example, a firm may have collection costs of $50,000 when its receivables are $800,000. This ratio is 50/800, or 6.25 percent. If the firm adopts a policy that increases receivables to $1.2 million, the collection costs might rise to $75,000 ($1,200,000. 0625).

   It should be pointed out that the relationship between collection costs and receivables usually holds even though firms may be making sales to riskier customers when they relax credit terms. It might be argued that collection costs should be higher for sales to customers with lower credit ratings. Two factors refute this position. First, higher costs are offset to some degree by economies that accrue with the larger collection activities. Second, the firm will probably make an effort to hold collection costs in line with previous expenditures.

2. **Bad-Debt Losses.** If a firm increases credit sales by a fixed percentage, bad-debt losses often rise by a larger percentage. A relaxing of credit terms allows more time for something to go wrong for customers. In addition, customers experiencing liquidity problems may increase their purchases or switch suppliers to obtain longer payment periods. More delinquencies and bad debts would be expected with these customers.

   The new level of bad debts with a change in the terms of trade is a highly subjective estimate at best. Still, it should be undertaken with the assistance of the Marketing and Accounting Departments. As an example, a firm may estimate $30,000 of bad debts with receivables of $5 million. If receivables double to $10 million, bad debts might be forecast to more than double, say $70,000.

Forecasting Financing Costs

If a change in credit policies causes an increase in receivables, this increase must be financed. If receivables decline, the firm is freeing money for other purposes. In either case, a financing cost or benefit is imputed. With an increase, higher interest costs are assumed. With a decline, lower interest costs are included in the analysis.

As an example, suppose receivables are currently $4 million and the incremental cost of funds is 15 percent. The firm is evaluating two credit policies. The first will increase receivables to $5 million, and the second will decrease receivables to $3.2 million. What is the financing cost or benefit with each policy?

The answer is a cost of $150,000 with the increase in receivables ($1,000,000*.15), and a benefit of $120,000 with the reduction ($800,000*.15).

Forecasting Discounts Taken

If the firm is evaluating terms of trade that include discounts for prompt payment, these discounts that are taken by customers must be forecast as a reduction of revenues. Past data or the experience of other firms may be helpful in estimating the percentage of customers who will accept the discount. Eventually, a percentage must be estimated in terms of the dollar value of sales.

The formula for discounts taken is

Discounts Taken	=	Percent Who Take Discount	*	Percent of Discount	*	Dollar Value of Sales

If it is estimated that 70 percent of customers will take the discount, a firm with sales of $30 million and terms of 2/10 net 30 will have discounts takes of $420,000 (0.70*.02 *30,000,000).

Forecasting the Receivables Balance

When forecasting the size of receivables with different terms of trade, a two step process is needed. First, we must estimate the receivables turnover. Then, it must be used to determine the balance of receivables. The estimated receivables balance is calculated by:

Credit Sales/Receivables Turnover

The accounts receivable turnover is calculated by taking a weighted average of those who take a discount and those who do not and then adding a lag factor in days. The formula is:

365 Days

Percent Taking Discount	*	Discount Period in Days	+	Percent Not Taking Discount	*	Net Period in Days	+	Lag Factor in Days

where the denominator of the formula is also called the **average collection period**.

In this formula, the lag factor is an estimate of the delays in payment as a result of mail and processing floats and customer slowness to pay. As an example, a net 30 policy may result in an average collection period of 45 days. This would be a lag factor of 15 days.

Another illustration would apply to a firm offering terms of 2/10 net 30. Forty percent of the customers will take the discount, and the lag factor is 12 days. The accounts receivable turnover will be 10.7, as follows:

$$ART = 365/(.40 * 10 + .60 * 30 + 12) = 10.7$$

Once we have the turnover and credit sales, we can forecast the size of receivables. If the turnover is 10.7 and annual credit sales are $10 million, the balance will be $934,579 (10,000,000/10.7).

For policies with no discount period, the percentage taking the discount is zero and the percentage paying the net amount is 100. Only the second half of the formula need be used. In our example above, with terms of net 30 and a 15-day lag factor the turnover would be

$$365/(1.00 * 30 + 15) = 8.1$$

After-Tax Profit

Once all the above items have been calculated, an income statement format is used to calculate net income. This is illustrated in the following solved problem.

A Solved Problem

To illustrate the use of cost-volume-profit analysis in evaluating terms of trade, we will work with a specific problem.

Data

A firm is evaluating changing its current policy of net 30. The proposed new terms of trade are to extend no credit at all, extend terms to net 60, or to offer discounts with policies of 2/10 net 30 or 2/10 net 60. A total of 90 percent of the firm's sales are made on credit, and this figure is not expected to change.

Working with the Marketing Department, the credit manager has developed a forecast of the likely sales with each policy. Should no change be made, a modest increase to $30 million is forecast. If the terms are extended to 60 days, it should be possible to enter new markets and achieve $35 million. The same level would apply for 2/10 net 60. On the other hand, terms of 2/10 net 30 would probably not increase sales at all. Refusing to extend credit would be disastrous, with a drop to $20 million. These estimates are based on a detailed knowledge of the market, prospective customers, and the fact that some of the firm's products are not available from other sources. Without credit, the marketing manager feels that most customers will not be happy, since they are used to having time to receive and inspect the goods before preparing a check for payment.

The cost of goods sold was developed in a meeting with the manager of cost accounting. At a $30 million sales level, the firm is at full production capacity for extended periods of time. The efficient utilization of plant and equipment will produce a cost of goods sold at 55 percent of sales. On the other hand, a drop to $20 million is really not efficient. Past data indicate that cost of goods sold runs at 60 percent of revenues at this level. The $35 million sales level is about the same, 60 percent. This level requires overtime work and higher expenses for maintenance on machinery. In addition, nonfinancial problems occur because of the extensive use of the machinery.

Administrative expenses are easy to forecast. With the exception of collection costs and bad debts, general and administrative (G & A) expenses will vary little within this range of sales. The lower sales level will not produce much savings, if any, and the higher sales level can be supported by existing overhead expenses. A $5 million number would be adequate to cover G&A, not including collection costs and bad-debt losses.

Collection costs and bad debts are another matter, since they definitely will vary with the terms of trade. If no change is made, collection costs should be about $1 million and bad debts $500,000. These costs would not change for the 2/10 net 30 policy. With 2/10 net 60 or net 60, they would rise to $2.2 million and $1.2 million, respectively.

The firm's income statement already includes $2.25 million for interest on debt. This is part of the financing for the existing level of receivables. Any savings or additional financing costs from a different level of receivables would produce a cost or savings at a 12 percent cost of funds. This is a before-tax cost and does not reflect the firm's tax rate of 40 percent.

Since two of the proposed policies involve discounts for prompt payment, the firm estimated the number of customers who will take the discount. With terms of 2/10 net 30, the credit manager estimates that 70 percent will take the discount. At 2/10 net 60, the discount is less attractive. Only 50 percent would be likely to accept it if the net amount were due in 60 days. In making these estimates, the credit manager recognizes that payments will not be made promptly in 10, 30, or 60 days. A 12-day lag factor seems to be at work. That is, cash is not available until 12 days after the terms, which means, on the 22nd day for terms of 2/10, the 42nd day for net 30, and the 72nd day for net 60.

The Solution

An evaluation of the five policies described above is presented in Figure 14-4. Each of the assumptions is identified in the input area. Then, the accounts receivable turnovers, average receivables balances, and income statements are displayed as outputs. Key formulas are as follows:

1. **Accounts Receivables Turnover.** An if/then statement is used here because no credit is one of the possibilities. If no credit is extended, the turnover and receivables balances will be zero. The problem is that the denominator of the formula contains zero when no credit is extended. Dividing by zero gives an error message with most spreadsheets. To avoid this problem, the following if/then statement has been used:

$$@IF(F15=0,0,365/(F13*F14+(1-F13)*F15+F16))$$

   If the cell containing the net period (F15) is zero, a zero is displayed. Otherwise, the formula for receivables turnover is computed. In our example, the turnover is 8.7 for net 30 and zero for no credit.

2. **Average Receivables Balance.** The balance is calculated by dividing credit sales by the turnover. Once again, an if/then statement is used to avoid dividing by zero at position F28. The formula is:

$$@IF(F27=0,0,(F10*F11)/F27)$$

3. **Discounts Taken.** This formual is equal to credit sales times the percent of customers taking the discount times the percent of the discount, or:

$$-F10*F11*F12*F13$$

4. **Savings (Cost).** This formula is the benefit from financing fewer receivables or the added cost of financing more receivables. It is calculated by taking the existing receivables at F28 and subtracting the average receivables calculated for each alternative. For the calculation in column G, in Figure 14-4 the formula is:

$$(\$F\$28-G28)*G22$$

where

        F28 is the receivables balance with the existing policy.
        G28 is the new receivables balance.
        G22 is the annual cost of tying up or freeing receivables.

Figure 14-4. Cost-Volume-Profit Model

Input Data	Col F	Col G	Col H	Col I	Col J
		No	*2/10*	*2/10*	
	Net 30	*Credit*	*Net 30*	*Net 60*	*Net 60*
6					
7					
8					
9					
10 Total Sales	30,000	20,000	30,000	35,000	35,000
11 Percent Credit Sales	0.900	0.000	0.900	0.900	0.900
12 Percent of Discount	0.000	0.000	0.020	0.020	0.000
13 Percent Taking Discount			0.700	0.500	
14 Discount Period Days	0	0	10	10	
15 Net Period Days	30	0	30	60	60
16 Lag Factor Days	12	12	12	12	12
17 CofGS	0.550	0.600	0.550	0.600	0.600
18 G&A	5,000	5,000	5,000	5,000	5,000
19 Collection Costs	1,000		1,000	2,200	2,200
20 Bad Debts	500		500	1,200	1,200
21 Current Interest	2,250	2,250	2,250	2,250	2,250
22 Cost of Money	0.120	0.120	0.120	0.120	0.120
23 Tax Rate	0.400	0.400	0.400	0.400	0.400
24					
25 **Output Screens**					
26					
27 Accounts Receivables Turnover	8.7	0.0	13.0	7.8	5.1
28 Average Receivables Balance	3,107	0	2,071	4,056	6,214
30		*No*	*2/10*	*2/10*	
31	Net 30	Credit	Net 30	Net 60	Net 60
32					
33 Revenues	30,000	20,000	30,000	35,000	35,000
34 Discounts Taken	0	0	(378)	(315)	0
35 Net Revenues	30,000	20,000	29,622	34,685	35,000
36 Cost of Goods Sold	(16,500)	(12,000)	(16,500)	(21,000)	(21,000)
37 Gross Margin	13,500	8,000	13,122	13,685	14,000
38 Administrative Expenses	(5,000)	(5,000)	(5,000)	(5,000)	(5,000)
39 Collection Costs	(1,000)	0	(1,000)	(2,200)	(2,200)
40 Bad Debts	(500)	0	(500)	(1,200)	(1,200)
41 Operating Income	7,000	3,000	6,622	5,285	5,600
42 Current Interest	(2,250)	(2,250)	(2,250)	(2,250)	(2,250)
43 Savings (Cost)	0	373	124	(114)	(373)
44 Earnings Before Tax	4,750	1,123	4,496	2,921	2,977
45 Taxes	(1,900)	(449)	(1,798)	(1,168)	(1,191)
46 Net Income	2,850	674	2,698	1,753	1,786

The end result of the cost-volume-profit model is a net income after taxes, in row 46. In our solved problem, the existing policy of net 30 provides the highest income, closely followed by 2/10 net 30. Other possibilities are considerably less profitable. Since the existing policy involves the least risk, it probably will be maintained. Still, the analyst might evaluate growth prospects or other factors that might make 2/10 net 30 an attractive alternative. Once a total viewpoint has been taken, the analyst can prepare a recommendation to management.

ESTABLISHING CREDIT LIMITS

A major component of credit policies is the establishment of a specific credit limit for each customer of the firm. Two groups of customers can be identified when viewing this task. Requests for small amounts of credit are fundamentally different from requests from customers who place large orders. In this section, we will examine both types of decisions.

Factors Affecting Small Orders

Many firms operate in industries where sales are divided among thousands of customers with average unit sales of $25 to $1,000. Even firms that have much larger unit sales will often have a number of credit sales for small dollar amounts. In these situations, three factors dominate the credit decision:

1. **Lack of Information**. When a firm receives an order for goods worth, say, $1,000, it is not likely that it will be accompanied by financial statements or other information that assist in evaluating financial strength. The firm placing the order probably has a number of suppliers and would not take the time to apply for credit with such a small order. The goods could be sold on cash terms, such as cash on delivery, but this might be cumbersome. The credit manager is more likely to make a credit decision without adequate information on financial strength.

2. **Cost-Benefit Relationship**. With a small order, the credit analyst faces a situation that is not cost effective. A credit decision requires time and expense. How much money should be spent on a small order? Whatever the time available, would it not be better used to evaluate customers who place larger orders and, hence, who cause greater exposure to the firm if they default? The credit manager may check with a credit agency or request a credit report from a service such as Dun and Bradstreet. Effort beyond this level is not likely to be cost effective.

3. **Size of the Markup**. The third factor is the amount of profit that is achieved on a sale. When selling goods or services with large markups, the credit decision is less critical. A few sales will more than overcome

a failure to pay. The situation is quite different if the markup is small. Then, an occasional default might wipe out profits entirely. If the markup is large, the credit decision can be almost automatic. If it is small, the firm might be forced to turn down most requests from unknown buyers.

Cash at Risk Approach to Small Orders

For small credit orders, the firm should pursue a policy that strives for a good balance between cash at risk and potential profits on a sale. The exact policy will vary with individual industries.

To deal with a large volume of small orders, the firm might develop a decision rule that is comfortable to its management. An example might be:

EXTEND CREDIT AUTOMATICALLY FOR ORDERS OF $1,000 OR LESS WHEN FIRST-YEAR PROFITS WILL EXCEED CASH AT RISK.

Using this decision rule, the firm compares its exposure with its potential profits and depends on the law of averages. Since only a small number of customers are likely to default in any given year, the firm will make money on small orders if profits exceed cash at risk during the one-year period.

To illustrate the application of this kind of approach, consider a firm selling products with a 20 percent profit margin. The Credit Department has received a purchase order for $5,000, along with an indication from the salesperson that first-year orders should total approximately $30,000 if credit is approved. On the basis of this information, the Credit Department calculates the first-year profit and cash at risk as shown in Figure 14-5. In this application example, the profit exceeds, risk and therefore the credit application falls within the established credit policy.

The major drawback of the decision rule approach using cash at risk is that it makes no attempt to come to grips with the basic creditworthiness of the customer. No effort is made to evaluate financial or operating strengths or to determine the credit capacity using standard analyses. For these reasons, many firms will not consider it. Still, it deserves some further consideration. As a practical matter, it is both difficult and expensive to monitor the credit-worthiness of hundreds or thousands of small accounts. Following a decision rule approach, the firm must recognize that the price of doing business includes moderate levels of collection costs and bad debts. As an example, these expenses might represent a dollar value of 5 to 10 percent of sales. If the firm has a markup of 20 to 40 percent, it will earn a profit on these orders.

To increase the benefits from a cash at risk approach, the firm might develop modified guidelines to screen particularly high-risk customers. As an example, the highest levels of default generally occur with firms that have been in business for three years or less. These firms are dealing with startup costs and other factors that produce higher levels of bankruptcy than occur with more established firms. The firm might use a cash at risk approach that applies only to customers that have been in business for a minimum period of time, say, three years. Thus, the firm can achieve the benefits of the high markup while reducing the difficulties of collection and defaults.

Figure 14-5. Cash at Risk Approach to Credit Limits.

Input Data	
Credit Requested	5,000
First-Year Estimated Sales	30,000
Cost of Sales, Percent	0.800
Outputs	
First-Year Sales	30,000
Less Cost of Sales	(24,000)
First-Year Profit	6,000
Credit Requested	5,000
Less Profit	(1,000)
Cash at Risk	4,000
Excess (Deficiency)	2,000

Limits for Large Accounts

A totally different approach is needed when making decisions on large orders. In these situations, the time spent to evaluate the credit application is small compared to the loss with default. The credit manager still recognizes the amount of the markup as a major factor, but time is spent evaluating financial and other information.

To avoid spending excessive time in making the decision on the credit limit, the analyst should use some guidelines in a systematic evaluation. In the following sections, we will develop a process for evaluating applications for large credit orders.

Broad Guidelines for All Customers

Every firm should establish some broad guidelines for the Credit Department. These guidelines are approved by the chief executive officer or top management team of the firm. They protect the firm from catastrophe on the extension of credit to any one customer or small group of customers. They also recognize some fundamental factors, such as the effect of the credit on the customer's financial position. Three such guidelines are common

1. **Maximum Credit to Any One Customer.** No matter how creditworthy, the extension of a certain credit level to a single customer is an unacceptable exposure to a firm. The credit decison should never have

the effect of "betting the firm" on any one sale. It is a duty of top management to determine the maximum amount of credit that can be outstanding to any one customer. This depends primarily on the size of the firm that extends the credit. A large firm can extend more credit to a single customer without risking the solvency of the firm itself.

2. **Percent of Customer Net Worth.** The term **net worth** refers to the equity reported on a balance sheet. The amount reported as net worth is an important indication of the owner's commitment to the firm. If net worth is small, two possibilities exist. First, it may never have been profitable, allowing it to retain earnings. Second, the owners may not be committed to it. They may have undercapitalized the firm initially by not providing adequate equity capital. Or, they may have declared excessive cash dividends with resultant low levels of retained earnings. Whatever the cause, a low net worth is a small commitment. Thus, the credit limit might be established to reflect the net worth of the customer.

3. **Percent of Customer Net Working-Capital.** The term **net working-capital** refers to the excess of current assets over current liabilities. If a company does not have adequate net working-capital, it may lack the liquidity to pay its bills. The credit decision might employ a guideline based on liquidity as measured by net working-capital.

Stable Liquidity Test

A separate component of the problem of the maximum credit to extend to a customer deals with liquidity. Does the customer exhibit a pattern of sufficient liquidity over time? To answer this question, the analyst can use the four ratios given in Chapter 13: current ratio, acid test, receivables turnover, and inventory turnover.

Once the ratios are calculated, two questions should be asked. The first is, "How does the firm compare to averages for similar firms?" This question simply involves a comparison with norms. The second is, "What are the trends in the firm's liquidity position over time?" This is designed to evaluate stability over time.

If these questions raise concerns as to the stability of liquidity of the potential customer, more information may be needed. If the firm has an unexplained pattern of liquidity fluctuations, it may be a high-risk customer that is likely to default or provide collection problems.

Stable Profitability Test

A different view when extending credit occurs by viewing profitability, once again against norms and over time. The analyst might choose a few quick measures of profitability, such as profit margin, return on investment, and return on equity. If the firm passes the tests, it may be viewed as having stable profits. If the ratios indicate problems, further information should be obtained.

Liquidation Coverage

A final element in establishing credit limits for large customers involves a liquidation analysis. A strong firm has a balance sheet that offers a margin of stability in the event of short-term problems. The strength of the balance sheet is most easily measured by calculating a net liquidation value. A large positive value indicates considerable safety from negative actions in the marketplace, whereas a small or negative value indicates less safety.

The technique used to evaluate liquidation coverage is fairly simple. Assets are valued at some percent that is likely in case of disaster in the market—a worst case scenario. For example, in the effort of forced liquidation, the cash would be worth 100 percent of value, receivables might be worth 90 percent, inventories 50 percent, and so on. Liabilities would have to be paid at 100 percent. When debt is subtracted from the liquidation value of the assets, a net liquidation value is obtained. If it is positive, this is a sign of strength in the balance sheet. If it is negative, the firm is less strong.

A Solved Problem

To illustrate a systematic approach to setting a credit limit for a large customer, let us consider a solved problem. Assume that we have received a request for credit in the amount of $300,000 from the Pollard Company, whose request for credit included a balance sheet and income statement for the past three years. We have converted the data into a format to be used in an electronic spreadsheet model, as displayed in Figure 14-6.

Figure 14-6. Financial Statements, Pollard Company (thousands).

	Two Years Ago	Last Year	This Year
Cash and Equivalents	1,428	1,555	1,320
Receivables	1,905	2,245	2,620
Inventories	2,230	1,640	1,580
Net Other Assets	3,305	3,415	3,210
TOTAL ASSETS	8,868	8,855	8,730
Current Liabilities	2,740	3,350	3,800
Long-Term Debt	2,770	3,280	3,635
Equity	3,358	2,225	1,295
Revenues	11,200	12,350	10,420
Cost of Goods Sold	7,400	7,320	6,245
General and Administrative Expenses	1,550	1,780	1,905
Interest Expenses	394	496	553
Taxes	687	950	675
Net Income	1,169	1,804	1,042

Our firm follows a systematic approach to determining the maximum credit limit to be approved for an individual customer. This is outlined in the model found in Figure 14-7. The components of the model are the input screen, calculations, and output screen.

1. **Input Screen.** The input screen contains the firm's norms and assumptions covering the decision to extend credit. It begins with the level of credit requested, $300,000. The maximum to one customer is identified as being $500,000, and supplemental guidelines are used with respect to net worth and net working capital. A series of financial norms to be applied in checks for stable liquidity and profitability are shown for seven ratios in the figure. The final item in the input area displays percentages for a liquidation analysis.

2. **Calculations.** This portion of the model calculates the seven ratios for the three year period.

3. **Output Screen.** The first area compares each norm with the calculated value for the ratio. If the ratio exceeds the norm, a YES is displayed; if the ratio fails to meet the norm, a NO is displayed. The next portion of the area compares the amount of credit requested with the maximum credit amounts calculated with each guideline. In addition, the model assumes liquidation of the assets at each appropriate percentage and subtracts liabilities at 100 percent to get a net liquidation value. The final two lines display credit limits with and without considering the net liquidation value.

Figure 14-7. Credit Limit Model, Pollard Company Example.

Input Screen

Credit Requested (000s)	300
Maximum to One Customer (000s)	500
Net Worth Guideline	0.10
Net Working-Capital Guideline	0.20
Current Ratio Norm	1.70
Acid Test Norm	1.10
Receivables Turnover Norm	7.00
Inventory Turnover Norm	6.00
Profit Margin Norm	0.19
Return on Investment Norm	0.16
Return on Equity Norm	0.12
Liquidation Percentages	
Cash	1.00
Receivables	0.95
Inventory	0.65
Other Assets	0.65

Calculations	Two Years Ago	Last Year	This Year
Current Ratio	2.03	1.62	1.45
Acid Test	1.22	1.13	1.04
Receivables Turnover	5.89	5.50	3.98
Inventory Turnover in Cash	5.02	7.53	6.48
Profit Margin	0.20	0.26	0.22
Return on Investment	0.25	0.37	0.26
Return on Equity	0.35	0.81	0.80

Output Screen	Norm	Does It Meet Norms?		
		Two Years Ago	Last Year	This Year
Current Ratio	1.700	Yes	No	No
Acid Test	1.100	Yes	Yes	No
Receivables Turnover	7.000	No	No	No
Inventory Turnover	6.000	No	Yes	Yes
Profit Margin	0.190	Yes	Yes	Yes
Return on Investment	0.160	Yes	Yes	Yes
Return on Equity	0.120	Yes	Yes	Yes

Credit Requested	300
Maximum Credit, One Customer	500
Maximum, Net Worth Basis	130
Maximum, Net Working Capital Basis	344
Net Liquidation Value	(513)

Credit Limit by Calculation	
Including Net Liquidation Value	(513)
Excluding Net Liquidation Value	130

What should we do with the application for Pollard Company, based on the results of Figure 14-7? Our analysis might be

1. **Broad Guidelines**. The request is below our maximum limit for one customer but above the guidelines for net worth and net working-capital.

2. **Stable Liquidity**. Some of the ratios do not meet our norms and have been declining. Still, they are not a disaster.

3. **Stable Profitability**. The firm's profits are stable.

4. **Liquidation Coverage**. The firm seems to have inadequate equity. The liquidation analysis shows a negative number.

Overall, we might conclude that Pollard is somewhat weaker than we desire when a $300,000 credit request is received. We might want to investigate further or propose a limit lower than $300,000. If we overlook the liquidation analysis, a limit of $180,000 seems justified. This can be approved pending further information on the downward liquidity and low level of equity.

Continued Evaluation

One of the major mistakes that credit managers can make is to fail to periodically review credit limits. In the case of Pollard Company, a $180,000 credit limit may have been approved. In a year or so, Pollard's good payment record might cause the firm to raise the limit to the $300,000 desired. Yet, Pollard may have continued its downward trend with respect to liquidity. To make the decision to raise the limit correctly, the Credit Department should secure new financial statements and conduct the evaluation with new numbers. Obtaining current financial data is entirely rational when argued but is not often followed in actual practice.

CONCLUSION

In this chapter, we have evaluated the practical approaches to establishing credit policies that support the firm's business operations. If the firm takes both a long-term and short-term view of profits, it can develop policies that extend credit where it is justified and withhold credit when the risks are excessive. As we saw with the cost-volume-profit method and credit limits for large customers, credit policies are an art, not a science. Still, they must be developed systematically and applied consistently if they are to make a proper contribution to the management of the firm.

HARDING SUPPLY COMPANY CASE—CREDIT POLICIES

The Harding Supply Company operates out of offices in Elkhardt, Indiana, and has been doing so since 1923. The company was founded by Gregory Daniels and ran as a one-man business until his death in 1967. Since 1976, Nancy Daniels Marsden, the daughter of the founder, has been running the business with the title of president.

Shortly after taking over the management of Harding Supply, Nancy Marsden began to question a number of practices. She tried different experiments with the distribution channels and discovered that she could eliminate many dealers' complaints while increasing her sales. By 1978, she felt comfortable with the firm's production activities and sales efforts. She then began to work on cash flow and credit problems. In 1981, Harding Supply sold most of its West Coast accounts to a subsidiary of a major steel company. The resulting cash from the sale of the accounts was used to modernize the firm's machinery for manufacturing plumbing supplies. Some of the funds were used to purchase new trucks for delivering supplies.

These actions considerably improved service for Harding's Midwest and East Coast customers and produced strong increases in sales. The 1988 net sales were forecast at $98 million if the firm continued to market its product as aggressively as it had done in the past.

At the end of 1987, Marsden began to analyze the impact of high interest costs on the firm's debt. She began with the firm's 1986 and 1987 balance sheets as prepared by the Accounting Department. She did not request a pro forma income statement because she liked to prepare her own. In addition to knowing the forecasted sales figure, she knew that the firm's cost of goods sold historically ran about 75 percent of sales. Of this 75 percent, labor accounted for 45 percent, raw materials 25 percent, depreciation 17 percent, and miscellaneous expenses 13 percent of the cost of goods sold. She expected these percentages to continue into 1988.

Marsden looked through the forecasted expenses for general and administrative items. The firm was budgeting three relatively stable items for 1988: office and marketing salaries, $4.5 million; sales expenses and promotion, $7 million; and miscellaneous overhead, $2.2 million. She knew that if the firm did not borrow any additional funds, Harding would be facing an annual interest expense of $3 million in 1988.

Having gathered these data, Marsden now needed to look at collection costs and bad-debt losses that were not included in the general and administrative expenses above. She decided to forecast these items using data from the firm's risk-class category that was reviewed on a regular basis. The credit manager normally prepared an estimate of the collection costs and bad-debt losses to be allocated to each category of customer. These estimates were compared against actual data at the end of each year, and for the past five years, the estimates have proven to be fairly accurate. The bad-debt losses were based on actual losses over the past six years, and the collection costs were allocated based on the routine expenses and special collection efforts required for each category of customer. The following table resulted from this process:

Harding Supply Company—Collection Costs and Bad-Debt Losses by Category of Customer

Risk Category	Collection Costs as a Percentage of Sales	Actual Bad–Debt Losses as a Percentage of Sales
1	1.0	0.5
2	1.5	1.0
3	2.0	2.0
4	5.0	3.0

After giving some thought to these data, Marsden sat down with Fred Morris, the firm's sales manager. Two months earlier, Morris had suggested that the firm increase its terms of trade to 2/10 net 60. He thought this would increase receivables, collection costs, and bad-debt losses, but would provide additional sales and profits to the firm. Morris estimated that selling expenses would rise by approximately $2 million and the level of receivables would also rise. If the additional profits were high enough, it would make sense to borrow money at 11 percent to finance these receivables. Marsden asked Morris whether the firm should also check out changing the terms of trade to net 15. This would reduce receivables and allow the firm to pay off a portion of the 11 percent notes that were owed to Manufacturer's National Bank. Morris indicated that selling expenses would probably drop by half a million dollars, but this savings would probably be more than offset by the loss of sales and profits. From this discussion, it appeared that Morris was willing to make an honest appraisal of both alternatives. He indicated that he would get back to Marsden with the effect of each alternative on sales.

Two weeks later, Morris sent Marsden the following forecast for 1988 sales with each alternative and the 1987 balance sheet.

Harding Supply Company Balance Sheet (December 31, 1987) (000s)

	1986	1987		1986	1987
Cash	$2,800	$3,000	Accounts	$5,500	$5,000
Marketable			Payable		
Securities	2,000	2,000	Notes Due		
Accounts			(current)	200	400
Receivable	6,800	7,700	Notes Due		
Inventories	11,000	13,000	(noncurrent)	1,400	1,200
Other Current			Mortgages	19,200	18,000
Assets	2,500	3,000	Long-Term Debt	14,000	14,000
Plant and			Common Stock		
Equipment	82,000	79,900	($1 par)	10,000	10,000
(Accumulated			Premium	13,000	13,000
Depreciation)	(23,000)	(22,000)	Retained		
			Earnings	20,800	25,000
Total Assets	$ 84,100	$ 86,600	Total Liabilities	$84,100	$86,600
			and Equity		

Harding Supply Company 1988 Sales Estimates with Varying Terms of Trade (000s)

	Net 15	2/10 Net 30	2/10 Net 60
Gross Sales	84,000	102,000	125,000
Less Returns	3,000	3,400	4,700
Less Discounts		600	300
Net Credit Sales	81,000	98,000	120,000
By Credit Category:			
1	26,000	30,000	30,000
2	37,000	42,000	48,000
3	18,000	24,000	24,000
4		2,000	18,000
Percent taking discount		0.30	0.10
Lag in payment, days	3	6	12

A quick check of Morris's calculations indicated to Marsden that they were in agreement on the 2/10 net 30 alternative. Since this was the case, she felt that she could rely on his estimates for the net 15 and 2/10 net 60 alternatives. She knew that the cost of goods sold would be approximately 75 percent at $81 million of sales, 73 percent at $98 million of sales and 70 percent at $120 million. The general and administrative expenses, with the exception of the collection costs, bad-debt losses, and selling expenses, were, in effect, fixed for 1988. Using these assumptions, she was prepared to develop the data and reach a decision on the appropriate credit policy for Harding Supply Company. She decided in advance that she would not change policies unless the new policy gave either an increase in sales of 20 percent or an increase in profits of 10 percent. She preferred both, but would accept a decline in sales of 25 percent or less as long as profits rose by 10 percent or more.

Required:
1. Prepare a separate schedule of collections costs and bad-debts losses with each policy.

2. What is the likely size of the accounts receivable with each policy if the firm has relatively steady sales over the course of a year?

3. Prepare a 1988 pro forma statement for Harding Supply with each of the three credit policies. (Use a 40 percent tax rate.)

4. Using Fred Morris's estimates, what reaction do you think he expects from Harding's competition if the new policies are adopted? What reaction from Harding's customers?

U.S.A Distributors Company—Credit Limit Case

Dynatronics International is a large manufacturer of petroleum and rubber-based products used in a variety of commercial applications in the fields of transportation, electronics, and heavy manufacturing. In the southwestern United States, many of the Dynatronics products are marketed by a wholly owned subsidiary, U.S.A. Distributors Company. Operating from a headquarters and warehouse facility in San Antonio Texas, U.S.A. Distributors has 850 employees and handles an annual sales volume of $75 million. All but $5 million of the sales represent items manufactured by Dynatronics.

James Maywood is the credit manager at U.S.A. Distributors. He supervises six employees who handle credit applications and collections on 4,500 accounts. The accounts range in size from $100 to $75,000. The firm sells on varied terms, with 2/10 net 30 as the most common. Sales fluctuate seasonally, and the average collection period tends to run 42 days. Bad-debt losses are less than 0.5 percent of sales.

Maywood is evaluating a credit application from Booth Plastics Incorporated, a wholesale supply dealer serving the oil industry. The company was founded in 1972 by Leland A. Booth and has grown steadily since that time. U.S.A. Distributors is not selling any products to Booth Plastics and had no previous contact with Leland Booth.

U.S.A. Distributors purchased goods from Dynatronics International under the same terms and conditions as Dynatronics used when it sold to independent customers. Although U.S.A. Distributors generally followed Dynatronics in setting its prices, the subsidiary operated independently and could adjust price levels to meet its own marketing strategies. Dynatronics' Cost Accounting Department estimated a 22 percent markup as the average for items sold to Texas Electronics. U.S.A. Distributors, in turn, resold the items to yield a 15 percent markup. It appeared that these percentages would hold on any sales to Booth Plastics.

U.S.A. Distributors incurred out-of-pocket expenses not included in the 15 percent markup. For example, Barbara Sanders, the salesperson who handled the Galveston area, would receive a 2 percent commission on all sales made to Booth Plastics. It would be paid whether or not the receivable was collected. Barbara would, of course, be willing to assist in collecting on any accounts that she had sold. In addition, the company would incur variable costs as a result of handling the merchandise for the new account. As a general guideline, warehousing and other administrative variable costs would run 2 percent of sales.

Maywood approached all credit decisions in basically the same manner. First, he considered the potential profit from the account. He estimated first-year sales to Booth Plastics of $55,000, with a maximum credit exposure of

$20,000 at any one time. And he projected future increases in sales to Booth at an 8 percent annual rate. Assuming that Leland Booth took the 2 percent discount, U.S.A. Distributors would realize a 15 percent markup on these sales since the average markup was calculated on the basis of the customer taking the discount. If Leland Booth did not take the discount, the markup would be slightly higher, as would the cost of financing the receivable for the additional period of time. In addition to potential profit, Maywood was concerned about exposure. He knew weak customers could become bad debts at any time and therefore required a vigorous collection effort whenever their accounts were overdue. His department probably spent three times as much money and effort managing a marginal account as compared to a strong account. He also figured that overdue and uncollected funds had to be financed by U.S.A. Distributors at a 13 percent rate. All in all, slow-paying or marginal accounts were very costly to U.S.A. Distributors.

U.S.A. Distributors follows certain guidelines for maximum credit to one customer. This includes a limit of 10 percent of the customer's net worth or 20 percent of net working capital.

With these considerations in mind, Maywood began to review the credit application for Booth Plastics.

Required: 1. What is the potential profit to U.S.A. Distributors on the first year of sales to Booth Plastics?

2. If James Maywood approves a $10,000 credit limit, what is the maximum cash exposure at any one time for U.S.A. Distributors?

3. Should the credit limit be approved? If not, how much credit should U.S.A. Distributors give to Booth Plastics?

Southwestern Credit Agency Report on Booth Plastics Incorporated.

March 10, 1987

Requested by: Credit Department, U.S.A. Distributors.

Reported for: Booth Plastics, Highway 6 Industrial Park,
                      Galveston, Texas.

Business: Sale and service of plastic and metal supplies and compo-
                      nents, primarily to Oil Industry, 1988 sales of $1.8 million,
                      16 employees.

Market area:	Texas Gulf.
Number of accounts:	Unknown, estimate perhaps 250.
Management:	Leland A. Booth, 96 percent owner and company president. No other significant shareholders.
Background:	Leland Booth started the business as a sole proprietorship in June 1972 with an estimated $60,000 in capital. Business was incorporated on June 30, 1980. Firm appears to be growing rapidly from estimated 1980 sales of $1.5 million.

Dun and Bradstreet Report

Booth Plastics Inc.
12 Waterford Drive
Galveston, Texas
Tel: (713)446-2235
Leland A. Booth, Pres.
No other officers

Rating: EE2
Payments discount—prompt
Sales: $1,745,360
Worth: $155,000
Employs: 14-16
Record: Clear
Condition: Good
Trend: Steady to up

Payments	High Credit	Owes	Term	Payment
	$72,345	17,000	2/10 net 30	discount
	27,200	4,500	net 30	net + 10
	2,432	2,432	net 30	net
	17,525	7,450	2/10 net 30	discount

Financial statements not available. Booth (president) estimates current balance sheet as follows:

Cash	$27,500	Trade Payables	$135,000
Receivables	225,000	Notes Due Bank	70,000
Inventory	175,000	Taxes Due	32,000
Equipment	25,000	3-Year Note	360,000
Fixed Assets	230,000	Equity	95,500
Other Assets	10,000		
Total Assets	$692,500	Total liabilities & Equity	$692,500

Booth reports steady improvement in business for past 3 years, from $1,525,312 to $1,745,360 at a growth rate of 7.2 percent. Current income statement is:

Sales	$1,745,360
Expenses	1,374,000
Commissions	115,000
Net Income	256,360
To Owner	150,000
To Taxes	85,000
Retained	21,360

History

Founded by Leland Booth in 1972. Largely borrowed funds. Has been increasing equity holdings on regular basis each year. Has expanded storage twice (1979 and 1982).

Wholesale supply dealer to energy industry, principally oil. Handles assorted plastic and rubber-related items for medium to heavy industrial use. Sixteen major customers; 200-300 small accounts. Facilities seem adequate for storage.

Financial position seems sound. First National Bank of Galveston offers secured line in five figures. No adverse reports.

15

Collection Policies and Government Regulation

As described in Chapters 13 and 14, the primary concerns for the firm when it is making credit decisions are: (1) the capacity of the customer to pay for the goods or services; and (2) the profits or other benefits that will accrue to the firm as a result of extending credit. Recognizing these considerations, the credit manager must be prepared to deal with two other dimensions of credit decisions. The first of these occurs because some customers will be slow to pay their bills and collection efforts are needed. Since laws governing collection practices exist, the firm should be aware of their key provisions and requirements. Second, the government has regulations dealing with the extension of credit in the first place. Firms should exercise care to protect themselves from accidental violation of the law.

In this chapter, we will examine some important federal government regulations that apply to many decisions when extending credit or collecting receivables.

TRUTH IN LENDING

The Truth in Lending Act was effective July 1, 1969, and has been amended since that date. The purpose of the Act is to assure customers needing consumer credit that they will be given meaningful information on the cost of that credit. Sufficient information is required so that the consumer can compare credit terms available from different sources and avoid the uninformed use of credit. In addition, the Act allows a customer to rescind credit transactions in certain circumstances if they result in a lien against his or her home. The Act further prohibits the issuance of unsolicited credit cards, limits cardholder liability, and establishes requirements to be followed in the event of disputes.

The Truth in Lending Act is published as Regulation Z of the Federal Reserve System and may be obtained from that source. The materials provide questions and answers to guide firms in making consumer credit decisions. In the following sections, some of the common questions and answers are provided. For exact information on what must be done to comply with the current law and regulations, the credit manager should obtain a copy of the updated Regulation Z.

General Questions and Answers

1. **What is the purpose of Regulation Z?**

   To let borrowers and consumers know the cost of credit so they can compare costs among various credit sources and avoid the uninformed use of credit. It regulates issuance of credit cards and sets maximum liability for their unauthorized use. It provides a procedure for resolving billing errors. It informs lessees of the costs of consumer leasing and places restrictions on the lessee's liability.

2. **What kinds of business are affected?**

   Regulation Z applies to organizations that extend credit for which a finance charge is payable or which is repayable in more than four installments. It also applies to personal property leases. It applies to banks, savings and loan associations, credit unions, finance companies, mortgage brokers, department stores, automobile, furniture and appliance dealers, plumbers, electricians, doctors, dentists and other professional people, and hospitals.

3. **What types of credit transactions are covered under Regulation Z?**

   Generally, credit extended for personal, family, household or agricultural uses, not exceeding $25,000. But all real estate credit transactions for these purposes are covered regardless of the amount, except agricultural credit over $25,000.

4. **What types of credit transactions are not covered?**

   a. Business and commercial credit—except agricultural credit.

   b. Credit to federal, state, and local governments.

   c. Transactions in securities and commodities.

   d. Transactions under certain public utility tariffs.

   e. Credit over $25,000—except real estate transactions.

   f. Agricultural credit over $25,000—including real estate transactions.

5. **What types of lease transactions are covered under Regulation Z?**

   Leases exceeding four months of personal property primarily for family use.

6. **What types of lease transactions are not covered?**

   a. Business, commercial, and agricultural leases.

   b. Leases to organizations.

   c. Leases for a period of time less than four months.

   d. Leases under $25,000.

   e. Leases which meet the definition of a credit sale.

   f. Leases of personal property which are incident to the lease of real property.

7. **Can a state law be substituted for Regulation Z?**

   Yes, provided the Federal Reserve Board makes that determination as provided by law.

8. **Do disclosures have to be made in the order they appear in the Regulation?**

   No, but they must be listed in an order that will be meaningful to the customer.

9. **What terms are used to describe credit transactions in the Regulation?**

   The Regulation divides consumer credit into two categories: open end credit and other.

10. **How long should a firm keep records?**

    Evidence of compliance is required for two years.

11. **Will anyone inspect the records?**

    If asked by the proper agency, a firm must show records relating to disclosure and evidence of compliance.

12. **Are there provisions for enforcement?**

    Specific responsibilities for enforcement of Regulation Z are divided among nine federal agencies. A complete list of these agencies and types of businesses they cover can be found in the Regulation itself.

13. **Are there penalties for violating the Act?**

    If an individual or firm fails to make disclosures as required under Truth in Lending, it may be sued for actual damages plus twice the amount of the finance charge in the case of a credit transaction, and for 25 percent of the total monthly payments in the case of a consumer lease, as well as court costs and attorney's fees. The finance charge and consumer lease portions of damages are subject to a minimum of $100 and a maximum of $1,000. If convicted in a criminal action, an individual can be fined $5,000, imprisoned for one year, or both. In addition, a $50 forfeiture penalty applies to any failure to comply with the Fair Credit Billing provisions.

Questions and Answers on Finance Charges

1. **What is the finance charge?**

    It is the total of all costs the customer must pay, directly or indirectly, for obtaining credit.

2. **What costs are included in the finance charge?**

    a. Interest.

    b. Loan fee.

    c. Finder's fee or similar charge.

    d. Time price differential.

    e. Amount paid as a discount.

    f. Service, transaction, or carrying charge.

    g. Points.

    h. Appraisal fee (except in real estate transactions).

    i. Premium for credit life insurance.

    j. Credit report fee (except real estate).

3. **In what form is the finance charge to be shown to the customer?**

    Clearly typed or written, stating dollars and cents total and annual percentage rate. The words "finance charge" and "annual percentage rate" must stand out clearly.

4. **Are maximum or minimum rates specified in Regulation Z?**

    No.

5. **How accurate must the firm compute the annual percentage rate?**

    To the nearest one-quarter of 1 percent.

Questions and Answers about Open End Credit

1. **What is open end credit?**

    It covers most credit cards, revolving charge accounts in retail stores, and check overdraft plans in banks.

2. **What must an open end credit customer be told?**

    The customer must receive these items in writing:

a. The conditions under which the finance charge may be imposed and the period in which payment can be made without incurring a finance charge.

b. The method used in determining the balance on which the finance charge is imposed.

c. How the actual finance charge is calculated.

d. The periodic rates used and the range of balances to which each applies.

e. The conditions under which additional charges may be made along with details of how they are calculated.

f. Descriptions of any lien on the property.

g. The minimum payment required on each billing.

h. A statement of the customer's rights under the Fair Credit Billing Act.

3. **Are periodic statements necessary on open end accounts?**

Yes, where there is a balance over $1.

4. **What sort of information must accompany a monthly statement?**

a. The balance at the start of the billing period.

b. A copy of the sales voucher or written identification of the transaction.

c. Amounts and dates of payments made, as well as returns, rebates, and adjustments.

d. The finance charge in dollars and cents.

e. The rates used in calculating the finance charge plus the range of balances to which they apply, the corresponding annual percentage rate, and any minimum charge.

f. The unpaid balance.

g. The closing date and the balance at that time.

h. A statement of the customer's rights under the Fair Credit Billing provisions.

i. An address for billing error inquiries.

5. **How is the annual percentage rate determined on open end credit?**

The finance charge is divided by the unpaid balance. This gives the rate per month. The result is multiplied by 12. Other methods for calculating the rate are detailed in the Regulation.

Questions and Answers about Credit Other Than Open End

1. **What type of credit is included?**

   Both loans and sales credit. Typically, buying or financing the purchase of "big ticket" items such as an automobile, washing machine, television set, or other major appliance.

2. **What must the credit customer be told in writing?**

   a. The total dollar amount of the finance charge.

   b. The date on which the finance charge begins.

   c. The annual percentage rate.

   d. The number, amounts, and due dates of payments.

   e. The total payments, except mortgages on dwellings.

   f. The charges for any default or delinquency.

   g. Description of any security held.

   h. Penalty charges for prepayment of principal.

   i. The method used to compute finance charges.

3. **In the case of a loan, what else must be provided?**

   a. The amount of credit to be given to the customer. This includes all charges that are part of the amount of credit extended but are not part of the finance charge. This information must be itemized.

   b. Amounts that are deducted as prepaid finance charges and required deposit balances.

4. **Where must this information be given?**

   It must be included in the instrument evidencing the obligation above the customer's signature.

5. **Are monthly statements required?**

   No, except for credit cards.

Questions and Answers about Real Estate

1. **Is real estate credit covered under Regulation Z?**

   Yes, when it is to an individual and not for business purposes, except that agricultural purposes in excess of $25,000 are exempt.

2. **Does such real estate credit cover more than mortgages?**

   Yes, any nonbusiness credit transaction that involves security interest in real estate is covered.

3. **Are there special provisions that apply to real estate credit?**

   Yes:

   a. The lender does not have to show the dollar amount of the finance charge for the purchase of the customer's dwelling.

   b. The customer has the right to cancel a credit arrangement within three business days if his or her residence is used as collateral.

4. **Must a creditor inform his or her customer of the right to cancel?**

   Yes, he must furnish the prescribed notice.

5. **What must the customer do to cancel a real estate transaction under the Regulaton?**

   a. Sign and date the notice to customer and either mail the notice or deliver it to the creditor at the address shown.

   b. Send a telegram to the creditor.

   c. Prepare a letter that includes a brief description of the transaction and mail it or deliver it.

6. **Can the customer telephone the cancellation?**

   No, WRITTEN notice is required.

7. **What if the Lender does not receive the notice of cancellation in three days?**

   He or she should allow for a mailed letter to be delivered.

8. **Does this right of cancellation apply to mortgages?**

   A first mortgage to finance the purchase of the customer's dwelling carries no right to cancel. A first mortgage for any other purpose or a second mortgage on the dwelling may be canceled.

9. **What happens regarding cancellation of a mechanic's lien acquired by a craftsperson?**

   The customer has a right to cancel within three business days. Unless there is an emergency, the craftsperson should wait three days before starting work.

10. **Suppose a customer needs emergency repairs and cannot wait three days?**

    A customer may waive the right to cancel to meet a bona fide emergency if failure to start repairs would endanger the customer, the family, or property. Preprinted waiver forms may not be used.

Questions and Answers about Credit Cards

1. **Are there restrictions on issuance of credit cards?**

Yes, a credit card may not be issued except in response to a request or application.

2. **What is an accepted credit card?**

It is a credit card which the cardholder has requested and received, or has signed, or has used, or has authorized another person to use. A credit card issued in renewal of an accepted credit card becomes accepted when received by the cardholder.

3. **Does Regulation Z apply to credit cards issued for business purposes?**

Yes, special provisions on liability may apply to credit cards issued for business purposes.

4. **Is a cardholder liable for unauthorized use of a credit card?**

Yes, if:

a. It is accepted.

b. The liability does not exceed the lesser of $50 or the amount obtained prior to notification to the issuers.

c. The issuer has given adequate notice of unauthorized use.

d. The issuer has provided the cardholder with an addressed postage-paid notification to be mailed in event of loss.

e. The issuer has provided a method whereby the user of the card can be identified as the person authorized to use it.

Question and Answer about Credit and Lease Advertising

1. **Does Regulation Z affect credit and lease advertising?**

Yes, it affects all advertising to aid or promote consumer credit or any consumer lease. This includes television, radio, newspapers, magazines, leaflets, flyers, catalogs, public address announcements, direct mail literature, window displays, and billboards.

FAIR CREDIT BILLING ACT

The Fair Credit Billing Act deals with credit cards and charge accounts, as well as with consumer lending by banks and financial institutions. It covers the rights of borrowers and procedures to be followed with respect to billings and errors in billing. The provisions of this Act have been incorporated into Regulation Z. Some common questions and answers are provided in the next section.

Questions and Answers on Fair Credit Billing

1. **Must all creditors comply with the Fair Credit Billing Act?**

   No, it applies to open end creditors, such as credit card issuers.

2. **How should a customer notify the creditor of suspected errors on a periodic statement?**

   Send a written notice within 60 days with the suspected error. The notice should contain the customer's name and account number, the amount in error, and the reasons there is an error.

3. **What is a billing error?**

   A mistake made in identifying a transaction or the failure to send a periodic statement to the customer's correct address. A customer may also allege as a billing error that the item was not delivered as agreed by the merchant.

4. **What must the creditor do in response to written notification of a billing error?**

   It must acknowledge the inquiry within 30 days and give a written response within two billing cycles. If there is an error, it must be corrected. If the lender does not agree with the customer, it must explain in writing and send documentary proof of the indebtedness.

5. **How should the amount alleged to be a billing error be treated during the resolution process?**

   Neither the amount in dispute nor charges imposed on that amount need be separately identified. Payment of the amount in dispute is not required pending compliance with the Fair Credit Billing Act.

6. **Must the lender comply with any requirements regarding credit reporting after an error notice is received?**

   Yes, until the lender has completed the response, it may not threaten to report adversely the customer's credit standing.

7. **Are there prohibitions on closing an account because a customer fails to pay a disputed amount?**

   Yes, an account may not be closed or restricted during the time the resolution procedure is pending, solely because the disputed amount is not paid.

8. **After completion of the error resolution procedure, how must finance charges be adjusted?**

   If there was an error, no finance charges may be collected.

9. **How are minimum payments treated?**

During the error resolution procedure, the lender may not require a minimum payment on the amount in dispute. After the error is resolved, the customer may be required to make up missed minimum payments.

10. **May a customer assert against the card issuer claims regarding unsatisfactory merchandise or services obtained by use of a credit card?**

   Yes, if:

   a. The customer first attempts to settle the problem with the merchant.

   b. The original transaction was in excess of $50.

   c. The transaction took place within the customer's home state or 100 miles of the home address.

11. **Must the lender inform the customer of his or her rights and duties under the error resolution procedure?**

   Yes, two notices are provided. The longer form must be given to all new customers when they open an account. A shorter form is provided which can be sent with each periodic statement.

12. **Can funds held in a deposit account for a customer be applied against his or her debt on a credit card?**

   Only if the customer agrees in writing; otherwise, only pursuant to a court order.

13. **What should a creditor do if a customer pays more than is owed?**

   It may credit the customer's account with the entire amount sent. If this is done, the creditor must return the excess if requested.

14. **Are there any requirements concerning how quickly payments must be credited to an account?**

   Yes, there are also requirements regarding how promptly refund credits for returns must be credited.

15. **Are there other provisions of which a credit card issuer should be particularly aware?**

   Credit card issuers cannot prohibit merchants who honor their cards from offering a discount to customers who pay cash. Nor can card issuers require merchants to procure services not essential to the credit card plan.

EQUAL CREDIT OPPORTUNITY

The Equal Credit Opportunity Act was effective October 1975. Its purpose is to forbid discrimination on the basis of sex or marital status by institutions granting credit. The Act has been amended to extend this prohibition to discrimination on the basis of race, color, religion, national origin, and age.

The Act is published as Regulation B of the Federal Reserve System. Parts are extracted below. Note that these materials are needed to complete the case at the end of this chapter.

Extracts from Regulation B

Equal Credit Opportunity—Section 2021

(a) **Authority and scope**. This Part comprises the regulations issued by the Board of Governors of the Federal Reserve System pursuant to Title VII (Equal Credit Opportunity Act) of the Consumer Credit Protection Act and applies to persons who are creditors.

(b) **Administrative Enforcement**. This function is assigned to the Comptroller of the Currency, Board of Governors of the Federal Reserve System, Board of Directors of the Federal Deposit Insurance Corporation, Federal Home Loan Bank Board, Administrator of the National Credit Union Administration, Interstate Commerce Commission, Civil Aeronautics Board, Secretary of Agriculture, Farm Credit Administration, Securities and Exchange Commission, and Small Business Administration. Except to the extent that administrative enforcement is specifically committed to other authorities, compliance will be enforced by the Federal Trade Commission.

(c) **Penalties and Liabilities**. Any creditor who fails to comply with the Act is subject to civil liability for actual and punitive damage. Liability for punitive damages is restricted to nongovernmental entities and is limited to $10,000 in individual actions and the lesser of $500,000 or 1 percent of the creditor's net worth in class actions, plus the awarding of costs and reasonable attorney's fees. Section 706(c) relieves a creditor from civil liability resulting from any act done in good faith in conformity with any rule of the Board of Governors of the Federal Reserve System. A civil action may be brought in a United States District Court without regard to the amount in controversy within two years after the date of the violation.

(d) **Interpretations**. A request for a formal Board interpretation must be addressed to the Director of the Division of Consumer Affairs, Board of Governors of the Federal Reserve System, Washington, D.C. 20551. Each request must contain a complete statement, signed by the person making the request, of all relevant facts of the credit arrangement. True copies of all pertinent documents must be submitted. The relevance of such documents must be set forth in the request, and the documents must not merely be incorporated by reference. The request must contain an analysis of the facts and specify the pertinent provisions of the regulation. Within 15 business days of receipt of the request, a response will be sent to the person making the request.

Section 2022—Definitions and Rules of Construction

The following definitions and rules of construction shall apply:

(a) **Account** means an extension of credit. When employed in relation to an account, the word **use** refers only to open end credit.

(b) **Act** means the Equal Credit Opportunity Act (Title VII of the Consumer Credit Protection Act).

(c) **Applicant** means any person who requests or who has received an extension of credit from a creditor.

(d) **Application** means an oral or written request for an extension of credit. A **completed application for credit** means an application in connection with which a creditor has received all the information that the creditor regularly obtains and considers in evaluating application.

(e) **Consumer credit** means credit extended to a natural person in which the money, property, or service is primarily for personal, family, or household purposes.

(f) **Credit** means the right granted by a creditor to an applicant to defer payment of a debt.

(g) **Credit card** means any card, plate, coupon book, or other single credit device existing for the purpose of being used from time to time upon presentation to obtain money, property, or services on credit.

(h) **Creditor** means a person who, in the ordinary course of business, regularly participates in the decision of whether or not to extend credit.

(i) **Discriminate against an applicant** means to treat an applicant less favorably than other applicants.

(j) **Elderly** means an age of 62 or older.

(k) **Good faith** means honesty in fact in the conduct or transaction.

(l) **Inadvertent error** means a mechanical, electronic, or clerical error that a creditor demonstrates was not intentional.

(m) **Marital status** means the state of being unmarried, married, or separated, as defined by applicable state law. For the purposes of this Part, the term unmarried includes persons who are single, divorced, or widowed.

(n) **Person** means a natural person, corporation, government agency, trust, estate, partnership, cooperative, or association.

(o) **Prohibited basis** means race, color, religion, national origin, sex, marital status, or age.

(p) **A demonstrably and statistically sound, empirically derived credit system** is a system

(1) in which the data used are obtained by using appropriate sampling principles

(2) which is developed to predict the creditworthiness of applicants with respect to the legitimate business interests of the creditor, including, but not limited to, minimizing bad-debt losses and operating expenses

(3) which separates creditworthy and noncreditworthy applicants at a statistically significant rate

(4) which is periodically revalidated as to its predictive ability by the use of appropriate statistical principles.

A creditor may use a demonstrably and statistically sound, empirically derived credit system obtained from another person or may obtain credit experience from which such a system may be developed.

(q) **Public assistance program** means any federal, state, or local governmental assistance program that provides a continuing, periodic income supplement. The term includes Aid to Families with Dependent Children, food stamps, rent and mortgage supplement or assistance programs, Social Security, and unemployment compensation.

(r) **State** means any state, the District of Columbia, the Commonwealth of Puerto Rico, or any territory or possession of the United States.

Section 202.4—General Rule Prohibiting Discrimination

A creditor shall not discriminate against an applicant on a prohibited basis regarding any aspect of a credit transaction.

Section 202.5—Rules Concerning Applications

(a) **Discouraging applications**. A creditor shall not make any oral or written statement, in advertising or otherwise, to applicants or prospective applicants that would discourage on a prohibited basis a reasonable person from making or pursuing an application.

(b) **General rules concerning requests for information**. A creditor may request any information in connection with an application provided it is not prohibited by Regulation B. A creditor shall not request an applicant's race/national origin, sex, and marital status.

(c) **Information about a spouse or former spouse.** Except as permitted in this subsection, a creditor may not request any information concerning the spouse or former spouse of an applicant. A creditor may request information concerning a spouse or former spouse if:

(1) the spouse will use the account; or

(2) the spouse will be liable upon the account; or

(3) the applicant is relying on the spouse's income as repayment of the credit; or

(4) the applicant resides in a community property state; or

(5) the applicant is relying on alimony, child support, or maintenance payments as a basis for repayment.

A creditor may request an applicant to list any account on which the applicant is liable and to provide the name and address in which such an account is carried. A creditor may also ask the names in which an applicant has previously received credit.

(d) **Information a creditor may not request.** If an applicant applies for an individual, unsecured account, a creditor shall not request the applicant's marital status, unless the applicant resides in a community property state. Where an application is for other than individual, unsecured credit, a creditor may request an applicant's marital status. Only the terms married, unmarried, and separated shall be used. A creditor shall not inquire whether income stated in an application is derived from alimony, child support, or maintenance payments, unless the creditor discloses that such income need not be revealed if the applicant does not desire the creditor to consider such income in determining the applicant's creditworthiness. A creditor shall not request the sex of an applicant. An applicant may be requested to designate a title on an application form (such as Ms., Miss, Mr., or Mrs.) if the form discloses that such title is optional. An application form shall otherwise use only terms that are neutral as to sex. A creditor shall not request information about birth control practices, intentions concerning the bearing or rearing of children, or capability to bear children. This does not preclude a creditor from inquiring about the number and ages of dependents or about dependent-related financial obligations or expenditures, provided such information is requested without regard to sex, marital status, or any other prohibited basis. A creditor shall not request the race, color, religion, or national origin of an applicant. A creditor may inquire as to an applicant's permanent residence and immigration status.

(e) **Application forms.** A creditor need not use written applications. If a creditor chooses to use written forms, it may design its own, use forms prepared by another person, or use model application forms.

Section 202.6—Rules Concerning Evaluation of Applications

(a) **General rule concerning use of information.** Except as otherwise provided in the Act, a creditor may consider any information as long as it is not used to discriminate against an applicant on a prohibited basis.

(b) **Specific rules concerning use of information.** A creditor shall not take a prohibited basis into account in any system of evaluating the creditworthiness of applicants. A creditor shall not take into account an applicant's age or whether an applicant's income derives from any public assistance program. In a statistically sound credit system, a creditor may use an applicant's age as a predictive variable, provided that the age of an elderly applicant is not assigned a negative factor or value. In a judgmental system of evaluating creditworthiness, a creditor may consider age or whether income derives from any public assistance program only for the purpose of determining a pertinent element of creditworthiness. A creditor may consider age of an elderly applicant when such age is used to favor the elderly applicant. A creditor shall not use assumptions or aggregate statistics that any group of persons will bear or rear children or, for that reason, will receive diminished or interrupted income in the future. A creditor shall not take into account the existence of a telephone listing in the name of an applicant for consumer credit. A creditor may take into account the existence of a telephone in the residence of such an applicant.

A creditor shall not discount or exclude from consideration the income of an applicant or spouse because of a prohibited basis or because the income is derived from part-time employment, an annuity, pension, or other retirement benefit. A creditor may consider the amount and probable continuance of any income. Where an applicant relies on alimony, child support, or maintenance payments, a creditor shall consider them to the extent they are likely to be consistently made. Factors that a creditor may consider are whether payments are received pursuant to a written agreement or court decree, the length of time they have been received, the regularity of receipt, the availability of procedures to compel payment, and the creditworthiness of the payor.

When evaluating credit history, a creditor shall consider

(1) Accounts that the applicant and a spouse are permitted to use, for which both are contractually liable

(2) Any information the applicant may present tending to indicate that the credit history being considered does not accurately reflect the applicant's creditworthiness

(3) Any account reported in the name of the spouse or former spouse that the applicant can demonstrate reflects creditworthiness.

A creditor may consider whether an applicant is a permanent resident of the United States, the applicant's immigration status, and additional information to ascertain its rights and remedies regarding repayment.

(c) **State property laws.** A creditor's consideration or application of state property laws shall not constitute unlawful discrimination.

Section 202.7—Rules Concerning Extensions of Credit

(a) **Individual accounts.** A creditor shall not refuse to grant credit on the basis of sex, marital status, or other prohibited basis.

(b) **Designation of name.** A creditor shall not prohibit an applicant from maintaining an account in a birth-given first name and surname, the spouse's surname, or a combined surname.

(c) **Action concerning existing open end accounts.** In the absence of evidence of failure to repay, a creditor shall not take any of the following actions regarding an applicant who is contractually liable on an existing open end account on the basis of the applicant's reaching a certain age or retiring, or on the basis of a change in the applicant's name or marital status:

(1) Require a reapplication.

(2) Change the terms of the account.

(3) Terminate the account.

A creditor may require a reapplication regarding an open end account on the basis of a change in an applicant's marital status where the credit granted was based on income earned by the spouse if the applicant's income alone at the time of the original application would not support the credit extended.

(d) **Signature of spouse or other person.** A creditor shall not require the signature of spouse or other person, if the applicant qualifies under the creditor's standards of creditworthiness. If an applicant requests unsecured credit and relies in part on property to establish credit-worthiness, a creditor may consider state law, the form of ownership of the property, its susceptibility to attachment, and other factors that may affect the value. The creditor may require the signature of the spouse or other person under applicable state law to make the property available to satisfy the debt in the event of default.

If a married applicant requests unsecured credit in a community property state, a creditor may require the signature of the spouse. If an applicant requests secured credit, a creditor may require the signature of the spouse or other person under applicable state law to make the property available to satisfy the debt in the event of default. If the personal liability of an additional party is necessary to support the credit requested, a creditor may request a co-signer, guarantor, or the like. The spouse may serve as an additional party, but a creditor shall not require that the spouse be the additional party.

(e) **Insurance.** A creditor shall not refuse to extend credit or to terminate an account because insurance is not available on the basis of the applicant's age. Information about age, sex, or marital status may be requested in an application for insurance.

Section 202.9—Notifications

(a) **Notification of action taken.** A creditor shall notify an applicant of action taken within:

   (1) 30 days after receiving a completed application concerning approval or adverse action.

   (2) 30 days after taking adverse action on an uncompleted application.

   (3) 30 days after taking adverse action regarding an existing account.

   (4) 90 days after the creditor has notified the applicant of an offer to grant credit other than the amount or terms requested.

(b) **Content of notification.** Any notification given to an applicant against whom adverse action is taken shall be in writing and contain the action taken, the provisions of section 701(a) of the Act, the name and address of the federal agency that administers compliance, and

   (1) a statement of specific reasons for the action taken; or

   (2) a disclosure of the applicant's right to a statement of reasons within 30 days after requesting them.

(c) **Multiple applicants.** If there is more than one applicant, the notification need only be given to one of them, the primary applicant where one is apparent.

(d) **Multiple creditors.** If a transaction involves more than one creditor and the applicant accepts the credit offered, this section does not require notification of adverse action by any creditor.

(e) **Statement of specific reasons.** Reasons shall be sufficient if specific and indicate the principal reason(s) for the adverse action. A creditor may formulate its own statement of reasons in checklist or letter form, or may use all or a portion of the sample form provided.

(f) **Failure of compliance.** A failure to comply with this section shall not constitute a violation when caused by an inadvertent error. Upon discovering the error, the creditor must correct it as soon as possible.

(g) **Notification.** A creditor notifies an applicant when a letter addressed to the applicant is delivered or mailed to the applicant's last known address or when the creditor communicates orally with the applicant.

Section 202.10—Furnishing of Credit Information

(a) For every account established, a creditor shall

    (1) Determine whether an applicant's spouse is permitted to use it.

    (2) Designate any such account to reflect the fact of participation of both spouses.

(b) If a creditor furnishes information concerning an account to a consumer reporting agency, it shall furnish the information in a manner that will enable the agency to provide access to the information in the name of each spouse.

(c) If a creditor furnishes information concerning an account in response to an inquiry regarding a particular applicant, it shall furnish the information in the name of the spouse about whom such information is requested.

Section 202.11—Relation to State Law

Inconsistent state laws. This Part alters, affects, or preempts state laws that are inconsistent with this Part to the extent of the inconsistency. A state law is not inconsistent with this Part if it is more protective of an applicant.

Section 202.12—Record Retention

(a) **Preservation of records.** For 25 months after the date that a creditor notifies an applicant of action taken, the creditor shall retain

    (1) The application form and written information used in evaluating the application.

    (2) A copy of the notification of action taken and the specific reasons for adverse action.

    (3) Any written statement submitted by the applicant alleging a violation of the Act.

(b) **Failure of compliance.** A failure to comply with this section shall not constitute a violation when caused by an inadvertent error.

FAIR DEBT COLLECTION PRACTICES

An important part of the management of the credit function deals with the practices and policies for collecting on loans. The firm has a choice between tight and relaxed approaches to granting credit in the first place. Similarly, it can be aggressive or liberal in collecting on overdue accounts. Four situations are thus possible as conceptual categories:

1. **Strict Approvals and Aggressive Collecting.** This is the most conservative approach to administering the credit policy. Generally, no credit is extended for small orders; for larger orders, a complete credit investigation is undertaken. Once a customer is late on loan payments or past the net period for credit purchases, active collection efforts begin. This policy is suitable for firms or financial institutions operating in a highly fluid environment with sizable bankruptcies or defaults. It is generally unsuitable when it results in sizable lost sales to competitors.

2. **Liberal Approvals and Relaxed Collecting.** This is the most liberal approach and is the opposite of the prior credit policy. Credit is granted or loans are made freely, and collections are not begun until payments are long overdue. This policy may be followed in situations where there are many small orders and the markup on each is large enough to cover losses. It is not suitable in most business and banking situations.

3. **Strict Approvals and Relaxed Collecting.** With this policy, the firm or bank hopes to catch most of its credit problems before the credit is extended. Sometimes this works; sometimes it does not. This policy is suitable for situations in which where collection costs are very high compared to the amount collected or where approved customers will pay without being reminded of their obligations. It is not suitable in environments in which approvals are costly or in which customers will not pay until reminded.

4. **Liberal Approvals and Aggressive Collecting.** With this policy, the firm or bank extends credit to most applicants and then collects vigorously as soon as the due date is passed. For business firms, this is usually a cost effective policy; for banks, it is not. Finance companies, however, often use this approach. This method is suitable when credit investigations are costly or not helpful and when the markup is sufficiently large so as to cover a certain level of losses. It is not suitable in low-profit situations or when collection costs are high.

Whatever the overall policy, it is important for the firm or bank to establish its collection procedures at the same time that it develops its credit policies. Collections are an art, not a science; they are also an integral part of any program of credit administration.

Fair Debt Collection Practices Act

Effective March 20, 1978, the Fair Debt Collection Practices Act outlines collection practices that may be used for consumer borrowings. Under certain circumstances, banks are considered third-party collectors under the provisions of the Act and must comply with it. As a general statement, the Act merely systematizes standard collection practices and forbids abusive and deceptive actions by collectors.

The following sections contain information on major provisions of the Act. These pages are needed to complete the case at the end of the chapter.

Fact Sheet on Banking Institutions and Fair Debt Collection Practices Act

The Fair Debt Collection Practices Act is designed to eliminate abusive and deceptive debt collection practices and to ensure that reputable debt collectors are not competitively disadvantaged.

Coverage

Not all persons or businesses that collect debts are covered by the Act. The Act defines "debt collector" as any person who regularly collects or attempts to collect, directly or indirectly, consumer debts asserted to be owed to another person. Consumer debt is incurred by an individual primarily for personal, family, or household purposes. Debt incurred for business or agricultural purposes is not covered.

The Act is applicable to banks that regularly collect debts for other institutions. A bank might solicit the help of another bank in collecting a defaulted debt of a customer who has relocated. A bank is subject to the requirements of the Act if it uses a name other than its own in its collection efforts.

A bank will <u>not</u> be a debt collector subject to the Act when it

- Collects debts due another only in isolated instances.
- Collects, in the bank's own name, debts owed to the bank.
- Collects debts which it originated.
- Collects debts not in default when obtained.
- Collects debts obtained as security for a commercial credit transaction involving the bank.
- Collects debts incidental to a bona fide fiduciary relationship or escrow arrangement.
- Collects debts for another person to whom it is related by common ownership or corporate control.

Others who are not covered by the Act are

- An officer or employee of the bank when collecting, in the bank's name, debts owed to the bank.
- Attorneys-at-law collecting debts on behalf of the bank.
- Legal process servers.

Requirements

The Act requires debt collectors to

- Cease further communication with a consumer upon written request, except to advise the consumer that the debt collector's further efforts are being terminated, or to notify the consumer that specified remedies may or will be invoked.
- Apply payments in accordance with the consumer's instructions.
- Notify the consumer in writing, within five days of initial contact, of the amount of the debt, the name of the creditor, and advise the consumer of the debt collector's duty to verify the debt if it is disputed. If the consumer disputes the debt within 30 days, the debt collector must stop collection efforts until verification is sent to the consumer.

Prohibitions

The Act prohibits

- <u>Abuse and Harassment</u>. Threatening violence or using profane language.
- <u>False and Misleading Representation</u>. Threatening to communicate false credit information, or giving a false impression that collection documents represent legal process.
- <u>Unfair Practices</u>. Misusing postdated checks or communicating by postcard.

Among the activities specifically prohibited are

- Contact with third parties, including employers, except to obtain information concerning the consumer's location.
- Communication with the consumer at place of employment if there is reason to believe that the employer prohibits such communications.
- Contact with a consumer at any unusual time or place, unless agreed to by the consumer.

- Initiation of a debt collection action in a jurisdiction other than those permitted by the Act.

Civil Liability

Private civil action must be brought within one year from the date of the violation. In the case of an individual action, the debt collector is liable for actual damages plus punitive damages of up to $1,000 for each named plaintiff and the lesser of 1 percent of net worth or $500,000 for all other class members.

Administrative Enforcement

The bank regulatory agencies are responsible for enforcing the Act under the Federal Deposit Insurance Act. This means that bank regulators may use their authority to issue cease and desist orders which may include provisions requiring affirmative action to correct conditions resulting from violations.

Questions and Answers about the Fair Debt Collection Practices Act

1. Q: When is a bank a debt collector?

   A: A bank that regularly participates in any arrangement, including reciprocal service agreements, with another person to collect defaulted consumer debts for that person, is a debt collector for those debts only. If a bank uses a name other than its own in collecting its own consumer debts, it is a debt collector.

2. Q: When is a debt in default?

   A: The Act does not define when a debt is in default. In determining whether a debt is in default, we will consider the bank's customary policies and practices, terms of the contract, determinations by the originator, and state law.

3. Q: May a bank ever regularly collect for another person without becoming a debt collector?

   A: Yes, if the bank is related to the other institution by common ownership or corporate control, it may collect consumer debts for that institution without becoming a debt collector.

4. Q: Is a bank a debt collector if it collects a consumer debt in an isolated instance for a nonrelated person?

A: <u>No</u>.

5. Q: When does a bank <u>regularly</u> collect debts due another?

A: The Act does not define "regularly." For purposes of examination, the following should be considered:

- Whether the bank has a formal agreement with another person to collect third-party debts, such as the Amercian Banking Association's reciprocal service agreement program.

- Whether the bank has established procedures for collection of third-party debts.

- The ratio of third-party defaulted debts collected during the past 12 months to all defaulted debts collected.

- The amount of time the bank spends in third-party debt collection.

6. Q: Are bank trust departments debt collectors?

A: <u>No</u>, the activities of trust departments and other bona fide fiduciary or escrow activities are exempt.

7. Q: Are banks debt collectors if they collect consumer debts held as security for an extension of commercial credit?

A: <u>No</u>, this activity is specifically exempted.

8. Q: Are employees, officers, or attorneys of banks considered debt collectors?

A: <u>No</u>, as long as they collect the bank's debts in the bank's name.

9. Q: May a bank communicate with persons other than the consumer to determine the location of the consumer?

A: <u>Yes</u>. However, the communication must be limited to location information such as place of residence, phone number, or place of employment. The bank may not identify itself as a debt collector, and nothing may be said concerning debt collection.

10. Q: May a bank discuss the debt with anyone other than the consumer?

A: Yes, the bank may contact its own attorney, the consumer's attorney, the creditor or creditor's attorney, consumer reporting agencies, the consumer's spouse, parent, guardian, executor, or administrator, and any other person obligated to pay the debt.

11. Q: In general, what means of debt collection are banks prohibited from using?

A: The bank cannot threaten violence or harm, swear, publish the consumer's name as an individual who allegedly refuses to pay debts, advertise the sale of the debt to coerce payment, make excessive telephone calls or fail to disclose the bank's identity on the telephone. Any other action that would harass, oppress, or abuse is prohibited. The bank also cannot make false representation about itself, the debt, its rights, or the consumer's rights.

12. Q: May a bank contact a consumer at the consumer's place of employment?

A: Not if it is against the consumer's wishes or if the bank knows that the employer forbids such contacts.

13. Q: May the bank be made to stop communicating with the consumer concerning the debt?

A: Yes, if the consumer notifies the bank in writing that the consumer refuses to pay the debt or simply does not want any further contact. However, at that point the bank may notify the consumer of possible further actions.

14. Q: May the bank accept postdated instruments?

A: Yes. However, the Act provides very specific rules for accepting these instruments.

15. Q: May a postcard be used in collection efforts?

A: No.

16. Q: May the bank threaten to repossess property?

A: Yes, only when there is a present right and intention to take possession of the property.

17. Q: May the bank use an envelope that contains any language or symbol indicating debt collection when communicating with a consumer?

   A. <u>No.</u>

WESTERN FINANCE COMPANY CASE—
GOVERNMENT REGULATION

Charles Barney, Senior Credit Analyst, at the Western Finance Company has recently taken over the task of responding to inquiries from the field offices. Western Finance operates 314 offices located in California and four other western states. The company is very active in installment sales financing, dealing directly with consumers for purchasing the paper of merchants and medical-dental practitioners. The company has grown rapidly during the 1980s and expects to grow at a slower rate during the 1990s.

Upon assuming his new responsibilities in the San Francisco corporate offices, Barney began to go through his mail. He immediately saw why the company had assigned him the task of interpreting and explaining recent government legislation with respect to consumer lending. On his desk were a number of questions from lending officers in the field offices. The questions dealt primarily with issues of truth in lending and equal credit opportunity. Barney made a note that one of his first tasks would be to publish a manual answering the major questions raised by these items of legislation. But first, he decided to give specific answers to specific questions raised by the field offices. The questions are summarized as follows:

1. We have been looking at financing the sale of $40,000 worth of wool bolts of cloth to a medium-sized tailoring outfit. The rate on the loan looks good, and our exposure would only be 90 days. But I have a question. Would this transaction be covered under Regulation Z—Truth in Lending?

2. We frequently have the problem that women want to open credit accounts in their maiden names. Generally, the woman uses her husband's name for all other purposes and is not even recognized under her maiden name. For example, one woman recently had her license, bank account, and credit cards in her married name. Yet she wanted to open an account in her maiden name. Do we have to honor this kind of request?

3. I recently had the opportunity to finance a credit purchase that is covered under Truth in Lending. The customer decided to rescind the transaction on the second day after the sale. He called the department store and told the firm of his intention on the afternoon of the third day, and he sent back the items on the fifth day by registered mail. The department store wants to know if this rescission is legally binding. Can you tell me?

4. We recently had a woman apply for a loan. I asked her how she would repay the loan. She told me that she received 80 percent of her income from alimony payments. Last year, she received only 9 of the 12 payments required in her divorce settlement, and this year only 7 of 12. She has a court order for her ex-husband to make the payments, but she explained that he had several unexpected layoffs from a job that he has held for the past eight years. Given these facts, do you think I can deny this woman credit?

5. We are working on financing the sale of some miscellaneous electronics items in the amount of $15,000 to the Internal Revenue Service in its Sacramento office. Will this transaction be covered under Regulation Z?

6. Two weeks ago, I turned down an employed man who applied for a loan. Everything about his application looked good except that he had a bad credit report from the local credit bureau. He asked me for the name and address of the Credit Bureau. Must I give it to him?

7. We recently financed the sale of $18,000 of farm equipment to a Tulsa, Oklahoma cooperative. Should this transaction have been financed in accordance with the Truth in Lending legislation?

8. A woman who recently applied for credit had no income other than her husband's salary. I asked that her husband co-sign the note, but he refused. Can I turn this woman down if her husband continues to refuse to sign the application?

9. We recently considered purchasing a note from a firm that had made a credit sale but failed to comply with Regulation Z. The firm knew of the requirements but the president decided not to bother since it was a lot of work, would not be very helpful to the customer, and, anyway, could not be enforced by the government. We decided not to purchase the note, but I am curious. Can anything happen to the president of that firm?

10. We were recently asked to help collect a loan due to Citizens National Bank. The loan was for $14,000 plus accrued interest and was 150 days overdue. If we agree to assist in collection on this loan, will we become a debt collector as defined in the Fair Debt Collection Practices Act?

11. One of our offices has a bad debt with a man who has moved three times in the past six months. We hired a debt collector who called the man's employer for the current address. The employer asked why he wanted the information. What can he respond?

12. We have an attorney who is a regular debt collector for us. He uses a reminder notice that simply states "Debt Overdue. Please pay promptly to avoid further action, including litigation." He is considering having it pre-printed on a 4 by 6 postcard in green and yellow letters. Can he

send such a postcard to the place of employment of an individual whose debt is overdue by more than 90 days?

Required: Prepare the answer for each of the questions raised in the letters to Charles Barney.

VI.

Consumer and Business Lending

16

Consumer Loans

OVERVIEW

A highly industrialized society depends to a great extent on direct sales to individuals, whether for expensive consumer goods or for equipment needed to start small businesses. Similarly, banks and financial institutions must evaluate the capacity to repay loans when such capacity is based on personal rather than business characteristics. Few individuals publish periodic balance sheets, income statements, and other documents reflecting their successful activities in the past.

In this chapter, we will deal with decisions to extend credit to individuals. We will cover some of the major features of consumer loans and develop an approach to evaluating personal credit capacity.

Purposes of Consumer Loans

A **consumer loan** may be defined as a borrowing by an individual, when such funds are lent based on a personal evaluation of the capacity of the borrower to repay the loan. Three purposes are commonly identified.

1. **Consumer Hard Goods**. This category includes automobiles, household appliances, and similar large ticket items that are used in the home or to meet personal needs. The weekend sailboat and the riding tractor for mowing the yard would be included here.

2. **Consumer Services**. This category includes the trip to Europe or the Far East, tuition for a child's schooling, hiring someone to paint the house, and similar borrowings where no goods are identified as collateral for the loan.

3. **Business Equipment or Services**. This category includes the cost of inventory, equipment, or other items for a commercial venture. Generally, it involves startup costs for a small business where the business activity is not sufficiently developed so as to allow the firm to become the borrower. Instead, an individual borrows the money directly and turns it over to be used to provide working-capital and fixed assets.

Kinds of Consumer Loans

Two categories of consumer loans may be identified: installment credit and noninstallment credit.

1. **Installment Credit**. In this loan agreement, the principal amount is repaid in a series of weekly or monthly payments. In most cases, the payments are equal in size. In some cases, the final payment is larger than earlier payments. This arrangement is said to have a balloon payment. Installment credit is so–called because the loan is repaid in a series of installments.

2. **Noninstallment Credit**. In this loan agreement, the money borrowed is repaid in a single lump sum payment covering both principal and interest. This approach to repaying the loan is relatively uncommon for consumer borrowing. Banks and financial institutions reduce their risk by requiring periodic payments against an outstanding loan balance. This matches a consumer pattern in which individuals receive salaries or other income periodically. The noninstallment credit approach is usually found in loans to individuals with high personal net worth. If an individual owns large illiquid assets, the bank views such assets as protection on the loan. Hence, the loan can be repaid in a lump sum in the future, perhaps coinciding with the sale of a large asset.

Direct and Indirect Borrowing

Consumer loans by financial institutions may be either direct or indirect.

1. **Direct Loan**. This transaction occurs when an individual goes to the bank or financial institution and arranges for a loan. In most cases, the individual is a customer of the bank, maintaining a demand deposit or interest-bearing account or taking advantage of other services. The customer completes a credit application, which includes identifying the purpose of the loan, and signs a loan agreement provided by the bank if the loan is approved.

2. **Indirect Loan**. This transaction occurs when a merchant or other business makes the arrangements for financing the purchase of goods or provisions of services. The seller facilitates a lending arrangement between the customer and a financial institution. As an example, an automobile dealer may offer 36–month financing as a related service when purchasing an automobile. Once the consumer has signed the note, the automobile dealer may sell it to a bank and the individual will make payments directly to the bank. This type of arrangement, also called installment sales financing, is fairly widespread. It is commonly

used for the financing of department store purchases, medical and dental services, home improvements, and various other consumer goods and services.

Collateralized Borrowing

In order to reduce the risk when lending to consumers, banks and financial institutions have designed lending agreements whereby large, valuable assets can be pledged as collateral for the loan. The most common agreement is to mortgage real estate, generally the home of the borrower. A first mortgage on a dwelling is usually held by the bank that provided financing to purchase the unit in the first place. After a number of years have passed, the mortgage is reduced. At the same time, the actual value of the house may have risen considerably. The result is an asset that can be pledged as collateral on an additional loan. Such a pledging is called a second mortgage in financial terms. In newspaper advertisements, it is called a variety of names, such as home equity loan, equity credit line, and homeowner loan.

Collateralized borrowing poses possible difficulties that should be recognized by all parties. Usually, it is an indirect loan with three points of view. The merchant is seeking to sell goods or services and is not concerned about the financial stability of the purchaser. The individual wants to make a purchase and may or may not have the earnings or other cash flow to repay a loan. The bank wants to make a loan that is fully secured, and ensure that the value of a home is sufficient to pay off first and second mortgage holders in the event of a default on the loan. The problem arises because the purchase bears no relationship to the source of repayment. The bank is often willing to make any loan, as long as the equity in a home is adequate to guarantee repayment. This can lead to an overextension of the individual's ability to repay and serious problems of foreclosure and legal action.

Characteristics of Consumer Loans

Direct and indirect consumer lending has developed to meet the needs of a credit society. The instruments and arrangements are refined on a continuing basis to reflect the concerns or goals of consumers, businesses, and financial institutions alike. Consumers are able to locate merchandise or services that are desired almost immediately, merchants can provide them, and financial institutions can make loans with attractive rates of return for the degree of risk involved.

Whatever the structure of the agreement, two characteristics of consumer loans are of special importance. These are as follows:

1. **Promissory Notes**. This is a written agreement to pay a sum of money or series of such sums on a given date or dates. The note has a drawer,

who is the consumer, and a drawee, who is either the merchant or the financial institution. Once properly signed in accordance with applicable laws, a promissory note is a separate legal instrument that is unrelated to the underlying transaction. It will have a life of its own and can be sold or transferred to third parties.

2. **Recourse.** An **endorser** is a person who signs the back of a draft or note for the purpose of transferring it to another party or guaranteeing payment. Recourse is the legal term whereby a purchaser of a note has the right to demand payment from another party other than the maker if the maker defaults on payment. If a merchant endorses the promissory note, the bank can collect first from the consumer, who is also the maker of the note. If this fails, the bank has recourse to the merchant who is liable as an endorser. Such an arrangement reduces the risk of consumer lending from the viewpoint of the bank and increases the exposure to the merchant.

In many cases, a financial institution will purchase a note **without recourse** and thus cannot collect from the merchant in the event of default. This situation may result in greater risk from indirect lending as compared to direct lending. Since the bank does not interview the customer with indirect lending, it is not in a position to evaluate the ability of the individual to pay off the loan. This risk can be reduced if the merchant takes proper action. If the seller follows acceptable credit–granting procedures, the loan may offer no greater risk than directly placed loans. Of course, if loans are made with recourse to the merchant, an indirect loan is less risky than a direct loan.

Credit Card Lending

An important form of consumer lending occurs when banks issue a credit card that may be used worldwide to charge goods and services at restaurants, airlines, hotels, department stores, and other outlets. In effect, the bank is approving a general level of credit similar to a credit line for a business. The individual may take advantage of the credit to make any purchase at any time.

Two kinds of credit may be extended when an individual uses a credit card. These are noninterest period and installment period.

1. **Noninterest Period.** To obtain credit, a consumer presents an embossed plastic card to a merchant. For large purchases in the United States, the merchant contacts the issuer of the card, either electronically or by telephone. This verifies that the card is valid and that the sale does not exceed the credit limit. In other countries, the card is checked with the passport of the purchaser. If acceptable to the merchant, the sale is completed. Each month, the individual is sent a statement

reflecting purchases with the card and the total due. Purchases in foreign currencies are translated into the domestic currency. The individual will then have a certain number of days, less than a month, to pay the charges. If this is done, no interest accrues and the credit was extended for a period of a few weeks at zero cost. This is the noninterest period of the credit.

2. **Installment Period.** If the individual does not pay the entire balance presented by the deadline, the issuer of the credit card will charge interest. The individual is advised that a minimum payment is due each month and that the loan can be repaid in a series of installments. These installments will vary as the individual uses the card to make additional purchases, since the amount of the installment is calculated each month based on the outstanding balance.

Checklike Consumer Borrowing

Banks and financial institutions have developed a variety of techniques to facilitate borrowing by creditworthy customers. In effect, the customer only has to write a check to activate a loan. Two categories of borrowing by using checks are common.

1. **Overdraft Borrowing.** An **overdraft** occurs when a person withdraws money from a bank account in excess of the amount in the account. Most banks offer **check-credit plans** that allow individuals to borrow by overdrafting their demand deposit accounts. When the check arrives creating the overdraft, the amount is automatically converted to an installment loan that must be repaid on a similar basis to other consumer loans. The loan information will commonly appear on the customer's monthly statement. The credit approval for such an arrangement is made in advance, and a credit limit is established by the financial institution.

2. **Draft Credit Lines.** A similar plan allows individuals to write their own loans without using overdrafts from their demand deposit accounts. A bank will provide blank drafts that look just like checks. When an individual fills one out and uses it for a purchase, the bank creates a loan equal to the face amount of the draft. This allows an individual to maintain a working balance in a regular checking account while borrowing money in a convenient manner. This arrangement gives the appearance of being overdraft borrowing, even though technically it is a preapproved line of credit that is activated by a draft.

CREDIT CAPACITY OF BORROWERS

As discussed in Chapter 13, the decision to extend credit should be made after an evaluation of the **credit capacity** of the potential borrower. We will now discuss credit capacity when the borrower is a consumer. In this section, we examine three major areas that assist in determining the consumer's ability to repay a loan.

Periodic Cash Flow

The primary source of repayment for the bulk of consumer loans is regular earnings or other cash flow to the borrower. In most cases, the individual will be employed by an organization that conducts steady business or has a regular source of funding. The person's employment history will show stability with limited interruptions between jobs. For individuals who are self-employed, a good credit risk occurs when the person has a specific skill in a business that offers relatively steady revenues. This applies to the professions, such as law or medicine, to the trades, such as plumbing, and to merchants, such as a retail store owner.

Once it is determined that an individual has a periodic cash flow, this cash flow must be matched against routine expenses. If an individual has a high level of fixed obligations, such as rent, mortgage payments, insurance premiums, or other liabilities, he or she may not be a good credit risk for additional borrowing. The lender looks, in effect, for a net cash inflow. If earnings are low or expenses are high compared to the earnings, the evaluation of credit capacity might be that the individual is a poor risk.

Net Assets

Net assets are defined as the market value of cash, real estate, securities, and tangible personal assets less the mortgages, loans, notes, credit card balances, and other liabilities that the individual personally owes.

Determining net assets is often a tricky job for a credit analyst. Determining the market value of real estate involves a subjective estimate and must recognize the costs of finding a buyer. Time delays are also expected since real estate is not highly liquid. Investments in financial securities have values that can fluctuate rapidly with changes in interest rates or movements in the stock market. Tangible personal assets may or may not be salable. A diamond ring, for example, may have cost $5,000 but to a jeweler may have a market value of only half that amount.

Determining the value of liabilities is usually more straightforward, since it can be assumed that they must be paid off at face value. The difficulty here is that there is no way of ensuring that all liabilities are listed on a credit application.

Even though net assets are not viewed as the primary means of repayment, a large net asset value, also called **net worth**, offers protection on a loan. A low net asset value does not provide a solid secondary source of payment for the loan.

Historical Stability

One of the strongest indicators of an individual's creditworthiness is past behavior. Thus, most financial institutions prefer to lend to consumers who can demonstrate a stable pattern of behavior. Several forms of stability are sought.

1. **Housing**. Has the individual lived in apartments or houses and met all obligations therein? People who move often, particularly to different cities or areas of the country, may be transients who are running away from obligations. People who purchase homes may have a greater commitment to fulfilling obligations than individuals who rent on a short-term basis.

2. **Employment**. Has the individual worked in a career field or for companies so that future employment is likely on a sustained basis? An individual who is a "jack of all trades" may offer more risk than a technician who has steadily advanced up a career ladder. An individual who has been employed for a number of years with large corporations or a municipal government exhibits stability by remaining in the workforce.

3. **Financial History**. Has the individual borrowed money in the past and met all obligations for repayment? In effect, the lender is seeking a credit history. Individuals who have repaid prior obligations are better risks than individuals who have never borrowed and faced the responsibility of diverting current income into the repayment of a loan.

When viewing stability, the lender has a moral and legal obligation to restrict the evaluation to valid lending criteria. Prejudices and broad generalities should never be used to deny credit to a worthy applicant. As an example, an applicant who has been a taxi driver for 3 weeks following a three-month period of unemployment raises valid stability issues. To refuse to lend to all taxi drivers would be an incorrect application of a stability standard.

Risk Categories

The risk-class approach to receivables management discussed in Chapter 14 is also used to divide loan applicants into different classes based on financial or other criteria. A **risk category** is a group of individuals of similar credit capacity, for whom capacity is measured against a scaled number of factors that indicate creditworthiness. Such factors are generally developed by the financial institution based on historical data and are not highly scientific. Typical factors include annual salary, net worth, and employment history.

The use of risk categories is illustrated in the case at the end of this chapter.

Conclusion

Consumer lending is an art, not a science, and involves many judgments that are best made by experienced lending officers. At the same time, the techniques and principles outlined in this chapter can be useful in coming to grips with the nature of the consumer credit decision. The case that follows offers a practical opportunity to apply some of the principles outlined in this chapter. The objective is to make recommendations on the credit capacity of a borrower and the interest rate to be charged on a loan while considering a number of factors.

CITY CENTRAL STATE BANK CASE—CONSUMER LOANS

Annette Simpson is the Assistant Manager of the downtown office of City Central State Bank. In this position, she handles a variety of customer services, special problems, and recommendations on individual and installment loans. She often interviews loan applicants and gathers the needed information so that a credit decision can be reached. In addition, she frequently deals with local automobile dealers and department stores on the bank's purchase of financing contracts. Once she makes a recommendation, the loan application and supporting file are forwarded to a bank vice-president for final approval. In virtually all cases, her recommendations are accepted.

Simpson's judgment is widely respected by her superiors for a number of reasons. One reason is that she carefully gathers all the informaton required under the bank's policies. She never forwards a loan without having obtained a completed loan application and performing a credit check. Another reason is that she carefully assigns each applicant to one of the bank's risk categories for individual loans. Management requires each loan officer, branch manager, or assistant manager to classify applicants into four risk categories, A through D, based on factors such as net worth of the individual, income, and current debt. These classifications are used to determine the amount of the loan and the interest rate to be charged on it.

Characteristics for Identifying Individual Applicant into Risk Category for Consumer Loans

	Category A	Category B	Category C	Category D
Net Worth (Good Assets less Liabilities)	$100,000+	$50-100,000	$20-50,000	Below $30,000
Family Income	$50,000+	$30-50,000	$20-30,000	Below $20,000
Equity in Home or	Over 40%	25-40%	15-25%	Below 15%
Monthly Rent	Over $1,200	$800-1,200	$400-800	Below $400
Total Non-housing Debt Divided by Annual Income	Under 20%	20-35%	35-50%	Over 50%

Once the checklist has been used to determine the risk classification, the bank's policy requires three other checks. If the applicant fails to meet any one of the three standards, the loan application is dropped one category. As an example, an applicant might be Category B based on net worth, income, and other debts. But the applicant might not have any other bank references. Thus, the applicant would become a Category C risk. The three standards that must be met are as follows:

1. The applicant must have been employed for at least 24 months with a single employer during the past five years and must not have been unemployed for more than 90 consecutive days during the past five years.

2. A "clear" bank reference must be available, either from City Central State Bank or another bank.

3. A clear credit report must be available from the local credit agency.

If any one of these standards is not met, the applicant is dropped one risk category.

Annette Simpson is aware of the bank's concern for the proper pricing of all loans. The bank wants to earn a satisfactory profit on its activities and therefore must lend money at rates that cover all costs plus provide a profit. The **spread** is defined as the difference between the effective loan rate and all costs associated with the loan. This may be expressed in a formula as

$$\text{Spread} = \begin{array}{c}\text{Effective}\\\text{Loan}\\\text{Rate}\end{array} - \begin{array}{c}\text{Average}\\\text{Cost of}\\\text{Funds}\end{array} - \begin{array}{c}\text{Administrative}\\\text{and Collection}\\\text{Costs}\end{array} - \begin{array}{c}\text{Bad–Debt}\\\text{Writeoffs}\end{array}$$

Simpson calculates the spread on all the loan recommendations that she forwards for approval. She begins with the **average cost of funds** which is defined as the bank's cost of its money. The bank receives its funds from several sources, including demand deposits, various kinds of time deposits, and capital. To calculate the **average cost** of these funds, the bank identifies each category of funds and "weights" its cost compared to the other categories. Once the bank has calculated its average cost of funds, it then estimates the cost in future periods. The forecasted cost of funds will depend on a number of factors, including the level of interest rates and the ability of the bank to attract depositors. To get the average cost in the spread formula, Simpson uses the forecasted cost for each year. For example, for a three-year loan, the average cost of funds would be

Average
Cost of   Next Year's   Second Year's   Third Year's
Funds for =   Cost   +   Cost   +   Cost
3-Year
Loan

Simpson does not have to perform the cost of funds calculation for her loan recommendations. The bank employs a part-time economist who performs the calculations every quarter. The economist begins with the bank's balance sheet given in Figure 16-1. The economist then weighs the individual sources of funds and the cost of each as is done in Figure 16-2. The result is an average cost of funds. An actual cost is calculated for the past period, and, based on projections of interest rates and likely sources of future financing for the bank, the cost of funds is estimated for the next five years. The bank's current situation is shown in Figure 16-3.

Not all areas of the bank employ the average cost of funds in pricing loans. In the commercial loans area, the **marginal cost of funds** is used for pricing large business loans. The marginal cost is defined as the bank's cost if it has to borrow additional funds to participate in a financing; it is usually based on the rate for large certificates of deposit. In the consumer loans area, however, the lower cost demand deposit funds are viewed as part of the bank's resources for individual lending. Thus, the average cost is used rather than the marginal cost.

City Central Bank has established clear-cut policies for pricing consumer loans, according to the risk category of the borrower. To be eligible for a loan, an individual must have sufficient income or other cash inflow so the loan payment does not constitute a serious strain on his or her resources. This rule is used for both secured and unsecured loans. A secondary consideration is the collateral or other assets that an individual pledges as part of the loan agreement. The bank stresses the importance of financial strength and collateral as a safeguard, but feels that it is better business practice to rely primarily on income or other inflows.

Figure 16-1. Balance Sheet, City Central State Bank,
End of Year (thousands).

Assets

Coin and Currency Held in Vault	$5,780
Deposits, Demand, with Federal Reserve District Bank	13,651
Deposits, Demand, with Correspondent Banks	825
Checks in Process of Collection	6,215
Holdings of U.S. Treasury and agency securities	3,577
Holdings of State and Municipal Securities	1,445

Other Securities	
Loans Outstanding:	
Business	88,407
Mortgage	78,512
Individual	39,415
Other	2,395
Federal Funds Sold	1,600
Bank Premises, Fixtures, and Miscellaneous	22,590
Total Assets	$264,412

Liabilities

Demand Deposits:	
Individuals	28,414
Companies or Businesses	49,835
Time and Savings Deposits:	
Individuals	141,565
Companies or Businesses	3,752
Deposits of U.S. Government	2,410
Deposits of States or Municipalities	710
Certified and Cashier's Checks	355
Federal Funds Bought	
Other Liabilities:	
Checks in Process	6,215
Large Certificates of Deposit	5,800
Other	100
Total Liabilities	$239,156

Capital	
Common Stock—par Value $1	400
Surplus	3,200
Undivided Profits	21,306
Reserve for Contingencies and Other Reserves	350
Total Capital	25,256
Total Liabilities and Capital	$264,412

Figure 16-2. Cost of Funds, Past Year—City Central State Bank

Source of Assets	Dollar Amount (thousands)		Cost or Required Return		Cost of Funds
Demand Deposits	78,249	x	0	=	0
Time Deposits	145,317	x	0.0652	=	9,474.67
Government deposits	3,120	x	0	=	0
Certified Checks	355	x	0	=	0
Federal Funds Bought	0	x	0	=	0
Checks in Process	6,215	x	0	=	0
Large CDs	5,800	x	0.0878	=	509.24
Other	100	x	0.0790	=	7.90
Capital	25,256	x	0.1750	=	4,419.80
Total Assets	264,412		Total Cost		14,411.61

Funds Available to Lend or Invest

Source of Assets	Dollar Amount		Adjustment		Funds Available
Demand Deposits[a]	78,249	x	1 - 0.125	=	68,467.88
Time Deposits[a]	145,317	x	1 - 0.030	=	140,957.49
Other Demand[a]	9,690	x	1 - 0.125	=	8,478.75
Large CDs[a]	5,800	x	1 - 0.030	=	5,626.00
Other	100	x	1 - 0.000	=	1 - 0.000
Capital[b]	25,256	x	1 - 0.894	=	2,677.14
			Available Funds		226,307.26

Cost of Funds

Financing Component (Average Fund Cost)
14,411.61/226,307.26 = 0.0637

[a]Adjusted for appropriate reserve requirement.
[b]Adjusted for nonearning premises and equipment

Figure 16.3. Average Cost of Funds.

Period	Average Cost of Funds
Past Year—Actual	0.0637
Next Year—Estimated	0.0684
2nd Year—Estimated	0.0705

3rd Year—Estimated	0.0740
4th Year—Estimated	0.0710
5th Year-Estimated	0.0685

Once it is established that the individual has adequate income, the applicant is assigned to a risk category and the pricing begins. The average cost of funds is calculated first; then a premium is added for administrative costs and bad-debt writeoffs. The bank uses its historical experience with consumer loans to estimate each of these costs by risk category. At the present time, administrative costs, which include collection costs, range from 0.5 percent for category A loans to 4.8 percent for category D loans. Bad debts similarly range from 0.2 percent to 3.7 percent. The complete data are given in Figure 16-4.

Figure 4. Administrative Costs and Writeoffs by Risk Category for Consumer Loans.

Risk Category	Administrative Costs (Including Collection Costs) as a Percentage of Loan Amount	Bad–Debt Write offs as a Percentage of Loan Amount
A	0.005	0.002
B	0.015	0.009
C	0.033	0.017
D	0.048	0.037

Once all the costs are included in the analysis, Simpson follows the bank's statement on required spreads. A different schedule is used for secured and unsecured loans and the spread varies by the size of the loan. A large loan requires relatively less administrative costs than a small loan, so the spread is less. The required spreads are given in Figure 16-5.

Figure 16.5. Bank Policy Manual, by Secured and
Unsecured Individual Loans, by Size of Loan.

Risk Category	$20,000 +	$10-20,000	$5-10,000	Below $5,000
Secured Loan				
A	0.020	0.025	0.030	0.035
B	0.030	0.035	0.040	0.045
C	0.035	0.040	0.045	0.050
D	—	0.050	0.055	0.060
Unsecured Loan				
A	0.035	0.040	0.045	0.050
B	0.040	0.045	0.050	0.055
C	—	0.055	0.060	0.065
D	—	—	—	—

After calculating the effective loan rate, Simpson forwards the recommendation and supporting loan application for approval. This process usually takes less than 24 hours.

Required: Prepare the recommendation on the attached loan application (Figure 16-6). Use the loan pricing worksheet (Figure 16-7.)

Figure 16-6. Loan Application #39664.

City Central State Bank

The undersigned hereby make application for a loan of $80,000, net repayable in 72 monthly installments on the 5th day of each month beginning April, 1989. The purpose of the loan is:

TO FINANCE THE PURCHASE OF A "WINDMAKER"
26-foot pleasure craft, Model #A-36578,
initial registration 1986.

The collateral offered is: LIEN ON THE BOAT

Borrower Sandy Fraser   Age 36 SS# 465-38-9014

Address 97 Barclay Drive, Winchester, Md. Length of time at this address 3 yrs.
Own X Rent _____ Landlord or Mortgage holder City Central State Bank

Previous address 291 Charlesgate, Houston, Texas Length of time 4 yrs.

Co-borrower None (Co-borrower, if any, to fill out separate sheet)
Previous loans with CCSB ____Yes _x_ No

Checking account at CCSB ____Yes _x_ No

Employment history (past 5 years only)

Employer Xerox Corp, 1214 Stratford Industrial Park   Since June 84

Title Senior Marketing Representative Current Income $68,000

Previous Employer J&J Industries, Akron, Ohio Period 1979-84

Previous Employer_____Period _____

Previous Employer _____Period _____

The undersigned represents that the statements made in this application (including the Personal Financial Statement which is part of this application) are true and correct and have been made to convince the bank to grant a loan to the undersigned with knowledge that the bank will rely thereon. No other obligations exist to the undersigned (either primarily, jointly, or as co-signer) that are not disclosed in this application. The undersigned authorize the bank to obtain any information required to verify this application.

Signed (s) S. Fraser   Date March 5th

Signed _____Date _____

As of _March 1989_

Borrower _Sandy Fraser, 97 Barclay Drive, Winchester, Md._

Occupation ___Sr. Marketing Rep ___ Employer _Xerox Corp. Stratford Indus Park_

I/we make the following statement of all my/our assets and liabilities at the date given above:

ASSETS		LIABILITIES	
Cash on hand	100	Installment loans	
Cash in banks(itemize)	1,000	1st National Bank	9,200
Securities(marketable)	16,500	Xerox Credit Union	5,700
Securities(not readily		GMAC	6,300
marketable)	13,200		
		Credit Cards	
Real estate	146,000		
		American Express	1,600
Automobile(s)	14,000		
		Visa	150
Other assets			
Household, etc.	6,000		
		Mortgage	
		Original amt 68,000	
		Balance	63,000
		Other debts(itemize)	None
TOTAL ASSETS	196,800	TOTAL LIABILITIES	85,950

Assets (Itemize)

Liabilities (Itemize)

Cash in bank—CCSB Acct #25934-1

Sec(Mktable)—100 shares of RSB
common stock, $165 recent price

Sec (Non–Mkt)—rights to family
business operated by father;
no current dividends

Real estate—home, purchased for
$110,000

Auto—total value, both cars

Household, etc. estimated value
of furniture, jewelry, etc.

1st Nat'l Bank—Home Improvement Loan,
$202 monthly payment

Xerox Credit—appliances and vacation
borrowing, $324 total monthly payments

GMAC—auto loan, $440 monthly payment

Mortgage—CCSB, $578 monthly payment
(does not include taxes ($2,600 annually)
and insurance ($700 annually.)

Life Insurance (Itemize Insuror, kind of insurance, and amount)
$65,000 whole life, Prudential, $115 per month payment

Identify any assets above that are pledged for other loans:

  one auto to GMAC; market secs to 1st Nat'l

I/we certify that the statements above are true and give a correct showing of my/our financial condition as of the date indicated. In the event of material change in my/our financial condition, I/we agree to notify the City Central State Bank immediately in writing.

Signed _(s) S. Fraser_____Date March 5th

Signed _____Date _____

Figure 16-7. Loan Pricing Worksheet, Consumer Loans, CCSB.

---

1. Risk Category of Applicant

Borrower ___S. Fraser_____

Total Assets   _____
Minus assets of questionable market value   _____
Minus total liabilities   _____
NET WORTH   _____

Family income   _____

Equity in home: Market value _____less mortgage _____= Equity

Monthly rent   _____

Total liabilities _____ minus mortgage _____= Nonhousing debt
                                             divided by annual income
                                             Ratio
Risk Category   _____

   a. Employed 24 months with single employer in past 5 years; not unemployed for 90 consecutive days in past 5 years? __x__Yes _____ No

   b. Clear bank reference (Bank: CCSB. __x__ Yes _____ No

   c. Clear credit report(Agency: ___Consolidated___) __x__Yes _____ No

<u>Revised Risk Category</u>

2. <u>Effective Loan rate</u> (Maximum loan period, consumer loans, 5 years)

Average cost of funds
   Next year
   + 2nd year   _____
   + 3rd year   _____
   + 4th year   _____
   + 5th year   _____

   Total _____divided by _____ years = _____

Administrative and collection costs. . . . .   _____
Bad debt writeoffs. . . . .   _____
Required spread. . . . .   _____
Effective Loan Rate. . . . .   _____

4. Analyst <u>Annette Simpson</u>
RECOMMEND:
Approval_____Refusal of Loan _____ (s) _____
                                                    signed

3. Recommendation

On the basis of the attached financial statements and loan pricing
worksheet, I recommend

APPROVAL _____   REFUSAL _____

of the attached loan application. If approved, I recommend

a loan in the amount of $_____for a period of _____

with installments payable every _____in the amount of _____

and a final payment of $ _____. The effective cost of this

loan is _____percent.

                                          <u>(s)</u> _____
                                          signed

17

Small Business Loans

OVERVIEW

When making loans or extending credit to large businesses, the analyst can use a variety of financial techniques to assess liquidity and profitability. Balance sheets, income statements, and historical data are often available to assist in making a decision. The situation is quite different when credit decisions must be made for small firms. The bank or credit analyst is working with different levels of detail and must use a wider range of subjective skills before making a credit decision.

In this chapter, we will examine some key features of lending to small businesses. These features also apply when evaluating credit decisions about selling goods or providing services to small firms.

Credit Philosophy

The starting point for processing small business loans is the development of policies by the top management of the bank or financial institution. Three general approaches are common

1. **Conservative Policy.** Some financial institutions follow policies that are quite restrictive when granting credit or approving loans to small businesses. The organization limits the dollar amount both to a single business and for small business loans as a percentage of the bank's commercial loan portfolio. Banks that follow a conservative policy believe that an appropriate risk-return relationship cannot be achieved when making loans to small businesses. The cost of a detailed credit investigation is high and might not be justified with the profit from a small loan. If the bank takes a shortcut on conducting the investigation, the bank feels that it might not know the degree of risk being accepted. The loans that are made by such a bank will be limited to established firms with stable markets and profits.

2. **Moderate Policy.** Banks following this policy are willing to accept some risks that would not be acceptable to financial institutions following a

conservative policy. The credit investigation might not be as thorough, and credit might be extended in larger amounts and to riskier customers. These banks will generally lend to established businesses that have sufficient assets to provide a measure of security for the loan.

3. **Liberal Policy.** Some financial institutions are relatively lenient in granting credit. With this philosophy, no credit investigation is conducted for prominent customers, and a limited investigation might be undertaken on unknown firms. With such an approach, it is not surprising that the lending institution must have a vigorous collection policy. Careful attention is paid to the business activities of borrowers, particularly the amount of cash in bank accounts and the status of receivables. In spite of aggressive collection practices, a number of bad-debt cases can be expected with liberal lending policies to small businesses. Such bad debts, as well as the high collection costs, must be overcome by higher interest rates on the loans.

Factors Affecting Lending Policies

The policies followed by the bank will reflect a number of factors, such as

1. **Competition.** A major factor influencing bank policy on small business loans is competition in the marketplace. The same is true for an industrial firm that is extending credit. If banks and financial institutions in the general area are making loans on lenient terms, an individual bank may be forced to be more liberal in order to maintain a market position. If competing firms are providing goods or services on liberal credit terms, a business may feel forced to follow suit. Conversely, limited competition may allow a firm to exercise tight restrictions on credit or allow a bank to lend only to strong firms with stable earnings and unencumbered assets.

2. **Management Philosophy.** Whatever the competitive pressures, the view of risk held by management or the board of directors will significantly influence policies on extending credit to small businesses. The bank's board may simply not believe that small business loans are sound business. Or the board itself may be composed of owners of small businesses and they may believe they are knowledgeable about lending in that area.

3. **Markup.** To be compensated for accepting risk, the bank or firm must have sufficient profit as a result of extending credit. This is fairly easy for most firms, since goods and services often are sold at 50 to 100 percent above the cost of manufacturing or providing them. The large markup justifies liberal credit, as long as the firm is not at 100 percent capacity in its business. The story is different for banks. As an example,

a bank may pay 7 percent to depositors and have administrative costs equal to 2 percent of loans outstanding. If the bank is lending at 12 percent, it has only a 3 percent spread to cover bad debts and provide a profit. If nonperforming loans to small businesses reach 5 to 10 percent of the portfolio, the bank will be losing money on small business loans. Thus, banks must usually exercise more care than business firms when making decisions to extend credit because their "markup" is less.

4. **Inventory Level.** Sometimes a firm will be holding excess inventory that is not easily sold and may become obsolete or otherwise unsalable. To move the inventory, the firm might liberalize credit decisions for small businesses. The bank parallel occurs when the bank has large deposit balances and limited opportunities to invest them at high returns. Rather than hold government or corporate securities, the bank may prefer to seek out small businesses that meet their credit requirements. This offers a chance to reduce the "inventory" of securities and replace them with higher return commercial loans.

THE CREDIT DECISION

Aside from the philosophy, the firm or bank must be prepared to make a credit decision. Some of the factors affecting the decision will be covered in this section.

Dun and Bradstreet

A credit investigation may involve the collection of data from a variety of sources. Credit reports from Dun and Bradstreet are probably the most widely used source of credit information on an individual firm.

D&B reports are compiled on thousands of companies and may be purchased by institutions and firms that extend credit to businesses. The reports contain historical and financial information on companies and give a rating based on Dun and Bradstreet's evaluation of a firm's creditworthiness. A D&B report is contained in the case at the end of this chapter.

Figure 17-1 shows the current key to D&B ratings. Firms are ranked on estimated financial strength from HH to 5A. Then, a composite credit appraisal is reflected in rankings from 4 to 1, which is a ranking from weakest to strongest. Thus, HH4 indicates a firm that is small and is not considered to have a strong financial position. The rating 5A4 is a much larger firm but is not viewed as having financial strength.

In addition to numerical ratings, the D&B report provides other information, as reflected in Figure 17-2. D&B points out that some firms are not suitable for financial ratings, but lenders and creditors may desire at least a size indication. This indication is provided by an Employee Range Designation showing the number of full-time employees in the business. The assumption would be that larger firms have more stability and hence might be better credit risks. In fact, this is generally true.

A final factor in D&B ratings is a suggested maximum credit limit for each category with a good or high composite credit appraisal. This information is shown in Figure 17-3, along with a disclaimer that they are not suggested credit limits. In fact, they really are. D&B apparently intends to point out the danger of using them without considering other factors, such as size of the markup and changes that may have occurred since the firm was rated. Even with these caveats, the D&B ranking is a useful guideline.

Figure 17-1. Key to Dun and Bradstreet, Incorporated, Ratings.

Estimated Financial Strength				*Composite Credit Appraisal*			
				High	Good	Fair	Limited
5A	Over		$50,000,000	1	2	3	4
4A	$10,000,000	to	50,000,000	1	2	3	4
3A	1,000,000	to	10,000,000	1	2	3	4
2A	750,000	to	1,000,000	1	2	3	4
1A	500,000	to	750,000	1	2	3	4
BA	300,000	to	500,000	1	2	3	4
BB	200,000	to	300,000	1	2	3	4
CB	125,000	to	200,000	1	2	3	4
CC	75,000	to	125,000	1	2	3	4
DC	50,000	to	75,000	1	2	3	4
DD	35,000	to	50,000	1	2	3	4
EE	20,000	to	35,000	1	2	3	4
FF	10,000	to	20,000	1	2	3	4
GG	5,000	to	10,000	1	2	3	4
HH	Up	to	5,000	1	2	3	4

**Classification for Both Estimated Financial
Strength and Credit Appraisal**

Financial Strength Bracket	**Explanation**
	When only the numeral (1 or 2) appears it is an indication that the estimated financial
1. $125,000 and over	strength, while not definitely classified, is presumed to bewithin the range of the figures
2. 20,000 to 125,000	in the corresponding bracket and that a condition is believed to exist which warrants credit in keeping with that assumption.

"INV" shown in place of a rating indicates that the report was under investigation at the time it went to press. It has no other significance.

Absence of a Listing

The absence of a listing is not to be construed as meaning a concern is nonexistent or has discontinued business, nor does it have any other meaning. The letters "NQ" on any written report mean "not listed in the Reference Book."

Year Business Started

The numeral shown in the last digit of the year indicates the date when the business was established or came under the present control of management. That is, 8 means 1968, and 9 means 1969. No dates go past ten years; thus, the absence of a numeral indicates ten years or more. This feature is not listed with branch listings.

Absence of Rating Designation Following Names Listed in the Reference Book

The absence of a rating expressed by two hyphens (–) is not to be construed as unfavorable but signifies circumstances difficult to classify within condensed rating symbols. It suggests the advisability of obtaining a report for additional information.

Figure 17-2. Employee Range Designations.

Employee Range Designations in Reports or Names not Listed in the Reference Book	Key to Employee Range Designations		
Certain businesses do not lend	ER 1	Over	–	1000 Employees
themselves to a Dun & Bradstreet	ER 2	500	–	999 Employees
rating and are not listed in the	ER 3	100	–	499 Employees
Reference Book. Information on	ER 4	50	–	99 Employees
these names, however, continues	ER 5	20	–	49 Employees
to be stored and updated in the	ER 6	10	–	9 Employees
D&B Business Data Bank. Reports	ER 7	5	–	9 Employees
are available on these businesses	ER 8	1	–	4 Employees
but instead of a rating they carry	ER N			Not Available
an Employee Range Designation (ER) which is indicative of size in terms of number of employees. No other significance should be attached.				

Strengths and Weaknesses of D&B Reports

The primary value of a D&B report lies in the historical data and descriptive information provided in the writeup. The creditor can gain, if you will, a "feel" for the potential borrower. Principals of the business, line of business, and reported financial and credit activities are all useful. Of particular value is information regarding affiliations of the firm. The creditor may discover that the firm is owned by an individual or a corporation with a known and strong credit rating. Such a relationship is probably an indication of creditworthiness, even though it should not be used as the sole basis for extending credit. It is also valuable to see if the report contains any negative items. If, for example, suppliers are reporting credit problems, the lender may wish to avoid entering a deteriorating or otherwise difficult situation.

Figure 17-3. Reference Book Suggested Credit Limit Chart for Processing Orders.

Composite Credit Approval	1	2	3	4
Estimated Financial Strength Rating				
5A	REQUIREMENTS			
4A	REQUIREMENTS			
3A	REQUIREMENTS			
2A	25,000	15,000		
1A	10,000	5,000		
BA	7,500	3,500		
BB	5,000	3,000		
CB	4,000	2,500	I N Q U I R E	
CC	3,500	2,000		
DC	3,000	1,500	O N A L L	
DD	1,500	1,000		
EE	1,000	750		
FF	900	500		
GG	500	300		
HH	100	100		
1	2,000			
2	500			

Important Note

The average lines indicated above are not intended to suggest limits, but are offered merely as a guide to help process orders. It is suggested that inquiry be made on orders in excess of these amounts or when slowness or past due items exist. Most credit executives consider it good business to inquire on all first orders.

The weaknesses of D&B reports are widely known to bankers and credit managers. Much of the information is provided by the business itself. Audited financial statements may not be available, and D&B does not have the ability to verify the accuracy of balance sheet and income statement items provided to it. A second problem occurs because the names of suppliers are often provided by the company being investigated; perhaps only suppliers who are paid on time were reported. Thus, it is not a full credit picture. Finally, D&B reports on small businesses may be out of date. A report with data compiled a year ago will not reflect current activities that may be markedly different if the firm is experiencing problems.

All in all, the D&B report is a useful document to include in a credit investigation on a small business. However, the lender or creditor must recognize its limitations and use it as a supplemental tool for evaluating credit capacity.

Other Sources of Credit Information

A number of regional and local credit agencies, some tied together nationally by electronic means, are in the business of providing credit ratings. These services can be used to determine whether a firm is paying its bills on time.

As with the D&B service, the lender must exercise care in evaluating credit reports from different agencies. Such reports are not necessarily complete for a variety of reasons. Some agencies are not careful in compiling data. Others do not check widely with companies in their local area to find problems. Still, these reports can be useful, particularly if they contain negative items.

An increasingly useful source of credit information is an industry or trade grouping. Lending officers and credit managers may be members of an informal network sharing credit information. Meeting once a month or on some other periodic basis, a group of bankers may discuss some of the problems they are having collecting debts. This information can be useful in making decisions on the direction of an industry or a potential customer.

Bankers and creditors must exercise care when making credit statements in informal groupings. As a general rule, negative statements on specific customer transactions should be avoided. To state that a specific firm is not paying its bills on time has legal and moral overtones. It may damage the company in its home community and this is not fair. In addition, a lender making a negative statement may expose the bank to legal problems at a later date.

Informal discussions without specific customer identification can be highly valuable. As an example, a bank may report problems collecting from building contractors. This difficulty could be an early warning of a downturn in housing or other construction. Knowing this information, the bank might increase its requirements before lending to small businesses that are seeking to expand because they believe the local economic conditions are strong.

CONCLUSION

The decision to extend credit to small businesses builds on the elements of credit capacity discussed in earlier chapters. It must be refined by techniques such as those discussed in this chapter. The following case affords an opportunity to see the kind of information that might be provided by a small business requesting a loan. It shows the mixture of personal and business data that is needed when making a credit decision. One should be alert to possible contradictions when solving the case. If analyzed properly, it should be possible to identify gaps in knowledge or possible errors in reporting data and prepare a list of questions to ask the customer before making a final decison on the loan.

NORTH JERSEY CARPET COMPANY CASE — CREDIT DECISION

On July 30, 1988, the North Jersey Carpet Company, Incorporated, applied for a $100,000 loan from the main office of the National Bank of New Jersey. The application (Exhibit A) was forwarded to the bank's commercial loan department.

Harry Bernard, the president and principal stockholder of North Jersey Carpet, applied for the loan in person. He told the loan officer that he had been in business since February 1986, but that he had considerable prior experience in flooring and carpets since he had worked as an individual contractor for the past 14 years. Most of this time, he had worked in Ohio, Indiana, and Michigan. He finally decided to "work for himself," and he formed the company with John Walters, a former co-worker. This information seemed to be consistent with the Dun and Bradstreet report obtained by the bank (Exhibit B).

According to Bernard, the purpose of the loan was to assist him in carrying his receivables until they could be collected. He explained that the flooring business required him to expend considerable cash to purchase materials, but his customers would not pay until the job was done. Since he was relatively new in the business, he did not feel that he could compete if he had to require a sizable deposit or payment in advance. Instead, he could quote for higher profits if he were willing to wait until completion of the job for payment. To show that his operation was sound, he included a list of customers and projects with his loan application (Exhibit C). He also included a list of current receivables (Exhibit D).

Bernard told the loan officer that he had monitored his firm's financial status closely and that he had financial reports prepared every six months. He said that he would send a copy to the bank (Exhibit E). In addition, he was willing to file a personal financial statement with the bank (Exhibit F).

Required: Prepare your recommendation on North Jersey Carpet Company.

Exhibit A. Loan Application.

NATIONAL BANK OF NEW JERSEY
211 Sinclair Lane
Morristown, New Jersey 07931

DATE: 7/30/88

The undersigned hereby make application for a loan of $100,000 net repayable in 60 monthly installments on the 5th day of each month beginning September 1988. The purpose of the loan is:

TO FINANCE RECEIVABLES

The collateral offered is:

LIEN ON RECEIVABLES; LIEN ON FIXED ASSETS

Business form: CORPORATION   Kind of business: COMMERCIAL
CARPETING/FLOORING

Business Address: 502 Main St.   Tel: (201) 762-4410
          Morristown, N.J. 07925

Previous loans with NBNJ? _____ Yes ___x___ No Established Feb. 1986

Checking account at NBNJ? __x__ Yes _____ No

Landlord: DANNEMANN REALTY Lease expires: 8/1/89.   Annual Rent: $2,400

Name of partners, officers, or stockholders

	Title	Shares owned	Percent Owned
1. HARRY BERNARD	Pres	900	90
2. ESTELLE BERNARD		50	5
3. JOHN WALTERS	V-P	50	5

The undersigned represents, warrants, and affirms that the statements made in this application are true and correct and have been made to induce you to grant a loan to the undersigned with knowledge that you will rely thereon. The undersigned also affirms that no obligations exist by the undersigned or company except as disclosed with this application. You are authorized to obtain any information you may require to verify this application. Any status changes by undersigned with respect to items furnished herein will be reported promptly to the bank.

NORTH JERSEY CARPET CO., INC.
Name of applicant

By: (s) Harry Bernard, Pres.

Exhibit B. Dun and Bradstreet Report.

| SIC | 57 | 13 | D-U-N-S | 06-279-4140 | May 9, 1988 |

Started: February 1986   Rating: EE2

North Jersey Carpet Co., Inc.   Summary
502 Main Street
Morristown, N.J. 07925   Payments   disc–ppt
Tel: 201-762-4410   Sales $612,000
Harry Bernard, Pres   Worth $65,410
No other officers   Employs   4-10
                                                 Record   Clear

Payments	HC Owes	Terms	Condition	Good	
	7,000	1,000	30	Trend	Up

FINANCE: On this date, Bernard, Pres., submitted following statement dated March 31, 1988.

Cash	$7,236	Accts pay	$268,058
Accts rec	220,553	Notes pay	21,800
Inventory	62,140	Taxes	5,851
Notes rec	27,924		
Ppd exp	1,720		
Current	$319,573	Current liabs	$295,709
		L-T liab–other	14,500
Fix & equip	24,900	Capital Stock	1,000
Deposits	1,250	Retained Earnings	34,514
Total assets	$345,723	Total	$345,723

1988 annual sales $612,000; cost of goods sold $440,840; gross profit $171,160; operating expenses $26,466; net income $86,828. Prepared from statements by Lawrence and Whitlow, CPA. Prepared from books without audit.

Above financial statement indicates a good condition exists. Majority of current assets are centered in accounts receivable, are sufficient to finance operations. Suppliers report a good account.

History: Incorporated NJ Feb. 1986. Business started Feb. 1986 by Harry Bernard and John Walters. Relocated Aug. 1987 from 6545 Orange Avenue, East Orange. Starting capital $15,000 from savings.

Walters, former partner, left business in 1987. No reason given. No compensation given to Walters.

H. Bernard born 1940, married. Prior to 1986 not residing in NJ.

Operation: Retails and installs carpets and floor coverings. Terms net 30. Sells to industrial concerns. Territory NJ. Rents 400 sq. ft. on 2nd floor of 2 story bldg. Premises are neat. Maintains 1,000 sq. ft. warehouse space at 12 Seney Road, East Orange.

Exhibit C. Customers and Projects,
North Jersey Carpet Company, Incorporated.

July 25, 1988

Completed and Billed

Hankins Bros.	Singelton Storage	$19,249
Hankins Bros.	Locklin Hardware Supply	1,325
G & R Construction	Diesel Fuel Marketers	5,666
Saddle Brook	Town Hall Tile	1,470
Armine Inc.	Flooring	1,685
Dynamic Industries	General Processing	1,850
Garbaldi Corp.	Whalen Products	7,310
John Reynolds	Lighting of Central Jersey	2,350
Central Processors	Carpeting and tile	1,840
Petroci Bros.	Bullock Interiors	8,387

In Process

Contractor	Project	Amount	Billed	Receivable
Lyons Bros.	Main Office	$96,050	$19,500	$19,500
Jannell Corp.	Pub. School #12	16,422	6,500	2,400
Shoemaker Co.	Reception area	34,860	34,860	34,860
Midway Constr.	E. Orange Recreation	41,876	27,420	16,510
Hankins Bros.	Warehouse tile	23,900	23,900	23,900

Summary

Completed and billed, 1988	$51,132
In process, billed, 1988	122,180
Accounts receivable, current but not shown in schedule above	49,151
Contracts not started	492,440
Contracts in process, not billed 152,930	
Total	$867,833

Exhibit D. Current Receivables,
North Jersey Carpet Company, Incorporated.

July 15, 1988

Hankins Bros.	7/15/88	$42,150
G & R Constr.	7/2/88	21,666
Saddle Brook	6/29/88	470
Lyons Bros.	6/29/88	19,500
Jannell Corp.	6/29/88	6,500
Armine Inc.	6/29/88	10,685
Dynamic	6/17/88	5,850
Shoemaker Co.	6/17/88	14,860
Garbaldi	6/7/88	15,309
Midway Constr.	6/1/88	27,420
John Reynolds	5/24/88	2,350
Central Processors	5/18/88	2,600
Fleming Realty	5/4/88	14,350
High Ridge Inc.	4/23/88	26,421
Roundtop Co.	4/17/88	5,781
Benjamin Bros.	3/27/88	<u>11,414</u>
	TOTAL	$227,326

<u>Aging Schedule</u>

1-30 days	$121,681
31-60 days	47,679
61-90 days	46,552
Over 90 days	<u>11,414</u>
	$227,326

Exhibit E. Financial Statements,
North Jersey Carpet, Company, Incorporated.

LAWRENCE AND WHITLOW
Certified Public Accountants
160 East Linden Avenue
South Orange, N.J. 07079
(201) 487-8560

Ronald Lawrence,   CPA Gilbert Whitlow, CPA

North Jersey Carpet Company, Inc.
502 Main Street
Morristown, N.J. 07925

Dear Mr. Bernard:

In accordance with your request, we have prepared the following financial statements from the books, records, and inventories furnished to us without verification.

The financial statements submitted herein were not audited by us according to generally accepted auditing standards; therefore, we do not express an opinion on them.

Respectfully submitted,

(s) Ronald Lawrence, CPA

Balance Sheet
North Jersey Carpet Company

March 31, 1988

	As of March 31, 1988	As of September 30, 1987
Current Assets		
Cash	$7,236	$3,523
Accounts Receivable–Trade	220,553	135,596
Inventory at Cost	62,140	8,523
Loans Receivable	27,924	0
Prepaid Expenses	1,720	835
Total Current Assets	$319,573	$148,477

Other Assets		
Auto Equipment	$14,300	$4,200
Office Equipment	10,600	10,900
Deposits	1,250	220
Total Other Assets	$26,150	$15,320
Total Assets	$345,723	$163,797
Current Liabilities		
Notes Payable–due in one year	$21,800	$21,800
Accounts Payable	268,058	122,080
Payroll Taxes Payable	5,851	1,518
Total Current Liabilities	$295,709	$145,398
Long-Term Liabilities		
Notes Payable–due after 1 year	$14,500	$3,000
Equity		
Capital	$1,000	$1,000
Retained Earnings	34,514	14,399
Total Equity	$35,514	$15,399
Total Liabilities and Equity	$345,723	$163,797

Statement of Profit and Loss
North Jersey Carpet Company, Inc.

March 31, 1988

	12 Months Ending March 31, 1988	6 Months Ending Sept. 30, 1987
Sales		
Gross Sales	$615,000	$219,048
Less Returns and Allowances	3,000	750
Net Sales	$612,000	$218,298
Cost of Sales		
Beginning Inventory	$450	$450
Purchases	267,900	109,752
Salaries and Wages	87,350	49,381
Subcontractors	82,500	34,600
General and Administrative—direct	22,780	952
Less Ending Inventory	(20,140)	(8,723)
Cost of Goods Sold	$440,840	$186,412
Gross Profit on Sales	$171,160	$31,886
Operating Expenses		
Payroll Taxes and Assessments	$12,045	$7,443
Union Fees and Insurance	6,981	3,723
General and Administrative—indirect	7,420	3,800
Total Operating Expenses	$26,446	$14,966
Net Profit for Period	$144,714	$16,920

Exhibit F. Personal Financial Statement, Harry Bernard.

As of July 31, 1988

Harry and Estelle Bernard, 206 Morris Avenue, Morristown, N.J. 07925
Occupation: Self-employed
Business Address: 502 Main St., Morristown, N.J. 07925

I/we make the following statement of all my/our assets and liabilities at the time of business on the date above:

Cash on hand	$ 850	Notes to banks–secured	
Cash in banks (itemize)	4,500	Notes to banks–unsecured	
Securities–marketable		Notes to others–secured	27,200
Securities–not readily marketable	35,000	Notes to others–unsecured	
		Mortgage payable	67,500
Real estate	108,000	Other liabilities	
Automobile(s)	15,000		
Other assets			
Jewelry, furs, antiques, household, misc.	35,000	None	
Total assets	$198,350	Total liabilities	94,700
		Net Worth	$103,650

1. Banking relations: None in N.J.
2. Detail of notes: N/A
3. Life insurance: Self–$20,000 with Mutual of Omaha, term
   Wife–$110,000 with Liberty Mutual, whole life
4. Securities: $35,000 face value of worth in North Jersey Carpet Co.
5. Real Estate: Own home–$108,000 value; mortgage–$67,500, purchased in 1986 for $85,000.
6. Age: 48 years Dependents: 3
7. Pledged Assets: None
Contingent Liabilities: None
Legal Actions: None
Insurance Coverage: Sufficient

I certify that the statements above are true and give a correct showing of my financial condition as of the date indicated. In the event of material change in my financial condition, I agree to notify the National Bank of New Jersey immediately in writing.

Signed this 31st day of July, 1988   (s) Harry Bernard

18

Credit Scoring Systems

A **credit scoring system** is a device for determining the amount of credit to be extended to a person or firm applying to borrow money or receive goods or services without immediate payment. Such systems are often used to provide a mechanical approach to credit evaluation. In this chapter, we will examine the benefits and weaknesses of such systems.

OVERVIEW

A credit scoring system has a number of characteristics, including

1. **Credit and Stability Variables.** The bank or company extending the credit will measure two kinds of variables. The first type is related to credit capacity, or the ability to pay, and might include items such as earnings and assets owned. The second category contains stability variables, or the likelihood that an individual or business is motivated to pay debts in the future. Typical variables are years of continuous employment or years of successful business activity.

2. **Single Numerical Value.** The goal of the system is to create a single number that indicates creditworthiness for a customer. This is called **an index number**, defined as a numerical value that may be used for the purpose of ranking alternatives. Each variable is assigned a weight, and all variables will total to a single index number. As an example, the entire scale for a system applying to individuals seeking personal credit might be 0 to 100 points. Ten of these points may be allocated to salary. Each $6,000 of annual salary might be assigned a value of 1 point. Thus, an individual who earns $36,000 per year will be given 6 points (36,000/6,000) in the weighting system. If the individual receives 85 points as a total of all the other variables, the final single value will be 91 points.

3. **Credit Scale.** A credit scoring system usually employs a credit scale that matches against a maximum dollar amount of funds that may be

lent or credit that may be extended. For example, a loan office may have a maximum credit limit of $10,000 for any one individual. To obtain such an amount, an individual must score 90 or above on a credit scale from 0 to 100. Between 80 and 90, the limit may be $7,000, 70 to 90 may yield $4,000, 60 to 70 may yield $1,000, and below 60 may result in a credit denial.

4. **Relative Ranking of Scores.** A numerical value has no meaning outside the rank-order system that generates it. Within the system, it is used only for comparing different applications. A high number indicates a good credit risk and a low number indicates a poor credit risk. The analyst knows that an applicant with a score of 80 is a better credit risk than an individual with a score of 40. This does not mean that the applicant with 80 is twice as creditworthy as the one with 40. The index numbers merely show that one applicant is higher than the other.

Design of Credit Scoring Systems

Commercial banks, finance companies, and industrial corporations make extensive use of credit scoring systems. As might be expected, the systems vary considerably, reflecting factors such as the following:

1. **Industry Environment.** The nature of the business will affect the structure of the credit scoring system. A firm making decisions to extend credit in heavy manufacturing will look for different characteristics than a firm extending credit for consumer purchases.

2. **Centralization or Decentralization of Credit Decisions.** If all credit decisions are made at a single location, a system can be designed to afford flexibility to the analyst. The credit decisions are made by individuals who can communicate with each other, and this might standardize decisions. On the other hand, some firms extend credit with decisions made on a decentralized basis. A finance company with 600 offices is one such example. If each office manager has the authority to approve loans, a specific and somewhat inflexible system may be established. This approach can be used mechanically by inexperienced managers without exposing the company to unapproved variations.

3. **Subjective Views of Management.** The firm's top managers often have specific views on what constitutes a creditworthy customer. Some individuals value years in business more than annual profits. Other managers have the reverse view. The weighting of each variable will reflect these subjective views of a firm's management.

4. **Historical Experience.** Because firms have been extending credit for many years, managers have experience as to what works and what does not. This applies to factors in the credit scoring system. In one industry,

the most important indicator of creditworthiness may be the net worth of the creditor. In another, the level of revenues may be correlated historically with the repayment of debts. These historical considerations will affect the design.

Construction of a System

The ability to construct a credit scoring system depends on a number of other factors. The key characteristics are as follows:

1. **Variables That Can Be Identified.** The firm or financial institution must be operating in an environment in which it can identify the variables that correlate to good credit. Then the institution must be able to blend the variables in a model that produces good results.

2. **Simple Structure.** A credit scoring system should be constructed so that it is not excessively complicated. An overly complex system will not be understood, cannot easily be modified to reflect changing circumstances, and may even be undermined by the persons charged with applying it.

3. **Reliable Results.** Even as it must be simple in structure, the system should also be sufficiently complex so as to be a good indicator of creditworthiness. Individuals who receive scores of 80 should pay their bills more quickly than individuals who receive scores of 60.

BENEFITS AND WEAKNESSES

A number of benefits and weaknesses can be identified when using credit scoring systems. In this section, we will examine some of them.

Benefits

Credit scoring systems are widely used because they bring a number of specific benefits to the process of making credit decisions.

1. **Objective Factors.** The system represents an attempt to identify factors related to the credit capacity and stability of the potential borrower. Such data add an element of objectivity to the decision making process. As an example, the salesperson may want a sale and thus inadvertently represents a potential customer as more creditworthy than is the actual case. By processing the request on a scale related to capacity to pay, the firm knows that the credit decision does not give excessive weight to the salesperson's feelings.

2. **Routinization of Decisions.** An important benefit of a credit scoring system is that it helps a firm or bank to standardize credit decisions. A firm can always expect to have unusual circumstances that might influence the ability to pay. Still, the vast majority of credit decisions are fairly routine. Decisions on these applications can be made routinely, a process that is assisted by credit scoring systems. This approach is particularly important in two situations. First is the finance company with many offices and decisions being made by office managers. Second is the company that evaluates thousands of new credit applications each year. By employing a credit scoring system, decisions in both environments can be made consistently from one applicant to the next.

3. **Variety of Factors Considered.** Credit capacity is not the result of a single factor, but rather is made up of a number of variables. A credit scoring system allows the firm to consider a list of factors that form a composite view of creditworthiness. For individual loans, a person's ability to pay is influenced not only by income and asset value, but also by other considerations. Similarly, a business's ability to pay will be reflected in a number of operating and financial factors. A credit scoring system allows the analyst to bring together many variables into a single model that correlates with the amount of credit that can properly be extended to an individual or business.

4. **Weighting of Key Variables.** A final advantage to a credit scoring system is that it ties together factors in a single model that allows varied weighting. The analyst is able to give different degrees of importance to each variable in the model. Earnings can be weighted at 20 percent and years living at one address can be 10 percent, even as both variables are considered in a single model. Once the variables have been identified and given a proper weighting, the system produces a single output that can be used to make the final credit decision.

Weaknesses

Credit scoring systems also have a number of weaknesses, including:

1. **Mechanical Structure.** A major weakness of a credit scoring system lies in its mechanical nature. The structure does not rely on a common sense assessment by the analyst based on the individual facts in a situation. Rather, a standardized set of facts must be gathered and plugged into the model. When the analyst receives the results, they will be based on assumptions and logic that were used when the model was constructed. Furthermore, they will not reflect any unusual circumstances of the individual or firm applying for credit. If the assumptions are no longer valid, the model will produce false results. If individual

circumstances are important, the mechanical structure of the model will not incorporate additional factors into the final decision.

2. **False Objectivity**. One of the advantages of a credit scoring system has been identified as its objectivity. In fact, the system may not be objective at all. The selection of variables to be included in the model is, by its very nature, a subjective process. The person constructing the system may not have any evidence that the variables are related to credit capacity or the willingness to pay off debts. The biases or unsupported beliefs of the individuals constructing the model will be reflected in the final system. The result may be a selection and weighting of variables that gives the appearance of objectivity without any of the positive results that are expected with a properly designed model.

3. **Limited Application**. A final weakness of a credit scoring system lies in the effort to develop one approach to cover the majority of credit decisions. The final model may be so broad as to have limited application in specific situations. As an example, consider a bank that uses a model for evaluating consumer loans. The system may use home ownership as an important indicator of the potential borrower's stability. Under such an assumption, an individual who rents an apartment or house will appear to be less creditworthy than individuals who own their own homes. As a general rule, the ownership of assets provides an indication of stability. Still, apartment dwellers who have invested in real estate partnerships run by others may have similar indicators of stability. Does the model provide for individuals who seek the advantages of an apartment but who invest in real estate anyway? If not, the model might not be suitable for evaluating applications from such individuals.

CONCLUSION

The development and use of credit scoring systems must reflect the firm's operating and financial environment. We will make no attempt to construct such a system here. Instead, let us analyze the system in the following case. The goal is to comment on the structure of the credit scoring system and on the validity of the results obtained.

LYLE ELECTRONICS COMPANY CASE— CREDIT SCORING SYSTEMS

Lyle Electronics Company is an operating division of General Technologies Incorporated, a major manufacturer of machinery and supplies for the industrial market. Lyle is set up as a semiautonomous unit and, with the exception of its financing requirements and legal needs, operates independently of General Technologies. Lyle has three major product lines: (1) burglar and sensor alarms which are used for plant and site security and are sold worldwide; (2) industrial timers which are used in computer applications in steel processing and the chemical industry; and (3) security and time clocks which are purchased for general industrial use and for specific requirements in vaults and similar areas where access is restricted.

Lyle Electronics sells primarily to large customers and has little interest in making small sales. The firm's average sale is approximately $23,000, although it is not uncommon for a complex security system to produce revenues of $1.5 million. On the other hand, numerous sales are made to small retailers and distributors who may occasionally place orders for only a few hundred dollars. Of the firm's 900 accounts, 50 percent produce orders in excess of $20,000, 30 percent range between $2,000 and $20,000, and the balance average under $2,000.

Tom Jennings has recently been hired by Lyle Electronics in the position of credit manager. Jennings' previous business experience is in the area of general accounting, although he did spend 3 years on the retail side of a medium-sized commercial bank. For the past three months, he has been examining the customer base and credit reports that are provided by the data processing department on a regular basis. After reviewing the overall situation, Jennings now feels comfortable establishing credit limits for new customers and reviewing the limits for existing customers.

Lyle Electronics employs a credit scoring system to make decisions on the initial extension of credit. The company believes that five factors are the key variables to creditworthiness in their domestic customers. The first of these is the existence of collateral to back the receivable. For some of the items, particularly the alarms and time clocks, the product itself can be used as collateral. For example, if Lyle Electronics is selling to distributors who will stock the items, Lyle can repossess the products in the event of slow payment or default. The same is true if the alarms or clocks are installed in warehouses or factories, although repossession is sometimes impractical in these cases. For some products, such as specialized sensing devices or timers, the product cannot easily be converted to other uses. If a default occurs, the item offers a minimal value as collateral.

462

The next three factors deal with the background of the customer. A major concern is the length of time that the customer has been in business. New customers who are also new to the business are viewed as being highly risky. Another concern is whether the owners or principals of the business have declared bankruptcy in the immediate past. This action is viewed as an indication that a creditor might not be inclined to honor his or her debts in the future. A third concern is the background of the customer in the firm's credit record. Do Dun and Bradstreet and other credit agencies give the customer a clean credit report?

A final factor is the financial strength of the firm placing the order. Lyle examines the application form and related financial statements to determine the size of the firm's assets and the liabilities that exist against them. A firm with a high level of assets that are not pledged to meet other extensions of credit and a low level of debts is viewed as being a good credit risk; the reverse would not be a good exposure for Lyle.

The firm uses a credit scoring system to evaluate the new customer. Once a weighted score is determined, by completing the form in Figure 18-1, the credit limit is determined by applying percentages to three factors: (1) net worth, which is defined as the total assets less the liabilities; (2) accounts payable; and (3) credit sales. The percentage to be applied is based upon the weighted score. These percentages are given in Figure 18-2.

As an example of the use of the system, suppose a firm had a net worth of $300,000, payables of $120,000, and credit sales of $800,000, and the firm scored a "0" under the credit scoring system. The initial credit limit would be $8,000, as follows:

Factor	Amount	Percentage		Value
Net Worth	300,000	x	0.05	= $15,000
Accounts Payable	120,000	x	0.10	= 12,000
Credit Sales	800,000	x	0.01	= 8,000 lowest amount

The $8,000 reflects a firm that scores exactly zero on the scale. The limiting factor is the 1 percent that is applied to credit sales. If this firm increased its credit sales, it would be entitled to more credit under Lyle Electronics Company's scoring system. The next limiting factor would be the 10 percent of accounts payable restriction. Lyle uses the lowest amount to protect the firm against abnormal situations. As an example, a firm may have excessive payables, a factor that places it in a high-risk category. Still, the firm would be entitled to sizable credit if only the payables balance were considered. Using the lowest of three variables helps avoid this kind of error.

Tom Jennings noted that his firm used the credit scoring system for initial orders only. For established customers, the firm used no formal system at all.

If a customer had a good payment record and increased his or her orders gradually, the orders would be filled. A sizable jump in order size would be investigated and, with a logical explanation, would also be honored. Lyle's management felt that the firm had no choice to reduce or eliminate a customer's credit if the customer had a record of paying on time. At the same time, the company reviewed slow-paying customers annually. The firm tried to determine whether sales to such customers produced satisfactory profits. The policy, which is explained in Figure 18-3, was applied only to customers who placed orders larger than $2,000. It considered the cost of tying up funds in receivables, collection costs, and the size of markup on the differing product lines. It also considered the cash at risk on a credit sale. The final decision would be made by comparing the cash at risk with the potential profit from the sale.

Figure 18-1. Credit Department Policy Statement—Business Application.

Item	Value		Weight	Weighted Average
Collateral				
Good	10	x	0.20	=
None	0			
Clear Credit Report				
Yes, active	10	x	0.20	=
Yes, inactive	0			
No	-10			
Been in Business for				
More than 6 years	5	x	0.20	=
3-6 years	0			
Less than 3 years	-5			
Assets				
High level, unpledged	10	x	0.20	=
Medium-high or some pledged	5			
Medium or sufficient	0			
Medium-low or insufficient	-5			
Low or inadequate or pledged	-10			
Bankruptcy declared in past 10 years by principal				
Yes	-10	x	0.20	=
No	0			
Total Score				_____

Figure 18-2. Credit Limits, First Order

Score	(Below -1)	-1 to +1	+1 to +3	+4 to +7
Credit limit is lowest of following percentages applied to each item				
To Net Worth	0	5%	10%	15%
To Accounts Payable	0	10	15	20
To Credit Sales	0	1	3	5

Note: Any other approvals or later orders in excess of these limits must be approved as exceptions to policy.

Figure 18-3. Credit Limit—Approved Customers Who Are Slow to Pay.

Lyle Electronics does not desire to make sales to customers who are slow paying bills unless it is earning a reasonable profit on such customers after considering the cost of financing the sales. The following procedure will be followed to evaluate existing customers who are slow to pay.

1. This analysis applies only to customers who place orders in excess of $2,000. For smaller orders, continuing delays in payment will result in the customer being placed on a "cash before delivery" basis on future orders.

2. All large customers ($2,000 is the cutoff) will be evaluated once a year. Any customers whose average payment period exceeds 60 days will be reviewed in detail.

3. The company's cost of money tied up in receivables is estimated to be 2 percent per month, including time value of funds and collection costs.

4. The company sends reminders to customers who are slow paying. Thus, the 2 percent cost of money applies during the first 30 days as well as after the receivable is overdue.

5. The markups on the individual product lines must be considered. We have a 15 percent markup on burglar and sensor alarms, a 25 percent markup on industrial timers, and a 35 percent markup on security and time clocks. These markups do not consider selling commissions. A 10 percent commission is paid on the total sale within 30 days after the sale is made. If the sale is not collected within a one-year period, the salesperson must return the commission.

6. The analysis is performed in four steps:

    a. Calculate the present value of the profit on the sale.

    b. Calculate the cash exposure on the sale by deducting the amount of the markup from the selling price.

    c. Calculate a breakeven point on the likelihood of default.

    d. Draw a conclusion on whether the account is sufficiently profitable so as to justify future credit sales.

The financing cost for receivables was measured at 2 percent a month and included collection costs. This was applied to the full sale price of the goods, not just the out-of-pocket costs. The company reasoned that most receivables could be factored at roughly 2 percent a month on their face values; therefore, an account that did not meet the standards for factoring was costing the company money at a rate of 2 percent of its face value. For the cash exposure calculation, a different reasoning was used. If a customer defaulted, the markup was not viewed as a cash loss since the profit had never been earned by the company. Only the out-of-pocket expenses were viewed as lost.

The final decision would be based on a breakeven analysis. The company used the following formula:

Present Value of Profits	x	Probability of Payment	=	Net Cash Exposure	x	Probability 1 - of Payment

and solved for the probability of payment. Suppose, for example, that the probability of payment determined by the formula is 50 percent. This means that, if the firm sells to customers who offer only 50 percent likelihood of paying for the goods, then the firm will break even—that is, neither make a profit nor sustain a loss. The breakeven point, where the profits earned equal the defaults, will be 50 percent. If 95 percent of the customers actually pay, the firm makes a profit; if only 30 pay, the firm suffers a loss.

This formula is a form of utility analysis that offers a measure of the margin of profit from selling to a group of customers. If the breakeven point is 75 percent and only 85 percent actually pay their bills, the firm will have narrow profits on sales to this group of customers. On the other hand, if the breakeven point is 60 percent and 98 percent eventually pay, the firm is making money on this group of customers.

The firm's credit manual gives a specific example of the application of this formula to the Barney Security Systems, as shown in Figure 18-4.

Tom Jennings was in the process of evaluating two requests with respect to credit. Thompson Industries was new to Lyle Electronics, even though it had been in business for 12 years. Thompson's purchasing manager had applied for $12,000 of credit and sought an open line to renew the credit on a regular basis. A local credit bureau reported an active record for Thompson, that was basically clear, although there were some reports of slow payment and one report of "lengthy delays" in remitting. Dun and Bradstreet reported some slowness in paying but indicated that the company was relatively profitable and had a sound balance sheet. No owners of the firm had been involved in bankruptcy proceedings in the past 20 years. Financial data reported by the credit bureau based on a report submitted by Thompson are shown in Figure 18-5.

Jennings, second request came from the company's controller. Union Jewelry Distributors sold certain sensing devices to wealthy individuals for use in protecting their homes and valuables. For the past five years, Union had paid its bills regularly, but recently the payments had slowed considerably. As an example, two years ago the firm paid in 37 days. For the past 16 months, the average has been 135 days. Telephone calls have produced no satisfactory explanation. Union's average order is $6,000, with roughly 40 percent of the items coming from the security and time clocks line and the balance coming from burglar and sensor alarms. The controller wanted a recommendation on whether to continue extending credit to Union Jewelry.

Figure 18-4. Credit Manual Example—
Evaluating Approved Customers Who are Slow to Pay.

Assumptions and Financial Data

Average Order Placed, Dollar Value	45,000
Markup on Each Product	
Industrial Timers	0.25
Time Clocks	0.35
Percent of Each Product	
Industrial Timers	0.30
Time Clocks	0.70
Average Collection Period, Days	165
Average Collection Period, Months	5.50
Sales Commission	0.10
Cost of Financing, monthly	0.02

Outputs

PRESENT VALUE OF PROFITS

Average Order

Industrial Timers	13,500	
Time Clocks	31,500	
		45,000

Average Profits at Stipulated Markups

Industrial Timers	3,375	
Time Clocks	11,025	
		14,400
Less Sales Commission		(4,500)
Less Financing Costs		(4,950)
Present Value of Profit on Sale		4,950

CASH EXPOSURE

Average Order	45,000
Less Profit	(14,400)
Net Cash Exposure	30,600

BREAKEVEN ON LIKELIHOOD OF DEFAULT

Probability of Payment is the unknown:

$$4,950 * X = 30,600 - 30,600 * X$$
$$X = 0.8608$$

CONCLUSION

To break even with this customer, the firm must collect 86.08 percent of the time. Stated differently, we can accept only a 13.92 percent chance of default before profits are wiped out. If the percentage risk is too high, credit should be halted.

Figure 18-5. Thompson Industries Financial Data.

Cash	$29,512
Receivables	153,414
Inventories	117,984
Other Assets	206,217
ASSETS	$507,127
Trade Payables	$120,557
Other Liabilities	64,483
3-Year Notes	97,813
Equity	224,274
TOTAL	$507,127
Cash Sales	7,485
Credit Sales	683,554
Less Cost of Sales	375,987
Less Overhead	174,542
Before-Tax Profit	140,510

Required: Prepare Jennings' recommendations on the credit requests from Thompson Industries and Union Jewelry Distributors.

VII.

Inventory

19

Inventory Management

In addition to cash and receivables, a third major area of working-capital management deals with inventories that allow the firm to conduct its business. The inventories can arise from production activities or they can represent goods purchased from other firms. In either case, the funds committed to handling, storing, or protecting these assets are managed appropriately under the working-capital policies of the firm.

In this chapter, we will examine the conceptual framework for the management of inventories. Some basic techniques will be used to illustrate the principles of efficient management and the tradeoffs needed when making decisions on inventory types and levels. Some mathematical examples will be used to provide frameworks for more complicated analyses not within the scope of this chapter.

NATURE OF INVENTORIES

Inventories are all goods held specifically for resale, whether by a manufacturing firm or by a distributor or other business that has purchased finished goods. A variety of factors influence the kinds of goods held and benefits therein. In this section, we will examine issues involved with holding inventories.

Role in Working-Capital

Inventories are a component of the firm's working-capital and, as such, represent a current asset. Some characteristics are important in the broad context of working-capital management, including

1. **A Current Asset.** It is assumed that inventories will be converted to cash in the current accounting cycle, which is normally one year. In some cases, this is not entirely true. For example, a vintner may require that the wine be aged in casks or bottles for many years. Or, a manufacturer of fine pianos may have a production process that

exceeds one year. In spite of these and similar problems, we will view all inventories as being convertible into cash in a single year.

2. **Level of Liquidity.** Inventories are viewed as a source of near-term cash. For most products, this description is accurate. At the same time, most firms hold some slow-moving items that may not be sold for a long time. With economic slowdowns or changes in the market for goods, the prospects for sale of entire product lines may be diminished. In these cases, the liquidity aspects of inventories become highly important to the manager of working-capital. At a minimum, the analyst must recognize that inventories are the least liquid of current assets. For firms with highly uncertain operating environments, the analyst must discount the liquidity value of inventories significantly.

3. **Liquidity Lags.** Inventories are tied to the firm's pool of working-capital in a process that involves three specific lags, namely:

   a. **Creation Lag.** In most cases, inventories are purchased on credit or are initially created with cash payment occurring at a later time. Raw materials may be purchased on credit, creating an account payable. When the raw materials are processed in the factory, the cash to pay expenses is transferred at future times, perhaps a week, month, or more. Labor is paid on payday. The utility that provided the electricity for manufacturing is paid after it submits its bill. Or, for goods purchased for resale, the firm may have 30 or more days to hold the goods before payment is due. Whether manufactured or purchased, the firm will hold inventories for some time period before payment is made. This liquidity lag offers a benefit to the firm.

   b. **Storage Lag.** Once goods are available for resale, they will not be immediately converted into cash. First, the item must be sold. Even when sales are moving briskly, a firm will hold inventory as a backup. Thus, the firm will usually pay suppliers, workers, and overhead expenses before the goods are actually sold. This lag represents a cost to the firm.

   c. **Sale Lag.** Once goods have been sold, they normally do not create cash immediately. Most sales occur on credit and become accounts receivable. The firm must wait to collect its receivables. This lag also represents a cost to the firm.

4. **Circulating Activity.** Inventories are in a rotating pattern with other current accounts. The expenses of paying for inventories can be represented by payables—accounts payable, wages payable, utilities payable, and others. Thus, the value represented in the firm's current accounts circulates from payables to inventories to receivables to cash.

Kinds of Inventories

As a reflection of the role of inventories in the business activity of a firm, three types of inventories can be identified

1. **Raw Materials.** These items must receive further processing before they can be sold by the firm. In a manufacturing environment, they are the items that have not yet been committed to the production process. Examples are microprocessor chips that are used by a manufacturer of computers, or steering wheels that are used by a firm that builds automobiles. It should be noted that one firm's finished product may be another firm's raw material. For the manufacturer of a computer chip, the raw material might be silicon and the final product is the chip. This chip then becomes a raw material for the computer manufacturer.

2. **Work in Process.** Once an item of raw material enters the production stream, it becomes work in process. The computer chips are now part of a larger product and may no longer be separately identifiable. During this stage, the inventory is more than a raw material but less than a product that can be readily sold.

3. **Finished Goods.** Once products have passed through the manufacturing phase and are approved for sale, the inventory consists of finished goods. These items meet the specifications of the Marketing Department and are salable without further processing.

The composition of the firm's overall inventory depends on many factors. The level of raw materials is influenced by production plans, seasonality of sales, technology, the reliability of supply sources, and scheduling and operating needs. The level of work in process varies with the kind of goods and the complexity of the manufacturing process. The finished goods inventories will depend upon market factors and expectations of customers.

Purpose of Inventories

The purpose of holding inventories is to allow the firm to separate the processes of purchasing, manufacturing, and marketing of its primary products. The goal is to achieve efficiencies in areas where costs are involved and to achieve sales at competitive prices in the marketplace. Within this broad statement of purpose, we can identify specific benefits that accrue from holding inventories.

1. **Avoiding Lost Sales.** Without goods on hand which are ready to be sold, most firms would lose business. Some customers are willing to wait, particularly when an item must be customized or is not widely available from competitors. In most cases, however, a firm must be prepared to deliver goods on demand. **Shelf stock** refers to items that are stored by

the firm and sold with little or no modification to customers. An automobile is an item of shelf stock. Even though customers may specify minor variations, the basic item leaves a factory and is sold as a standard item. The same situation exists for many items of heavy machinery, consumer products, and light industrial goods.

2. **Gaining Quantity Discounts.** In return for making bulk purchases, many suppliers will reduce the price of supplies and component parts. The willingness to place large orders may allow the firm to achieve discounts on regular prices. These discounts will reduce the cost of goods sold and increase the profits earned on a sale.

3. **Reducing Order Costs.** Each time a firm places an order, it incurs certain expenses. Forms have to be completed, approvals have to be obtained, and goods that arrive must be accepted, inspected, and counted. Later, an invoice must be processed and payment made. Each of these costs will vary with the number of orders placed. By placing fewer orders, the firm will pay less to process each order.

4. **Achieving Efficient Production Runs.** Each time a firm sets up workers and machines to produce an item, startup costs are incurred. These are then absorbed as production begins. The longer the run, the smaller the costs to begin producing the goods. As an example, suppose it costs $12,000 to move machinery and otherwise begin an assembly line to produce electronic printers. If 1,200 printers are produced in a single three-day run, the cost of absorbing the startup expenses is $10 per unit (12,000/1,200). If the run could be doubled to 2,400 units, the absorbtion cost would drop to $5 per unit (12,000/2,400). Frequent setups produce high startup costs; longer runs involve lower costs.

These benefits arise because inventories provide a "buffer" between purchasing, producing, and marketing goods. Raw materials and other inventory items can be purchased at appropriate times and in proper amounts to take advantage of economic conditions and price incentives. The manufacturing process can occur in sufficiently long production runs and with preplanned schedules to achieve efficiency and economies. The sales force can respond to customer needs and demands based on existing finished products. To allow each area to function effectively, inventory separates the three functional areas and facilitates the interaction among them.

This role of inventory is diagrammed in Figure 19-1.

5. **Reducing Risk of Production Shortages.** Manufacturing firms frequently produce goods with hundreds or even thousands of components. If any of these are missing, the entire production operation can be halted, with consequent heavy expenses. To avoid starting a production run and then discovering the shortage of a vital raw material or other component, the firm can maintain larger than needed inventories.

Figure 19-1. Why Firms Hold Inventories.

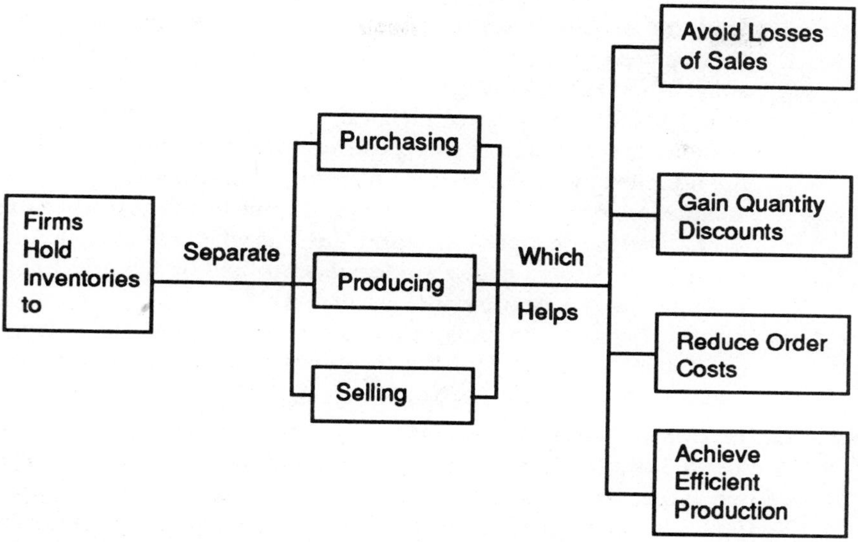

Costs Associated with Inventories

The holding of goods for future sale involves four categories of costs for the firm.

1. **Carrying Costs.** These costs consist of the expenses of storing and safeguarding the inventory. Typical carrying costs include

   a. **Storage and Handling.** The firm must provide storage space, usually through the operation of a warehouse, supply room, or similar facility. Workers must be employed to receive, distribute, move, clean, count, and protect the goods. Equipment, such as forklifts or carts, may be needed. All activities dealing with the physical handling of the goods are included in storage costs.

   b. **Damage or Theft.** Once received, goods must be safeguarded. Unscrupulous employees, customers, or other persons with access to the storage area can steal items. Careless procedures can cause damage that makes an item unsuitable for sale. Despite the best efforts, some goods will be damaged or stolen. A portion of these expenses will not be covered by insurance and will represent an expense to the firm.

   c. **Insurance.** The inventory, as well as the warehouse and accompanying equipment, should be covered by insurance in order to offer protection against fire, accidents, and similar hazards. Larger amounts of inventory will require more insurance. Insurance premiums represent a carrying cost to the firm.

d. **Spoilage or Obsolescence.** When firms hold goods, they expose themselves to the possibility that the goods will not be salable at some future time. **Spoilage** refers to a situation in which a product is not salable because of physical deterioration, such as when perishable subsistances rot, plants or flowers die, textile products are attacked by moths, carpets discolor, or chemicals decompose. **Obsolescence** occurs when a firm is unable to sell goods because of changes in the market demand, such as when styles of clothing change, Christmas markets become saturated by too many competing toys, or new technology creates features not found on existing home stereo units. If goods spoil or products are no longer desirable in the market, the inventory must be liquidated at a fraction of its cost, or destroyed.

2. **Order Costs.** These are the variable costs of placing an order for additional inventory. Each separate shipment from a supplier involves certain expenses connected with requesting and receiving goods. Examples include typing the order, inspecting the goods upon arrival, and moving the goods from the loading dock to the proper storage area in the warehouse. If the firm makes fewer individual orders, it will incur lower variable order costs.

3. **Funds Tied Up.** When funds are committed to inventory, they are tied up and cannot be invested elsewhere. Such an action involves a cost of funds. A portion of the inventory will be financed by trade credit from suppliers, and this involves no cost. Or goods may be sold before the firm must pay for them. An example might be a firm that purchased copying machines on terms of net 30 and sold the machines in 20 days. In most cases, however, a large portion of inventory is being financed by general funds, and this involves a cost.

The cost of funds tied up is particularly noticeable when the firm is contemplating an expansion of its inventory. The firm may have to borrow to obtain funds, and the new debt will involve additional interest. Or, if the firm finances additional inventory with existing cash, it loses the opportunity to invest the cash elsewhere to earn a profit. The lost profit represents a cost. Whatever the source of funds, inventory has a cost in terms of financial resources; excess inventory represents an unneeded cost.

4. **Cost of Running Out of Goods.** Whenever the firm is not able to respond to a production line need or a customer's order because of a shortage of inventory, it incurs a cost. If the production line must shut down because of missing parts or raw materials, production will be

inefficient. If customers cancel orders, the firm will lose profits. Adequate inventory helps avoid loss of sales, loss of customer goodwill, and interruptions to the manufacturing process.

INVENTORY MANAGEMENT

The goal of inventory management is to minimize the total costs of carrying and financing goods while providing full support to the marketing efforts of the firm. In this section, we will examine some of the issues involved in minimizing the costs of inventory. Then, we will develop a systematic approach to inventory management.

Inventory Level Indicators

An efficient production operation will have sufficient inventory to support production without exposing the firm to undue risks or costs from maintaining excessive items in warehouses or elsewhere. Aside from the specific carrying and financing costs, the manager must pay particular attention to four indicators that affect the level of inventory, namely:

1. **Production Requirements.** The manufacturing area will have production plans in place, perhaps for a month, a quarter, or longer. The inventory on hand or on order must match these plans. This process is quite different from the overall level of inventory. It is possible to have huge inventories, and yet not have the items needed for the next quarter's production runs.

2. **Sales Forecasts.** The Marketing Department has its goals and plans for the next months. Advertising may be scheduled for some items but not others. A market may be emerging for televisions but not for audio tape decks. It is not enough to have a large inventory. The firm must maintain an inventory of items that will be sold in the future.

3. **Seasonal or Cyclical Factors.** For most firms, sales levels will vary, either by season or by some expected cycle. When sales are high at the top of a cycle, the firm should anticipate the future. If it is likely that sales will begin to decline, inventory should be cut back. If sales are low but will increase in the future, inventory must rise in advance of the rising cycle.

4. **Changes in Technology.** Some of the horror stories in inventory management have occurred as a result of failures to anticipate emerging technologies. This is the case of the manufacturer of buggy whips who failed to see the automobile replacing the horse and buggy. Modern examples occur almost daily. New electronic items replace last year's

best sellers. Clothing styles change overnight, causing textile manufacturers to hold enormous obsolete inventories. Fads enter the scene and
burn out in a few months.

As we discuss inventory management in this section, these four factors provide
the framework for all elements of the system. It will be assumed that the firm
is in touch with its markets, pays attention to business cycles and technology,
and is interested in matching inventory to production plans.

Total Cost Objective

To manage inventory as a specific task of working-capital management, the
firm establishes a goal of minimizing a total cost function. This is illustrated
in Figure 19-2. The important factors are order costs, carrying costs, safety
stock level, and total costs.

1. **Ordering Costs**. Note that this is a downward sloping line. With larger
   orders, the individual order costs decline. Frequent small orders involve
   high costs to process the paperwork and handle each delivery.

2. **Carrying Costs**. This is an upward sloping line. If large volumes are
   ordered each time, it costs more to store and insure them; the firm
   incurs greater risks of damage, theft, or obsolescence.

3. **Safety Stock Level**. To avoid running out of goods to sell, the firm may
   stock extra inventory. This raises carrying costs and thus total costs.

4. **Total Costs**. This is the sum of the costs. It is minimized as a tradeoff
   between order costs and carrying costs.

In the figure, the total cost for an item of inventory is minimized when the firm
holds an average of 30,000 units. The technique for arriving at this optimal level
will be discussed shortly.

Manage the Important Items

A specific technique for minimizing inventory costs does not follow a comprehensive system at all. Rather, it argues that the important items should receive
special attention and that other items deserve markedly less concern. As an
example, if a firm can run out of an item and yet not lose a sale or disappoint
a customer, it can be argued that it is a waste of money to manage the item
closely. When an item accounts for relatively few sales dollars, it is possible to
spend more money managing the item than will be earned in profits from it.
Such situations encourage the firm to make cost distinctions when managing
inventory.

Figure 19-2. **Minimizing Total Costs.**

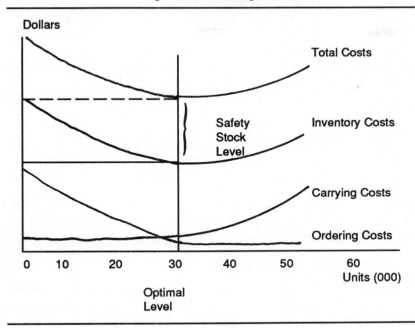

As a general rule, three types of inventory may be viewed as important to manage agressively:

1. **High-Cost Items.** If a firm is holding relatively expensive and valuable inventory, such as a jeweler or a manufacturer of electronic components, the loss of a single item can be very costly. No one wants to be the individual who lost the Star Sapphire of India, nor can the firm stand the loss of a $6 million item of inventory. High-cost items should be managed carefully to ensure against loss or damage and to minimize the high carrying and financing costs of such items.

2. **High-Volume or High-Profit Items.** Some items represent the bread and butter business of the firm. To run out of these items is to have a serious impact on revenues or profits. These items, as well as the components included in them, should be managed with special care.

3. **Bottleneck Items.** These components are needed to complete finished goods. In many cases, a few items are needed in most production runs. An example might be common transistors used in different electronics products. If bottleneck items are not available, the entire production process may be forced to shut down. To avoid such costly inefficiencies, these items deserve individual attention.

A Computerized Management System

The daily activities of inventory management for firms, large or small, require the use of a computerized system. Such a system is needed for recordkeeping as well as for analyzing stock levels and preparing management reports.

Most firms employ a systems approach to the task of inventory management. A number of subsystems are tied together to achieve the single goal of minimizing the cost of maintaining inventory. When tied into the capabilities of computers, fast response time is possible. For example, information on an order can be entered so that production personnel know that an item has been reordered. Or, when an item is removed from inventory because it is used in production or sold, the computer can automatically flag the item to be reordered. With advanced systems, the computer can actually create the purchase order without manual processing.

A system for managing inventory will involve three subsystems: economic order quantity; reorder point; and stock level. In the next sections, each will be examined in turn.

The Economic Order Quantity Subsystem

The **economic order quantity** (EOQ) refers to the order size that will result in the lowest total of ordering and carrying costs for an item of inventory. If a firm places unnecessary orders, it will incur unneeded order costs. If it places too few orders, it must maintain large stocks of goods and will have excessive carrying costs. By calculating an economic order quantity, the firm identifies the number of units to order that results in the lowest total of these two costs.

A number of mathematical models are available to calculate the economic order quantity. Generally, they minimize a cost function. Numerous models exist, as the field of inventory management is highly developed and can be studied in college programs such as operations research and production management. Without getting into highly refined decision models, we can illustrate the concept of economic order quantity with a basic mathematical model. As with all models, we must carefully spell out the limitations and restrictions on its use. For our model, the constraints and assumptions are

1. **Demand Is Known**. Although it is difficult to predict accurately the firm's level of sales for individual items, the marketing manager must provide a sales forecast. Using past data and future plans, the manager can often make a reasonably accurate prediction of demand. This is expressed in units sold per year.

2. **Sales Occur at a Constant Rate**. This model may be used for goods that are sold in relatively constant amounts throughout the year. A more complicated model is needed for firms whose sales fluctuate in response to seasonal or other cyclical factors.

3. **Costs of Running out of Goods Are Ignored.** Costs associated with shortages, delays, or lost sales are not considered. These costs are considered in the determination of safety level in the reorder point subsystem.

4. **Safety Stock Level Is Not Considered.** The safety stock level is the minimum level of inventory that the firm wishes to hold as a protection against shortages. Because the firm must always be above this level, the EOQ formula need not consider the costs of maintaining the safety stock level.

The best formula for calculating economic order quantity under these conditions is derived using calculus. We will not derive it but rather will state it as follows:

$$EOQ = \sqrt{\frac{(2)(U)(OC)}{(CC\%)(PP)}}$$

where

2 = mathematical factor that occurs during the derivation of the formula

U = units sold per year, a forecast provided by the Marketing Department

OC = cost of placing each order for more inventory, provided by cost accounting

CC% = inventory carrying costs expressed as a percentage of the average value of the inventory, an estimate usually provided by the Cost Accounting Department

PP = purchase price for each unit of inventory, supplied by the Purchasing Department

As an example of the use of this formula, a firm anticipates 50,000 units of annual sales of a product that costs the firm $10. The cost of placing an order is $10, and the carrying costs have been estimated by cost accounting as 10 percent of the inventory value. The economic order quantity is

$$EOQ = \sqrt{\frac{(2)(50,000)(10)}{(10\%)(10)}} = \sqrt{\frac{1,000,000}{1}} = 1,000 \text{ units}$$

Thus, the firm should order 1,000 units if it places an order to minimize total costs.

Example: A firm estimates sales of 200,000 units of a product in the next year. Each order would cost the firm $50. The firm pays $60 per unit for the product and estimates that inventory carrying charges are 20 percent of the inventory value. What is the economic order quantity for this product?

Answer: 1,291 units. The formula is:

$$(2 * 200000 * 50)/(.20 * 60) = 1,291$$

Reorder Point Subsystem

An important question in any inventory management system is, "When should an order be placed so that the firm does not run out of goods?" The answer, expressed in terms of units of inventory, is provided by the reorder point subsystem.

The reorder point is the level of inventory at which the firm places an order in the amount of the economic order quantity. If the firm places the order when the inventory reaches the reorder point, the new goods will arrive before the firm runs out of goods to sell.

In designing a reorder point subsystem, three items of information are needed as inputs .

1. **Usage Rate**. This is the rate per day at which the item is consumed in production or sold to customers. It is expressed in units. It may be calculated by dividing annual sales by 365 days. If the sales are 50,000 units, the usage rate is 50,000/365, or 137 units per day.

    A more complicated analysis may be used with computer-based reorder point subsystems. The usage rate can be adjusted to reflect seasonal or cyclical factors and will result in differing reorder points at different times in the year.

2. **Lead Time**. This is the amount of time between placing an order and receiving the goods. This information is usually provided by the Purchasing Department. The time to allow for an order to arrive may be estimated from a check of the company's records and the time taken in the past for different suppliers to fill orders.

3. **Safety Stock Level**. This minimum level of inventory may be expressed in terms of several days' sales. The level can be calculated by multiplying the usage rate times the number of days that the firm wants to hold inventory as a protection against shortages. As an example, the firm may wish to hold sufficient inventory for 15 days of production in the event its order for raw materials does not arrive on time. In this case,

the safety stock level is 15 days, and it is calculated in terms of units of inventory by multiplying 15 times the daily usage rate.

Determining the number of days of safety stock to hold involves a number of variables. Some questions that must be answered are the following:

a. How much variation exists in the usage rate, and how likely is it that the firm will run out of the goods?

b. How much does it cost in terms of lost revenues and profits if the firm runs out for one day? two days? one week?

c. At what point are the carrying costs higher than the lost revenues due to shortages?

Mathematical models exist to help the inventory manager deal with these issues. These models are beyond the scope of this chapter. We will assume that such models are used when appropriate to estimate the number of days of safety stock needed for a product.

To calculate the reorder point, the following formula is used:

$$\text{Reorder Point} = \text{Usage Rate} * \left(\text{Lead Time} + \text{Days of Safety}\right)$$

As an example of the use of this formula, consider a firm with a usage rate of 137 units per day, a lead time of 6 days, and a safety stock desired of 20 days of sales. The reorder point is:

$$137 * (6+20) = 3{,}562 \text{ units}$$

In this case, the firm will place an order for the economic order quantity when the inventory gets down to 3,562 units.

Example: A firm expects annual sales of 9,125 units, desires to maintain a 12-day safety stock level, and has an 8-day lead time for orders. What is the reorder point for the firm?

Answer: 500 units. The formula is:

$$9125/365 \text{ days} = 25 \text{ units daily}$$
$$25 * (8+12) = 500 \text{ units}$$

The Stock Level Subsystem

The stock level subsystem keeps track of the goods held by the firm, the issuance of goods, and the arrival of orders. It is made up of the records accounting for the goods in stock. Thus, the stock level subsystem maintains records of the current level of inventory. For any period of time, the current level is calculated by taking the beginning inventory, adding the inventory received, and subtracting the cost of goods sold. Whenever this subsystem reports that an item is at or below the reorder point level, the firm will begin to place an order for the item.

TOTAL SYSTEM

The three subsystems are tied together in a single inventory management system. This may be illustrated graphically by charting units of inventory on one axis and time on the other. Figure 19-3 shows a system for an item with a reorder point of 1,960 units, a safety stock level of 1,120 units, and an economic order quantity of 1,000 units. The firm reorders at 1,960 units and continues to use its inventory until 1,120 units, when the order of 1,000 units arrives to return the inventory to 2,120 units.

The inventory management system can also be illustrated in terms of the three subsystems that comprise it. Figure 19-4 ties each subsystem together and shows the three items of information needed for the decision to order additional inventory. The computer or analyst compares the level of the ending inventory with the reorder point for the items. If the ending inventory is less than the reorder point, an order should be placed for the economic order quantity.

Figure 19-3. **Inventory Management System.**

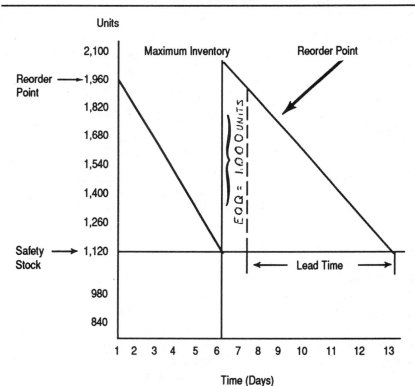

Figure 19-4. Three Subsystems of the Inventory Management System.

Economic Order Quantity Subsystem

From Purchasing	Purchase Price
From Marketing	Sales Forecast
From Cost Accounting	Order Cost Carrying Costs

Stock Level Subsystem

Beginning Inventory	Accounting Records
+ Inventory Received	Warehouse
- Inventory Issued	Warehouse
= Ending Inventory	Accounting Records

EOQ

Reorder Point Subsystem

From Purchasing	Lead Time
From Marketing	Sales Safety Stock Level

Reorder Point   Ending Inventory

If ending inventory is greater than reorder point, do nothing.

If ending inventory is less than or equal to reorder point, order an amount equal to economic order quantity.

DRAPER CORPORATION CASE—MANAGEMENT OF INVENTORIES

Draper Corporation had a good year in 1988 as it benefited from a period of high demand for medical diagnostic equipment. From its hand–held scanner to the permanently installed DiagScan X10, the firm expected steady sales for the next three years. With revenues reaching almost $70 million, the firm counted on continuing success in its primary markets in New England, New York, and the mid-Atlantic states.

Bob Jordan, the operating vice president, was working recently on refinements to the 1989 budget. A major item was the firm's inventory and related costs. The warehouse was adjacent to the manufacturing facility in Long Island and was literally overflowing. Increasingly, bottlenecks occurred when items were being moved in and out of the building. The situation became acute on days when trucks were loading or unloading at the dock. Boxes were piled in the aisles, a procedure that caused considerable confusion. Because the firm paid for the trucks by the hour when they did not unload promptly, the company experienced unnecessary costs when trucks could not be unloaded and had to remain parked at the warehouse overnight.

Bob Jordan was not convinced that the company was handling its inventories efficiently. He asked for records on the items maintained in the warehouse. Basically, the entire inventory consisted of nine components, labeled A through I on the firm's records. Different combinations of each product were used in different diagnostic scanners. Once the items were finished according to customer specifications, the final product was shipped out the same day. This avoided the need to maintain a finished goods inventory but placed a premium on accurate management of the nine components. If any item was missing, the fabrication might stop and a sale might be lost. This encouraged management to maintain large quantities of each item.

To better understand the efficiency of the inventory management activities, Jordan began to collect some data. First, he requested a listing of the stock on hand for each item at the close of a recent Friday. He also asked for an estimate of the order cost on each item. He was given the information in Figure 19-5. Then, he asked for some cost data and was given the information in Figure 19-6, which displays annual usage in units and cost per unit to Draper.

Jordan discussed his project to evaluate inventory levels with the warehouse manager. The manager went through his records and then advised Jordan on estimated carrying costs. The manager based the costs on a percentage of the purchase price of each item. He also gave Jordan the lead time between placing an order and receiving the goods. Then, he responded to Jordan's request for a safety stock estimate for each item. This estimate would be based on the cost of running out for each item. Items A and G posed the most problems if they ran out, so they would have the highest safety stock requirements; items D and I were the least critical. The complete data on carrying costs, lead time, and safety stock level are given in Figure 19-7.

Figure 19-5. Stock on Hand, Actual, and Order Costs.

Item	Stock on Hand (Units)	Order Cost
A	2420	90
B	4060	50
C	2990	70
D	480	120
E	1340	60
F	600	80
G	2300	110
H	1530	100
I	960	130

Figure 19-6. Annual Usage and Cost to Purchase Each Unit.

Item	Annual Usage (Units)	Purchase Price
A	7,500	610
B	15,200	440
C	23,000	90
D	900	3,100
E	4,200	900
F	1,300	700
G	8,500	2,200
H	2,600	130
I	6,400	220

Figure 19-7. Carrying Costs, Lead Times, and Safety Stock Levels.

Item	Carrying Cost (Pct)	Lead Time (Days)	Safety Stock (Days)
A	0.05	65	50
B	0.10	15	40
C	0.12	30	30
D	0.08	25	20
E	0.06	90	40
F	0.14	45	30
G	0.06	55	50
H	0.18	10	40
I	0.11	20	20

Required:

1. What is the economic order quantity for each item of inventory?

2. What is the reorder point in units for each item?

3. Compare the actual on-hand inventory with the safety stock level provided by the warehouse manager. How many excess units of each item were carried on a recent Friday? Were any items below the safety stock level?

4. What actions should the firm take?

20

Inventory Planning

An important task of working-capital management is to ensure that inventories are incorporated into the firm's planning and budgeting process. All too often, this is not the case. Sometimes, the level of inventory reflects the orders received by the general manager of the plant without serious analysis as to the need for the materials or parts. This lack of planning can be costly for the firm, either because of the carrying and financing costs of excess inventory or the lost sales from inadequate inventory.

The firm's **budget** is the formal plan expressed in dollars that forecasts revenues and expenses. Implied in a properly prepared budget is an assumption that the organization has set goals and seeks to reach them. Prior to preparing a budget, the firm may involve itself in a planning process in which events are predicted and alternative scenarios are explored. In most organizations, the budget process is coordinated by a department, with one or more persons designated as corporate planners, long–range planners, or similar titles.

The inventory requirements to support production and marketing should be incorporated into the firm's planning process in an orderly fashion. In this chapter, we will tie the level of inventory into the firm's budget. The components of inventory will be matched against a sales forecast. Then, profits on each product line will be used to identify a margin of safety with each item stored in inventory. Finally, we will determine the required level of each inventory item in accordance with production goals and assumptions.

THE PRODUCTION SIDE

The first step in inventory planning deals with the manufacturing mix of inventory items and end products. In this section, we will examine the production side of inventory planning. A single example will be followed through the rest of this chapter.

Inventory Components

Every product is made up of a specified list of components. For example, a computer may have a video display screen, keyboard, disk drives, power supply, miscellaneous cables, internal boards, and a protective case. In order to manufacture 100 computers, each of the parts will be needed in proportion to the requirements on the list of components. If one display screen is used per computer, 100 display screens will be required. If six internal boards are used in each computer, 600 such boards will be required in inventory.

In our example, we will assume a firm is manufacturing three finished goods identified as X, Y, and Z. Product X will be consist of four components, A, B, D, and E, as shown in Figure 20-1. Thirteen units of component D will be required for each unit of X, four each of B and E, and five units of A. Similarly, product Y requires a different mix but not the same four components. Z requires five components, once again in a different mix from either X or Y.

To forecast the required level of each inventory item A through E, the analyst must recognize the different mix of components in each finished product.

Cost of Inventory Items

Each item maintained in inventory will have a cost. This cost may vary based on volume purchases, lead time for an order, historical agreements, or other factors. For the purpose of preparing a budget, each item must be assigned a unit cost. The purchase price of each item in our example is given in Figure 20-2. Item C is a relatively costly component. Item E is less costly.

Materials Cost of Each
Final Product

Once the mix of components is known and each component has been assigned a value, the analyst can calculate the materials cost for each product. This cost is a weighted average of the components and their individual costs, and it is shown in Figure 20-3.

To illustrate the calculation of materials cost, consider the $12,800 cost of product X. A total of $4,000 of this amount involves component A, which requires five units at $800 each. Similarly, four units of B at $600 each give a $2,400 cost of component B. When the same process is followed for D and E, the total cost is $12,800.

Figure 20-1. Inventory Components

	X	Y	Z
A	5	3	2
B	4	0	7
C	0	15	8
D	13	10	3
E	4	2	5

Figure 20-2. Unit Cost of Inventory Items.

A	800
B	600
C	1,200
D	400
E	300

Figure 20-3. Materials Costs for Each Product.

	X	Y	Z
A	4,000	2,400	1,600
B	2,400	0	4,200
C	0	18,000	9,600
D	5,200	4,000	1,200
E	1,200	600	1,500
	12,800	25,000	18,100

THE MARKETING SIDE

The second step in inventory planning involves a forecast of unit requirements during the future period. Both a sales forecast and an estimate of the safety level to support unexpected sales opportunities are required. The Marketing Department should also provide pricing information so that higher profit items receive more attention. In this section, we will examine the marketing inputs to inventory planning.

Sales Forecast in Units

Working with the expectations of the sales force, demographic trends, the level of competition, and other factors, the marketing manager will develop an estimate of sales for each product. (See Figure 20-4). Product X shows a rising trend over five months, then it begins to decline; Y declines; then recovers; and Z declines. These patterns may reflect seasonal or cyclical sales patterns, with important consequences for the firm's inventory management.

Required Inventory During Each Period

Once the sales forecast has been reviewed and accepted, the firm is ready to develop the levels of required inventory for each period and each product. Essentially, a four step process is involved here.

1. **Identify the Profit Contribution of Each Product.** Some products have a high markup and offer a relatively large profit to the firm. These products should always be available for sale since a missed sale has a large impact on operating income. Other products have smaller markups; thus, occasional missed sales have less impact on profits. A strict approach to managing inventory will allow a larger safety margin for high–margin products.

    In our example, we will use the gross profit margin as a measure of profit contribution. (See Figure 20-5.) Products X and Z have higher markups than Y. Even so, there are variations by month for each product. The variations may reflect discounts offered on a seasonal basis, higher selling costs during slow periods, or other factors. By identifying the relative profitability by month, the firm can vary its inventory. During a period when the markup is small, a smaller safety margin can be maintained for a product.

2. **Match the Profit Contribution with the Safety Margin.** Figure 20-6 matches the gross profit margin with a safety margin for inventory. To illustrate the use of the figure, consider a product offering a 45 percent gross profit. The firm will establish a safety margin of 21 percent. Thus, assume that a sales forecast is for 100 units. The manufacturing unit will plan for available inventory of 121 units, calculated by

    $$\text{Sales Forecast} * (1 + \text{Required Margin})$$

    or $100*(1 + 0.21) = 121$. When the gross profit declines to 35 percent as a result of seasonal variations, the margin will decline to 18 percent, according to the figure.

A major question in inventory planning involves the selection of the required margin. How does the manager pick 18 percent at one gross profit level and 24 percent at another? The answer is that many factors play a role in the process. The most important is the tradeoff between the cost of lost sales and the cost of maintaining inventory. Other considerations are the availability of funds to finance inventory, space available for storage, and competitive impacts when customers are not served on a timely basis. A number of mathematical techniques have been developed to optimize these factors. The calculations are beyond the scope of this book. Still, the reader should recognize that a required margin should be matched against gross profit in some way that supports business operations and optimizes long-range income and cash flow.

3. **Match Safety Margins with Each Product.** Figure 20-7 matches the margin of safety for each product and period, based on the gross profit margin in the period. As an example, consider product X in month 4. From Figure 20-5, we can see that X offers a gross profit margin of 55 percent in month 4. From Figure 20-6, we can see that a 55 percent gross profit margin has a required safety margin of 24 percent. In Figure 20-7, product X shows a 24 percent margin in month 4. The same comparison is made for the other products, and margins of safety vary cyclically based on changes in the gross profit margin.

One comment might be made with respect to Figure 20-6, which is identified as a lookup table. Many spreadsheets offer a lookup function so that Figure 20-7 can automatically be calculated from the data in Figures 20-5 and 20-6. Using a function such as @LOOKUP, we can enter formulas in Figure 20-7. The formula will identify the gross profit margin in Figure 20-5 and match it with the closest safety margin in Figure 20-6. For values exactly in the middle, the lower required safety margin is chosen. If the manager is using Lotus 1-2-3 or another spreadsheet that contains this function, it should be used to create the figures in Figure 20-7.

4. **Calculate Required Inventory in Units.** Figure 20-8 is the final step in the process. Forecasted sales is multiplied by the number of inventory components needed per unit, and then by one plus the safety margin to get the inventory needed for each product for each month. Figure 20-9 displays the same information in dollars. The units from Figure 20-8 are multiplied by the costs in Figure 20-2 to get dollars.

Figure 20-4. Sales Forecast in Units.

	Month 1	Month 2	Month 3	Month 4	Month 5	Month 6
Product X	100	125	150	175	200	175
Product Y	70	60	50	50	60	70
Product Z	150	150	125	125	100	100

Figure 20-5. Gross Profit Margins.

	Month 1	Month 2	Month 3	Month 4	Month 5	Month 6
Product X	0.65	0.60	0.55	0.55	0.60	0.60
Product Y	0.50	0.50	0.45	0.45	0.40	0.40
Product Z	0.55	0.60	0.60	0.60	0.65	0.65

Figure 20-6. Lookup Table for Required Safety Margins.

	Gross Profit on Sale				
	0.35	0.45	0.55	0.65	0.75
Safety Margin	0.18	0.21	0.24	0.27	0.30

Figure 20-7. Calculated Margins of Safety Against
Shortages Based on Contributions to Profit.

	Month 1	Month 2	Month 3	Month 4	Month 5	Month 6
Product X	0.27	0.24	0.24	0.24	0.24	0.24
Product Y	0.21	0.21	0.21	0.21	0.18	0.18
Product Z	0.24	0.24	0.24	0.24	0.27	0.27

Figure 20-8. Required Inventory with Margin, in Units.

	Month 1	Month 2	Month 3	Month 4	Month 5	Month 6
A	1,261	1,365	1,422	1,577	1,706	1,587
B	1,810	1,922	1,829	1,953	1,881	1,757
C	2,759	2,577	2,148	2,148	2,078	2,255
D	3,056	3,299	3,488	3,891	4,313	4,028
E	1,607	1,695	1,640	1,764	1,769	1,668

Figure 20-9. Required Inventory with Margin, in Dollars.

	Month 1	Month 2	Month 3	Month 4	Month 5	Month 6
A	1,008,880	1,091,840	1,137,200	1,261,200	1,365,120	1,269,440
B	1,086,000	1,153,200	1,097,400	1,171,800	1,128,600	1,054,200
C	3,310,200	3,092,400	2,577,000	2,577,000	2,493,600	2,706,000
D	1,222,400	1,319,600	1,395,200	1,556,400	1,725,200	1,611,200
E	482,220	508,560	492,000	529,200	530,580	500,460
	7,109,700	7,165,600	6,698,800	7,095,600	7,243,100	7,141,300

Some Clarifications

Note that Figures 20-8 and 20-9 switch from products X, Y, and Z to components A through E. Note further that no labor costs are included in the numbers. This ommision reflects the specific task we have undertaken. We are not performing the job of the Cost Accounting Department to measure inventory levels. Rather we are planning for the purchase of raw material items A through E. The level we maintain depends upon the need for completed products X, Y, and Z. We have calculated a required inventory of raw materials based on the need for finished products.

It should be noted further that a different process is needed to calculate the required levels of X, Y, and Z. The fact that 100 units is forecast to be sold in a month does not mean that 100 plus units must be on hand all month. The actual ending inventory will vary with the pattern of sales. We have only calculated raw materials needed to support the final products.

One further item is missing from this approach. This involves the timing of raw materials versus the manufacture of the final product. We assume that the finished goods can be manufactured immediately upon availability of raw materials. This may not be the case. For example, to produce finished good X, the firm may have to process raw materials A and B for a few weeks, add D for a week, then add E, and wait three weeks before the product X can be sold. These timing delays must be considered in the planning process. Still, such factors only complicate the mathematics; the concept is the same. Planning for raw materials levels must be based on the need for finished goods, as estimated in sales forecasts, and in consideration of profit contributions.

THE INVENTORY DATA BASE

An important component of inventory planning involves access to an inventory data base. Essentially, we are working with a structured framework that contains the information needed to effectively manage all items of inventory, from raw materials to finished goods. This information includes the classification and amount of inventories, demand for the items, cost to the firm for each item, ordering costs, carrying costs, and other data. In this section, we will examine the record–keeping of inventory planning.

Nature of Inventory Data Bases

A **data base** is a collection of data items arranged in files, fields, and records.

1. **File.** A file is a storage area with a name. In a filing cabinet, this could be a manila folder with the heading "List of Spare Parts." In a computer, this is an area of memory in the computer or space on a diskette, disk, or tape where data are stored under a file name and can be retrieved by using appropriate software. Figure 20-10 shows a portion of a sample data base for customers of a firm. The file is called "customer listing" for its paper name and "CUSLIST" for its electronic name.

2. **Field.** The category of information that identifies similar data items is known as a field. In Figure 20-10, the fields are NAME, ADDRESS, CITY, and STATE. A data base needs to identify fields in order to search and locate information. For example, suppose a firm wants to mail a letter to Mason Furniture but does not know its address. By searching the field called NAME, it can locate Mason Furniture. Then, it can check other data items for the address, city, and state. If the data base were not set up with fields, every item of data would have to be checked to see if it was called Mason Furniture.

3. **Record.** A collection of related data items is called a record. In our example, Mason Furniture is one data item —the name of the customer. A related data item is 555 Waverly Ave., since this is the physical location of Mason Furniture. Two other related data items are Newark and NJ, since these are the city and state where we can find 555 Waverly

Ave. and Mason Furniture. The four data items—Mason Furniture, 555 Waverly Ave., Newark, and NJ—are a record in this data base.

Figure 20-10. Portion of Sample Data Base.

Customer Listing, Cuslist

Name	Address	City	State
Simpson-Agro Inc.	234 Morris Ave.	Baltimore	MD
Durso Industries	10 Ward Place	Maplewood	NJ
Alonso Stores	4 Edison Drive	Hartford	CT
Mason Furniture	555 Waverly Ave.	Newark	NJ

Activity Data

The first component of an inventory data base deals with the movement of individual items. Inventory management is an active and dynamic process, with daily or even hourly changes. Raw materials arrive and are placed in a warehouse or other storage area. At some point, they are transferred to the manufacturing area where they become components of work in process and then finished goods. Items that are finished are sold and removed from the inventory. All of these activities must be monitored on a continuing basis in order to ensure adequate goods for production or sale.

An inventory management system for a manufacturing facility will have hundreds or even thousands of items. A variety of activity fields can be created to show the full movement through the manufacturing process. To illustrate activity data, we will use a simplified sample problem. Figure 20-11 shows a portion of the activity data for a sample data base. In this example, we have a number of items of inventory, listed in the left hand column. Four data fields are identified.

1. **Starting Levels for Period.** The firm has a number of units on hand at the start of a period. These levels for each product are given in the column marked On Hand, Start.

2. **Removals from Inventory.** As the period progresses, some items are removed from the storage area. They may become part of work in process or finished goods, or they may be sold. Such removals are displayed in the column called Issued This Period.

3. **Receipts of Items.** Just as some items are removed, others are received or manufactured. These are displayed in the column named New Stock.

4. **Ending Balances.** When removals are subtracted from the starting balance plus new receipts, the result is the inventory on hand at the end of the period. This is displayed for each item under Ending Balance.

Reorder Data

A second important component of inventory management data involves information needed to make decisions on reordering or replenishing the items. This category can consist of a variety of items, depending on whether the item is manufactured, ordered, or obtained by a combination of both processes. In our example, we will assume that all items are ordered from an outside supplier. In this situation, four items of information are needed.

1. **Inventory on Hand.** Before any decisions can be made to order additional items, the firm must have accurate records of availability in the warehouse or other storage areas. This process is one of maintaining data on activity, as was done in the previous section. In our example, we will assume that the ending balance in Figure 20-11 is the inventory on hand for reorder purposes.

   In most management settings, the inventory on hand will be calculated using a large computer system. It may be part of accounting or other operational activities. The reorder system may be separate, either on a mainframe or using software on a stand-alone computer system. If two systems are used, the ending balances may be transferred electronically in summary form to the reorder system.

2. **Units Already Ordered.** Some items of inventory will have been ordered in past periods. These items will not appear on the availability reports but must be considered before reorder decisions can be made. In Figure 20-12, the prior order column shows units that have been ordered but have not yet been received.

3. **Reorder Point.** In the previous chapter, we discussed the determination of a reorder point for each item of inventory. This reflects the lead time for the arrival of goods plus a safety level. In Figure 20-12, the reorder point for each item is displayed.

4. **Economic Order Quantity.** In the previous chapter, we also discussed an economic order of goods, once the reorder point has been reached. This reflects a number of factors, including the cost of storage, cost of placing an order, and possible damage or spoilage to the goods. In the figure, the economic order quantity is displayed for each item.

Cost Data

A final element of inventory data commonly used for making decisions involves the unit cost of each item. With such information, the manager can make a number of decisions with respect to managing high–cost, high–volume items. Reports can also be prepared using dollar amounts to identify excessive levels of inventory. Unit cost data are displayed in Figure 20-12 for each item of inventory.

INVENTORY REPORTS

A major purpose of maintaining accurate inventory data is to allow the firm to make management decisions on the level and appropriateness of different items of inventory. A wide variety of reports can be prepared to assist managers in making operational or marketing decisions. In this section, we will use a few reports to illustrate the kind of information managers can expect from the inventory planning system.

Figure 20-11. Product Availability Report, Sample Problem

The following represents the status report of inventory available as of the start of the current week.

Item	On Hand Start	Issued This Period	New Stock	Ending Balance
DEC LN12	23	9	15	29
VECTOR 2020	41	16	0	25
DIABLO 3	52	6	0	46
EPSON 214	75	23	0	52
STARJET	23	7	0	16
STARJET 2	19	11	0	8
RITEWAY 4A	11	2	15	24
JUKI 550	45	21	0	24
NASHUA 16B	60	14	0	46
PARK TECH 601	26	17	0	9
PARK TECH 45	31	4	0	27
LESTER LINE	31	8	10	33
GOLDATA 4	6	1	0	5
STATGRAPH	33	0	15	48
STATGRAPH 3	16	7	0	9
MACROTECH 741	48	14	0	34
MICROHOT 5	22	13	0	9
FOCUS II	78	39	5	44

Figure 20-12. Reorder Information and Cost Data, Sample Problem.

Item	Prior Order? Units	Re-Order Point	EOQ	Unit Cost
DEC LN12	0	30	15	165
VECTOR 2020	0	15	20	225
DIABLO 3	30	18	30	110
EPSON 214	0	35	60	220
STARJET	0	25	10	180
STARJET 2	25	6	20	260
RITEWAY 4A	0	8	20	90
JUKI 550	0	30	15	520
NASHUA 16B	20	40	20	150
PARK TECH 601	0	21	10	230
PARK TECH 45	0	35	25	290
LESTER LINE	0	14	15	175
GOLDATA 4	12	10	15	205
STATGRAPH	0	10	5	320
STATGRAPH 3	0	15	10	135
MACROTECH 741	10	30	15	255
MICROHOT 5	0	25	16	220
FOCUS II	0	50	40	275

Exception Reports

An **exception report** identifies a deviation from an established policy or norm with respect to the management of inventory. This deviation may be expressed as a variance from the norm. Figure 20-13 identifies two common exceptions in an inventory management system: order variance and reorder variance.

1. **Order Variance.** This exception exists when the firm has placed an order for a different number of units than the economic order quantity. In many cases, this is done for a good reason. One example would be when a supplier has a special price for a large volume order. The firm might then double its order to take advantage of a limited price offer. A second example might occur when a supplier reports a shortage of the product. The firm might place an order for an amount smaller than the EOQ at the request of the supplier.

Even though such variances can be explained, they still should be reported as exceptions. This is done in the figure. The level of existing orders is displayed in the prior order column and the EOQ levels are also given. The variance is displayed with two assumptions:

a. **No Prior Order.** In the spreadsheet format, an if/then statement is used to display a zero if no prior order has been made. Thus, even though a difference exists between the zero in the one column and EOQ in the other, no variance will be shown.

b. **Prior Order Versus EOQ.** If any value is shown in the prior order column, it will be compared to the EOQ. If the two numbers do not match, a variance is displayed. A manager can then visually check each positive or negative value to determine whether such variance really exists and whether it can be explained.

2. **Reorder Variance.** This exception occurs when the availability report shows a level of inventory below the reorder point, yet no order has been processed for more inventory. The report totals the inventory on hand at the end of the period and the total units on prior order. Then, the sum is compared to the reorder point. If the sum is less than the reorder point, a variance is displayed. This allows the firm to ensure that it is not running out of goods without placing a replenishment order.

The two exception reports in the figure offer a fairly simple view of such reports. In a complex manufacturing environment, exceptions occur as a result of manufacturing processes, as well as replenishment through outside orders. Such reports must reflect the production schedule, including seasonal or cyclical variations in manufacturing. Still, the principle is the same. The manager must monitor the level of inventory and compare it to the needs of production or marketing. Then, the inventory must be replenished in amounts needed and on a timetable that supports the firm's business. Exception reports are a way to ensure that information is available to make correct decisions on inventory levels and activities.

Figure 20-13. Exception Report, Sample Problem.

The following lists items that are exceptions to stated policy for inventory management in the prior period:

Item	Prior Order? Units	EOQ	Order Variance	Re- Order Point	On Hand Start	Prior Order? Units	Reorder Variance
DEC LN12	0	15	0	30	23	0	-7
VECTOR 2020	0	20	0	15	41	0	0
DIABLO 3	30	30	0	18	52	30	0
EPSON 214	0	60	0	35	75	0	0
STARJET	0	10	0	25	23	0	-2
STARJET 2	25	20	5	6	19	25	0
RITEWAY 4A	0	20	0	8	11	0	0
JUKI 550	0	15	0	30	45	0	0
NASHUA 16B	20	20	0	40	60	20	0
PARK TECH 601	0	10	0	21	26	0	0
PARK TECH 45	0	25	0	35	31	0	-4
LESTER LINE	0	15	0	14	31	0	0
GOLDATA 4	12	15	-3	10	6	12	0
STATGRAPH	0	5	0	10	33	0	0
STATGRAPH 3	0	10	0	15	16	0	0
MACROTECH 741	10	15	-5	30	48	10	0
MICROHOT 5	0	16	0	25	22	0	-3
FOCUS II	0	40	0	50	78	0	0

Cost Reports

The essential nature of inventory management involves two types of information. The first deals with operations. Will the firm have enough raw materials, work in process, and finished goods to conduct its business properly? The second deals with the cost of maintaining inventory. Is the firm efficiently managing the resources committed by management to the inventory area?

Figure 20-14. Inventory and Items on Order, Dollar Values, Sample Problem.

Item	Balance at End	Inventory Value	Prior Order?	Value on Order	Total Value
DEC LN12	29	4,785	0	0	4,785
VECTOR 2020	25	5,625	0	0	5,625
DIABLO 3	46	5,060	30	3,300	8,360
EPSON 214	52	11,440	0	0	11,440
STARJET	16	2,880	0	0	2,880
STARJET 2	8	2,080	25	6,500	8,580
RITEWAY 4A	24	2,160	0	0	2,160
JUKI 550	24	12,480	0	0	12,480
NASHUA 16B	46	6,900	20	3,000	9,900
PARK TECH 601	9	2,070	0	0	2,070
PARK TECH 45	27	7,830	0	0	7,830
LESTER LINE	33	5,775	0	0	5,775
GOLDATA 4	5	1,025	12	2,460	3,485
STATGRAPH	48	15,360	0	0	15,360
STATGRAPH 3	9	1,215	0	0	1,215
MACROTECH 741	34	8,670	10	2,550	11,220
MICROHOT 5	9	1,980	0	0	1,980
FOCUS II	44	12,100	0	0	12,100
		109,435		17,810	127,245

To measure inventory costs, a variety of reports can be prepared. Two such reports are shown in Figure 20-14.

1. **Resources Committed to Existing Inventory.** The inventory on hand must be purchased or manufactured. The larger the number of units, the greater the resources committed to supporting operations and marketing. The figure multiplies the units on hand times the unit cost and shows the money tied up in the different items, as well as a total dollar amount committed to inventory.

2. **Near–Term Cash Needed to Pay for Prior Orders.** When a firm places an order for inventory, a process is set in motion. Once the goods arrive, a payable is created. Then, cash is needed in 30 or so days to pay the invoice. Similarly, when the firm produces an item of finished goods, costs are incurred. The figure shows the dollars that will soon be needed to pay for items ordered.

Once again, a complex manufacturing environment will involve many other cost reports. These assist the firm in decisions to allocate resources and determinations on whether such resources are being used efficiently.

Reorder Instructions

A third category of report involves the ordering of items for the inventory. The reorder instructions in Figure 20-15 are an example of a report that can be transmitted to the Accounting or Purchasing Department so that goods can be replenished. This report is set up using if/then statements; therefore, the computer calculates reorder instructions automatically based on the level of reported inventory, prior orders, reorder points, and economic order quantities.

The first step in the report is to compare the potential inventory with the reorder point. If the ending inventory for the period plus prior orders exceeds the reorder point, a zero is displayed as the amount to order. When this is not the case, the report displays an amount to order that is equal to the EOQ for the item.

Three items should be noted with respect to this report.

1. **Automatically Generated**. It is not necessary for anyone in Inventory Management or the Data Processing Department to prepare this report. It can be calculated automatically using data already maintained in the system.

2. **Accuracy of Recordkeeping**. Since the report is automatic and is sent for action to another department, its accuracy is highly important. If the firm maintains inaccurate records on the level of inventory, the Purchasing Department will be ordering goods that are not needed, or will fail to order items that must be available for production or marketing. Thus, accurate entries to change inventory levels and identify reorder points and EOQs are required if the report is to be valid.

3. **Manual Override**. The report can be changed manually by individuals responsible for inventory management. It can even be done while the report is still on the screen. If the system has failed to record inventory received or another error is known to the inventory clerk or department head, the report can be modified before it is forwarded for action.

Figure 20-15. Reorder Instructions, Sample Problem.

The following items should be ordered in the amounts indicated:

Item	Balance at End	Prior Order?	Poten-tial	Re-Order Point	EOQ	Amount to Order
DEC LN12	29	0	29	30	15	15
VECTOR 2020	25	0	25	15	20	0
DIABLO 3	46	30	76	18	30	0
EPSON 214	52	0	52	35	60	0
STARJET	16	0	16	25	10	10
STARJET 2	8	25	33	6	20	0
RITEWAY 4A	24	0	24	8	20	0
JUKI 550	24	0	24	30	15	15
NASHUA 16B	46	20	66	40	20	0
PARK TECH 601	9	0	9	21	10	10
PARK TECH 45	27	0	27	35	25	25
LESTER LINE	33	0	33	14	15	0
GOLDATA 4	5	12	17	10	15	0
STATGRAPH	48	0	48	10	5	0
STATGRAPH 3	9	0	9	15	10	10
MACROTECH 741	34	10	44	30	15	0
MICROHOT 5	9	0	9	25	16	16
FOCUS II	44	0	44	50	40	40

CONCLUSION

The task of inventory planning can be highly complex in manufacturing environments. At the same time, it rests on fundamental principles. The system used for inventory must tie into the operations of the firm. In this chapter, we have coupled inventory management and planning with the production and marketing activities of the firm. Goods must be available to support economical and efficient fabrication of finished goods. An equally important consideration is that the proper mix of goods must be on hand to meet the needs of customers and to allow the firm to compete in the marketplace.

We have used a number of techniques to illustrate inventory decisions and the systems and reports needed to make them correctly. Although the actual environments are more complex, the fundamentals are known. Inventory planning and management must be responsive to the needs of the firm. Data must be maintained in an accurate fashion and must be retrievable in formats that provide useful information. The firm should design systems, including reports, that allow it to make proper business decisions.

ROBIN SPORTING GOODS—MANAGING INVENTORIES

The Robin Sporting Goods Company is located in Minneapolis, Minnesota, but has a worldwide market for its line of hockey equipment. The firm is the primary manufacturer of chest protectors, elbow pads, and face guards for professional hockey teams in the United States, Canada, and Western Europe. Even some teams in Eastern Europe and the Soviet Union have made bulk purchases of its goods.

Sears has become the newest customer for Robin Sporting Goods. Sold under the SPORTPRO name, the firm has a licensing agreement with the National Hockey League (NHL) and a distribution agreement through 1,400 Sears stores and outlets. The basic contract covers chest protectors, face guards, helmets, shin guards, elbow pads, and shoulder pads in the colors of every team in the NHL. In the near future, the firm hopes to add gloves, jerseys, goalie pads, leggings, stockings, undershirts, wrist bands, and other items. The future will be bright indeed if the firm is successful in its initial efforts with Sears and the NHL.

In addition to its Minnesota manufacturing facility, Robin Sporting Goods has established a joint venture operation in Hangzhou, China. The Chinese operation is managed by Chen Ruowei, a former representative of the China Council for the Promotion of International Trade and a U.S.-trained cadre member in China. Working with a labor force of 120 employees, Miss Chen runs a simple fabrication unit, converting raw materials into three finished products. The raw materials, including textile items, chemicals, wire, and metal clips, are purchased from Shanghai and Hong Kong and shipped to Hangzhou. There, they are converted into chest protectors, elbow pads, and face guards, which are shipped in bulk to the United States. Emblems and logos are added to the basic items in Minneapolis, after Robin Sporting Goods receives specific orders.

Chen Ruowei operates the factory on a highly cyclical basis. This approach has caused some difficulties with the workforce and municipal government in Zhejiang Province, but these problems have largely been solved. The basic timetable for the next year is as follows:

July	Receipt of order from Minnesota for next year's products and placing of order for raw materials.
Sept.-Oct.	Receipt of raw materials. Logging of items into inventory.
Nov.-April	Manufacture of finished goods.
May-June	Packing, customs inspections, and shipments to United States.
July-Aug.	Cleanup of plant and vacation.

In her planning, Miss Chen has identified 12 items of raw materials that are needed in the manufacturing process. These are identified in Figure 20-16. The item number is assigned by Robin Sporting Goods' Accounting Department. The other information in the figure is used for various purposes. As an example, elastic fabric is purchased on spools measured in yards, at a cost of $1.50 per yard. The joint venture agreement specifies payment in U.S. dollars, even though the fabric is manufactured in Nanjing and is shipped to Hangzhou by river. The "on hand" column in the figure shows the leftover inventory from last year. Thus, the factory has 250 yards of elastic fabric, 630 metal clips, 26,500 yards of vinyl stripping, and so forth available at the present time.

These raw materials are used in different proportions to manufacture each item. The amount of each component is shown in Figure 20-17. A face guard, for example, requires 4 yards of roll wire, a half gallon of rubber paint, and 2/10ths of a gallon of blue dye. Even though the factory identifies the face guard as a finished good, more work is needed after it leaves the factory. Once this unit is shipped to the United States, it must be inserted into a partial headgear unit before it can be sold.

On June 27, Chen Ruowei received the order for next year's finished goods. Robin Sporting Goods wants 22,000 chest protectors, 33,000 elbow pads, and 17,000 face guards. After receiving this order, Miss Chen checked the leftover inventory. She discovered that the factory had 450 chest protectors, 500 elbow pads, and 1,000 face guards that were not finished in time for last year's shipment but were on hand for shipment this year.

As part of her planning, Miss Chen has identified labor costs to be matched with each product. These are calculated by dividing the total expenses of the factory by the output. Her estimate of the labor cost to manufacture a chest protector is $8 per unit. Similarly, an elbow pad costs $3.50 and a face guard costs $11. The actual labor is paid in yuan, but the joint venture contract specifies some hard currency obligations for Robin Sporting Goods. These considerations are handled in Minnesota and do not affect Chen Ruowei's planning.

Required: 1. Assume that the current finished goods inventory is carried at $25 for a chest protector, $8 for an elbow pad, and $15 for a face guard. What is the factory's current inventory in units and dollars?

2. What is the level of each raw material that will be needed for production next year?

3. What is the level of each raw material that must be purchased for next year's production?

4. Assume that Chen Ruowei wants to start the month of November with an inventory equal to 60 percent of next

year's needs. What is the level of inventory of each item that should be on hand on November 1?

5. Excess inventory can be defined as raw materials that will not be needed next year. Does the factory have any such inventory on hand at the present time?

6. Calculate the materials and labor costs for next year's production.

7. Calculate the unit cost of each finished goods item that will be manufactured next year.

Figure 20-16. Raw Materials Inventory.

Item	Item #	Container	Units	On Hand	Unit Cost
Elastic Fabric	RM120	Spool	yds	250	1.50
Metal Clips	RM210	Lot	units	630	1.35
Vinyl Stripping	RM220	Roll	yds	26,500	2.25
Nylon Board Cloth	RM221	Roll	yds	750	1.25
Injecto Foam	RM230	Drum	gallons	120	7.00
Blue Dye	RM240	Can	gallons	350	6.00
Black Dye	RM242	Can	gallons	190	4.50
White Dye	RM243	Can	gallons	40	5.50
1/4" Backing	RM260	Spool	yds	150	0.70
Nylon Thread	RM271	Roll	yds	1,600	0.25
1/8" Roll Wire	RM272	Spool	yds	225	2.45
Rubber Paint	RM283	Drum	gallons	160	6.80

Figure 20.17. Raw Materials as Components of Finished Goods.

Item	Item #	Amount
Chest Protector		
Elastic Fabric	RM120	0.50 yd.
Metal Clips	RM210	4.00 units
Vinyl Stripping	RM220	0.50 yd.
Nylon Board Cloth	RM221	1.25 yd.
Injecto Foam	RM230	0.75 gal.
Blue Dye	RM240	0.25 gal.
1/4" Backing	RM260	1.00 yd.
Nylon Thread	RM271	6.00 gal.
Elbow Pad		
Elastic Fabric	RM120	0.10 yd.
Nylon Board Cloth	RM221	0.60 yd.
Injecto Foam	RM230	0.20 gal.
Black Dye	RM242	0.10 gal.
1/4" Backing	RM260	0.30 yd.
Nylon Thread	RM271	3.00 gal.
Face Guard		
1/8" Roll Wire	RM272	4.00 yd.
Rubber Paint	RM283	0.50 gal.
Blue Dye	RM240	0.20 gal.

Mini Vehicles Case–
Inventory Management

Mini Vehicles, Inc. will never offer serious competition to the major automobile manufacturers in Michigan, Japan, or West Germany. Still, it has carved out a small and stable market for small gas-powered vehicles. When a policeman riding a small, two-person conveyance pulls up to an illegally parked car and tickets it, that policeman can write the ticket in the comfort of his or her own vehicle. IWhen it is raining, the plastic doors can be closed. In cold weather, a small duct allows the engine heat to enter the passenger area. On the back, a small compartment allows the officer to carry his or her lunch, a change of clothes or other items. If all of these things are true, the chances are good that the officer is driving the police version of a product produced by Mini Vehicles Incorporated.

The company is equally successful with its two recreational vehicles. The Custom Golf Cart is widely respected on fairways from Europe to Australia. A recent shipment of 60 units was purchased by a company in Thailand for use in that country's resorts. Similarly, the Senior Citizen Vehicle has been successful in a variety of areas. Widely purchased in Florida and Arizona, it provides transportation in retirement communities. It is also purchased in small volume by resorts and hotels. It is even used on college campuses as a security vehicle.

Mini Vehicles Inc. has begun its inventory planning for next year. The planning is conducted for five quarters on a rolling basis; that is, as one quarter ends, a new quarter is added to the end of the planning period. The goal is to maintain only those inventories that are needed to support operations while minimizing lost sales. Inventories are adjusted cyclically, to reflect changing sales patterns of its three products.

Figure 1 shows the components used to manufacture the police, golf, and senior citizen versions of the mini vehicle. All three units use the same steering component, but motors, tires, chassis, and accessories vary. The figure shows the number of each component in each vehicle, along with the unit cost for the component.

Figure 2 is a production forecast for the next five quarters. This is based upon the sales forecast provided by the marketing vice president. As might be expected, the firm matches its inventory needs with the forecast.

Figure 1. Inventory Components and Prices.

	Police	Golf	Sr. Cit.	Unit Price
Steering Unit	1	1	1	1,400
Motor "A"	1	0	0	2,800
Motor "B"	0	1	1	1,800
Tires "A"	2	2	4	80
Tires "B"	0	2	0	50
Chassis "A"	1	0	0	1,600
Chassis "B"	0	1	0	900
Chassis "C"	0	0	1	800
Style Pkg "A"	1	0	0	400
Style Pkg "B"	0	1	0	200
Style Pkg "C"	0	0	1	600
Parts Kit "A"	2	0	0	240
Parts Kit "B"	1	3	2	160
Parts Kit "C"	3	1	1	130
Parts Kit "D"	2	1	1	190
Parts Kit "E"	0	2	4	225

Figure 2. Production Forecast in Units.

	Qtr. 1	Qtr. 2	Qtr. 3	Qtr. 4	Qtr. 5
Police	310	220	140	120	320
Golf	400	250	20	100	420
Sr. Citizens	150	170	160	150	160

Figure 3 shows the manufacturing costs associated with each vehicle during the next five quarters. These costs vary, based on seasonal factors, the mix of full and part time employees, and other factors. Each number is expressed in terms of dollars per vehicle.

Figure 4 shows the markup for each vehicle, which also varies cyclically. This figure is applied to the total manufacturing cost. As an example, suppose it costs $6,000 for materials and $4,000 for labor to manufacture a police vehicle, and it has an 80 percent markup for the quarter. The selling price for one unit would be calculated as

$$(6000+4000) * (1+.80) = 18,000$$

When preparing its forecasts, the firm assumes level general and administrative expenses over the course of a year. For the next five quarters, these are projected at $2.7 million per quarter, which includes interest costs on the firm's debt.

Figure 5 contains one additional item of information for inventory management. It is a safety margin above the forecast. As an example, if the firm projected sales of 100 units and had a 20 percent safety margin for the period, the inventory level would be

$$100 *(1+.20) = 120 \text{ units}$$

In using this safety margin, the firm assumes that it wants to begin each quarter with the full inventory needed to support that quarter's sales, plus the safety margin. This is the case because production in a quarter is designed to support the following quarter's sales.

Required: 1. What is the unit cost to manufacture each of the three inished goods?
2. Prepare an income statement (down to earnings before taxes), for the next five quarters.
3. What is the required inventory of raw materials in units for each quarter? In dollars?

Figure 3. **Manufacturing Costs, Including Labor but Excluding Materials, Each Unit.**

	Qtr. 1	Qtr. 2	Qtr. 3	Qtr. 4	Qtr. 5
Police	1,300	1,300	1,600	1,600	1,200
Golf	1,100	900	900	950	950
Sr. Citizens	950	950	1,050	1,050	1,050

Figure 4. Markup above Materials and Manufacturing Costs, Each Vehicle.

	Qtr. 1	Qtr. 2	Qtr. 3	Qtr. 4	Qtr. 5
Police	0.70	0.60	0.60	0.35	0.65
Golf	0.30	0.55	0.55	0.55	0.45
Sr. Citizens	0.25	0.25	0.30	0.30	0.30

Figure 5. Safety Margin, Finished Goods above Sales Forecast.

	Qtr. 1	Qtr. 2	Qtr. 3	Qtr. 4	Qtr. 5
Police	0.20	0.20	0.10	0.20	0.20
Golf	0.10	0.10	0.00	0.10	0.10
Sr. Citizens	0.15	0.15	0.05	0.15	0.15
General & Admin.	2700000	2700000	2700000	2700000	2700000

VIII.

Appendix A

Time Value of Money Tables

Compound Value of $1 [($1) (CVF)].

Period	2.00%	4.00%	6.00%	8.00%	10.00%	12.00%	14.00%	16.00%	18.00%	20.00%
1	1.020	1.040	1.060	1.080	1.100	1.120	1.140	1.160	1.180	1.200
2	1.040	1.082	1.124	1.166	1.210	1.254	1.300	1.346	1.392	1.440
3	1.061	1.125	1.191	1.260	1.331	1.405	1.482	1.561	1.643	1.728
4	1.082	1.170	1.262	1.360	1.464	1.574	1.689	1.811	1.939	2.074
5	1.104	1.217	1.338	1.469	1.611	1.762	1.925	2.100	2.288	2.488
6	1.126	1.265	1.419	1.587	1.772	1.974	2.195	2.436	2.700	2.986
7	1.149	1.316	1.504	1.714	1.949	2.211	2.502	2.826	3.185	3.583
8	1.172	1.369	1.594	1.851	2.144	2.476	2.853	3.278	3.759	4.300
9	1.195	1.423	1.689	1.999	2.358	2.773	3.252	3.803	4.435	5.160
10	1.219	1.480	1.791	2.159	2.594	3.106	3.707	4.411	5.234	6.192
11	1.243	1.539	1.898	2.332	2.853	3.479	4.226	5.117	6.176	7.430
12	1.268	1.601	2.012	2.518	3.138	3.896	4.818	5.936	7.288	8.916
13	1.294	1.665	2.133	2.720	3.452	4.363	5.492	6.886	8.599	10.699
14	1.319	1.732	2.261	2.937	3.797	4.887	6.261	7.987	10.147	12.839
15	1.346	1.801	2.397	3.172	4.177	5.474	7.138	9.265	11.974	15.407
16	1.373	1.873	2.540	3.426	4.595	6.130	8.137	10.748	14.129	18.488
17	1.400	1.948	2.693	3.700	5.054	6.866	9.276	12.468	16.672	22.186
18	1.428	2.026	2.854	3.996	5.560	7.690	10.575	14.462	19.673	26.623
19	1.457	2.107	3.026	4.316	6.116	8.613	12.055	16.776	23.214	31.948
20	1.486	2.191	3.207	4.661	6.727	9.646	13.743	19.461	27.393	38.337
21	1.516	2.279	3.399	5.034	7.400	10.804	15.667	22.574	32.323	46.005
22	1.546	2.370	3.603	5.436	8.140	12.100	17.861	26.186	38.141	55.205
23	1.577	2.465	3.820	5.871	8.954	13.552	20.361	30.376	45.007	66.247
24	1.608	2.563	4.049	6.341	9.850	15.178	23.212	35.236	53.108	79.496
25	1.641	2.666	4.292	6.848	10.834	17.000	26.461	40.874	62.667	95.395
30	1.811	3.243	5.743	10.062	17.449	29.960	50.949	85.849	143.367	237.373

Compond Value of an Annuity (Regular) of $1 [($1)] (CVFa).

Period	2.00%	4.00%	6.00%	8.00%	10.00%	12.00%	14.00%	16.00%	18.00%	20.00%
1	1.000	1.000	1.000	1.000	1.000	1.000	1.000	1.000	1.000	1.000
2	2.020	2.040	2.060	2.080	2.100	2.120	2.140	2.160	2.180	2.200
3	3.060	3.122	3.184	3.246	3.310	3.374	3.440	3.506	3.572	3.610
4	4.122	4.246	4.375	4.506	4.641	4.779	4.921	5.066	5.215	5.368
5	5.204	5.416	5.637	5.867	6.105	6.353	6.610	6.877	7.154	7.442
6	6.308	6.633	6.975	7.336	7.716	8.115	8.535	8.977	9.442	9.930
7	7.434	7.898	8.394	8.923	9.487	10.089	10.730	11.414	12.141	12.916
8	8.583	9.214	9.897	10.637	11.436	12.300	13.233	14.240	15.327	16.499
9	9.755	10.583	11.491	12.488	13.579	14.776	16.085	17.518	19.086	10.799
10	10.950	12.006	13.181	14.487	15.937	17.549	19.337	21.321	23.521	25.959
11	12.169	13.486	14.972	16.645	18.531	20.655	23.044	25.733	28.755	32.150
12	13.412	15.026	16.870	18.977	21.384	24.133	27.271	30.850	34.931	39.580
13	14.680	16.627	18.882	21.495	24.523	28.029	32.088	36.786	42.218	48.496
14	15.974	18.292	21.015	24.215	27.975	32.392	37.581	43.672	50.818	59.196
15	17.293	20.023	23.276	27.152	31.772	37.280	43.842	51.659	60.965	72.035
16	18.639	21.824	25.672	30.324	35.949	42.753	50.980	60.925	72.938	87.442
17	20.012	23.697	28.213	33.750	40.544	48.883	59.117	71.673	87.067	
18	21.412	25.645	30.905	37.450	45.599	55.749	68.393	84.140		
19	22.840	27.671	33.760	41.446	51.158	63.439	78.968	98.603		
20	24.297	29.778	36.785	45.762	57.274	72.052	91.024			
21	25.783	31.969	39.992	50.422	64.002	81.698				
22	27.299	34.248	43.392	55.456	71.402	92.502				
23	28.845	36.618	46.995	60.893	79.542					
24	30.421	39.082	50.815	66.764	88.496					
25	32.030	41.645	54.864	73.105	98.346					
30	40.567	56.084	79.057	113.282						

Present Value of $1 [($1) (PVF)]

Period	2.00%	4.00%	6.00%	8.00%	10.00%	12.00%	14.00%	16.00%	18.00%	20.00%
1	.980	.962	.943	.926	.909	.983	.877	.862	.847	.833
2	.961	.925	.890	.857	.826	.797	.769	.743	.718	.694
3	.942	.889	.840	.794	.751	.712	.675	.641	.609	.579
4	.924	.855	.792	.735	.683	.636	.592	.552	.516	.482
5	.906	.822	.747	.681	.621	.567	.519	.476	.437	.402
6	.888	.790	.705	.630	.564	.507	.456	.410	.370	.335
7	.871	.760	.665	.583	.513	.452	.400	.354	.344	.279
8	.853	.731	.627	.540	.467	.404	.351	.305	.266	.233
9	.837	.703	.592	.500	.424	.361	.308	.263	.225	.194
10	.820	.676	.558	.463	.386	.322	.270	.227	.191	.162
11	.804	.650	.527	.429	.350	.287	.237	.195	.162	.135
12	.789	.625	.497	.397	.319	.257	.208	.168	.137	.112
13	.773	.601	.469	.368	.290	.229	.182	.145	.116	.093
14	.758	.577	.442	.340	.263	.205	.160	.125	.099	.078
15	.743	.555	.417	.315	.239	.183	.140	.108	.084	.065
16	.728	.534	.394	.292	.218	.163	.123	.093	.071	.054
17	.714	.513	.371	.270	.198	.146	.108	.080	.060	.045
18	.700	.494	.350	.250	.180	.130	.095	.069	.051	.038
19	.686	.475	.331	.232	.164	.116	.083	.060	.043	.031
20	.673	.456	.312	.215	.149	.104	.073	.051	.037	.026
21	.660	.439	.294	.199	.135	.093	.064	.044	.031	.022
22	.647	.422	.278	.184	.123	.083	.056	.038	.026	.018
23	.634	.406	.262	.170	.112	.074	.049	.033	.022	.015
24	.622	.390	.247	.158	.102	.066	.043	.028	.019	.013
25	.610	.375	.233	.146	.092	.059	.038	.024	.016	.010
30	.552	.308	.174	.099	.057	.033	.020	.012	.007	.004
35	.500	.253	.130	.068	.036	.019	.010	.006	.003	.002
40	.453	.208	.097	.046	.022	.011	.005	.003	.001	.001
45	.410	.171	.073	.031	.014	.006	.003	.001	.001	.000
50	.372	.141	.054	.021	.009	.003	.001	.001	.000	.000

Present Value of Annuity (Regular) of $1 [($1) (PFVa)].

Period	2.00%	4.00%	6.00%	8.00%	10.00%	12.00%	14.00%	16.00%	18.00%	20.00%
1	.980	.962	.943	.926	.909	.893	.877	.862	.847	.833
2	1.942	1.886	1.833	1.783	1.736	1.690	1.647	1.605	1.566	1.528
3	2.884	2.775	2.673	2.557	2.4787	2.402	2.322	2.246	2.174	2.106
4	3.808	3.630	3.465	3.312	3.170	3.037	2.914	2.798	2.690	2.589
5	4.713	4.452	4.212	3.993	3.791	3.605	3.433	3.274	3.127	2.991
6	5.601	5.242	4.917	4.623	4.355	4.111	3.889	3.685	3.498	3.326
7	6.472	6.002	5.582	5.206	4.868	4.564	4.288	4.039	3.812	3.605
8	7.326	6.733	6.210	5.747	5.335	4.968	4.639	4.344	4.078	3.837
9	8.162	7.435	6.802	6.247	5.759	5.328	4.946	4.607	4.303	4.031
10	8.983	8.111	7.360	6.710	6.145	5.650	5.216	4.833	4.094	4.192
11	9.787	8.760	7.887	7.139	6.495	5.938	5.453	5.029	4.656	4.327
12	10.575	9.385	8.384	7.536	6.814	6.194	5.660	5.197	4.793	4.439
13	11.384	9.986	8.853	7.904	7.103	6.424	5.842	5.342	4.910	5.533
14	12.106	10.563	9.295	8.244	7.367	6.628	6.002	5.468	5.008	4.611
15	12.849	11.118	9.712	8.560	7.606	6.811	6.142	5.575	5.092	4.675
16	13.578	11.652	10.106	8.851	7.824	6.974	6.265	5.669	5.162	4.730
17	14.292	12.166	10.477	9.122	8.022	7.120	6.373	5.749	5.222	4.775
18	14.992	12.659	10.828	9.372	8.201	7.250	6.467	5.818	5.273	4.812
19	15.679	13.134	11.158	9.604	8.365	7.366	6.550	5.877	5.316	4.843
20	16.352	13.590	11.470	9.818	8.514	7.469	6.623	5.929	5.353	4.870
21	17.011	14.029	11.764	10.017	8.649	7.562	6.687	5.973	5.384	4.891
22	17.658	14.451	12.042	10.201	8.772	7.645	6.743	6.011	5.410	4.909
23	18.292	14.857	12.303	10.371	8.883	7.718	6.792	6.044	5.432	4.925
24	18.914	15.247	12.550	10.529	8.985	7.784	6.835	6.073	5.451	4.937
25	19.524	15.622	12.783	10.675	9.077	7.843	6.873	6.097	5.467	4.948
30	22.397	17.292	13.765	11.258	9.427	8.055	7.003	6.177	5.517	4.979
35	24.999	18.665	14.498	11.655	9.644	8.176	7.070	6.215	5.539	4.992
40	27.306	19.793	15.046	11.925	9.779	8.244	7.150	6.233	5.548	4.997
45	29.490	20.720	15.456	12.108	9.863	8.283	7.123	6.242	5.552	4.999
50	31.424	21.482	15.762	12.234	9.915	8.305	7.133	6.246	5.554	4.999

Index

Acceptance,banker's, 179
Acceptances, yields, 181
Accounts payable, 233
Accounts receivable, 231
Accounts receivable, turnover, 267
ACH credits, 77
Acid test, 265
Activity data, 499
Advances, factors, 312
Advances from customers, 306
Aging schedule, 363
Annual compounding, 167
Approval fee, 289
Arbitrage, 201
Arbitrage, space, 205
Arbitrage, time, 205
Ask quote in forward market, 201
Asset turnover, 334
Assets, 231
Assets, quick, 264
Assignment of receivables, 309
ATMs, 29
Availability, bank policies, 57
Availability fee, 289
Available funds, 56
Average collection period, 267, 369
Bad debt losses, 361
Balance sheet, 230
Balance sheet, uses of, 236
Balance sheet projection, 116
Bank, depository, 52
Bank, disbursing, 52
Bank debenture ratings, 179
Bank holding company, 32
Bank processing float, 52
Bank wire, 72
Banker's acceptance, 179
Banks, size of, 33
Baumol model, 149
Bayesian statistics, 142
Bearer, 27
Bernoulli process, 152
Bid, competitive, 174
Bid quote in forward market, 201
Billing float, 51

Bogus collateral, 308
Bond, treasury, 175
Borrowing capacity, 284
Bottleneck item, 481
Branch, 32
Broker, 195
Budget, 491
Business risk, 171
Call, foreign exchange, 218
Capital budget, 107
Capital indicators, 338
Capital structure, 268
Carrying costs, 477
Cash, 229
Cash, adequacy of, 263
Cash at risk approach to credit, 374
Cash balance, optimal, 149
Cash budget, 107
Cash cycle, 107
Cash flow analysis, 229
Cash forecast, 110
Cash forecasting, 107
Cash forecasting, 141
Cash inflows in forecast, 111
Cash item, 56
Cash management, international, 195
Cash management system, 51
Cash needs, planning for, 120
CD, 176
CD yields, 181
Certificate of deposit, 29, 176
Check credit plan, 423
Check processing float, 52
Checkable deposits, 36
Circulating working capital, 5
Citicash Manager package, 76
Cleanup, 284
Clearing, 56
Clearinghouse, 66
Coefficient of correlation, 139
Collateral, 307, 325
Collected balances, 56
Collection costs, 361
Collection item, 56
Collections, managing, 55

Commercial bank packages, 75
Commercial paper, 177, 305
Commercial paper ratings, 180
Commissions, factoring, 313
Common stock, 234
Comparative balance sheet, 236
Comparative ratios, 262
Compensating balance, 45, 169, 289
Competitive bid, 174
Compound interest, 166
Compounding, 166, 290
Compustat, 262
Concentration bank, 54
Concentration banking, 54
Consumer loan, 419
Continuous probability distribution, 122
Controlled disbursing, 65
Correspondent banking, 41
Correspondent relationship, 62
Cost data for inventories, 500
Cost reports, inventory, 504
Cost volume profit approach, 365
Covenant, 289
Creation of money, 38
Credit capacity, 323, 424
Credit capacity, analyzing, 340
Credit card lending, 422
Credit limits, establishing, 373
Credit norms, 325
Credit policies, 359
Credit scale, 457
Credit scoring system, 457
Credit swap, 224
Currency option, 218
Currency strength, 201
Current assets, 231
Current assets, adequacy of, 264
Current liabilities, 232
Current ratio, 264
Cyclical factors, 8
Daily compounding, 166
Data base, 498
Dealer, 195
Debt equity ratio, 339
Delayed payments, effect of, 297
Demand deposit, 28
Depository bank, 52
Depository transfer check, 53, 77
Deposits, checkable, 36
Deposits, classification of, 28
Deposits, derivative, 43
Deposits, Fed, 41
Deposits, primary, 43
Derivative deposits, 43
Direct send, 62
Disbursements, managing, 64

Disbursing, remote, 65
Disbursing bank, 52
Discounts in forward market, 198
Discounts taken, forecasting, 368
Discrete probability distribution, 122, 141
Diversification, 187
Dividend payout, 340
Draft, 196
DTC, 53
Dun and Bradstreet, 262, 441
Earnings per share, 338
Earnings power, 337
Economic order quantity, 149, 482
Economics of short term loans, 290
Effective cost, 290
Effective cost of single payment note, 292
Effective cost of standby financing, 296
Effective cost of working capital, 296
Effective cost with fees and balances, 294
EFT, 53, 64
Electronic funds transfer, 53, 64
Electronic payments service, 85
Electronic transfer, 67
Endorser, 422
EPS, 338
Equal Credit Opportunity Act, 398
Equity, 233
Establishing credit limits, 373
Eurocurrency, 42
Eurodollar deposit rates, 183
Eurodollar market size, 182
Exception reports, inventory, 502
Excess reserves, 42
Exchange rates, 184
Expected return, 163, 168
Expected value, 122
External analysis, 259, 326
Factoring commissions, 313
Factoring receivables, 311
Factor's reserves, 312
Fair Credit Billing Act, 396
Fair Debt Collection Practices, 407
Fed deposits, 41
Fed wire, 72
Federal funds, 42
Federal Reserve Membership, 31
Federal Reserve System, 63
Fees, 169, 289
Field warehouse, 307
Finance paper, 177, 305
Financial analysis, 259
Financial future, 190
Financial norms, 270
Financial Ratio, 260
Financial risk, 171
Financial statement, 229

Financing, receivables, 309
Financing, short term, 283
Finished goods, 475
Finite stochastic process, 152
Fixed assets, 231
Float, 51
Floating lien loan, 308
Floor planning, 308
Flow of funds statement, 242
Forecasting inflows, 111
Forecasting receivables, 368
Forecasting sales, 366
Forecasts, increasing accuracy, 119
Foreign exchange, 195
Foreign exchange, needs for, 197
Foreign exchange futures, 216
Foreign exchange market, 195
Forward market, 198
Forward market, ask quote, 201
Forward market, bid quote, 201
Forward market, discount, 201
Forward market, premium, 201
Four C's of credit, 20
Full bodied money, 26
Full exposure, foreign exchange, 209
Funds available to lend, 45
Funds from operations, 243
Funds tied up, 298, 478
Future market, 190
Futures, foreign exchange, 216
Futures contracts, use of, 217
Good funds, 56
Gross margin, 242, 334
Hedging, 206
Hedging decision, 213
Hedging guidelines, 215
Hertz, David, 142
IMM, 216
Income statement, 237
Index number, 457
Input screen, 110
Installment credit, 420
Installment financing, 299
Institutional deposits, 27
Interest rate differential, 200
Interest rate risk, 175
Internal analysis, 260
International cash management, 195
International Monetary Market, 216
Intrabank clearing, 62
Intrinsic value of money, 26
Inventories, 231
Inventories, purpose of, 475
Inventory, 473
Inventory data base, 498
Inventory lags, 474

Inventory management, 479
Inventory planning, 491
Inventory reports, 501
Inventory turnover, 265
Investing excess cash, 163
Investment account, 53
Invoice, 51
Lag, 108
Lead time, 484
Least squares, 127, 138
Left side risks, 11
Legal reserves, 41
Legal tender, 26
Level of significance, 139
Liabilities, current, 232
LIBOR, 286
Lien, 308
LIFFE, 216
Line of credit, 285
Linear regression, 127
Liquidation coverage, 377
Liquidity, flow of, 330
Liquidity, magnitude of, 329
Liquidity guidelines, 330
Liquidity indicators, 327
Liquidity ratios, 263
Lockbox, 53, 68
London Interbank Offered Rate, 286
Lost opportunity costs, 150
Mail float, 52
Managing collections, 55
Managing disbursements, 64
Manual transfer, 160
Marginal contribution, 242
Marginal cost of funds, 429
Market line, 171
Markov chain, 152
Materials cost, 492
Miller-Orr Model, 152
Modified income statement, 118
Money creation, 38
Money market fund, 188
Money supply, 25
Money supply, measures of, 35
Moody's bond ratings, 177
Negotiable CD, 29
Net worth, 425
Norm, financial, 236
Normal probability distribution, 122, 141
Norms, credit, 325
Norms, financial, 270
Norms, industry, 325
Notification basis, pledging, 310
NOW account, 28
Operating account, 52
Operating assets, 335

Operating budget, 107
Optimal cash balance, 149
Order costs, 478
Order variance, 502
Output screen, 110
Overdraft, 423
Payables, 233
Periodic compounding, 166
Permanent working capital, 5
Phoenix Hecht, 96
Pledging receivables, 309
PNB Compulink package, 84
Portfolio, 185
Portfolio risk, 186
Portfolio theory, 185
Preferred stock, 234
Premium, establishing, 203
Premiums in forward market, 198
Price earnings multiple, 339
Primary deposits, 43
Prime bank, 176
Prime rate, 286
Private loans, 306
Pro forma financial statement, 250
Probability distribution, 121, 141
Profit and loss statement, 237
Profit margin, 333
Profitability, 263
Profitability indicators, 331
Promissory note, 421
Put, foreign exchange, 218
P/E multiple, 339
Quick assets, 264
Quick ratio, 265
Rate of return, riskless, 171
Ratio, 260
Ratios, comparative, 262
Ratios, kinds of, 263
Ratios, users of, 260
Raw materials, 475
RCPC, 62
Receipts and disbursements, 110
Receivables, aging, 363
Receivables, factoring, 311
Receivables, pledging, 309
Receivables, purpose of, 359
Receivables financing, 309
Receivables policies, 359
Receivables turnover, 267
Recourse, 312
Regional check processing center, 62
Regulation B, 399
Regulation Z, 390
Remote disbursing, 65
Reorder data, 500
Reorder instructions, 506

Reorder variance, 503
REPO, 181
Repurchase agreement, 181
Required reserves, 41
Reserves, factor, 312
Reserves, role of, 40
Restrictive covenant, 289
Retained earnings, 234
Return on equity, 336
Return on investment, 335
Revolving credit agreement, 286
Right side risks, 12
Risk, business, 171
Risk, financial, 171
Risk, identifying sources of, 179
Risk, interest rate, 175
Risk, measuring, 174
Risk, nature of, 171
Risk, portfolio, 186
Risk, secondary sources, 181
Risk, systematic, 186
Risk, unsystematic, 186
Risk and return, 170
Risk category, 425
Risk class, 363
Riskless rate of return, 171
Rollover effect, 284
Safety level, 115
Safety margin for inventory, 494
Safety stock level, 483, 484
Seasonal factors, 8
Secured loan, 307
Secured short term sources, 307
Security agreement, 307
Security risk, 186
Selective basis, 309
Shelf stock, 475
Short term financing, 283
Short term financing, sources of, 285
Shortage, 115
Sigma, 124
Simulation models, 141
Single payment note, 285
Small business loans, 439
Sources and uses of funds, 242
Space arbitrage, 205
Spot market, 197
Stable liquidity test, 376
Stable profitability test, 376
Standard and Poor's, 262
Standard deviation, 124, 142
Standby line of credit, 286
Stochastic model, 152
Stock level subsystem, 485
Subjective probability, 142
Surplus, 115

Surplus, factor, 312
Symptoms of problems, 362
Systematic risk, 186
Terminal warehouse, 307
Terms of trade, 268, 362
Thrift institutions, 28
Time arbitrage, 205
Time value of money, 164
Times interest earned, 337
Transactions accounts, 41
Transactions costs, 150
Treasury bond, 175
Treasury note, 175
Treasury securities, 174
Trust receipt loan, 308
Truth in Lending Act, 389
Turnover, inventory, 265
Turnover, receivables, 267
Unit banking, 32
Unsecured short term loans, 285
Unsystematic risk, 186
Usage rate, 484

Variable working capital, 5
Vault cash, 41
Wages payable, 233
Warehouse receipt loan, 307
Weak currency, 202
Wire transfer, 72
Without recourse, 422
Work in process, 475
Working capital, adequacy of, 259
Working capital, circulating, 5
Working capital, extrapolation, 119
Working capital, financing, 14
Working capital, nature of, 4
Working capital, needs for, 8
Working capital, policies, 3
Working capital, pool, 242
Working capital, practices, 17
Working capital, ratios, 263
Working capital, strategies, 9
Zero balance account, 64
Zero balance account system, 161